THE WAR FROM WITHIN

THE LEGACY OF THE GREAT WAR

A Series sponsored by the Historial de la Grande Guerre Péronne-Somme

General Editor
JAY WINTER

Previously published titles in the Series

Antoine Prost
IN THE WAKE OF WAR
'Les Anciens Combattants' and French Society

Patrick Fridenson
THE FRENCH HOME FRONT 1914-1918

Stéphane Audoin-Rouzeau
MEN AT WAR 1914-1918

Gerald D. Feldman
ARMY, INDUSTRY, AND LABOR IN GERMANY 1914-1918

Rosa Maria Bracco
MERCHANTS OF HOPE

Adrian Gregory
THE SILENCE OF MEMORY
Armistice Day 1919-1946

THE WAR FROM WITHIN
German Working-Class Women in the First World War

BY UTE DANIEL

TRANSLATED BY MARGARET RIES

Oxford · New York

First published in 1997 by
Berg
Editorial offices:
150 Cowley Road, Oxford, OX4 1JJ, UK
70 Washington Square South, New York, NY 10012, USA

Translation from the German with permission of Vandenhoeck &
Ruprecht, Göttingen. © Vandenhoeck & Ruprecht, Göttingen.

Berg is an imprint of Oxford International Publishers Ltd.

Library of Congress Cataloging-in-Publication Data

A catalogue record for this book is available from the
Library of Congress.

British Library Cataloguing-in-Publication Data

A catalogue record for this book is available from the British Library.

ISBN 0 85496 892 X (Cloth)
       1 85973 147 3 (Paper)

Typeset by JS Typesetting, Wellingborough, Northants.
Printed in the United Kingdom by WBC Book Manufacturers,
Bridgend, Mid Glamorgan.

Contents

Foreword

That my book, originally published in German in 1989 as *Arbeiterfrauen in der Kriegsgesellschaft. Beruf, Familie und Politik im Ersten Weltkrieg* by Vandenhoeck & Ruprecht (Göttingen), is now being published in English is due to the contribution of many individuals. I would like to take this opportunity to thank them. Jay M. Winter was the first to suggest the idea of a translation of my book, and then organized the means that would turn that idea into reality. Margaret Ries translated the work, in consultation with Fabian Hilfrich. For the purposes of this publication, I have rewritten and shortened my original text. When it first appeared in Germany, this book was part of a transformation in gender and social history, and the theoretical approach adopted in the book was much less widely accepted than it is today. The theoretical foundation of the book remains here as originally presented, and I have only updated the literature on the social and gender history of the First World War in a few places.

Ute Daniel, Braunschweig

List of Abbreviations

AfS	*Archiv für Sozialgeschichte*
AK	Armeekorps (Army Corps)
BA	Bundesarchiv Koblenz
BA/MA	Bundesarchive/Militärarchiv Freiburg i. Br.
BDF	Bund Deutscher Frauenvereine (Federation of German Women's Associations)
Bd.	Band (volume)
Bl.	Blatt (a sheet from a paginated document)
Bufa	Bild- und Filmamt (Photograph and Film Office)
CEH	*Central European History*
DNHV	Deutschnationaler Handlungsgehilfenverband (German National Association of Commercial Clerks)
FAZ	Frauenarbeitszentrale (Headquarters for Women's Labor)
Fs.	Festschrift
Gd	*Geschichtsdidaktik*
GG	*Geschichte und Gesellschaft*
GLA	Generallandesarchiv Karlsruhe
GWU	*Geschichte in Wissenschaft und Unterricht*
HStA	Hauptstaatsarchiv
HStA/Kr	Hauptstaatsarchiv/Kriegsarchiv München
HZ	*Historische Zeitschrift*
IWK	*Internationale wissenschaftliche Korrespondenz zur Geschichte der deutschen Arbeiterbewegung*
JbWG	*Jahrbuch für Wirtschaftsgeschichte*
JCH	*Journal of Contemporary History*
JIH	*Journal of Interdisciplinary History*
JMH	*Journal of Modern History*
KZSS	*Kölner Zeitschrift für Soziologie und Sozialpsychologie*
MGM	*Militärgeschichtliche Mitteilungen*

List of Abbreviations

MSPD	Mehrheits-Sozialdemokratische Partei Deutschlands (Majority Social Democratic Party of Germany)
NL	Nachlaß (i.e. estate of a deceased)
NPL	*Neue Politische Literatur*
OHL	Oberste Heeresleitung
PVS	*Politische Vierteljahresschrift*
RABl	*Reichsarbeitsblatt*
SPD	Sozialdemokratische Partei Deutschlands (Social Democratic Party of Germany)
StA	Staatsarchiv
Stellv. Gen.kdo	Stellvertretendes Generalkommando (Deputy General Command)
Ufa	Universum-Film AG (Universe Film Company)
USPD	Unabhängige Sozialdemokratische Partei Deutschlands (Independent Social Democratic Party of Germany)
VSWG	*Vierteljahresschrift für Sozial- und Wirtschaftsgeschichte*
Wumba	Waffen- und Munitions-Beschaffungsamt (Weapons and Munitions Procurement Agency)
ZfG	*Zeitschrift für Geschichtswissenschaft*
ZGO	*Zeitschrift für die Geschichte des Oberrheines*
ZStA	Zentrales Staatsarchiv

List of Tables

List of Tables

1

Introduction

When one sees how the awful, senseless, insane facts of life are later twisted into history and how they finally read so harmlessly and easily in the tradition of history, as if all the pain and all the need and the entire suffering of the soul had been stripped away..., then one could think that human beings do not intend history to be a rendering of life's events, but instead, the reverse: their convalescence and redemption from all the torturous events of their fate... Expressed in neat numbers, the so-called First World War, which killed approximately 10 million people between 1914 and 1918, cost the human race 6,000 Marks for every second of its duration... There would not be any more miserable, hungry people on this earth, if this value and energy had been put at the service of reason instead of at the service of a self-destruction whose impact will be felt for centuries. In the year 1930, however, historians will prove that all this was historically necessary: The great War for the great Revolution, the great Revolution for the great War; and so on into infinity, because we human beings are - intellectual creatures.

                                                                Theodor Lessing[1]

The cultural philosopher Theodor Lessing, who published his indictment of German culture *Geschichte als Sinngebung des Sinnlosen* in 1919, was murdered in 1933 at the instigation of the National Socialists. He was murdered, in other words, by representatives of that political orientation for which the lost war of 1914-1918 served as apt justification for preparing for the next. In 1945, this war, too, was lost, and the world's changed political contours led to a situation in which the contradictions and oppositions within Europe were increasingly overshadowed by the global dichotomy of the two superpowers and where, correspondingly, the demands made on the First World War for political objectives were increasingly infrequent. Lessing's critique of historiography, in so far as it was aimed at history's role as a claqueur in the political struggle for the meaning-endowment (*Sinnstiftung*[2]) of the First World War, has consequently become less relevant.[3] What remains extremely relevant for any effort to turn the First World War into the subject of an historical study, however, is Lessing's methodological critique of "*Vergemütlichung.*" Lessing saw this act of "making (something) more comfortable" as contraband, which every description after the fact smuggles into the analysis, namely by the unintended "way in which one separates history from the facts . . . until everything historical" becomes "the subject of novelists."[4] Lessing's verdict that historiography is the pastoral poetry of the modern age pertains both to theoretical reflections of what history is and to the actual practice of doing history. It refers to the unavoidable problem confronting every effort to transform lived experience, either our own or that of another, into descriptions and analyses, concepts and images, a problem which results from the fact that the very process of mediation presupposes the imaginability of even the most "unimaginable" emergency and death situations. The conceptual-pictoral version of experience that is produced through this process "arrests," as it were, even the most miserable and offensive situations and thereby renders them harmless. In historiographical practice, however, the problem addressed by Lessing can and must be taken as a warning against a surplus of meaning-endowment – whether the paths into the past present are forged from "above" or "below," from "the left" or from "the right."

In West German historiography, this problematic has played itself out in the recent dispute over the so-called history of everyday life. Although the details of this dispute and its present status cannot be elaborated here,[5] it remains of prime importance for our concerns that, during the course of this discussion, Lessing's problematic was taken up and made more precise from the standpoint of contemporary historiography. This debate revolved around one question: Where do we find the "true" subject of history, from which historiography may not free itself without giving up its function of enlightenment, and from which it may not abstract? Do we find it in an understanding of anonymous processes and structures, which are not authored by the reciprocal intentions of individual actors, or in the experiences, lifeworlds and means of perception of those individuals, who live, suffer and possibly perish under these structures and processes?

2

The recognition that this dichotomy is by no means necessary can by now be considered a consensual result of the discourse between the history of everyday life and historical social science. The issue of how this general postulate could be theoretically grounded and then realized in an empirical historical investigation has not yet been clarified, however. One of my objectives in this work is to offer a possible solution to this dilemma.

It is also my hope that, in its methodological approach of combining the history of everyday experience with structural history, this work will prove of specific use to those engaged in doing gender history and research. Since the 1970s, research into women's history, because of the groundwork it laid and the issues it addressed, has been immensely helpful in bringing the deficits of the traditional means of writing social history to light, particularly with respect to the connection between the analysis of structural history and that of the history of everyday experience. The more intensively women's life and work experiences were made the subject of historical investigation, the more obvious it became that their formation could not be analyzed without taking the general societal context into account and that, on the other hand, the formation of society could not be analyzed without reference to the experience and lives of individual women. Research into women's history has succeeded in establishing as a prerequisite of both argument and content that it is not only possible, but imperative, that gender be established "as the fundamental category of social and historical reality, perception and research."[6]

The correction and refinement that "Herstory" brings to "History" can be summarized, in short, as the discovery and subsequent examination of the gender-specific dialectic between the particular and the general.[7] Works of women's history have proven the distinct power of the socio-historical category of gender, above all, where they could show that such supposedly gender-neutral concepts as class, social protest and the family, when used without reflection, actually conceal essentially gender-specific lines of differentiation and that the men's and women's houses of more "primitive" societies continue to exist, if not as actual physical buildings, then as social and mental constructs.[8] Conversely, the use of the concept "gender" as a socio-historical category opens the possibility of attaining a new level of generalization in the history of society, in that it allows for "the fixation of women's place in the social system."[9] This means that the conditions of a specific society will be examined, on the one hand, in terms of the gender-specific structures that they shape, and, on the other, in terms of the ways in which women were involved in the development, maintenance and/or change of these societal structures. With this work, I hope to make a contribution to these methodological efforts to write women's history in the context of actual society.

My choice of the First World War as an object of study was influenced by three decisive factors. Firstly, the First World War offers the historian the enormous advantage of being an event-packed historical phenomenon. As when we throw a rock into water, the event of the Great War

> creates waves, stirs up mud from the ground, thus unearthing what creeps and flies under the foundation of life ... Due to its extraordinary, sensational, surprising, and unsettling character, the event triggers a multitude of critical relationships, a sort of swarm of discourses ... [Because] of this thaw of words, things will be uttered that are normally concealed, that are not spoken about, because they belong to the realm of the banal, of the everyday, and because no one thinks of informing us about them, as long as things take their usual course.[10]

If we begin with the event of "the First World War," we can then reach conclusions about socio-historical phenomena that, under "normal" conditions, seem so self-evident that they never find entrance into the social reality that is handed down in written sources. This eloquent silence of past normality is a notorious problem of socio-historical analyses of classes that were scarcely or not at all involved in the societal production of symbols and meaning. This is also a problem that plagues examinations of such basic social structures as the role of women in society, the relationship between the state and the people, or the interdependence of individual reproduction and that of the entire society. The total war of 1914–1918 brought with it a literal "eruption of words," which affected not only those segments of society that belonged to the deep semantic structure of the German Empire, but also those which con-stituted the basis, but only rarely the subject, of handed-down verbalizations. The First World War thus gave expression to a plethora of facts, perceptions and judgments about topics such as the role of women in society or the attitude of the population to the state, all of which also had significance beyond the war itself.

Although the experiential and historical consequences of the First World War are often heatedly discussed in academic and political circles, the history of everyday life and experience during the war has never been examined in depth, either with regard to the civil population as a whole or with regard to individual social groups within the context of wartime society.[11] This was my second reason for choosing the First World War as the historical frame of reference.

The third and most important reason was the prominant status that the secondary literature has ascribed – and continues to ascribe – to the years 1914–1918, seeing in them the processes of change that transformed women's societal role in the nineteenth century to that of the twentieth. Whether the increase in female labor during the war or the introduction of women's suffrage at the end of it is used as evidence of the First World War's assumed hand in this transformation, the "modernizing"[12] impact of the war – which is often only vaguely defined – on women's position in society is frequently surmised.[13] Any description of the First World War from a gender-history perspective must consequently and clearly declare its position on the question of whether the effects of the war on the situation of women in German society were "emancipatory" or not. The answer to this question should, in my opinion, be as close to the sources and as detailed as possible, so that the discussion about the "emancipation of women" in general and during the First World War in particular can be conducted on more solid ground than it has been heretofore. For the objectives of women's historical studies, "emancipation" proved to be a questionable analytical category as soon as these studies shifted their predominant focus from the history of women's movements to the social history of women outside these organizational-political contexts. This change in perspective cast doubt on the traditional view that women's history could be written as a success story about the fight for a share of political power, or as the tardy, but ultimately linear process of the modernization of one segment of society. Such progressive models started to crumble as it became clear, for example, how ambivalently the modernization of jurisprudence between the end of the eighteenth and the beginning of the twentieth century had affected the position of women.[14] They also lost in persuasive power the more clearly works of women's and family history could show that the creation of the modern family and household not only brought "emancipatory" reliefs and new freedoms, but new burdens and restrictions as well.[15]

I shall address the question of what "emancipatory" effect – if any – the First World War had on women in two stages. The main section of the work is grounded in the methodology of the history of everyday experience, which will be outlined below, and analyzes the living and working conditions of women workers between 1914 and 1918. Disregarding one exception, which will be handled later, I give the term "emancipation" neither heuristic nor analytic value here. This decision is based on the premise that any concept of emancipation can only grasp historical reality when it is historically constructed, not when it is posited a priori. In a second step, my concluding remarks serve both as an attempt to define "emancipation" based on the history of everyday life, and to answer the question of how "emancipatory" the results of the war were on the women examined in the entire study.

At the heart of this study stand working women, women, in other words, who worked for wages and those who did not, but who came from working-class families. Within this broader group, I have chosen to focus on urban working-class women and their professional and familial experience. Two reasons were decisive for this delimitation.

Firstly, through this singular focus on working women in urban areas, a stratum of women is delimited for which a certain homogeneity in terms of reproduction, of patterns of perception, shaped through socialization, everyday knowledge and everyday communication, as well as of socio-economic situation within wartime society can be assumed. For the chosen theoretical approach of this study, this posited homogeneity was both necessary and sufficient.

Secondly, I performed this delimitation under the assumption that, both for men and for women, membership in a specific class and stratum represents a constitutive element of their social situation and perception, from which a researcher cannot abstract. It is exactly this stratum- and class-specific limitation, therefore, that offers us the possibility of examining such areas of life as family and profession, which are normally considered in isolation, in their inner correlation. In specific instances in this study, however, I consciously overstep the bounds of this methodological construct. I do this, for one, where the source material is not sufficiently differentiated; this is particularly the case with the statistics about the demographic development during the war. Secondly, the use of a gender-history approach leads to a further and, in this work, theoretically significant break with the chosen class-specific analytic schema: Already inherent in this approach is the imperative to look for those places where class-specific connections are clearly eclipsed, and perhaps even "invalidated" by those of gender. Such is the case with the societal group "war wives" (*Kriegerfrauen*), which, composed of the wives of conscripted soldiers, by no means only included working-class women. This group, consequently, will be examined as to whether its members nevertheless identified themselves – based on a recognizable homogeneity of socio-economic position, resulting either from their classification as a uniform group by other societal groups or institutions and/or from their own self-understanding – as belonging to the group "war wives." Likewise, the question of women's sexual behavior during the war was acute not only for working-class women. Here, we must not only consider female workers who befriended prisoners of war working in their companies, but also female farmers who had sexual relationships with imprisoned agricultural workers who were assigned to work for them. A last example of where issues of gender necessarily predominate over those of class exists in women's specifically female attitudes to the war and wartime society and their resulting collective behavior. At first glance, the sources already seem to verify that, of all women, it was working-class women who expressed their critical stance toward the war the earliest, developed it the most radically and who participated the most frequently in collective action such as strikes or food riots. I will attempt to show, however, that when we consider German war society as a whole, one of the lines dividing the population into those increasingly critical of the war and those who wanted to "stick it out" to the end ran between "the" women and "the" men. Correspondingly, it was necessary here, as well, to replace the original class-specific analysis of my study with a gender-specific analysis.

Using the example of working women in the First World War, I shall thus attempt to show that it is not only possible to link the relationships of their everyday world with the spheres of economic and political decisions and social structures that transcend them, but also imperative to do so. The necessity for this arises from the fact that, if we handle each of these areas as though it were a quasi-autonomous segment of society, certain constellations of conditions fall out of the analytical framework, constellations which, in the end, decisively shape and unite these two areas. We must then ask if the state's wartime labor-market policy to mobilize and train women to work in the war industry did not ultimately founder because the life situations of these women, as well as the way in which they perceived their role in wartime society, were not compatible with the objectives of the state's policy. I will, similarly, examine the ways in which people were provided with money and food during the war in terms of the extent to which the logic and practice of state rationing and social policy was frustrated by the logic and practice of individual strategies, particularly those of working-class women, for obtaining provisions. And when considering the increasingly critical attitude toward the war, which the great majority of the population had manifested, at the latest, by 1916, we need to ask how far and under what circumstances could everyday ways of thinking develop political force. Here, it is of prime importance to determine what influence the thoughts and behavior of anonymous, unorganized masses of people had on the development of political structures, as when, for example, the government, in reaction to public morale, expanded its catalog of functions to include mass propaganda.

Conversely, I would contend that working-class women's life-world relations, whether they concerned wage work or housework, women's familial situation or their political consciousness and activity, cannot be analyzed without considering the state's labor-market and rationing policy, demographic structural data, hypotheses about patterns of collective behavior, and so forth. For the theoretical underpinnings and problematization of this book's effort to unite "micro-" and "macro-"history, I have had recourse to the discursive foundations already prepared by phenomenological sociology, on the one hand, and by Marxist social science of the Lukácsian mold, on the other. Phenomenologically oriented sociology was shaped primarily by Alfred Schütz, who, in turn, utilized Edmund Husserl's recognition theory and Max Weber's sociology of understanding as his starting points. In the last twenty years or so, this strain of

8

sociology has been developed into a theory of the construction of social reality.[16] The essential points of this theory that are relevant for the present work are outlined below.

It is precisely society's dual nature, i.e. as objective fact and as subjectively experienced and interpreted construct ("the subjective sense"), that renders it "reality *sui generis*." "Objective" and "real" are those phenomena that, in a given society at a specific point in time, are always present, independent of intentional acts. The subjective sense should not be understood as an individual category, but rather as a social construct. Human beings construct a way of perceiving social reality that, historically changeable and dependent on their specific societal position, can be seen as socially learned and mediated "knowledge" about the reality and constitution of phenomena.

This knowledge regulates individuals' behavior in everyday life. It is mediated through communication, which is, in varying degrees, standardized. Everyday, face-to-face communication is communication at its least standardized; the forms and contents of anonymous communication at its most standardized. We can speak of a form of anonymous communication when a standardized sender addresses himself to a standardized recipient. Such is the case, for example, when the "authorities" address the "population." The contents of anonymous communication are such that they are shaped by concepts not normally used in everyday-world discourse, as, for example, the symbolic language of science, art or politics.

Everyday knowledge is ordered according to its particular relevance, which arises from the immediate, practical goals of the "knowers" and the actors and their concrete position in society. This scale of relevance then shapes individuals' ways of perceiving and acting.

Individuals are introduced into the objective world of a given society through socialization, which is at once historical and gender-, race- and class-specific. During the process of socialization, which is molded partly by the family and partly by other societal institutions, such as school, professional organizations, mass media, etc., individuals, social groups and classes internalize social reality as their framework for action. The everyday, never-ending internalization of social reality and its changes occurs because of "the reality-creating power of discussion."[17]

In societies based on a division of labor, the categorization of institutional order and the concomitant heterogeneous allocation of knowledge leads to the necessity of creating, both on the individual, group and class level and on that of the entire society, a coherence of meaning that is capable of integrating and ordering the fragmentary experiences and supplies of knowledge of individuals and of individual groups into a meaningful individual or social context. The problem of the legitimation and acceptance of institutional regulations originates from this.

When the everyday world is in crisis, the overall coherence of meaning-endowment, now having become problematic, can disintegrate into "sub-worlds of meaning." These sub-worlds form according to the varied criteria of society's concrete categories, such as age, gender, class, religion or even a common, similarly experienced oppression, and are distinguished from one another by their incompatible patterns of action and perception.

Following in the footsteps of George Lukács, Agnes Heller, in particular, has developed a Marxist sociology whose fundamental assumptions come very close to those outlined in "knowledge-sociological" terminology above.[18] Based on a materialistic theory of behavior, Heller's sociology proceeds from a narrower conception of everyday life than that used in phenomenological sociology.[19] Since Heller's sociology facilitates the socio-historical functionability of the term "everyday life," and since it takes into greater account the increased burden of proof to which the use of this term is subjected in contemporary social sciences, this study relies on her concept of everyday life, which, coincidentally, is completely compatible with the Berger–Luckmannish approach:

> Everyday life is the totality of individuals' activities for their reproduction, which subsequently create the possibility of society's reproduction . . . The reproduction of society, however, does not spontaneously come about through the self-reproduction of the individual. A person is only capable of reproducing himself *in fulfilling his societal function: Self-reproduction becomes a moment in the reproduction of society.* The everyday life of one person consequently conveys, at the individual level, a picture of the reproduction of the respective society . . . *Everyday life* [thus conveys] . . . *the extraordinary and is simultaneously its nursery school.* In this respect, [it is] the secret yeast of history . . . in that, out of the conflicts of everyday life emerge those larger conflicts of the entire society, it is there that they search for an answer, and as soon as

these societal conflicts are resolved, they return to everyday life, which they then restructure and transform ... [20]

In "normal" times, i.e. those of society that are shaped neither by revolutionary processes nor by society-restructuring wars, everyday life is the "foundation" of conscious and organized political activity. This activity, however, simultaneously transcends its everyday basis, in that it abstracts from it and only then leads to organized class action. In times of radical revolutionary change or total war, the boundaries between proto-political everyday thought and behavior and "true" politics blur. In such crisis situations of everyday life, the prerequisite for the politicization of societal conditions no longer lies in the abstraction from the realm of everyday communication and activity, but rather the everyday situation itself becomes a political issue.[21]

These two theoretical approaches result in several central conclusions for the objectives of socio-historical analysis in general and for those of the First World War in particular.

Firstly, all forms and contents of individual reproduction in a given society at a given point in time, as well as those means of perception and processes of justification that are linked to and influence them, are possible subjects of analysis. In this work, I have chosen to examine central aspects of female wage labor, of the situation of working-class families and of working-class women's participation in the meaning-endowment of domestic politics during the First World War. In concentrating on work, family and ways of perceiving the war, I have taken into account the fact that it is through these three areas that everyday knowledge and everyday behavior, as defined above, reveal themselves.

A second conclusion is that the spheres of individual reproduction need to be analyzed in terms of the way in which and to what extent they were formed by factors outside the realm of everyday life, as well as how far, in turn, their consequences went beyond the context of the everyday world. The theoretical approach employed here does not constitute the "history of everyday life" in a narrower sense, because entirely "traditional" historiographical topics from the areas of politics, economics and culture are recognized as relevant subjects of analysis. This approach requires, however, the historian, when examining such topics, also to consider how far these "traditional realms" structure the everyday life and behavior of a specific social group or class and in what way(s) they are then reflected in the perception of those affected. Conversely, this approach also identifies the everyday life of a particular group or class, as defined above, as a subject of investigation, but for the express purpose of clarifying the connections between everyday behavior and perception and higher structures. In this work, I attempt to do this in chapter 2, after a short description of the first months of the war.

There, I try to elucidate the connections between the quantitative development of women's wage work, the state's labor-market policy, the socio-economic position of potential or actual female workers, and their perception of their situation. In a similar vein, chapter 3 describes the relations between state economic and family policy, demographic structures, homework, wartime child-bearing and -rearing, and women's perception of these.

Finally, one needs to examine what form the knowledge about social institutions, political circumstances, etc. that develops in the everyday relationships of specific groups and classes takes; how and through whom it is communicated; in what relation this knowledge stands to the politico-institutional meaning-endowment "from above" and whether it is revealed in distinguishable "subworlds of meaning." Equally, politico-institutional meaning-endowments themselves must be analyzed, particularly in terms of their contents and methods, their success or lack thereof in constructing, stabilizing or changing worlds of symbols. Both of these occur in the third section of this work, when I investigate the contents and structures of informal communication and state propaganda during the war.

A theoretical heuristics with these emphases necessarily reaches the limits of the source material. For many areas of everyday thinking and action, the lack of sources is just as notorious as that regarding the effects of everyday structures on the "larger" realm of politics. This lack should not be taken as a discouragement, however, but as a challenge: With the help of the available social history sources, the historian can endeavor to reconstruct these connections by forming justifiable hypotheses about things that are not directly revealed. I have primarily attempted such a reconstruction, with regard to patterns of perception, in chapter 3.

Two unusual features of the manner of description I have

chosen remain to be mentioned. Although they could potentially prove to be problematic, I believe that, in this case, these descriptive peculiarities are justified by the theoretical approach of this work. They characterize the work especially in those places where the interaction between the ways of perception "from above" and "from below" is analyzed. The first involves the frequent alternation of the description between the two perspectives, in particular where the connection between the two is analytically reconstructable or itself part of a reciprocal process of perception. Thus, for example, the description alternates between the level of official action and perception pertaining to women and families and the perception of these women themselves.

The second distinguishable descriptive feature of these above-mentioned places is my use of lengthy and frequent quotations. This is not the result of a "childish desire to impose everything verbatim on the reader that oneself has read for consolation instead of allowing it to form the silent and reassuring background of one's own discourse."[22] Rather, the quotations here serve as the sediment out of which the patterns of perception can be read. They can, consequently, only partially be replaced by paraphrasing. There is a further reason for my detailed, verbatim quoting of the letters of "war wives" to the front, the reports about the population's morale, the rumors that circulated, etc., one that refers back to the beginning of this introduction: Theodor Lessing. The quoted statements convey at least an impression of how the war might have been experienced as a reality by working-class women and others – instead of serving simply as a "silent and reassuring" background for the description of a noisy and restless time, during which people lived and died. Their distress and misery should not be "rendered more comfortable"[23] than necessary by detached scientific analysis.

Notes to Chapter 1

1. Theodor Lessing, *Geschichte als Sinngebung des Sinnlosen* (München, 1983), 156, 216.

The War from Within

2. *Sinnstiftung* is a word frequently used in academic and philosophical writing. It is not one, however, that I ever found translated in an English–German dictionary. It means to endow (*stiften*) something with meaning (*Sinn*). Since the text usually required the use of a noun instead of a verbal phrase, I have generally utilized the correct, if less elegant word "meaning-endowment" where *Sinnstiftung* appeared in the German text. [Translator]

3. Wrote Lessing, "Just as the success of a theatrical performance, no matter whether the acted play is good or meaningless, is always codependent on the actions of a paid or voluntary claque, judgments about the theater of life depend on the historians. The latter, however, be they voluntary or forced, are just an organized claque, paid by their state or party not to let a certain play fail. And for this, they receive their food and a free, privileged seat in the parquet. That is how they are bought; they clap their hands bloody, and all the while are allowed to believe that they are the judges of the world." Ibid., 119-120.

4. Ibid., 156ff.

5. For more information on this debate, see, among others: D. Peukert, "Arbeiteralltag - Mode oder Methode?" in H. Haumann, ed., *Arbeiteralltag in Stadt und Land* (Berlin, 1982), 8-39; R. M. Berdahl et al., *Klassen und Kultur. Sozialanthropologische Perspektiven in der Geschichtsschreibung* (Frankfurt/ M., 1982); J. Kocka, "Klassen oder Kultur? Durchbruch und Sackgassen in der Arbeitergeschichte," *Merkur* 36 (1982): 955-965; M. Broszat, "Plädoyer für Alltagsgeschichte. Eine Replik auf Jürgen Kocka," *Merkur* 36 (1982): 1244-1248; H.-U. Wehler, "Neoromantik und Pseudorealismus in der neuen 'Alltagsgeschichte,'" in H.-U. Wehler, *Preußen ist wieder chic* (Frankfurt/M., 1983), 99-106; V. Ullrich, "Alltagsgeschichte. Über einen neuen Geschichtstrend in der Bundesrepublik," *NPL* 29 (1984): 50-71; D. Peukert, "Neuere Alltagsgeschichte und historische Anthropologie," in H. Süssmuth, ed., *Historische Anthropologie. Der Mensch in der Geschichte* (Göttingen, 1984), 57-72; J. Kocka, "Historische-anthropologische Fragestellungen - ein Defizit der historischen Sozialwissenschaft?" in Süssmuth, *Historische Anthropologie*, 73-83; H. Medick, "'Missionare im Ruderboot'? Ethnologische Erkenntnisweisen als Herausforderung an die Sozialgeschichte," *GG* 10 (1984): 295-319; K. Tenfelde, "Schwierigkeiten mit dem Alltag," in *GG* 10 (1984): 376-394; H. Nagl-Docekal and F. Wimmer, eds., *Neue Ansätze in der Geschichtswissenschaft* (Wien, 1984); H. Heer and V. Ullrich, eds., *Geschichte entdecken. Erfahrungen und Projekte der neuen Geschichtsbewegung* (Reinbek, 1985); F. J. Brüggemeier and J. Kocka, eds., *Geschichte von unten - Geschichte von innen. Kontroversen um Alltagsgeschichte* (Hagen, 1985); J. Kocka, "Sozialgeschichte in der Bundesrepublik. Entwicklungen seit Mitte der 70er Jahre," in J. Kocka, *Sozialgeschichte. Begriff - Entwicklung - Probleme* (Göttingen, 1986); P. Borscheid, "Alltagsgeschichte - Modetorheit oder neues Tor zur Vergangenheit?" in W. Schieder and V. Sellin, eds., *Sozialgeschichte in Deutschland* (Göttingen, 1987), 3: 78-100; A. Lüdtke, ed., *Alltagsgeschichte. Zur Rekonstruktion historischer Erfahrungen und Lebensweisen* (Frankfurt/M. and New York, 1989); U. Daniel, "Kultur und Gesellschaft. Überlegungen zum Gegenstandsbereich der Sozialgeschichte," in *GG* 19 (1993): 69-99; R. Sieder, "Sozialgeschichte auf dem Weg zu einer historischen Kulturwissenschaft?," in *GG* 20 (1994), 445-468; W. Schulze, ed., *Sozialgeschichte, Alltagsgeschichte, Mikro-Historie* Göttingen, 1994).

Introduction

6. G. Bock, "Historische Frauenforschung: Fragestellungen und Perspektiven," in H. Haumann, ed., *Frauen suchen ihre Geschichte. Historische Studien zum 19. und 20. Jahrhundert.* (München, 1983), 34. For questions and investigations concerning West German women's history, also see K. Hausen, "Women's History in den Vereinigten Staaten," *GG* 7 (1981): 347-363; G. Pomata, "Die Geschichte der Frauen zwischen Anthropologie und Biologie," *Feministische Studien* 2 (1983): 113-127; J. C. Fout, "Current Research on German Women's History in the Nineteenth Century," in J. C. Fout, ed., *German Women in the Nineteenth Century* (New York and London, 1984), 3-54; H. Nagl-Docekal and F. Wimmer, eds., *Neue Ansätze in der Geschichtswissenschaft* (Wien, 1984); G. Bock, *Zwangssterilisation im NS. Untersuchungen zur Rassenpolitik und Frauenpolitik* (Opladen, 1985); U. Frevert, *Frauen-Geschichte? Zwischen bürgerlicher Verbesserung und neuer Weiblichkeit* (Frankfurt/Main, 1986); U. Frevert, "Bewegung und Disziplin in der Frauengeschichte. Ein Forschungsbericht," *GG* 14 (1988): 240-262; G. Bock, "Geschichte, Frauengeschichte, Geschlechtergeschichte," *GG* 14 (1988): 364-391; U. Becher and J. Rüsen, eds., *Weiblichkeit in geschichtlicher Perspektive. Fallstudien und Reflexionen zu Grundproblemen der historischen Frauenforschung* (Frankfurt/M., 1988); K. Hausen and H. Wunder, eds., *Frauengeschichte – Geschlechtergeschichte* (Frankfurt/M. and New York, 1992); U. Frevert, *"Mann und Weib und Weib und Mann." Geschlechter-Differenzen in der Moderne* (München, 1995). In the last years, gender history got a very different shape under the influence of the "linguistic turn"; for this see among others: K. Canning, "Feminist Theory after the Linguistic Turn," *Signs* 19 (1994): 368-404.

7. This play on words was borrowed from its originator, Sheila Ryan Johansson; S. R. Johansson, "'Herstory' as History: A New Field or Another Fad?" in B. A. Carroll, ed., *Liberating Women's History. Theoretical and Critical Essays* (Urbana, Ill., et al., 1976): 400-430.

8. See the panel *"Frauenräume"* (Women's Rooms/Realms) at the 1985 Historians' Conference in Berlin and K. Hausen, "Frauenräume," *Journal für Geschichte* (1985): 12-15.

9. Hausen, "Women's History," 352.

10. G. Duby and G. Lardreau, *Geschichte und Geschichtswissenschaft. Dialoge* (Frankfurt/M., 1982), 63.

11. A survey of the relevant secondary literature concerning the First World War, particularly that from a social history or a history of mentalities perspective, is listed below.

In addition to those works cited in endnote 12, on women's work see: M.-E. Lüders, *Die Entwicklung der gewerblichen Frauenarbeit im Kriege* (München and Leipzig, 1920); U. Daniel, "Fiktionen, Friktionen und Fakten – Frauenlohnarbeit im Ersten Weltkrieg," in G. Mai, ed., *Arbeiterschaft 1914–1918 in Deutschland. Studien zu Arbeitskampf und Arbeitsmarkt im Ersten Weltkrieg* (Düsseldorf, 1985), 277-323; U. Daniel, "Women's Work in Industry and Family, 1914-1918," in R. Wall and J. Winter, eds., *The Upheaval of War: Family, Work and Welfare in Europe, 1914-1918* (Cambridge, 1988), 267-296; S. Augeneder, *Arbeiterinnen im Ersten Weltkrieg. Lebens- und Arbeitsbedingungen proletarischer Frauen in Österreich* (Wien, 1987); B. Guttmann, *Weibliche Heimarmee. Frauen in Deutschland 1914-1918* (Weinheim, 1989); Y.-S. Hong, "The Contradictions of Modernization in the German Welfare State:

15

The War from Within

Gender and the Politics of Welfare Reform in First World War Germany," *Social History* 17 (1992): 251-270. On wage work, the workers' movement and its internal administration, see: P. Graf Kielsmansegg, *Deutschland und der Erste Weltkrieg* (Frankfurt/M., 1968); K.-D. Schwarz, *Weltkrieg und Revolution in Nürnberg. Ein Beitrag zur Geschichte der deutschen Arbeiterbewegung* (Stuttgart, 1971); G. Hardach, *Der Erste Weltkrieg*, Geschichte der Weltwirtschaft im 20. Jahrhundert 2, W. Fischer, ed. (München, 1973); J. Reulecke, *Die wirtschaftliche Entwicklung der Stadt Barmen von 1910-1925* (Neustadt a. d. A., 1973); S. Miller, *Burgfrieden und Klassenkampf. Die deutsche Sozialdemokratie im Ersten Weltkrieg* (Düsseldorf, 1974); V. Ullrich, *Die Hamburger Arbeiterbewegung am Vorabend des Ersten Weltkriegs bis zur Revolution 1918/19*, 2 vols (Hamburg, 1976); J. Kocka, *Klassengesellschaft im Krieg. Deutsche Sozialgeschichte 1914-1918*, 2nd expanded ed. (Göttingen, 1978); D. Josczok, *Die Entwicklung der sozialistischen Arbeiterbewegung in Düsseldorf während des Ersten Weltkriegs* (Reinbek, 1980); M. Scheck, *Zwischen Weltkrieg und Revolution. Zur Geschichte der Arbeiterbewegung in Württemberg 1914-1920* (Köln and Wien, 1981); F. Boll, *Massenbewegungen in Niedersachsen 1906-1920. Eine sozialgeschichtliche Untersuchung zu den unterschiedlichen Entwicklungstypen Braunschweig und Hannover* (Bonn, 1981); H. J. Bieber, *Gewerkschaften in Krieg und Revolution. Arbeiterbewegung, Industrie, Staat und Militär in Deutschland 1914-1920*, 2 vols (Hamburg, 1981); C. E. Schorske, *Die große Spaltung. Die deutsche Sozialdemokratie 1905-1917* (Berlin, 1981); H. Schäfer, *Regionale Wirtschaftspolitik in der Kriegszeit. Staat, Industrie und Verbände während des Ersten Weltkriegs in Baden* (Stuttgart, 1983); G. Mai, *Kriegswirtschaft und Arbeiterbewegung in Württemberg 1914-1918* (Stuttgart, 1983); Mai, ed., *Arbeiterschaft*; H.-U. Ludewig, *Das Herzogtum Braunschweig im Ersten Weltkrieg. Wirtschaft - Gesellschaft - Staat* (Braunschweig, 1984); K. Schönhoven, ed., *Die Gewerkschaften in Weltkrieg und Revolution 1914-1919*, Quellen zur Geschichte der deutschen Gewerkschaftsbewegung im 20. Jahrhundert 1 (Köln, 1985); G. D. Feldman, *Armee, Industrie und Arbeiterschaft in Deutschland 1914 bis 1918* (Berlin and Bonn, 1985); H.-G. Husung, "Arbeiterschaft und Arbeiterbewegung im Ersten Weltkrieg: Neue Forschungen über Deutschland und England," in K. Tenfelde, ed., *Arbeiter und Arbeiterbewegung im Vergleich. Berichte zur internationalen historischen Forschung* (München, 1986), 611-664; E. Heinemann, *Für Kaiser und Vaterland. Hildesheim im Ersten Weltkrieg* (Hildesheim, 1989); K. Hartewig, *Das unberechenbare Jahrzehnt. Bergarbeiter und ihre Familien im Ruhrgebiet 1914-1924* (München, 1992); B. Sicken, "Die Festungs- und Garnisonsstadt Wesel im Ersten Weltkrieg: Kriegsauswirkungen und Versorgungsprobleme," in B. Kirchgässner and G. Scholz, eds., *Stadt und Krieg* (Sigmaringen, 1989), 125-222; A. Roerkohl, *Hungerblockade und Heimatfront. Die kommunale Lebensmittelversorgung in Westfalen während des Ersten Weltkriegs* (Stuttgart, 1991); M. Faust, *Sozialer Burgfrieden im Ersten Weltkrieg. Christliche und sozialistische Arbeiterbewegung in Köln* (Essen, 1992); J. Rund, *Ernährungswirtschaft und Zwangsarbeit im Raum Hannover 1914 bis 1923* (Hannover, 1992); V. Ullrich, "Kriegsalltag und deutsche Arbeiterschaft 1914-1918," *Geschichte in Wissenschaft und Unterricht* 43 (1992): 220-230. On the social and cultural history of the First World War, see: E. Jirgal, *Die*

Introduction

Wiederkehr des Weltkriegs in der Literatur (Wien and Leipzig, 1931); W. K. Pfeiler, *War and the German Mind*. *The Testimony of Men of Fiction who Fought at the Front* (New York, 1941); K.-L. Ay, *Die Entstehung einer Revolution. Die Volksstimmung in Bayern während des Ersten Weltkriegs* (Berlin, 1968); P. Fussell, *The Great War and Modern Memory* (London, 1975); H. M. Klein, ed., *The First World War in Fiction* (London, 1976); E. J. Leed, *No Man's Land. Combat and Identity in World War I* (Cambridge, 1979); H. M. Klein, "Class and Disillusionment in World War I," *JMH* 50 (1978): 680–699; R. Wohl, *The Generation of 1914* (Cambridge, Mass., 1979); K. Vondung, ed., *Kriegserlebnis. Der Erste Weltkrieg in der literarischen Gestaltung und symbolischen Deutung der Nationen* (Göttingen, 1980); T. Ashworth, *Trench Warfare 1914–1918. The Live and Let Live System* (London, 1980); B. Hüppauf, ed., *Ansichten vom Krieg. Vergleichende Studien zum Ersten Weltkrieg in Literatur und Gesellschaft* (Königstein/Ts., 1984); L. Burchardt, "The Impact of the War Economy on the Civilian Population of Germany during the First and Second World War," in W. Deist, ed., *The German Military in the Age of Total War* (Leamington, 1985), 40–70; J.-J. Becker, *The Great War and the French People* (Oxford et al., 1986); K. Möser, "Kriegsgeschichte und Kriegsliteratur. Formen der Verarbeitung des Ersten Weltkriegs," *MGM* 49 (1986): 39–51; P. Knoch, ed., *Menschen im Krieg 1914–1918* (Ludwigsburg, 1987); J. M. Winter, *The Experience of World War I* (London, 1988); Wall and Winter, eds., *The Upheaval of War*; P. Knoch, ed., *Kriegsalltag. Die Rekonstruktion des Kriegsalltags als Aufgabe der historischen Forschung und der Friedenserziehung* (Stuttgart, 1989); B. Murdoch, *Fighting Songs and Warring Words. Popular Lyrics of Two World Wars* (London et al., 1990); E. A. Marsland, *The Nation's Cause. French, English and German Poetry of the First World War* (London et al., 1990); S. Audoin-Rouzeau, *14–18: Men at War. Reports from the French Trenches* (New York et al., 1991); P. Fridenson, ed., *The French Home Front 1914–1918* (Oxford, 1992); G. Hirschfeld and G. Krumeich, eds., "*Keiner fühlt sich hier mehr als Mensch...*" *Erlebnis und Wirkung des Ersten Weltkriegs* (Essen, 1993); B. Ulrich and B. Ziemann, eds., *Frontalltag im Ersten Weltkrieg* (Frankfurt/M., 1994); H. Fries, *Die große Katharsis. Der Erste Weltkrieg in der Sicht deutscher Gelehrter und Künstler*, 2 vols (Konstanz, 1995); H. Cecil and P. Liddle, eds., *Facing Armageddon: The First World War Experienced* (London, 1996); B. Hüppauf, ed., *War, Violence, and the Modern Condition* (Berlin, 1997); B. Ziemann, *Front und Heimat. Ländliche Kriegserfahrungen im südlichen Bayern 1914–1923* (Essen, 1997); G. Hirschfeld et al., eds., *Kriegserfahrungen. Studien zur Sozial- und Mentalitätsgeschichte des Ersten Weltkriegs* (Essen, 1997).

12. For the use of the concept of modernization in contemporary historiography, see: B. H.-U. Wehler, *Modernisierungstheorie und Geschichte* (Göttingen, 1975); Th. Nipperdey, "Probleme der Modernisierung in Deutschland," *Saeculum* 30 (1979): 292–303; R. Scholz, "Gesellschaftsgeschichte als 'Paradigma' der Geschichtsschreibung," in R. Scholz, ed., *Kritik der Sozialgeschichtsschreibung* (Hamburg, 1991), 87–133.

13. See, for example, S. Bajohr, *Die Hälfte der Fabrik. Geschichte der Frauenarbeit in Deutschland 1914 bis 1945* (Marburg/L., 1979), 101, 119, 127; U. von Gersdorff, *Frauen im Kriegsdienst 1914–1945* (Stuttgart, 1969), 10. Von Gersdorff later toned down her position; see her article "Frauenarbeit und

17

The War from Within

Frauenemanzipation im Ersten Weltkrieg," *Francia* 2 (1974): 522; Bieber, *Gewerkschaften*, 207; Chr. Sachße, *Mütterlichkeit als Beruf. Sozialarbeit, Sozialreform und Frauenbewegung 1871–1929* (Frankfurt/M., 1986), 152. This assumption of the First World War's beneficial effect on the role of women in society runs through an immense number of other publications. See, for example, M.-E. Lüders, *Das unbekannte Heer. Frauen kämpfen für Deutschland 1914–1918* (Berlin, 1937), 226-229 and *passim*; Ch. Lorenz, "Die gewerbliche Frauenarbeit während des Kriegs," in P. Umbreit and Ch. Lorenz, *Der Krieg und die Arbeitsverhältnisse* (Stuttgart et al., 1928); 390 and *passim*; A. Seidel, *Frauenarbeit im Ersten Weltkrieg als Problem der staatlichen Sozialpolitik, dargestellt am Beispiel Bayerns* (Frankfurt/M., 1979), 3 and *passim*; A. Marwick, *War and Social Change in the Twentieth Century. A Comparative Study of Britain, France, Germany, Russia and the United States* (London, 1974), 49, 223 and *passim*.

14. For this, in particular see U. Gerhard, *Verhältnisse und Verhinderungen. Frauenarbeit, Familie und Rechte der Frauen im 19. Jahrhundert* (Frankfurt/M., 1981), and H. Schröder, *Die Rechtlosigkeit der Frau im Rechtsstaat. Dargestellt am Allgemeinen Preußichen Landrecht, am Bürgerlichen Gesetzbuch und an J. G. Fichtes Grundlage des Naturrechts* (Frankfurt/M. and New York, 1979).

15. See, for example, G. Bock and B. Duden, "Arbeit aus Liebe - Liebe als Arbeit. Zur Entstehung der Hausarbeit im Kapitalismus," in *Frauen und Wissenschaft. Beiträge zur Berliner Sommeruniversität für Frauen Juli 1976* (Berlin, 1977), 118-200; H. Rosenbaum, *Formen der Familie* (Frankfurt/M., 1982); U. Frevert, "The Civilising Tendency of Hygiene," in Fout, ed., *German Women*, 320-344.

16. P. L. Berger and Th. Luckmann, *Die gesellschaftliche Konstruktion der Wirklichkeit. Eine Theorie der Wissenssoziologie* (Frankfurt/M., 1982); A. Schütz and Th. Luckmann, *Strukturen der Lebenswelt*, 2 vols (Frankfurt/M., 1979/84); W. M. Sprondel and R. Grathoff, eds., *Alfred Schütz und die Idee des Alltags in den Sozialwissenschaften* (Stuttgart, 1979); K. Hammerich und M. Klein, eds., *Materialien zur Soziologie des Alltags. KZSS*-Special Edition, vol. 20, 1978 (Opladen, 1978); L. Landgrebe, "Lebenswelt und Geschichtlichkeit des menschlichen Daseins," in B. Waldenfels et al., eds., *Phänomenologie und Marxismus*, 2: *Praktische Philosophie* (Frankfurt/M., 1977), 13-58; A. Schütz, *Gesammelte Aufsätze*, 3 vols (Den Haag, 1971/72); A. Schütz and T. Parsons, *Zur Theorie sozialen Handelns. Ein Briefwechsel* (Frankfurt/M., 1977); Th. Luckmann, *Lebenswelt und Gesellschaft. Grundstrukturen und geschichtliche Wandlungen* (Paderborn et al., 1980); A. Giddens, *The Constitution of Society. Outline of the Theory of Structuration* (Cambridge, 1984).

17. Berger and Luckmann, *Konstruktion*, 164.

18. A. Heller, *Alltag und Geschichte. Zur sozialistischen Gesellschaftslehre* (Neuwied and Berlin, 1970); A. Heller, *Das Alltagsleben. Versuch einer Erklärung der individuellen Reproduktion* (Frankfurt/M., 1978).

19. Schütz and Luckmann, *Strukturen* 1: 25-130.

20. Heller, *Alltagsleben*, 24-25, 30, 86-87.

21. Ibid., 151, 278.

22. Th. Mann, *Betrachtungen eines Unpolitischen*, in *Gesammelte Werke* (Frankfurt/M., 1974), 12: 11.

23. Lessing, *Geschichte*, 156.

18

2

War as Event: August 1914 and the First Months of the War

War, war, the people have risen - it is as though they were not there at all before and now all at once, they are immense and touching.

K. Riezler, 14 August 1914[1]

In the evening of 31 July 1914, at 8 p.m., "an officer, accompanied by about half a platoon and one musician" appeared "in the [Hamburg] City Hall marketplace and, after a drumroll, read aloud a declaration of war. The parade had the effect that the entire market was immediately full of people. It was scarcely clear to the crowd what it was all about, and it quickly dispersed again."[2] The observer quoted above assumed that hardly any of those assembled before the Hamburg City Hall were in the position to recognize that this ritual was the execution of a 63-year-old Prussian law, which stipulated that a public proclamation of war be made by troops and to the "beat of drums or the sound of trumpets."[3] When we look back on the First World War, this assumption serves as a starting point: Was this "anachronistic parade" at the beginning of a war that has gone down in history as the first completely mechanized "human slaughterhouse"[4] more than a mere absurdity? And who, outside of the crowd of people gathered in the Hamburg City Hall marketplace, really knew "what it was about," what the drums announced? Both questions point to the same fact: Not only were the rituals that marked the beginning of the First World War anachronistic, but so were the conceptions, planning and equipment relevant to the war. And these anachronistic ideas affected the "spectators" and the "drummers," i.e. the population and the government and the military, equally. In March 1917, a man from Lower Bavaria noted in a letter: "this isn't a war anymore it's a slaughter of people, yuck."[5] This remark accurately describes the discrepancy

19

between the power of imagination and reality that characterized German society in the last months of 1914. In 1914, war was imaginable only as a military event, not as a permanent state of affairs that would last four years and embrace the whole of society. It was this anachronistic horizon of expectation[6] that gave the first months of the war their contradictory double countenance. The mass enthusiasm of German society, unaware of things to come, was coupled with the penetration of the requirements of war, unmitigated by any prior planning, into virtually every social and economic sector. What do these two characteristic aspects of the first months of war – i.e. the "August experience" and the collective *Burgfrieden* mentality on the one hand, and the precipitate and unplanned changes in society and the economy on the other – say about women? What was their part in the "immense" and "touching" entrance that the people, in Kurt Riezler's view, made onto the stage of history at the beginning of the First World War?

There can be no doubt that this initial, collective euphoria about the war actually existed, and that it was not an invention of the censored press or official announcements. However much the propaganda activities of the Naval League (*Flottenverein*) or of other sources and groups may have contributed to this mass enthusiasm, it was also fueled by the most varied political, social, and emotional hopes and needs. And although it remained primarily the privilege of writers of the middle classes to convey a sense of this euphoria to posterity,[7] the euphoria itself encompassed all classes. Berlin's police commissioner (*Polizeipräsident*) described this phenomenon as follows: "Those detectives who professionally have a lot of contact with workers' groups can't believe that the same people who just a short time ago were organizing protests and giving three cheers to the Internationale are now brimming over with patriotism."[8]

After the first victory on the Western Front, the police commissioner was of the opinion that it was only the shortage of flags that had put an end to the workers' patriotic decorating of their neighborhoods.[9] In his novel *Jahrgang 1902*, Ernst Glaeser used the image of the shooting fair (*Schützenfest*), during which small-town bourgeoisie, Social Democrats and trade unionists got drunk together on beer and patriotism, to capture the "August experience" and this *Burgfrieden*-euphoria. After several glasses of beer, the young protagonist of the novel has his own personal

War as Event: August 1914 and the First Months of the War

"August experience:" "Next to me, August said: 'Now everybody is the same. There aren't any differences anymore.' 'Yes,' I mumbled and futilely tried to bring a face into focus, 'I don't see any differences anymore, either.'"[10]

Nothing indicates that women's reaction to the First World War was in any way dissimilar to that of the rest of society. Men and women, adults and adolescents, workers and white-collar employees, city-dwellers and farmers collectively breathed life into the official symbolic interpretation of the war as a fight in defense of the German people. Independently of one other, rumors spread across the German Empire like an informal communication network, populating it with enemy well-poisoners, French automobiles that were supposedly transporting part of Paris' war treasure to Russia, and spies, who in many cases were said to be disguised as women. This flood of rumors was simultaneously an expression and an intensification of the "August experience," i.e. of the fundamental opinion that literally turned the proclaimed unity of the state and the people into an actual experience. The military threat to the state was experienced as a personal threat to individuals, and for this personal experience, the appropriate images of spies and well-poisoners were circulated. This basic stance of the population, which had materialized in the form of rumors, very often erupted in spontaneous, collective action:

> As we were in Nienburg, another train pulled in, which was transporting Austrian soldiers from Bremen to the French border. Suddenly the rumour spread that a Russian spy was hiding in the train. In no time, we thousand sailors had armed ourselves with rocks and boards and stormed the train, screaming with the wildest rage. All the cars were searched inside and out. "Here he is." Everybody rushed to the back of the train. "Here he is." Everybody rushed to the front. And then they found him under the locomotive. As he was pulled out, he got several bloody blows on the head, until he turned out to be one of our own people. He was on one side and had crept under the locomotive to look, and from the other side, someone had dragged him out as a spy.[11]

However, small, but not insignificant adjustments must be made to this uniform picture, as far as women are concerned.

The "community of the people" (*Volksgemeinschaft*) that was propagated and experienced at the beginning of the war included men and women to the same degree. To interpret this as a levelling out of prescribed gender differences would be incorrect, however. The role that was assigned to women in the official discourse of the first months of the war as their specific war contribution – i.e the societal paradigm[12] "woman in war" – indicates a greater stereotyping and thereby a solidification rather than a blurring of gender-specific attributes. With only slight exaggeration, we could summarize the public description of gender-specific differences, in so far as this was a reflection of the state of the war, as follows. "Man" was identical with "soldier," "woman" was identical with "what the soldier defends" and "who takes care of the soldier," as well as with "who supports the soldier's relatives." As the Bavarian Queen Marie Therese said in her appeal on 2 August 1914 to the women of Bavaria:

> Of you, who are not granted the privilege of defending the dignity of the Fatherland with blood and life, I ask most fervently that you contribute with all your strength to easing the suffering of every brave man wounded by the enemy bullet or thrown ailing to the ground by the hardships of war. Like my daughters Hildegard, Helmtrude and Gundelinde, put yourselves . . . at the service of the Red Cross. [Help was also needed at home.] My daughters Adelgunde and Wilt-rude are working in the welfare field . . . As in the campaign of 1870–1871, Bavaria's women and virgins will fulfill their patriotic duty, this I know, for such service of women is pleasing to God.[13]

In the next four years, the social paradigm of "woman (in war)" accumulated additional characteristic features. "Woman," for example, came to be equated with the individual "who supplies the soldier with ammunition." This paradigm also became, much more than in the first few months of war, the site of competing definitions. The complementary nature of the gender roles, as it was emphasized in the attributions at the war's outset, remained intact, however.

This complementarity in the assignment of gender roles was also repeated on another level. Analogous to the accentuated division between male and female participation in the war, an equally sharp line was drawn between women and men who were on one or the other side of the fronts. The images of the "patriotic woman" and the "enemy woman" played an important role in the war propaganda of all the belligerent nations, both in that directed abroad and in that aimed at a state's own population. The words of an 8-year-old newspaper reader provide a good summary of this second facet of society's picture of women.

War as Event: August 1914 and the First Months of the War

Monday, 17 August 1914. Today I read about countless atrocities. The Belgians are really very underhand people, and that's what one calls "Frankierisch" [*franctireur*] in German. They shoot out of the attic windows or they lure our soldiers into their houses, where they are poisoned and then murdered. There are also scoundrels in Belgium, and that's the women, who sit in hidden corners and start shooting when a soldier goes by, so that he is really frightened and also often falls down dead. But then the Belgians write in their newspapers that the Germans are cruel and blood-thirsty barbarians who nail their enemies to the ground, cut off their ears and noses and who, for no reason, gouge out the eyes of small children and infants and then eat them raw for breakfast. Papa doesn't believe, however, that German soldiers eat small children totally raw.[14]

In a later journal entry, this same avid newspaper reader wrote: "Many German women and girls fondle the French prisoners, which isn't right."[15] These words allude to the second correction that needs to be made to the "August experience" with regard to women. When the first transports of French prisoners of war rolled into Germany, they were given a warm reception in many places by women, the friendly tone of which raised a cry of indignation heard in newspaper articles, letters to the editor and petitions.[16]

Where we find this "undignified" behavior specified at all, the complaint lay in the perception that women allowed the prisoners, when they arrived at the train station or later in the prison camp, to receive too good provisions. In the eyes of the critics, the regaling of prisoners with wine and chocolate constituted an unpatriotic act. The orders of the Elberfeld rail commander to the train stations under his jurisdiction provide a good example of this sentiment. As he wrote: "During the transport of prisoners of war, German women and girls have sometimes behaved in an undignified manner. I request that station masters intervene in the strongest manner, as soon as our national honor is offended by such elements."[17]

Other military officers issued similar announcements and, in some cities, also reintroduced the stocks for such women. The Stuttgart General Command (*Generalkommando*), for example, ordered that they be taken into custody and their names published.[18] And the fact that a military staff doctor could slap a woman in public,[19] without being criticized for it, underlines once again what was actually at issue. The women concerned were not admonished for wasting food, but rather, for violating the code of patriotic behavior. These women's motives for acting in such a manner cannot be considered here. Their behavior and the consequent public reaction provide a sure clue, however, that contact between German women and foreign prisoners of war was a conflict-laden issue in the public perception and control of female behavior. The fact that prisoners of war had provisions did not cause offense in and of itself; the problem was, rather, that German women took care of "enemy" men. This attraction was confirmed later in the war when more and more prisoners of war were employed in factories and on farms, thereby constantly increasing the possibilities of their contact with the female population.

"A sudden consternation has taken hold of economic life."[20] The city of Neukölln introduced its war administration (*Kriegsverwaltung*) report with these words, but they are equally applicable as a description of the impact of the war's outbreak on working women. From a material standpoint, they suffered a general loss in pecuniary income. Conscripted men no longer served as wage-earners and working women themselves lost their jobs in innumerable cases as a result of the slowdown in production.

It is important to consider the extent of this collapse. By the end of 1914, roughly 40% of all men eligible for military service had been drafted.[21] If one assumes that, of these approximately 5½ million men, a good half were married – this was the proportion in 1915, when 5 million out of 9 million conscripted men were married, and thus well over one-third of all married men had been drafted[22] – then the number of husbands serving at the front or in the garrison at the end of 1914 amounted to approximately 2¾ million. The number of families and women who were financially affected by this mobilization of men needs to be calculated somewhat higher however, since not only married men supported relatives. And in 1914 and 1915, female unemployment was so high that, in the index of the 1915 *Archiv für Frauenarbeit*, it laconically read: "For Working Women, see Unemployment." According to the skilled workers' associations' statistics for August 1914, 19.9 out of every 100 male union members were unemployed and 31.9 out of every 100 female members. In many workers' associations, more than half of the organized women were out of work.[23] On 1 August, the

War as Event: August 1914 and the First Months of the War

Nuremberg Free Trade Unions (*Freie Gewerkschaften*) counted 2,084 unemployed individuals among their members, 21% of whom were women; on 1 September, 11,985 unemployed individuals, 43% of whom were women; and on 1 October, 8,183 unemployed individuals, 55% of whom were women.[24] There are several reasons why women constituted a disproportionately high percentage throughout the Reich of those made unemployed by the war. Of these reasons, the mobilization of soldiers, which increasingly reduced male unemployment in contrast to that of women, is the most obvious. Many unemployed men who did not belong to those age groups called up for service first tried to expedite this process on their own by seeking early conscription. As the commanding general of the 7th Army Corps Münster (*Armeekorps*, the army corps were the administrative arms of the military commanders at home) said in September 1914, many Home Guard (*Landsturm*) draftees went

> so far as to implore me to conscript them into the army, not only so that their worries about their livelihood should be relieved in this way, but also that their relatives might be blessed with state and local support. Of course I cannot fulfill these latter requests, since the army is not a welfare organization for financially weak individuals.[25]

The conscription of male labor created disproportionately high unemployment among women not only on paper, but also in reality. Because so many male skilled workers were drafted, countless departments within companies, as well as entire companies themselves, had to be closed and consequently, large numbers of unskilled (i.e. female) labor laid off. The other factors that caused this high female unemployment were structural in nature. Female labor, for example, was highly concentrated in those industries, such as the textile industry, that were particularly hard hit by the conversion to a war economy. In addition, the skill level of female workers was generally low and their mobility in the labor market, due to family obligations, limited; they were, as a result, less competitive and less employable than men. Finally, there were many unemployed female domestic servants who, partly out of panic and partly out of patriotism, had been discharged by their "masters."

After the outbreak of war, it became the principal task of government and community social policy to cushion, if not stop, the fall into poverty of widening circles of the population, in particular of working-class women and families. This was achieved primarily by giving financial assistance to the families of conscripted soldiers. This Family Aid (*Familienunterstützung*) was based on the "Law regarding the Support of Families of Men in Military Service" (*"Gesetz betreffend die Unterstützung von Familien in den Dienst eingetretener Mannschaften"*) of 28 February 1888 and 4 August 1914 and provided for the payment of imperial subsidies, to be first advanced by the cities and districts, to such families.[26] The law stipulated that the Empire's subsidy be further increased by the respective community, until the recipient's need was met.

Calculations based on the individual records kept by the Berlin aid authorities reveal the following "snapshot" of the change in "war families'" standard of living once they made the transition from earned income to Family Aid. The average income of a skilled worker's family with one child fell from 128.52 to 30.00 marks per month (23.34%); its rent, on the other hand, remained constant at, on average, 26.71 marks per month. As the number of children in a family increased – a factor that played a role in subsidy calculations – this ratio improved somewhat. The family of a skilled worked with four children, for example, received 49.56% of the husband's previous wage. Families of unskilled workers with one child saw their average monthly income drop from 99.62 to 30.00 marks, or 30.11% of what they had formerly earned. Their monthly rent on average 20.61 marks. In this instance, the existence of four children raised the percentage to 69.73%. Families of unskilled workers with at least nine children belonged to the rare category of wage workers who actually received a "salary increase" because of war welfare. They received 116.31% of the husband's former wage. (All figures quoted here include Berlin's municipal supplements of 100%.)[27] By the end of September, only 926 of the nearly 3,800 municipalities with more than 2,000 inhabitants had supplemented the exceedingly low subsidies from the Reich. By the end of January 1915, the figure had risen to 1,729, which included all big cities, apart from Saarbrücken.[28] In many communities, it was necessary to grant a special rent subsidy in order to prevent "war families" from being evicted.[29] Larger companies also participated in maintaining the families of their conscripted workers. Unemployment assistance, for which neither the Reich nor the separate German states acknowledged a responsibility at the beginning of the war, was paid by municipalities and trade unions. By the end of October 1914, consequently, the trade unions had spent 12.8 million marks on unemployment.[30]

What happens, then, when we place this rather static and necessarily statistical "snapshot" of the situation of working women in the first months of war again into its fluid historical context? The available sources make this possible for the administrative region (*Regierungsbezirk*) of Düsseldorf. In this first weeks of the war, the picture was still very uniform.[31] The rush of men to join the war effort was so great that many volunteers had to be rejected – the single exception here being the Hubbelrath Mayor's Office – and the "competition of married and unmarried women to become patriotically active"[32] did not leave working class women untouched. Industrial unemployment was just as common as the nascent increase in food prices, which was intensified by the "panic buying" of municipalities and of those families with enough disposable income. Countless municipalities enacted price freezes, which were designed to oppose the "dirty and unpatriotic usury efforts of the traders."[33] They were, however, usually rescinded after a few weeks. From this point on, the effects of the war on the social position of working-class women and families became much more differentiated. By the end of 1914, the establishment of military contracts had considerably reduced unemployment in many places, albeit generally more slowly for women than for men. In contrast to Duisburg, Essen, Mülheim, Oberhausen and Düsseldorf, which had already begun to complain about a lack of labor, cities such as Krefeld, Elberfeld and Barmen, whose production structure, specialized for the textile industry, impeded the transition to military contracts, recorded even higher levels of unemployment.[34] Another line of differentiation proved to be equally important for the social situation of working-class families. This line had already existed before the war, but now took on a completely new urgency, which intensified during the course of the war. On one side of this line stood those working-class families which relied almost exclusively on the market to reproduce themselves, i.e. who had to pay rent and buy their food. On the other side were those families which owned an apartment and/or piece of land, which they could then use to grow their own food. As a general rule of thumb, we could say that the higher the integration of a working-class family into the

market system and the more this family had to satisfy its everyday
needs through money transactions, the more detrimentally it was
affected by the war situation. The number of working-class families that could reproduce themselves using two "tracks," i.e. the
market and money, as well as domestic agricultural production
for either personal use or sale, appears to be substantial, even in
those areas that were highly industrial.[35]

At one end of the scale were those working-class and "war
families" whose social position deteriorated only slightly – and
sometimes even improved – at the beginning of the war. Women
from some of these families now had more cash at their disposal
than previously. They received this money directly, no longer
transmitted through male wage-earners, and, for many families,
conscription had meant the departure of their main consumers.
The fact that these women also spent this money generated
lasting public outrage. As the Landrat of Moers complained in
December 1914:

> Unfortunately, many women do not know how to handle money. An
> excessive amount of money is now, in particular, being spent in
> working-class circles on sweets, finery and other luxury items. In
> the absence of their husbands, many women are neglecting house-
> keeping and children, and, along with their children, are subsisting
> on bread, butter and meat. Without generalizing to undue proportions,
> one cannot deny, however, the grave social ills in working-class
> settlements. The cause lies, no doubt, in the fact that money is too
> easily acquired, not properly earned, and that many women, in losing
> their husbands, have also lost their stable support, which has not
> exactly been replaced by want.[36]

In the course of time, many more voices joined the Landrat in
his lament, which ran along the lines of "distress at home spares
the husband." These voices shaped the social paradigm of "war
wife" until the end of the war.

At the other end of the aforementioned scale were those families which did not own an apartment and/or land, did not receive
assistance from many outside sources and which, additionally,
probably fell more into debt. Debt was not uncommon among
"war families," since mobilization, which was aimed at young
men and husbands, often came at exactly that phase in the
family's cycle in which loans, taken out to establish the household, needed to be paid back.

Lists gathered in February 1915 from the cities and districts of the administrative region of Düsseldorf, in which several particularly needy individuals were recommended to receive an extraordinary donation from the poor fund, provide a glimpse into the situation of those women and families living at subsistence level.[37] From this group of 61 women – no men or, for that matter, complete families were included in the recommendation – 16 were widows. Only 6 of the women did not have children. The other 55 had, between them, 267 children under the age of 14. (The question of whether the high number of children was a criterium for selection or exclusively an expression of the difficult situation of large families must remain unanswered here.) That means that every woman had to take care of, on average, 4.8 children under 14. The average age of the women was 39. Only one, a 25-year-old cleaning woman, had earnings of her own, which amounted to 3 marks a week. A 29-year-old ironer and a 30-year-old laundress from Moers had lost their income at the beginning of the war, when their customers, primarily mine workers, were drafted. Before the war, one widow, with two children older than 14 and two younger, had earned a living by renting rooms to three male lodgers. Two of these were conscripted; the widow, consequently, earned hardly any income, but still had 40 marks in rent to pay a month. After her husband was called up, one married women from Düsseldorf, who had three children under 14, supplemented her 56 marks a month of war aid by delivering newspapers and taking in washing. Her doctor, however, ordered her to discontinue this work because of her heart problems. This woman's situation was further complicated by the fact that her husband, unknown to her, had taken out several large loans, which she then had to pay back if she did not want to have her possessions impounded. The wife of a conscripted plumber, who had six children under 14, only earned enough by renting out three apartment houses to cover the interest on their mortgages, since the apartments were either empty or the tenants themselves could not pay the rent. The other women included on the list do not seem to have had any personal income before the war, a conclusion also suggested by the large size of their families.

The information collected about the living conditions of the sixteen widows effectively proves that the situation of widowed women without their own resources – which, independent of the effects of war, was problematic enough – now approached the intolerable.[38] Twelve of these women had children. Two had one child, one woman had two children, three had three, three widows had four children and three had six, respectively. Only six of these women received family assistance. Five received no government support and the rest received public monies designated either for the poor or for widows and orphans, which ranged between 3.20 and 52 marks a month.

All the other women recommended to receive this special aid supplement were, with one exception, married to conscripted men. They received, on average, 65 marks a month. The lowest amount of 30 marks a month was alloted to a childless woman whose monthly rent was 22 marks; the highest, 122.50 marks a month, to a woman with 11 children under the age of 14. The average monthly rent was 18 marks. As a result of the more or less emphatic persuasion of the municipalities, many landlords had lowered their rents. They then recouped a portion of this loss from the municipalities.

It would be interesting to know how strongly these women themselves experienced their situation as an express consequence of the war and not "only" as the continuation of a plight that had already existed before its onset. This question, unfortunately, can only be answered approximately. We can assume that these women's own processing of their situation was conditioned, among other factors, by the extent to which they felt it to be a break from their pre-war existence. One such decisive rupture, i.e. the conscription of male family members and particularly of husbands, was certainly commonplace. More narrowly, the break in these women's material life situation can only be measured if we can ascertain their own criteria for comparison: What standard of living was normal for these women before August 1914 and could then serve as a basis for judging their present circumstances? One possible indicator is the husband's civilian profession, which hitherto had essentially determined a family's standard of living. Thirty-four of the women indicated their husband's occupation, which are as follows: three bricklayers, three factory workers, two day-laborers, two stone-cutters, a farmer, a tenant farmer (with a pre-war monthly wage of 33 marks), a weaver, an assembly-line worker, a dockworker, a mill worker, a dyer, a handyman (whose pre-war income had been 120 marks a month), a woodworker, a milkman, a sailor, a traveling salesman (who had earned approximately 150 marks a month), a warehouse manager, a plasterer, a coachman, a master baker, a bookbinder, a plumber (and owner of three apartment houses), a blacksmith (who had earned between 80 and 100 marks a month before the war), a cabinet maker, a self-employed carpenter, an independent building contractor (whose properties were in debt), a cutter (with a pre-war earnings of 110 to 112 marks a month) and a head waiter.

This list occasions a brief comment. The spectrum of professions cited here stretches from unskilled workers to members of the self-employed middle class. The fact that women and families of such varied backgrounds could suddenly appear on the same list of the needy possesses a significance that extends beyond these individual cases. It refers to the question of meaningful criteria for determining women's social differentiation, which poses itself anew for the war period. That the emphasis of this work lies on wage-working women and female members of working-class families should not be understood as the anticipated answer to this question. At this juncture, I would advance the following provisional thesis: The conscription of men created a separate class of women whose material situation was determined to a much greater extent by the effects of the First World War than by the social distinctions of the pre-war period. The class of "war wives" was differentiated according to the material impact of the war and the perception of their changed situation by women themselves. The "war wife" was normatively and clearly delimited in public discourse and, during the course of the war, she, in turn, developed her own self-understanding.

In his First World War narrative *Wir fordern Reims zur Übergabe auf*,[39] Rudolf G. Binding provides a memorable picture of the war's transition from momentary event to permanent state. When, in their advance on Paris, the German troops reached Reims in the first weeks of the war, the city was supposed to be asked to surrender peacefully. Commissioned with these orders, three members of the German army were sent in a "brave-looking" vehicle across enemy lines. They consisted of an aggressive young captain with the white flag of surrender, a chivalrous cavalry captain armed with his grandfather's saber, and an opera singer, who had freely volunteered for the war, with a bugle. The bugle was to take the place of the trumpet, which was just as necessary as the white flag, according to army regulations, for the ritual of surrender negotiations. As a result of a misunderstanding, the three peace envoys were arrested by the French as spies. The misunderstanding was resolved. The three Germans, however, were held for several weeks under the strictest information ban in order to ensure that, when they returned to their own lines, they could not bring any strategically important information with them. During this time, the battle of the Marne took place, after which the war on the Western Front was transformed from one of movement into one of position. The opposing armies fortified themselves in a system of trenches, from which, for the next four years, from the North Sea to the Swiss border, they would face one another. After their liberation, these three clueless soldiers, with their memories of a war that had not existed for a long time, seemed like ghostly Don Quixotes. Transplanted, with no transition, into this new, dug-in war, they experienced the expiration of their former categories of thought and their expectations about the war as a trauma, for which nothing had prepared them.

After the battle of the Marne, a rethinking and restructuring was not only imperative for the narrower interests of the military. The problem of how to cope with the war as a permanent state extended to society as a whole and, towards the end of 1914, imposed itself ever more urgently on the consciousness of the government and population on the home front. The army required reinforcements of men and materials. The population needed to learn how to survive. And the civil authorities – Reich, states and municipalities – and the military commanders somehow had to reconcile these two competing interests. The wheel was in motion; the spokes, however, still had to be put into place. The consequences of this process for wage-working women and how they handled them is the subject of the following account.

Notes to Chapter 2

1. K. D. Erdmann, ed., *Kurt Riezler: Tagebücher, Aufsätze, Dokumente* (Göttingen, 1972), journal entry from 14 August 1914.

2. Senatsreferent to Senatspräsident, 1 August 1914: StA Hamburg, Kriegsakten des Senats AIB.

War as Event: August 1914 and the First Months of the War

3. "Preußisches Kriegszustandsgesetz," 1851, rpt. in: I. Jastrow, *Im Kriegszustand. Die Umformung der öffentlichen Lebens in den ersten Kriegswochen* (Berlin, 1914), 134-138.

4. Such is the title of a novel published shortly before the First World War: W. Lamszus, *Das Menschenschlachthaus. Visionen vom Krieg*, 2 pts. (Leipzig, 1923).

5. Letter excerpt, March 1917: HStA/Kr, I. Bayerisches AK, 1979.

6. As one example of many, see for example, C. Delrück, *Die wirtschaftliche Mobilmachung in Deutschland 1914* (München, 1924), 63-92.

7. Regarding the "August experience" and the "ideas of 1914," see H. Lübbe, "Die philosophischen Ideen von 1914," in H. Lübbe, *Politische Philosophie in Deutschland* (München, 1974), 173-238; E. Koester, *Literatur und Weltkriegsideologie. Positionen und Begründungszusammenhänge des publizistichen Engagements deutscher Schriftsteller im Ersten Weltkrieg* (Kronberg/Ts., 1977), particularly 134-143; K. Vondung, "Deutsche Apokalypse 1914," in K. Vondung, ed., *Das Wilhelminische Bildungsbürgertum. Zur Sozialgeschichte seiner Ideen* (Göttingen, 1976), 153-171; K. Vondung, ed., *Kriegserlebnis. Der Erste Weltkrieg in der literarischen Gestaltung und symbolischen Deutung der Nationen* (Göttingen, 1980); R. Rürup, "Der 'Geist von 1914' in Deutschland. Kriegsbegeisterung und Ideologisierung des Kriegs im Ersten Weltkrieg," in B. Hüppauf, ed., *Ansichten vom Krieg. Vergleichende Studien zum Ersten Weltkrieg in Literatur und Gesellschaft* (Königstein/Ts., 1984), 1-30; *August 1914: Ein Volk zieht in den Krieg*, Berliner Geschichtswerkstatt ed. (Berlin, 1989); M. C. C. Adams, *The Great Adventure. Male Desire and the Coming of World War I* (Bloomington and Indianapolis, 1990). Recent publications relativize the impact of the "Augusterlebnis": J. Verhey, *The "Spirit of 1914". The Myth of Enthusiasm and the Rhetoric of Unity in World War I Germany* (Diss. Berkeley, University of California, 1991); W. Kruse, *Krieg und nationale Integration. Eine Neuinterpretation des sozialdemokratischen Burgfriedensschlusses 1914/15* (Essen, 1993); M. Stöcker, *Das Augusterlebnis 1914 in Darmstadt* (Darmstadt, 1994); Th. Raithel, *Das "Wunder" der inneren Einheit. Studien zur deutschen und französischen Öffentlichkeit bei Beginn des Ersten Weltkriegs* (Bonn, 1996); Chr. Geinitz and U. Hinz, "Das Augusterlebnis in Südbaden", in G. Hirschfeld et al., eds., *Kriegserfahrungen. Studien zur Sozial- und Mentalitätsgeschichte des Ersten Weltkriegs* (Essen, 1997), 20-35.

8. Bericht des Berliner Polizeipräsidenten, nos. 4 and 5, September 1914: ZStA Potsdam, Reichskanzlei 2398. These reports have since been edited and published; see I. Materna and H.-J. Schreckenbach, eds., *Berichte des Berliner Polizeipräsidenten zur Stimmung und Lage der Bevölkerung in Berlin: 1914-1918* (Weimar, 1987).

9. Ibid.

10. E. Glaeser, *Jahrgang 1902* (Berlin, 1931), 195-203, quotation, 201. See, as well, M. Stickelberger-Eder, *Aufbruch 1914. Kriegsromane der späten Weimarer Republik* (Zürich and München, 1983).

11. J. Ringelnatz, *Als Mariner im Krieg* (Reinbek, 1977), 12. Max Beckmann also experienced a spy chase, with himself as the leading character: M. Beckmann, *Briefe im Kriege 1914/1915* (München and Zürich, 1984), 14-17. The rumors circulating in Barmen at the outset of the war have been compiled by H. Haacke, *Barmen im Weltkrieg* (Barmen, 1929), 31ff. On the so-called

The War from Within

mobilization psychoses, see also P. Plaut, *Psychographie des Krieges*, in W. Stern and O. Lipmann, eds., *Beiträge zur Psychologie des Krieges*, Beihefte zur Zeitschrift für angewandte Psychologie 21 (Leipzig, 1920), 1–123. The police of Stuttgart issued the following order of the day to the policemen:

Policemen! The inhabitants are starting to go crazy! The streets are filled with old women of both sexes engaged in undignified activities. Everyone suspects his neighbor of being a Russian or French spy and assumes it is their duty to beat him and the policeman, who might try to help that person, to a pulp. At the very least, however, they hand the "suspects" over to the police, not without causing a great disturbance. The people take clouds for planes, stars for airships, and bicycle handlebars for bombs . . . One cannot imagine what would happen if times really got difficult. And it is proven that, up to now, nothing disquieting has happened here. Nevertheless, one gets the impression of being in an insane asylum. Policemen, stay cold-blooded, remain men instead of women, don't have the wind put into you and keep your eyes open, like you are obliged to do.
As cited in Jastrow, *Im Kriegszustand*, 49–50.

12. Without further theoretical claims and because it is concise and easily remembered, the term "societal paradigm" will be employed to abbreviate the compilation of various patterns of perception, which, in a given society, are directed toward a specific group in this society, a particular problem etc., and which thus construct the said group or problem in its social "meaning." The term has been borrowed from Paul Fussell and has been transposed from the literary to the social level. Fussell defines "cultural paradigms" as "systems of convention and expectation that extensively determine the extent to which objective phenomena intrude on individual experience, what the individual 'makes of the objects,' how he integrates new experiences into the schemata that his culture taught him to consider meaningful." P. Fussell, "Der Einfluß kultureller Paradigmen auf die literarische Wiedergabe traumatischer Erfahrung," in Vondung, ed., *Kriegserlebnis*, 175–176.
13. ZSta Potsdam, 61 Re 1/7966, 74.
14. E. Buchner (=Eduard Mayer), *1914–1918. Wie es damals daheim war. Das Kriegstagebuch eines Knaben* (Nürnburg, 1930), 24. See here as well, L. Wieland, *Belgien 1914. Die Frage des belgischen "Franktireurkriegs" und die deutsche öffentliche Meinung von 1914 bis 1936* (Frankfurt/M. et al., 1984).
15. Buchner, *1914–1918*, 50.
16. ZStA Potsdam, 61 Re 1/7966, *passim*; HStA/Kr, MKr 13346, *passim*. Also see Haacke, *Barmen*, 33–34.
17. *Berliner Lokal-Anzeiger*, 17 August 1914. ZStA Potsdam, 61 Re 1/7966, 76f.
18. ZStA Potsdam, 61Re 1/7566; *Kölner Volkszeitung*, 17 August 1914.
19. ZStA Potsdam, 61Re 1/7566; *Dresdner Nachrichten*, 20 August 1914.
20. *Kriegsverwaltungsbericht der Stadt Neukölln 1914–1918*, Statistisches Amt, ed. (Neukölln, 1921), 111.
21. "Bulletin der Studiengesellschaft für soziale Folgen des Krieges," *Deutschland* (Kopenhagen, 1919). The figures cited are an estimate.
22. *Die Kriegsvolkszählungen vom Jahre 1916 und 1917 in Bayern*. Beiträge zur Statistik Bayerns 89, Bayerisches Statistisches Amt, ed. (München, 1919), 87.

War as Event: August 1914 and the First Months of the War

23. L. Bendit, "Der Krieg und der deutsche Arbeitsmarkt," diss. Erlangen (1920), 11.

24. *Nürnberg während des Krieges. Wirtschaftliche Lage und soziale Fürsorge* 1.8.-1.11.1914 Statistisches Amt, ed. (Nürnberg, 1914), 13.

25. Kommandierender General of the 7th AK Münster to Oberpräsident Münster, 15 September 1914: StA Münster, Oberpräsidium 4123, Bl. 86.

26. This law is reprinted in Jastrow, *Im Kriegszustand*, 139ff.

27. M. Hoffmann, "Das Gesetz betreffend die Unterstützung von Familien in den Dienst eingetretener Mannschaften vom 28.2.1888/4.8.1914 und seine Anwendung," diss. (Berlin, 1918), 134ff.

28. P. Umbreit, "Die deutschen Gewerkschaften im Kriege," in P. Umbreit and Ch. Lorenz, *Der Krieg und die Arbeitsverhältnisse* (Stuttgart et al., 1928), 68-69.

29. In Barmen, by the end of September, the number of families who had received this rent subsidy amounted to approximately 10,200, i.e. almost a third of the 36,597 households counted in the 1910 census. In addition, almost all of these renters received a 10% reduction in rent from the owners of the respective apartment houses. Haacke, *Barmen*, 81. For further information about rent subsidies during the war, see also: W. Bierbrauer, "Die Einwirkungen des Krieges und der Nachkriegszeit auf die Wohnbautätigkeit unter besonderer Berücksichtigung von Rheinland und Westfalen," diss. (Münster, 1921); Hoffmann, *Gesetz*, 146-174; P. Hirsch, "Die Kriegsfürsorge der deutschen Gemeinden," *Annalen für soziale Politik und Gesetzgebung* 4 (1916): 270ff.; H. Kruschwitz, "Deutsche Wohnungswirtschaft und Wohnungspolitik seit 1913," in W. Zimmermann, ed., *Beiträge zur städtischen Wohn- und Siedelwirtschaft*, vol. 1., Schriften des Vereins für Sozialpolitik 177 (München and Leipzig, 1930), 11-21.

Wartime legislation to protect renters was impotent, however, against one basic social fact, the essence of which one "war wife," after losing a lawsuit against her landlord, summed up as follows: "Then, my opponent was a landlord, his lawyer was a landlord, the judge was a landlord and my lawyer was a landlord. And there I stood in the middle as renter, and not even a fully valid one, because I was a war wife." I. Linde, *Kriegserinnerungen eines Kindes* (Leipzig, 1936), 49.

30. *Deutschland im Ersten Weltkrieg* (Berlin, 1971), 1: 445. By 31 January 1915, the trade unions had spent 6.2 million marks on assistance to the families of their conscripted members. By 30 September 1918, the figure had reached 27 million marks. Umbreit, *Gewerkschaften*, 69. On the trade unions' war and unemployment benefits in the first period of the war, see also: H.-J. Bieber, *Gewerkschaften in Krieg und Revolution. Arbeiterbewegung, Industrie, Staat und Militär in Deutschland 1914-1920* (Hamburg, 1981), 1: 87-98.

31. The following information, unless otherwise noted, is taken from the Reports from the Mayors and District Administration Heads to the Chairman of the Düsseldorf Regional Council (Regierungspräsident Düsseldorf), re. the course of mobilization, August 1914: HStA Düsseldorf, Regierung Düsseldorf 14911, Bl. 199-287.

32. One of the essential components of women's patriotic activity during the First World War was the sending of "alms" to the front. A war correspondent for the *Daily Telegraph* of London described it so: "It was a standing joke in

35

Hindenburg's army that nobody could get a bar of chocolate without agreeing to take a pair of socks as well." J. M. de Beaufort, *Behind the German Veil: A Record of a Journalistic War Pilgrimage* (New York, 1918), 109.

33. Landrat Dinslaken to Regierungspräsident Düsseldorf, 4 December 1914: HStA Düsseldorf, Regierung Düsseldorf 15058. What follows, where not otherwise noted, is taken from this archival collection, which contains reports from chief mayors and district administration heads to the chairman of the Düsseldorf Regional Council on the economic situation in December 1914.

34. Regarding the transition of individual cities to the war economy and their respective economic problems. see J. Reulecke, "Wirtschaft und Bevölkerung ausgewählter Städte im Ersten Weltkrieg (Barmen, Düsseldorf, Essen, Krefeld)," in J. Reulecke, ed., *Die deutsche Stadt im Industriezeitalter. Beiträge zur modernen deutschen Stadtgeschichte* (Wuppertal, 1980), 114-126. On the changing position of the textile industry during the war, see: W. Niecz, "Untersuchung der Lage der weiblichen Arbeitskräfte in der Textilindustrie während der Kriegs- und Übergangszeit," diss. (Frankfurt/M., 1923/25).

35. See here, as well: J. Mooser, *Arbeiterleben in Deutschland 1900-1970* (Frankfurt/M., 1984), 160-178. For interesting material about this line of differentiation during the war and immediately after, see: H. Bundschuh, "Lohn- und Lebensverhältnisse der Arbeiter in der Industrie des Neckartals mit Beschränkung auf die standortlich gebundene Industrie," diss. (Heidelberg, 1923). Regions in which landholding and property were in the hands of industrial working-class families, i.e. those in which the husband worked in a factory and the wife and children farmed the land, suffered the least from the notorious wartime lack of agricultural labor, because their lots were small and because they had already divided farm work among the family members prior to the war. See, for example, Monatsbericht der Kriegsamtstelle Saarbrücken für März 1917, 3 April 1917, 2-3: BA/MA, PH 2/72.

36. Landrat Moers to Regierungspräsident Düsseldorf, 9 December 1914: HStA Düsseldorf, Regierung Düsseldorf 15058. See as well, 18. Bericht des Berliner Polizeipräsidenten, 30 November 1914: ZStA Potsdam, Reichskanzlei 2398/1, Bl. 53.

37. HStA Düsseldorf, Regierung Düsseldorf 33185a.

38. In terms of the war and post-war periods, see E. Frese, "Die deutschen Kriegerwitwen im Berufs- und Erwerbsleben und die diesbezügliche staatliche Kriegshintergebliebenenfürsorge unter besonderer Berücksichtigung der Verhältnisse in Hamburg-Altona und Bremen," diss. (Hamburg, 1923); H. B. Haugg, "Methodik und Systematik der Kriegsbeschädigten- und Kriegshinterbliebenenstatistik," diss. (Erlangen, n.d.[1922]); R. W. Whalen, *Bitter Wounds. German Victims of the Great War, 1914-1939* (Ithaca, NY, and London, 1984), 69-81; K. Hausen, "The German Nation's Obligations to the Heroes' Widows of World War I," in M. R. Higonnet et al., eds., *Behind the Lines. Gender and the Two World Wars* (New Haven, Conn., 1987), 126-140. See, as well, the relevant sources at the BA Koblenz - for example, R86/42, R431/705 and 706, R86/2319 - and the BA/MA - for example RM3/7271 and 7511.

39. R. G. Binding, *Wir fordern Reims zur Übergabe auf* (n.p., 1935).

3

Women's Wage Labor in the First World War

The more that is remembered, the greater the confusion in our historical knowledge. In our archives, one should breed mice, not catch them. How happy are the peoples who don't write anything down and for whom the events of yesterday morning have already become legends!

Franz Blei[1]

"Today, seamstresses, ironers, shopgirls and, in by far the greatest numbers, women who have never worked before and ladies' helpers are showering the enemy with bombs and grenades."[2] This is how contemporary observers saw female wage labor, and this view has persisted in histories of the First World War until today. The German war economy of 1914 to 1918 is said to have increased female employment to unprecedented proportions, as well as permanently changing its structure: "For the development of female labor in Germany, the First World War represented an important, if not the most important, break."[3]

This picture of women's wage labor during the war needs fundamental correction, however. In this chapter, I shall show that the increase in female employment was, in fact, relatively small and that any structural changes brought on by the war had no lasting effect beyond it. As indicators of direct or indirect structural changes in women's wage labor, the following shall be examined: the quantitative development of female wage labor; its distribution across specific sectors and branches of the economy; the qualification structure and the level of wages; the societal valuation of women's work, in particular that of the employer, the trade unions and the government; and the interpretation of the women involved of their wartime situation. If the assumption about the far-reaching effects of the First World War on women's wage labor does possess any validity, then we

37

should be able to observe clear and long-lasting changes in at least one of these indicators.

The Quantitative Development of Women's Wage Labor, 1914–1918

In 1916, a census of occupations was conducted across the entire German Empire.[4] The results, however, were only analyzed by a few of the federal states. Therefore, those authorities responsible for civil employment during the war had to content themselves with approximations in their analyses of the labor situation. They made do with compilations of data regarding the wartime development of wage work that came from the most varied sources, both in terms of where in the Empire it was collected and which official organ collected it. Since, like the employment authorities, socio-historical analysis also has no other fundamental access to the wartime labor situation, I shall roughly outline the statistical basis of this data below.

The reports of the Factory Inspectorate (*Gewerbeaufsicht*) recorded the level of employment for those businesses with ten or more employees. Thus, statistics were not collected about the employees of smaller companies, nor about those, such as agricultural workers, servants and homeworkers, who did not work in centralized commercial enterprises. These reports suggest an excessively large increase in women's wage labor during the war. The reason for this is that it was exactly these larger industrial concerns that increased their level of (female) employment during the war. In those industries included in the Factory Inspectorate's reports, the number of employed women and girls rose from 1,592,138 in 1913 to 2,319,674 in 1918.[5]

Employment exchanges' (*Arbeitsnachweise*) coverage of the labor market only gave information about how the number of those looking for work, of positions available and of those consequently occupied changed. As an individual's use of an employment exchange was voluntary and as he or she often found a job without its help, these figures cannot be taken as representative.

The level of employment for specific branches of industry was determined through various investigations conducted by governmental authorities, trade unions, etc. The results cannot be generalized. These investigations focused exclusively on the level of employment in those industries that, because of either their size or their particular branch of trade, were considered part of the "war industry," where the rise in the employment of women was disproportionately high.[6] Thus, although the significance of these investigations for the narrower area of the war industry is often quite relevant, they exaggerate the scope of women's wage labor as a whole.

Relatively speaking, the reports of local, trade-union and industry health-insurance companies about the individuals who were mandatorily insured by them provide information about the greatest number of employees. As a measure for the wartime development of employment, this material has several problems, however.[7] In comparison to the occupational census, "helpers" in agriculture, industry and trade are completely unaccounted for here. Of white-collar employees, only those whose yearly salary was under 2,500 marks were included. Servants, agricultural workers and those employed by public companies could, under certain conditions, be released from paying these compulsory insurance contributions; the consequent decrease is also not calculable. Men and women working in cottage industries are also only partially included in these figures, since, as of 1 September 1914, their obligation to be health-insured was abolished and was not reintroduced everywhere by local statute. The deficiency in the reporting led to the fact that even those individuals paying mandatory contributions were often not included. The Post Office's health-insurance company only rarely reported its statistics, and that of the miners' guild was completely exempt from such reporting. The number of individuals working in mines, therefore, never even appeared. In addition, some insurance companies only managed to file these obligatory reports sporadically during the war. As a result, the statistics of the health-insurance companies, in so far as they were published, only included approximately 70% of all employees making mandatory contributions. There was an additional shortcoming in health-insurance-company reporting, which, in this instance, led to an over- rather than an under-recording of the number of employees. All soldiers for whom employers, trade unions or communities continued to pay the insurance premium went down in the books as mandatorily insured individuals, something which seems to have occurred fairly frequently.

Despite all the qualifications listed above, the insurance-company reports still prove to be the most reliable statistics of those available.[8] What conclusions, then, can we draw from them about the development of women's employment during the First World War?

The answer to this question shall be based on a calculation comparing the number of female employees paying compulsory contributions with the number of health-insurance companies that filed a report on 1 July 1914 as well as on 1 July 1918 (see Table 1). Of the 6,319 insurance companies that filed a report on 1 July 1918, 5,328 also did so on 1 July 1914. They had 8.12 million insured employees, or 89% of the total of those insured by the companies that filed in 1918. Of the total number of employees in Germany, not just those with mandatory health insurance, the insurance companies' list registers approximately one-half to three-fifths. If we exclusively use the statistics of those health-insurance companies that filed both reports as a basis, and set the number of those individuals who, on 1 July 1914, were compulsorily insured at 100, then the index of female insurees had risen to 117 by 1 July 1918. Female employment, in other words, rose by 17% between 1914 and 1918.

What conclusions can we draw from this?

These figures are only conditionally useful as an indicator of the comparative development of female and male employment during the war. The relationship between the two did not change primarily because of the rise of female labor, but rather, because of the drafting of men. The drop in the number of male employees is also exaggerated here: Miners are not included, a group whose wartime figures fell less than those of the employed male population as a whole. When we posit the number of those miners employed during the second quarter of 1914 in Prussia at 100, then the absolute low point is reached in the third quarter of 1918 with 68.[9] Those prisoners of war that were employed in industries are also not counted; they numbered almost 400,000 in 1917.[10]

What is meaningful is a comparison of the number of female insurees before the start and in the final phases of the war. As mentioned, this rose by approximately 17%. This figure, above all, supports the argument that female employment increased inordinately during the First World War.[11] Plausible as this argument may appear at first glance, the significance of this 17% – and hence of the argument itself – becomes problematic as soon

Table 1. Female Employees with Mandatory Health Insurance, 1914 and 1918 (Statistics compiled from 5,328 local health insurance agencies)

Regional Insurance Offices	Female Employees with Mandatory Health Insurance*		Absolute Increase/ Decrease	Percentage** Increase/ Decrease
	1.7.1914	1.7.1918		
Aurich	4,470	8,959	+ 4,489	+ 100
Hannover	19,191	28,523	+ 9,332	+ 49
Dortmund	53,079	76,480	+ 23,401	+ 44
Sigmaringen	496	713	+ 217	+ 44
Danzig	35,292	49,965	+ 14,673	+ 41
Magdeburg	65,178	90,522	+ 25,344	+ 39
Arnsberg	7,397	10,177	+ 2,780	+ 37
Trier	21,349	29,078	+ 7,729	+ 36
Düsseldorf	208,279	279,210	+ 70,931	+ 34
Breslau	61,249	81,701	+ 20,452	+ 33
Königsberg	35,534	46,481	+ 10,947	+ 31
Stettin	50,874	65,226	+ 14,352	+ 28
Schleswig	73,409	94,191	+ 20,782	+ 28
Posen	43,792	55,818	+ 12,026	+ 27
Greater Berlin	459,519	572,718	+ 113,199	+ 25
Allenstein	18,896	23,496	+ 4,600	+ 24
Oppeln	57,041	69,808	+ 12,767	+ 22
Marienwerder	7,968	9,470	+ 1,502	+ 19
Wiesbaden	94,513	112,817	+ 18,304	+ 19
Cologne	85,771	101,202	+ 15,431	+ 18
Potsdam	48,799	57,012	+ 8,213	+ 17
Köslin	13,159	15,097	+ 1,938	+ 15
Stade	12,891	14,817	+ 1,926	+ 15
Kassel	54,500	62,692	+ 8,192	+ 15
Koblenz	13,811	15,368	+ 1,557	+ 11
Merseburg	61,676	68,319	+ 6,643	+ 11
Hildesheim	14,259	15,695	+ 1,436	+ 10
Stralsund	14,500	15,826	+ 1,326	+ 9
Minden in Westphalia	28,735	30,828	+ 2,093	+ 7
Osnabrück	11,018	11,426	+ 408	+ 4
Gumbinnen	11,263	11,617	+ 354	+ 3
Frankfurt on the Oder	65,024	66,869	+ 1,845	+ 3
Liegnitz	91,065	91,838	+ 773	+ 1
Bromberg	17,113	16,863	- 250	- 1
Münster in Westphalia	12,005	11,213	- 792	- 6
Lüneburg	2,736	2,530	- 206	- 7
Erfurt	31,695	28,694	- 3,001	- 9

The War from Within

Table 1. Female Employees with Mandatory Health Insurance, 1914 and 1918 (Statistics compiled from 5,328 local health insurance agencies) (*continued*)

Regional Insurance Offices	Female Employees with Mandatory Health Insurance* 1.7.1914	1.7.1918	Absolute Increase/ Decrease	Percentage** Increase/ Decrease
Aachen	40,022	36,573	- 3,449	- 9
Total for Prussia	**1,947,568**	**2,379,832**	**+432,264**	**+ 22**
Speyer	35,333	41,498	+ 6,165	+ 17
Landshut	19,104	22,202	+ 3,098	+ 16
Bayreuth	18,805	21,268	+ 2,463	+ 13
Regensburg	21,230	23,511	+ 2,281	+ 11
Augsburg	45,665	50,594	+ 4,929	+ 11
Munich	30,082	33,481	+ 3,399	+ 11
Nuremberg	72,908	78,639	+ 5,731	+ 8
Würzburg	17,383	17,929	+ 546	+ 3
Total for Bavaria	**260,510**	**289,122**	**+ 28,612**	**+ 11**
Dresden-Neustadt	163,984	180,944	+ 16,960	+ 10
Leipzig	143,470	154,459	+ 10,989	+ 8
Bautzen	53,288	47,619	- 5,669	- 11
Zwickau	102,695	79,826	- 22,869	- 22
Chemnitz	120,612	82,789	- 37,823	- 31
Total for Saxony	**584,049**	**545,637**	**– 38,412**	**– 6**
Stuttgart	157,306	179,117	+ 21,811	+ 14
Neckar District	*79,728*	*99,000*	*+ 19,272*	*+ 24*
Donau District	*20,955*	*25,022*	*+ 4,067*	*+ 19*
Black Forest District	*37,316*	*36,372*	*- 944*	*- 2*
Jagst District	*19,307*	*18,723*	*- 584*	*- 3*
Total for Württemberg	**157,306**	**179,117**	**+ 21,811**	**+ 14**
Karlsruhe	48,326	61,407	+ 13,081	+ 11
Mannheim	49,893	56,556	+ 6,663	+ 11
Freiburg im Breisgau	35,533	32,146	- 3,387	+ 10
Konstanz	9,688	8,128	- 1,560	+ 9
Total for Baden	**143,440**	**158,237**	**+ 14,797**	**+ 10**
Darmstadt	62,012	73,379	+ 11,367	+ 27
Rhine-Hesse Province	18,257	26,166	+ 7,909	+ 43
Starkenburg Province	27,305	31,493	+ 4,188	+ 15
Upper Hesse Province	16,450	15,720	- 730	- 4
Total for Hesse	**62,012**	**73,379**	**+ 11,367**	**+ 18**

42

Table 1. Female Employees with Mandatory Health Insurance, 1914 and 1918 (Statistics compiled from 5,328 local health insurance agencies) (*continued*)

Regional Insurance Offices	Female Employees with Mandatory Health Insurance*		Absolute Increase/ Decrease	Percentage** Increase/ Decrease
	1.7.1914	1.7.1918		
Bremen	16,661	25,110	+ 8,449	+ 51
Lübeck	8,691	12,525	+ 3,834	+ 44
Hamburg	82,933	108,958	+ 26,025	+ 31
Dessau	30,434	36,562	+ 6,128	+ 20
Gotha	43,744	50,503	+ 6,759	+ 15
Oldenburg	18,773	21,271	+ 2,498	+ 13
Neustrelitz	7,204	8,112	+ 908	+ 13
Detmold	9,797	11,070	+ 1,273	+ 13
Braunschweig	27,799	31,217	+ 3,418	+ 12
Schwerin in Mecklenburg	13,547	14,886	+ 1,339	+ 10
Arnstadt	6,725	6,840	+ 115	+ 2
Meiningen	14,152	14,357	+ 205	+ 1
Gera	38,422	35,895	- 2,527	- 6
Strasbourg	31,128	37,975	+ 6,847	+ 22
Metz	12,155	11,551	- 604	- 5
Mülhausen	25,878	17,559	+ 8,319	- 32
Total for Alsace-Lorraine	69,161	67,085	- 2,076	- 3
Railway Insurance Companies	7,053	74,001	+ 66,948	+ 949
German Empire	3,549,981	4,143,716	+ 593,735	+ 17

* Does not include women unable to work because of illness or those who had recently given birth.
** This is my own calculation.
Source: *RABl* 16 (1918): 657–658.

as we recall that rates of increase only make sense in relation to other data. In other words, no conclusions can be made about this 17% increase in the number of female insurees between 1914 and 1918 until we know what the corresponding rate was before the war.

In order to facilitate such a comparison, I have chosen the following figures from the period 1889–1913, divided, like the war, into four-year increments (see Table 2). These statistics refer to the entire female membership of health-insurance programs.

This fact does not change the comparability of the rates of increase, however, since the rate for the entire membership and that for those compulsorily insured ran parallel during the course of the war.[12]

Between 1889 and 1913, the rate of increase in female members of health-insurance programs, despite a rise in the absolute number of women employed, levelled off slightly. The wartime increase of 17% also lies completely within this trend. These two sets of insurance figures, when taken together, consequently suggest that the impact of the war on the qualitative development of female employment was amazingly low.[13] The modesty of this increase is all the more astounding when we consider that, because of the war, women who had recently married or were unable to get married because of the conscription of their fiancé, continued working, instead, as was the custom, of leaving the workforce. Their presence thus contributed to this wartime increase as well.[14]

The wartime statistics for women with mandatory health insurance therefore by no means indicate that the impact of the war on female employment was large – as has been asserted by traditional First World War histories. Instead, it was remarkably small. This surprising conclusion is strengthened by the results of the population and occupational census conducted in Bavaria on 1 December 1916.

Table 2. Female Members of Mandatory Health Insurance Programs, 1889–1913

Year	Total	Rate of Increase (in %)
1889	1,195,662	
1893	1,549,425	30
1897	1,886,995	22
1901	2,288,270	21
1905	2,834,697	24*
1909	3,444,425	22
1913	4,127,401	20

* In 1903, mandatory health insurance was expanded, to include sales help and apprentices.
Source: Statistik des Deutschen Reiches, new series (Berlin, 1921), 289: 55*.
The rate of increase is my own calculation.

Table 3. The Development of Female Employment in Bavaria, 1882–1916

	1882	1895	1907	1916
Female Employees*	956,797	52,114	1,413,718	1,235,611
In Agriculture	674,116	522,540	873,030	616,415
Number of Women, per 100 Female Employees, in Agriculture	70.4	54.9	61.7	49.9
In Industry	102,017	156,267	215,366	258,051
Number of Women, per 100 Female Employees, in Industry	10.7	16.4	15.2	20.9
Female Population	2,699,411	2,949,056	3,363,981	3,616,182
Number of Women Employed per 100	35.4	32.3	42.0	34.2

* Including women in domestic service, excluding the category "Self-Employed Women without a Profession".
** This is my own calculation.
Source: *Die Kriegsvolkszählungen vom Jahre 1916 und 1917 in Bayern.* Beiträge zur Statistik Bayerns 89, Bayerisches Statistisches Landesamt, ed. (München, 1919), 128–134, 139ff.

As Table 3 shows, female employment clearly decreased between 1907 and 1916. This decline, in all probability, was due to a formal statistical problem, namely that female agricultural "helpers" were "under-recorded" in 1916, whereas, in 1907, they were "over-recorded."[15] Nevertheless, there is nothing in these figures that suggests either a rise in women's employment in general, or a disproportionate rise in female industrial labor in particular. The image of the hordes of women who supposedly appeared on the labor market for the first time between 1914 and 1918 must consequently and definitively be abandoned.

This conclusion immediately raises new questions, however. For one, the fact, as such, requires explanation. How was it possible that, despite the celebrated labor shortage in the war economy and the consequent energetic efforts to rectify this shortage by mobilizing women, female employment did not increase more? To answer this question, it is necessary to go a bit further afield and subject the conditions, strategies and course of the general labor policy in the First World War to a more thorough analysis than they have yet received. This will be done in the present chapter. A second relevant question can be settled here, however: Where did the female workers employed in the war industry come from if not from the ranks of women who had never worked before? By "war industry" I mean, in particular, the metal, mechanical, electrical and chemical industries, since there is no doubt that female employment did increase exceptionally in each of these during the war. In 2,594 businesses of the metal industry, for example, the number of female workers employed in August/September 1916 was 266,530, as opposed to 63,570 before the war; this signifies an increase of 319.3%, almost all of which can be attributed to the war industry.[16] In the administrative sector of the 1st Bavarian Army Corps, those war-economy industries with 50 or more employees had, in February 1917, 11,499 female employees, in comparison to 1,304 in July 1914. This is an increase of 782%. For the 3rd Bavarian Army Corps' sector, the corresponding figures are 61,169 in comparison to 32,926, which means that the increase in the number of female employees between July 1914 and February 1917 was approximately 86%.[17]

We find an initial indication of the origins of those women employed in the war industry in Table 1, which reveals a decline in the number of women with mandatory health insurance for several administrative districts that ran counter to the prevailing trend. The drop occurred primarily in those areas – Aachen, Münster and Erfurt, Bautzen, Chemnitz and Zwickau, Konstanz and Freiburg im Breisgau and Upper Hesse – in which the textile industry predominated.[18] A portion of those female textile workers employed before the war transferred to the war industry between 1914 and 1918.[19] Other sectors of the economy also lost female labor to the war industry, as several investigations regarding the backgrounds of female war-industry employees verify. The 22,763 female employees, for example, who were counted in the Bavarian gunpowder factories on 1 December 1916, had been practicing the following trades on 1 July 1914 (see Table 4):

Almost half of the women working in Bavaria's gunpowder mills on 1 December 1916 were already factory workers before

Table 4. Pre-War Occupations of Bavarian Female
Gunpowder Workers

Previous Occupation	Absolute	in %
Agricultural Worker	633	2.8
Gunpowder Worker	8,488	37.3
Metal Worker	645	2.8
Spinner	430	1.9
Factory Worker (unspecified)	386	1.7
Weaver	344	1.5
Seamstress	313	1.4
Mechanical-Engineering Worker	311	1.4
Workers in the (Metal) Toy Industry	204	0.9
Total Number of Workers	*11,121*	*48.8*
Shop assistant	257	1.1
Maid	1,398	6.1
Wageworker in Domestic Service	222	1.0
Charwoman	219	1.0
Total Number in Domestic Service	*1,839*	*8.1*
No Trade/Unspecified	540	2.4
Not Previously Employed	6,053	26.6
Other	2,319	10.2
Total	**22,762**	**100.0**

Occupations with less than 200 women are jointly listed under "Other."
Source: Die Kriegsvolkszählungen vom Jahre 1916 und 1917 in Bayern.
Beiträge zur Statistik Bayerns 89, Bayerisches Statistisches Landesamt, ed.
(München, 1919): 204.

the war; a good 8% had been formerly employed in domestic
service and approximately 1% as shop assistants. Only just under
27% – to which some of those listed under the heading "No
Trade/Unspecified" could be added – had not been previously
employed. A significant portion of this 27% was made up of
female adolescents who, independent of the war, entered the
workforce during this time. Only after these adolescent girls
have been subtracted, can we assume that some of the women
remaining took up employment as a consequence of the wartime
situation and that, without it, they would probably have remained
unemployed.

An investigation, covering the period between March and August 1917, of the more than 90,000 women workers employed in the entire Bavarian war industry attests a very similar composition of the female workforce. Between 41 and 46% of these women had been working in factories prior to the war, 18% in domestic service, 2% as shop assistants and 1% in agriculture, and just under 28% had had no previous occupation, which, again, included adolescent girls just starting out.[20] As comparable statistics are unavailable for the years 1917 and 1918, the question of whether the number of women entering the workforce continued to increase substantially during that period must remain open. One indication, however, that there was also no great surge of formerly unemployed women, particularly of "war wives," into war-industrial jobs in 1917 or 1918 is the fact that the number of Bavarian "war wives" and/or women with children in the war industry – which was already not very high to begin with in 1917 – had decreased by the end of the war.[21]

Limiting the picture regionally to the federal state of Bavaria, as above, only modifies it in details, not in general tendency. This is confirmed by sample surveys, such as that conducted by the Board of Trade (*Gewerberat*) in Berlin Friedenau at the beginning of 1916 of three war-industry companies. Among the 68 female employees of one shell factory, 48 had worked in factories, 8 as maids, 6 as seamstresses and 1 as a hairdresser, an artisan, a shop assistant, a cook, a milliner and as a florist, respectively. In a smaller shell factory, the previous occupations of the 34 female workers broke down as follows: 16 factory workers, 14 maids, one ironer, one nurse, one seamstress and one shop assistant. The third business, an upholstery factory producing for the military, offered a similar picture: 12 women had been factory workers, 4 had been seamstresses, 2 quilters, 1 a cutter, a colorer and a tailor, respectively, and 15 had been servants.[22] Of the female armaments workers in the Factory Inspectorate district of Stettin and Stralsund – to give one last example – up to 50% of the women came from companies that had been shut down, 40% from households and 10% from agriculture.[23]

The female workforce employed in the war industry was recruited primarily from factory workers, employees in domestic service, shop assistants and agricultural workers, i.e. from those groups of the female population that were already employed before the war. The consequent decline in the number of female employees outside of the war industry can be seen with particular clarity in the example of domestic service. On 1 July 1914, 31,491 female servants were insured by the local insurance office in Munich; on 1 October 1918, that number was just over 20,584. For the same period of time, servants' share of the total number of female insurees declined from 31% to 17%.[24]

It is more difficult to prove the migration of female labor out of the agricultural sector. Although the government increasingly tried to prevent this migration with bans, the number of women who left the country for work was not insignificant. Where it was possible in terms of the distance, rural women did not settle permanently in the city – a situation that would have exacerbated the problems of insufficient food and appartments there – but rather, became weekend-commuters.[25] The suction effect the labor-hungry war industry had on female agricultural workers and rural servants could not be stopped, even by the threat of prison sentences. Against the more or less unchecked wartime labor market, such bureaucratic measures were impossible to carry out. Female agricultural workers seeking to transfer to the war industry responded to the Employment Office's (*Arbeitsamt*) references to the ban on migration "with a mocking smile and the dismissive comment that, 'if the Employment Office won't act as a mediator for us, then we'll go to the factories directly ourselves, where we'll always be taken. So and so many from our village have been taken already,' and so forth."[26] In February 1918, the Bavarian Ministry of the Interior (*bayerisches Innenministerium*) acknowledged that the migration of agricultural labor into the war industry could not have been prevented.[27]

It was not only in this instance that labor-market policy proved incapable of steering the development of women's wagework during the war to any great extent. Despite costly organizational and propagandist efforts at all governmental and administrative levels to reduce the chronic labor shortage through the mobilization of female labor, the increase in female employment during the war remained far short of expectations. To explain this, we must go a bit further afield and examine, on the one hand, working-class women's specific life situations, which were decisive for their conduct on the job market, and, on the other, the authorities' efforts, undertaken primarily in the second half of the war, to influence this conduct. This is the subject of the next section.

Labor-Market Policy and Women's Wage Labor

The Life Situations and Labor-Market Behavior of Working-Class Women

Why did working-class women not want to work in the war industry? What were the specific individual preferences that influenced these women's choice? In order to answer these questions, it is important to look a little closer at the women in question. Four of the most important categories of actual or potential wage-working women shall thus be outlined, in short, below.

For the group of women who had been working in jobs that were either poorly paid or restrictive of their personal freedom (such as servants) or who had lost their jobs because of company closures, the wartime economic situation facilitated their obtaining better positions. This "self-mobilization," which represented the biggest share of the increase in female employment in the war industry,[28] was a result of rational, economic behavior on the part of these women to improve their situation.

The receipt of Family Aid enabled another group of women to support themselves and their dependants without receiving additional income. The majority of these women lived in smaller cities or rural communities, where, as a result of the generally better food conditions or of their own farming or gardening, did not need any cash beyond that of the Family Aid. In comparison to "normal" times, these women's and families' need of money was astonishingly small. This fact reflected a structural problem of the war industry, one that would become increasingly acute during the course of the war: the partial collapse of the money economy. These women were not available to be mobilized as labor so long as their receipt of war aid was in jeopardy. "War wives" who lived in big cities, on the other hand, could scarcely ever survive on Family Aid alone. They often chose to earn additional income outside of the war industry, however, and took on such work as housecleaning, piecework or laundry.[29] Women with children in particular avoided factory work, since the income they could have earned would have to have been used, for the most part, to pay for childcare.[30]

A discussion, which was to last the entire war, quickly arose between the imperial government, municipalities and labor organizations about these untapped labor reserves. It began after several municipalities and Deputy General Commands (*stellvertretende Generalkommandos*), whose economies were based predominantly on agricultural production, attempted to combat the shortage of (agricultural) labor. The two entities either threatened "war wives" with the withdrawal of their Family Aid or, in more carefully formulated decrees – since such a refusal of aid to needy "war families" would have been illegal – with a renewed examination of their neediness – proof of which was requisite for receiving aid – if they did not declare themselves willing to work. The Social Democrats, who saw themselves as the representative of the interests of Family-Aid recipients and who then began to translate these interests into political action, denounced these measures as "forced labor for war wives."[31] In July 1915, Philipp Scheidemann, in a letter to the Imperial Ministry of the Interior (*Reichsamt des Innern*), demanded that the Reich authorities oppose such practices of the municipalities. The State Secretary of the Interior (*Staatssekretär des Innern*) answered with a statement that illuminated the position the imperial government would hold on this question until the end of the war: The Reich would not intervene in this situation, particularly since those women in question should not, through the receipt of Family Aid, lose the habit of performing a job which they had done without question before the war. It should be left to the municipalities themselves whether – and if yes, in what form – they wanted to make use of this pressure.[32]

From 1916, this was how things stood, as well, during the era of the Third Supreme Command (*Dritte Oberste Heeresleitung*). Despite the harsh words that General Chief of Staff Hindenburg had for the "war wives," who, in his eyes, were more or less useless and living off the state, no general withdrawal of Family Aid was ordered for those who refused to work. Two considerations, in particular, were decisive for this action. For one, in those cases where the local authorities believed that the repeated complaints they received about "war wives" who were unwilling to work and who supposedly used their Family Aid to live a life of luxury were justified, they already knew to take recourse in threatening these women with Family-Aid cuts.[33]

The imperial government also found it unwise to use family assistance for the purposes of labor mobilization because of the foreseeable repercussions this would have on soldiers' morale.

In his edict of 6 March 1917, the imperial chancellor (*Reichs-kanzler*) ordered the authorities to resist "every pettiness" in dealing with Family Aid. His reason for doing so was that

> The men who are fighting at the front and who daily risk their lives for the Fatherland are entitled to be relieved of the worry about theirs back home. They must have the knowledge that their families, for whom they can no longer provide themselves, are not suffering want, but rather, are receiving everything they require for their livelihood.

A woman's Family Aid, therefore, was only to be withheld "after a mature and thorough examination" and after every other possible means of influencing her had failed.[34]

The *Kriegsamt* (War Office) was instituted in 1916 as the central authority responsible for steering the war economy. It was, consequently, the War Office's idea not to settle this assistance question with a uniform regulation for the entire Empire, but to leave the examination of each case to the respective municipality, a practice which was followed until the end of the war.[35] In some respects, however, this solution "was asking for trouble." The communities of the Reich were thus left with the difficult problem of obtaining money for family war assistance from the money market, which, for civilian interests, was extremely tight. Those communities that were especially weak financially consequently had a marked interest in cutting family allowances, which they did with seeming regularity. How many women were thereby coerced to accept employment, either in agriculture or elsewhere, must remain open here. It is certain, however, that the complaints of women who suffered under such measures contributed to the continuous deterioration of the population's general morale.[36]

In rural cities and communities, where the income and ability to work of every individual inhabitant was common knowledge, it was easier for the local authorities, in deciding the individual cases, to force "war wives" to take up employment in agriculture. This method, however, was not transferable to larger cities and municipalities. Here, the authorities tried, instead, to induce female Family-Aid recipients either to look for a job or to remain working by only taking part of their earnings into account when calculating their level of assistance. The fact that women had traditionally earned notoriously low wages was now taking its toll, in that these wages proved to be a clear obstacle to women's mobilization. Although the level of Family Aid was, in many cases, below subsistence level, women's wages were often not much higher. If the difference between a woman's earnings and Family Aid was not very substantial, and if, additionally, she had to spend a part of that difference on transportation, increased wear and tear on clothing, child-care and the like, then it made little economic sense for her to go to work. Factory inspectors in Mönchengladbach pointed out this dilemma as early as December 1914. They noted, for instance, that if seamstresses received roughly 40 marks a month in Family Aid, but could only earn approximately 60 marks working, "it did not suit them" to work for an extra 20 marks a month. The inspectors suggested that women who earned so little be allowed to keep half of their Family Aid.[37] The majority of municipalities subsequently implemented this or a similar solution. Although the imperial government also left this question to the municipalities to regulate, it still recommended that 50% of a woman's earnings be disregarded when calculating aid deductions.[38] The conflict of interest between the Reich and the municipalities also proved to be a hindrance in this case. For many municipalities, the government's higher priority of labor mobilization took a backseat to their own urgent need to relieve their strained budgets by cutting family allowances. As the war dragged on, they consequently practiced a more restrictive deduction policy. In some cases, the municipalities unconditionally eliminated "war wives'" entire allowance when they started a job, and they regularly deducted other forms of assistance, such as that from employers.[39] These measures considerably decreased women's interest in either becoming or remaining employed:

> It infuriates war wives who have gotten a job that what they earn over 20 marks a month is currently subtracted from their Family Aid. These industrious women rightly consider this an unjustified severity, especially in comparison to those women who do not want to work at all. Five marks more a month seems insignificant compared to the bother and expenditure of energy and to having to leave their children with strangers. The women who do not work have a comfortable life, can take walks with their children and spare their clothing, while these women have to slave away for 20 marks.[40]

Conscripted husbands also took this practice amiss. In the spring of 1918, Agnes von Harnack, after discussions with former German prisoners of war, reported that many men found these deductions unfair. As one of them explained to her: "I wrote my wife, 'Who told you to work, when you know that, then, your aid will be cut.'"[41]

On the whole, the practice of deducting a woman's income from her Family Aid seems to have had a negative impact on the government's efforts to mobilize women to work. As Marie-Elisabeth Lüders said, looking back on the situation, many "war wives" had been

> kept from working by the general practice of the delivering agencies [i.e. the communities] of deducting working earnings from Family Aid. Understandably, the women did not consider the so-called "release of 50% of one's earnings" from the calculation of family allowances as a release, but as a withholding, and thereby as a kind of punishment of those who were willing to work; in many cases, this led directly to women giving up work they had already started, because the income that remained after deductions bore no relation to the work they performed and to their sacrifice of a well-run and orderly home.[42]

The third essential category of women that needs to be examined in terms of whether their individual preferences aided or impeded their mobilization for the war industry is composed of those women who were forced to earn money for the first time. This group included women whose husbands had been killed during the war – widows' pensions were still much lower than war support – those who had not applied for any aid – the "invisible poor" – as well as women whose need had not been recognized or those who could not live solely from war assistance. When these women, in their need of money, did look for work in factories, they were often directly employed in their conscripted or fallen husband's former position or at least in the same department.[43] More was involved than simply a pragmatic and formal arrangement, at least as far as these women were concerned. For them, holding their husband's position represented a transference of the content of family structures to the workplace. The fact of this transfer was not unique, but its scope, which included all emotional aspects of family life, was. One munitions worker who had been working in her husband's position suddenly quit without explanation after he was killed in the war. As she later wrote to the factory nurse:

> Perhaps you will understand me, when I tell you the reason. My beloved husband had worked there for years, and I did the same work

there for one and a half years, with his tools, everything, that he had brought there, and I was proud that, while he was fighting out there on the front, I could represent him here. During the 11 years of my marriage, we always got along well, but it was probably only in the last year that we first became one. It was not always pleasant in the factory. But I had my husband, whom I could always talk things over with in letters, and he answered me time after time and again, every letter gave me courage. And so, until that day, that job was sacrosanct to me. That's why I can't do it anymore, but I do want to work somewhere else, for our child.[44]

The practice of employing wives in the same position as their conscripted husbands seems to have been especially prevalent in the transportation industry. A census of the Transport Workers' Association (*Transportarbeiterverband*) in October and November 1915 found that, of the almost 14,000 women working on the street cars, 2,800 were the wives of street-car public employees currently in the army.[45]

This group of women who needed to earn money for the first time by no means represented a sure source of recruitment for the war industry, however. In many cases, women with no experience of factory work and, in particular, those with small children, whose accommodation would have been both problematic and expensive, preferred to support themselves with homework. Their interest in performing homework coincided with a relatively extensive supply of such work. The biggest customer was the army administration, which, directly or indirectly – i.e. through intermediary companies, women's organizations or other groups set up for this purpose – offered jobs sewing for the army. Many of these first-time female earners found employment in the home production of gunlock covers, sandbags, cartridge and shell baskets, leather belts, gas masks, rusk satchels and uniforms, while the civil and military authorities waited in vain for them to go to work in the war industry.[46] Along with the degeneration of the household economy into a quasi-subsistence economy, the spread of homework suggests that the development of the German war economy was more differentiated than has heretofore been understood. In strange contrast to its "modernizing" aspects, such as mass production and new techniques of production, the war industry simultaneously exhibited anachronistic features. Modes of production that had essentially been surpassed by developments in technology and the division of labor gained a new vitality. Roughly speaking, wartime homework was characterized by two different tendencies. On the one hand, some of its traditional concentration in certain regions or on certain types of production waned to the point of insignificance during the war: Either the raw materials or the demand was missing, or the workforce transfered to the war industry or, in some instances, to the agricultural sector. This trend was countered, on the other hand, by an expansion in those areas and branches of homework that could adapt themselves to the needs of army production, or that were actually created by these needs.[47] There is no statistical data available for the total extent of homework between 1914 and 1918. It is possible, however, to ascertain the increase in the number of women performing such work on a regional level. In Hamburg, for example, close to 8,400 homeworkers were registered in 1914, two-thirds of whom were women. Their wartime figure was estimated at approximately 15,000, of which roughly 10,000 were female.[48] And in the Prussian administrative district of Kassel, the number of female outworkers increased from 1,010 in May 1914 to more than 7,500 in September 1918.[49] The growing number of members in the Women Homeworkers' Union (*Gewerkverein der Heimarbeiterinnen*) can also be taken as further indication of the overall increase in this specific workforce (see Table 5).

With regard to labor-market policies and strategies, army sewing represented a strange conglomerate, in that it was supposed to

Table 5. Membership of the Women Homeworkers' Union, 1913–1919

1913	8,385
1914 (January)	8,400
1915 (March)	10,100
1916 (January)	12,915
1917 (January)	16,106
1918 (March)	17,100
1919 (January)	19,644

Source: E. M. Gravert, "Der Einfluß der wirtschaftlichen Demobilmachung auf die Entwicklung der Frauenarbeit," diss. (Hamburg, 1924–1925); Ch. Lorenz, "Die gewerbliche Frauenarbeit während des Krieges," in P. Umbreit and Ch. Lorenz, *Der Krieg und die Arbeitsverhältnisse.* (Stuttgart et al., 1928), 356.

be used simultaneously for completely heterogeneous purposes. Military sewing served as a socio-political means of providing work for unemployed women or for those who, because of health and family reasons, could not work in a factory.[50] At the same time, however, all women who could potentially be employed in the war industry or in agriculture were to be dissuaded from such work. For the first objective, military sewing commissions were supposed to provide those women dependent on outwork with an adequate income; for the second, it was to be effective in terms of production and to help relieve the armaments industry.[51] It was only in the second half of the war that a uniform regulation came into existence.[52] Before that point, no military or civil authority had had an overview, much less control, over the number of employees in wartime homework. The military authorities only intervened in the structure of wages, in order to counteract particularly blatant cases of wage depression, and thereby proved themselves once again as champions of the minimum wage, which was enthusiastically greeted by the trade unions.[53] The wages of many female homeworkers were exceedingly low. This was due, in particular, to the system of subcontractors that characterized wartime homework, a system in which women were often, literally, at the end of the receiving line. The lamentable level of women's wages even induced Berlin's police commissioner to socio-political comment:

> As serious as the state-establishment of minimum wages may seem in times of peace, the present extraordinary situation justifies the regulation of wages through these state authorities responsible for issuing commissions, in order to secure for the classes of low earners, which are already economically severely distressed, an appropriate share of the profits realized by employers.[54]

Orders from the Prussian War Ministry (*preußisches Kriegsministerium*) to its procurement offices in 1915 and subsequent military commanders' decrees, which further emphasized the point, forbid individuals working on military contracts to be paid less than certain agreed minimum wages. Seventy-five percent of the piecework-rate had to go to the homeworker, and in general, only one subcontractor was permitted.[55] In terms of social policy, wartime female homework proved to have an advantageous effect: Together with financial assistance from the Reich, the municipalities and larger businesses, it ensured that numerous "war families" at least received the income necessary to survive. From the point of view of governmental labor-market policy, however, this influx of women into homework was – and remained – a case of unwanted mobilization: Those individuals who sewed for the army were consequently unavailable to fill the labor needs of the armaments industry.

The fourth and final group of women for which the structural conditions of the mobilization of female labor for the war industry shall be elucidated is that of unemployed textile workers. A certain portion of these women did transfer to war-industry businesses and therefore belonged to the first group mentioned above, i.e. to those women who contributed to an increase in female employment in these branches of industry. The majority of unemployed or short-time female textile workers could not be mobilized for the war industry, however. The paradoxical situation thus arose that, while the shortage of labor was developing into one of the key obstacles to the intensification of weapons production, the German Empire, states and municipalities were spending large sums of money to support unemployed female textile workers.

The origin of this high unemployment in the textile industry was the shortage of raw materials. From about the middle of 1915, cotton, the industry's most important raw material, could no longer be imported, and if production had continued at its previous rate, the existing stocks would have only lasted for six months.[56] In 1915 and 1916, in order to ensure that the scarce supplies of cotton be reserved for the needs of the army, the imperial government imposed a series of production and working-hour restrictions on the clothing and textile industry. As the ensuing unemployment among textile workers was a direct consequence of state intervention, both the Reich and the individual states recognized – which was a novelty in the history of social policy – their resulting obligation to provide unemployment benefits. To accompany the production slowdowns, the imperial government introduced a state assistance program for textile workers (see Table 6). Its benefits applied to unemployed and short-time textile and clothing workers according to the level of their need. The municipalities were to determine the eligibility for assistance in each case.[57] In order to be able to judge the significance of this measure, in terms of its impact both financially and on labor-market policy, it is necessary to examine the number of workers – predominantly women – who were affected. This information for the textile industries of Westphalia, the Rhineland and the Kingdom of Saxony shall be outlined below.

Table 6. Production Restrictions and Unemployment Benefits in the Textile and Clothing Industry, 1915–1916

Production Restrictions	Unemployment Benefits
15 May 1915: Commissions for military fabric may only be assigned by the Clothing Procurement Office (*Bekleidungsbeschaffungsamt*). Only those companies commissioned by the Clothing Procurement Office for this purpose are still allowed to process such fabric.	
1 August 1915: General ban on the manufacture of cotton products.	
12 August 1915: Reduction in the work hours for workers in spinning, weaving and knitting mills to five days a week and a maximum of 10 hours a day.	
14 August 1915: Ban on the sale/processing of cotton; confiscation of cotton and cotton thread. Beginning on 4 September, the cotton industry can only produce for the needs of the army.	**18 November 1915**: The Bundesrat appropriates federal funds for unemployment benefits in the textile industry; communities receive at least half of these funds, retroactive as of 1 October 1915; in monostructural areas, a larger portion of the relevant expenses is refunded; Prussia reimburses another third of
7 December 1915: Ban on spinning cotton. Production in the individual spinning mills is limited to a specified fraction of the amount of raw	

Table 6. Production Restrictions and Unemployment Benefits
in the Textile and Clothing Industry,
1915–1916 (*continued*)

Production Restrictions	Unemployment Benefits
materials processed in peacetime. **31 December 1915**: Ban on the sale, processing and transport of weaving yarn, knitting wool and cotton jersey. Dying, twisting, weaving, knitting, etc. is only allowed for army purposes. **1 February 1916**: Confiscation of woven and knitted goods; reduction in the work hours in such factories to 40 hours a week maximum.	its communities' expenses so that they only have to pay one-sixth of unemployment costs. **5 January 1916**: Male and female home workers are included in unemployment benefits.
1 April 1916: Confiscation of cotton thread and yarn (spinning and weaving ban); replaces the decrees from 1 August, 14 August and 7 December 1915.	**13 April 1916**: Imperial Unemployment Benefits are extended to workers in the clothing industry; the need clause is made more stringent. (Need is only recognized in the event that the workers concerned, together with their dependants, can no longer provide for their livelihood.)

Before the war, the textile and clothing industry of West-phalia[58] had employed approximately 70,000 workers, almost half of whom were women. A survey, conducted by the Association of Westphalian Employment Exchanges (*Verband Westfälischer Arbeitsnachweise*) of 349 textile companies in the province in September 1915, revealed that, in comparison to before the war, the number of male workers had declined to 11,852, or 41%, and that of female workers to 3,309, or 15%. If we project this percentage onto the workforce as a whole, then, in September 1915, there would have been almost 30,000 women working in the Westphalian textile industry, but only 17,000 men. The remaining male workers had either already been conscripted or were now working in other industries and/or regions. While there was no unemployment to speak of among male textile workers in September 1915, some women were still unemployed, some had already lost their subsequent job and some were working a reduced number of hours. And then in January 1916, the sweeping reductions in textile production put approximately 50,000 women in Westphalia out of work.[59]

In September 1915, the chambers of commerce of the Rhine province announced that, in their area, at least 30,000 textile workers had been laid off, 17,500 of whom were women.[60]

The consequences of the production restrictions were particularly serious for the Kingdom of Saxony, which had been shaped by the textile industry. Of the approximately 380,000 textile and clothing employees before the war, almost 280,000 had been women.[61] Whereas almost one-third of the men had been drafted or had changed their occupation by the autumn of 1915, in July 1915, four-fifths of the female workers were still employed. In other words, a good 220,000 women were still working in factories directly affected by the production restrictions. After deducting those workers who were to be absorbed by other companies, the Saxon government was faced with well over 100,000 jobless individuals, all of whom would need financial assistance and the majority of whom were women.[62]

It was not only the large number of female employees in the textile and clothing industry that led to the fact that unemployment support became, predominantly, the support of unemployed women. In addition, these women, primarily because of their familial obligations, were often not in a position to relocate. The authorities took women's function as familial bread-winners into account and often accepted the fact that women were married and/or had children as convincing grounds for their refusal to accept employment in other regions. The consequence of this, however, was that women had to be further provided with unemployment benefits.[63] The apparent general consensus among governmental authorities to honor women's role as family providers in their social policy – in spite of the labor shortage in the armaments industry – reflects the value they placed on women ensuring the survival of the family under wartime conditions. The settledness exhibited by female textile workers was intensified still further by another factor: Numerous textile-worker families owned either their own house or a piece of arable property and were therefore unwilling to move.[64] This led to the peculiar situation that, as a large number of trained, female factory workers fell victim to either state-subsidized unemployment or shortened working hours, weapons production suffered increasingly from a labor shortage. Additionally, the acceptance of homework commissions from the army provided many female textile workers with an alternative to changing their trade and/ or their residence.[65] Despite several administrative attempts to induce at least a portion of these women to transfer to the war industry, the problem continued to exist until the second half of 1916. This "unsatisfactory state of affairs"[66] only changed when, in the summer of 1916, the introduction of pulp-yarn processing again improved the employment opportunities in the textile and clothing industry. In general, it seems that only one-fourth of the unemployed female textile workers were found positions in other industries.[67]

The most effective measure in mobilizing women to work for the war industry was the Bundesrat decree of 4 August 1914, which placed employment restrictions for women and adolescents in industrial jobs at the discretion of the administration.[68] This resulting dilution of industrial health and safety regulations did not obtain a single new employee for the war economy. It did, however, permit the women (and adolescents) already employed there to be more intensively exploited through longer working hours, night-shifts and health-endangering jobs. In October 1916, the Weapons and Munitions Procurement Office (*Waffen- und Munitions-Beschaffungsamt*, hereafter refered to as Wumba) ordered the responsible authorities, usually the Factory Inspectorate, to approve all applications from war suppliers to employ women, even if this employment ran counter to trade regulations – if, for example, women were employed in jobs, such as heavy labor, that were designated for men only. As an official of Wumba wrote to the chairman of the Aachen Regional Council: "I by no means underestimate the danger involved here for women's health. In these serious times, however, all the disadvantages women may suffer in these occupations must be tolerated, if this is required to safeguard the prompt production of the needs of the army."[69]

The majority of employers' applications for the authorization of night-shifts and overtime for women were approved, also in the first half of the war. It is thus fair to say that a considerable portion of the female labor mobilized for the war industry was derived from a relapse into the nineteenth century. Only then, before the introduction of health and safety regulations for female workers and factory inspections, was it possible to exhaust female labor to a similar extent. The women "mobilized" in this sense, who, in other words, worked night or double shifts, often did so because they could thereby increase their low female wages in order to be able to live on them, or because they could thus combine a night job in the factory with their daily work in the family.[70] This work in the war industry cost many women their health, however, and it even cost some their lives. Part of the reason was that many of the "typical" factory jobs for women during the war were also extremely dangerous, to both health and life. In addition to the repeated explosions,[71] women employed in gunpowder production and packaging had another, quieter danger to expect, namely the consequences of their constant contact with such chemicals as dinitrobenzol or trinitro-toluol. District autopsy findings, such as the "muddy brain" of one 19-year-old, previously healthy woman after four weeks in a gunpowder factory,[72] and unambiguous statements by factory doctors in the chemical industry referred explicitly to the extraordinary health risks that women endured while manufacturing weapons. The imperial government, however, did not see itself in a position to do more than recommend that women no longer be employed in such jobs *"as soon as circumstances permitted."*[73]

The Prussian trade minister's anticipation in 1915 that, because of the current conditions for women in explosives and armaments industries, the Factory Inspectorate's publication of its reports during the war would "meet with serious misgivings from the censorship office" was fully substantiated.[74] They were only published in 1920 – which was too late to prevent the general worsening of conditions for women in these and other industries of the war economy. The reintroduction of women into underground work in mines, for example, a measure that was repeatedly supported by heavy industry, was later vehemently combated by the Headquarters for Women's Labor (*Frauenar-beitszentrale*, or FAZ) in the War Office.[75] It could not be completely averted, however. Such extensive use was made of the "window of opportunity" opened by the Bundesrat decree of 4 August 1914, which authorized exceptions to the occupational restrictions for women and adolescents, that it effectively amounted to an abolition of worker-protection regulations. Fifteen-hour days for women and adolescents were no rarity, and 12-hour shifts for female night-workers the rule. In some cases, women even worked shifts that rotated every 24 hours. Employers' applications for exceptions were usually granted without any reservation and often without any time limit (i.e. "for the length of the war"). They also increasingly gave "rise to the objections" of the imperial government.[76] Consequently, in 1917, the October 1916 edict of the quartermaster (*Feldzeug-meisterei*) was repealed and it was recommended that these applications be screened more carefully and their approval granted more conservatively.[77] The regulation of exceptions, however, continued to be more charitable to those industries that asserted that, without them, they could not deliver their military commissions.[78]

After two years of war, the state of the labor mobilization was deemed to be unsatisfactory. The academic Commission for the Analysis of the War Economy (*Kommission zur Analyse der Kriegswirtschaft*) submitted a memorandum – which coincided with the preparation of the Auxiliary Service Law (*Hilfsdienst-gesetz*)[79] – in which it made the following rough calculations: By the end of 1916, approximately 8.5 million men had been conscripted,[80] 2 million of whom had received a deferment of military service in order to remain working in the war economy. Of the 6.5 million male workers lost to the front, approximately 4 million had been health-insured and thus stemmed predominantly from industry. The commission denoted prisoners of war and women as the only two important sources of replacement labor. "Since, in general, one forced laborer is probably equivalent to no more than two-thirds of a unforced one,"[81] the commission estimated that the prisoners of war had successfully replaced 750,000 male German workers in industry and agriculture. According to its calculations, the commission determined that the increase in female labor in some areas of the economy had roughly replaced an equal number of conscripted men. Including foreign labor from either neutral countries or occupied territories, there still remained 4.5 million male workers for whom a replacement had not been found. Nor was one in sight. At this juncture, the highest level of the military intervened in labor policy. The Supreme Command under Hindenburg and Ludendorff called for an end to improvizations and a complete reorganization of the war economy according to the interests and under the aegis of the military. From this point on, everything was to be different.

The Auxiliary Service Law, the War Office and the Organization of Female Labor

In the summer of 1918, Anny D., a day-laborer's daughter from Schweinfurt, pursued a rather unusual course in order to solve a pressing family problem. She sent a petition to King Ludwig III of Bavaria, asking him to enlist her father for auxiliary service (*Hilfsdienst*), since he was lazy and mistreated his wife and children.[82] Provided that the Bavarian authorities, to whom this petition was forwarded, had realized its declared intention and had ordered Kaspar D. to take up employment as a compulsory supplementary worker at the company Fichtel & Sachs, then the institution of the auxiliary service would have fulfilled, at least this time, one of the hopes held for it. This was not often the case. No other measure of labor-market policy during the war was burdened with so many demands, fraught with so much domestic turmoil and executed with such excessive institutional energy as the Auxiliary Service Law. And with no other measure was there such a glaring discrepancy between effort and outcome. Only the trade unions succeeded in drawing some benefit from this "changeling."[83] The law brought them long-sought official recognition as a constituent force in social policy, and they were decisively involved in both its materialization and implementation. In the longer term, however, the consequences of the Auxiliary Service Law also proved to be completely ambivalent for the workers' movement. Although women did not fall under the stipulations of the law, the mobilization of female labor during the second half of the war occurred within the professed organizational and political framework of the Auxiliary Service Law. I shall therefore briefly outline the origin and institutional establishment of the law below.

During the two great battles of 1916, Verdun and the Somme, it became evident that the German army's supply situation was in a critical condition. There was a shortage of munitions and war matériel, and the soldiers could not be replaced as quickly as they could be killed – from January to October 1916 alone, the military recorded 1.4 million "losses."[84] The Third Supreme Command under Hindenburg and Ludendorff, appointed in August 1916, initiated its activity with the announcement of the so-called "Hindenburg Program," an immense production program drawn up jointly by the Supreme Command and heavy industry. As Hindenburg wrote to the Prussian war minister (*preußischer Kriegsminister*) on 31 August 1916, in order to achieve the established objectives of the program – among others, the doubling of the current munitions and mortar production and the tripling of artillery and machine-gun production – and to compensate for the shortage of workers and soldiers, increased numbers of disabled veterans, prisoners of war, women and adolescents had to be put to work.[85] In September, Hindenburg and Ludendorff stated their demands more specifically: reductions in the number of deferments, an expansion of the draft to include men up to 50 years of age and, most important, the passing of a War Service Act (*Kriegsleistungsgesetz*). This law was to make compulsory conscription to work possible and would apply to women:

> There are countless thousands of childless war wives who only cost the state money. Equally, thousands of women and girls are running around who do not do anything, or at most, practice some useless trade. The principle "who does not work, shall not eat" is, in our situation, more than justified, *also with regards to women . . .* [Universities should be closed.] This, as well, is an act of justice, in that *men unfit for military service* and women are now outstripping students and others fighting on the battlefield and will, in the future, take away their jobs.[86]

Minister of State (*Staatsminister*) Helfferich drafted Imperial Chancellor Bethmann Hollweg's response to the demands of the Supreme Command. Although Helfferich's original draft was slightly more polished in tone, the letter from the chancellor on 30 September clearly let it be known that an unbridgeable rift existed between the new military leadership's understanding of politics and that of the Reich's civil leadership. Bethmann Hollweg declared that, apart from the conscription of 17–18-year-old and 45–50-year-old men – which was seen as only partially useful – all of the measures proposed by the Supreme Command had either already been attained or were impractical. He justified his rejection of compulsory work for women in particular detail. Although the final version of Helfferich's letter for the chancellor lacks his slip into folksy language – as he wrote, "The introduction of a general compulsory service for women would 'put the cart before the horse'" – that was exactly the sense intended:

> Without having to fear contradiction, one can maintain that . . . those tasks that could be expected to be performed by female workers are today already being discharged by such on the largest scale. However, it has not been possible to accommodate women who have become unemployed in other industrial branches even approximately in the war industry. According to the last months' statistics, for every 100 open positions, roughly 80 men apply, whereas 160 women are seeking work. Female labor is thus, in contrast to male, in much greater supply than demand. Consequently, the problem to solve with regard to women now and probably long into the future is not: How can one make more women workers available? but rather: How can one create additional suitable work for women? . . . The introduction of universal compulsory service for women would thus be an inappropriate measure, to which the most serious reservations, also in economic, moral and social respects, stand in the way. As long as there is not a complete change in this employment situation, I must counsel in the most urgent terms against following this path.

Helfferich's smug conclusion that "One can command an army, but not a national economy," was, however, withheld from the recipient.[87]

The Prussian war minister, to whom the military command sent both their own letter and that of the chancellor, also came out against a War Service Act in general and against forced labor for women in particular. In a letter to Hindenburg, he stated his reasons. Not only was there a surplus of female labor, as the chancellor had identified, but this was composed primarily of women who, for either physical or familial reasons, were not suitable for factory work.[88]

On 7 October, Hindenburg once again demanded that the chancellor abolish freedom of movement for the war-industry workforce and, additionally, that he should not reinstate industrial health and safety standards for women and adolescents. Shortly after, on 17 October, there was a meeting of those departments of Prussia and of the Reich that were involved in labor mobilization in the Imperial Office of the Interior (*Reichsamt des Innern*). As their conclusion, the participants stressed that forced labor for men as well as for women would "not be advisable:"

> On the one hand, the difficulties that, because of individuals' different levels of education and social status, would obstruct the practical implementation [of such a measure] are insurmountable. On the other hand, success commensurate to the intensity of the intervention is not to be expected. Male persons who are in some capacity able to work are already, with few exceptions, working in concerns that either directly or indirectly serve war objectives. And female workers are still available in sufficient numbers.

The abolition of the workforce's freedom of movement also found no support, on the grounds that, for domestic reasons, it would not be opportune.[89] The arguments that the imperial and Prussian governments raised against the plans of the military leadership were completely valid: In 1916, there was still a significant number of unemployed female (textile) workers, and many of the women who were theoretically available for employment in the war industry actually could not be mobilized because of family reasons.

The united front of the Prussian and imperial governments against the military leaders' program proved, for the time being, to be ineffective, however. In its letter to Bethmann Hollweg of 23 October 1916, the Supreme Command presented its old catalogue of demands in a new form. The extension of conscription to include men from age 15 to age 60 was to provide the basis for a general obligation to work and would automatically include the abolition of the workforce's freedom of movement. The demand that women also be required to work was raised again, as well. Hindenburg's letter to the chancellor is an informative document of the image of women held by a crucial societal institution, namely the military leadership. It shall consequently be quoted here in detail. The chief of the general staff (*Generalstabschef*) wrote:

> It is also my opinion that women's work should not be overestimated. Almost all intellectual work, heavy physical labor, as well as all real manufacturing work will still fall on men – in addition to the entire waging of the war. It would be good if clear, official expression were given to these facts and if a stop were put to women's agitation for

parity in all professions, and thereby, of course, for political emancipation. I completely agree with Your Excellency that compulsory labor for women would be an inappropriate measure. After the war, we will need the woman as spouse and mother. I thus strongly support those measures, enacted through law, prerogative, material aid, etc., aimed at that effect. In spite of the strong opposition to such measures, it is here that vigorous action needs to be taken, in order to extinguish the influence of this female rivalry, which disrupts the family. Your Excellency would please gather from the above that I am not only concerned with the war, but that I am also aware that, for the development of our people *after* the war, healthy social conditions, i.e. in the first place the protection of the family, are necessary.

If I *nevertheless* urge that the requirement to work be extended to all women who are either unemployed or working in trivial positions, now and for the duration of the war, I do so because, in my opinion, women can be employed in many areas to a still greater degree than previously and men can thereby be freed for other *work*. But first industry and agriculture must be urged even more to employ women. Further, the choice of occupation must not be left up to the women alone, but rather, it must regulated according to ability, previous experience and social status. In particular, I want to stress again that I consider it especially wrong to keep secondary schools and universities, which have been almost completely emptied of men by conscription, open only for women. It is valueless, because the scholarly gain is minimal; furthermore, because precisely that rivalry with the family that needs to be combated would be promoted; and finally, because it would represent the coarsest injustice if the young man, who is giving everything for his Fatherland, is forced behind the woman.[90]

With these views, the Supreme Command was, for the time being, able successfully to assert itself against the objections of the Empire's civilian leadership. During his visit to the main headquarters in Pleß on 26 October, Bethmann Hollweg agreed to introduce forced labor. While in Pleß, the chancellor met with General Groener, the designated head of the War Office. This central military authority, whose founding was pushed through simultaneously with the Auxiliary Service Law by the Supreme Command, was to play the primary role in the implementation of the augmented weapons program. This military "superauthority," equipped with essentially dictatorial powers and, as was the concomitant intention, freed from narrow-minded bureaucratic thinking, was to make the War Ministry (*Kriegsministerium*) "get a move on" and to render munitions production and labor mobilization more effective.[91] As head of the front railway system, Groener had made a name for himself as an efficient organizer, and, since May 1916, he had been the chief of the general staff's representative on the board of the newly founded War Food Office (*Kriegsernährungsamt*). And it was Groener who, even before the founding of the War Office on 1 November 1916, was ultimately successful in dissuading Ludendorff from the idea of compulsory labor for women.[92] The Supreme Command did not return to this particular demand before the Auxiliary Service Law came into effect.

However, it was not only the exclusion of women that strongly differentiated the Auxiliary Service Law as it was ultimately implemented on 5 December from the original intention of the military command. As the law could not be passed without the consent of the Reichstag, fairly significant concessions had to be made to the strongly represented Social Democratic Party – concessions which quickly gave the Supreme Command cause to distance itself from its own brainchild. The most important stipulations of the Auxiliary Service Law read as follows:

Every male German from the completion of his seventeenth to that of his sixtieth year, in so far as he has not already been conscripted for military service, is required to perform auxiliary labor. Those persons "who are employed in the governmental bureaucracy, bureaucratic institutions, in the war industry, in agriculture or forestry, in nursing, in war-economic organizations of every kind or in other occupations and enterprises that are either directly or indirectly important for the conducting of the war or the provision of the population" qualify as already being employed in the auxiliary service. The War Office runs the "patriotic auxiliary service." The assessment of which institutions fall under these stipulations is made by a so-called assessment committee, which is composed of one officer, two higher-ranking public servants and two representatives of the employer and the employee, respectively. The enlistment of persons who are employed by institutions other than those included here, is effected first through an order to report in writing, then, should this not be observed, through written notification by the so-called enlistment committee, to be composed of one officer, one civil servant and two representatives, respectively, from the employer and the employee. Upon receipt of written notification, the individual obligated for auxiliary service [*Hilfsdienstpflichtiger*] has two weeks in which to look for work that is recognized as auxiliary service. No one may employ an individual obligated for auxiliary service who already holds a position that is recognized as one of auxiliary service, if this individual does not present written confirmation (the so-called "Certificate of Employment Change" [*Abkehrschein*]) from his last employer, in which the latter consents to the change of employment. In the event of the employer's refusal to issue this certificate, the individual obligated for auxiliary service can address a so-called arbitration committee which is composed of a representative of the War Office as chairman and three representatives, respectively, for the employer and the employee. This committee can then issue the said certificate instead of the employer, if the former considers the change of employment justified; a change of employment to "better the work conditions" is also to be considered justified. Furthermore, this arbitration committee may be consulted in disputes about salary and work conditions in auxiliary service enterprises [*Hilfsdienst-betriebe*].[93]

Even though the arbitration committee would also possibly have to make decisions concerning the interests of working women, only adult male Germans were admitted as members of the committee, with the justification that the Auxiliary Service Law only referred to men.[94] Women were only eligible to become members in the internal workers' committees that were supposed to be established in all auxiliary-service companies with at least fifty employees.

The War Office's fate was similar to that of the Auxiliary Service Law. Here, as well, the military command had enough influence to get the project launched. However, the Supreme Command's ignorance of, or rather, its disregard for the complicated domestic power structure – consisting of parliaments, parties, the workers' movement and Prussian-German departmental particularism that the Supreme Command thought should be ignored – led in this case to an outcome that no one had desired, but which no one, Hindenburg and Ludendorff included, had the necessary political power to eliminate. The factors "responsible" for the development of the Auxiliary Service Law resulted primarily from the delicate balance of power between the government, the Reichstag and the workers' movement – Bethmann Hollweg's famous "politics of diagonals." In the case of the War Office, however, it was structures of constitutional law and practical administration that licked the Auxiliary Service Law into its final shape. In particular, the resistance of the War Ministry and other affected departments to giving up decisive areas of competence to the War Office led to the fact that "the existing administrative body... was not included in a central military office with dictatorial powers, but rather, was enlarged by a new office with unclear delimitations of competence, but with a rapidly swelling staff of several thousand."[95] The War Office was not placed over the Prussian War Ministry, but rather, at least nominally, subordinated to it. It took over the main departments of the war economy from the War Ministry, as well as the authority, granted by the emperor on 1 November 1916, to give directives to the Deputy General Commands in matters concerning military replacements, workers and the war economy. As the independent position of the Deputy General Commands was by and large retained, however, and as every commanding general could undertake what he deemed appropriate, Groener effectively created a new array of offices, that of the main and subordinate War Office bureaus (*Kriegsamtsstellen und -nebenstellen*). A bureau of the War Office was located wherever there was a Deputy General Command; this was not under its jurisdiction, however, but under that of the War Office. The results engendered by this organizational restructuring were completely mixed. The dualism between the War Ministry and the Deputy General Commands, which had impeded the labor-market policy of the first half of the war, was neutralized. From this point on, however, one had to reckon with the problematic relations between the Deputy General Commands and the War Office bureaus, and, more crucially, with the permanent conflict, smoldering at the highest level, between the War Office and the War Ministry and other departments. The icy relationship between the War Office and the other administrative departments made cooperation with the latter – imperative for the fulfillment of the War Office's task – impossible.

This politico-bureaucratic context shaped subsequent labor-market policy, including that of the mobilization of women. From this point on, this task also belonged to the War Office and was consequently subject to its specific problems.

With the addition of Alexander Schlicke from the German Metal Workers' Association (*Deutscher Metallarbeiterverband*), War Office Chief Groener brought a labor representative into his administration, which had been shaped by military officers and industrialists. In like manner, Groener added two members of the women's movement to his all-male staff. These two were to direct, "from women for women,"[96] the systematic recording of female labor and to achieve, against the opposition of employers and trade unions, its increased use in the war industry.[97] This incorporation of women's organizations into such a prominent place in the direction of the war economy institutionalized a development in the relationship between women's associations and the state which had already begun on a semi-official level in August 1914. Even before mobilization, Gertrud Bäumer, chairwoman of the Federation of German Women's Associations (*Bund Deutscher Frauenvereine*, hereafter referred to as BDF) – the umbrella organization of all those women's associations which claimed adherence to the women's movement in a strict sense – requested on 31 July 1914 that all member associations contact the Patriotic Women's Associations (*Vaterländische Frauenvereine*)[98] – a support organization of the Red Cross – the Red Cross, civil authorities and welfare organizations to avoid fragmentation of the incipient welfare activity. Under the banner of wartime national welfare, the women's organizations then concluded their own *Burgfrieden*. They formed the National Women's Service (*Nationaler Frauendienst*), in which the BDF, religious and patriotic women's organizations, and the social-democratic women's movement cooperated during the war. They likewise concluded a truce with the civil authorities: The Prussian Ministry of the Interior approved the plans that Bäumer and Hedwig Heyl presented on 1 August 1914, and municipal authorities, facing a severe shortage of personnel, were more than willing to transfer part of their war-welfare activity to honorary female social workers. The local branches of the National Women's Service, attached to local authorities, concerned themselves with food provision, the position of "war families" and job-placement for women. Furthermore, they functioned as a general counseling center in matters of war welfare. Initially, these local chapters were only rather loosely connected to one another. When they merged in January 1917 to form the National Women's Service of Germany (*Deutsche Zentrale des Nationalen Frauendienstes*), there were sixty local organizations.

It was not only its war-welfare activities, however, that qualified the women's movement(s) for a more institutionalized role in the organization of the war economy. In addition, the BDF, as the largest political women's movement in the original sense of the word, identified itself with the society of belligerent Germany to a degree never granted pre-war German society. If representatives of the BDF had conceived of alternatives to what it saw as the patriarchal "chilling of the world under the rule of reason, in service of greed" before 1914[99] – alternatives which reflected the conspicuous, albeit not antagonistic, distance the bourgeois women's movement placed between itself and the social conditions of its time – then it was in exactly this wartime society that the BDF saw the possibility of reviving its alternative plans. Not unlike certain tendencies in the workers' movement, the bourgeois women's movement expected that the weight of the events of the war would initiate a reorganization of societal relations in line with its own objectives, one result of which would be a permanent improvement in women's chances of participation. In retrospect, Bäumer described this as follows:

> A different order than the materialistic, technical one of the nineteenth century prevailed and we felt an enormous feeling of liberation. An order not of achievement and reward, risk and profit, effort and advantage, but of life and death, blood and strength, effort as such, absolute, in every case. This is what we experienced then: being lifted into a totally different order, one that opposed the individualistic principle of achievement. It was, in a special form, the decisive *antithesis* of the industrial-capitalistic way of life. Public feeling was completely transformed, taken off the hinges of rational connections and transported up to the world of values such as: homeland, soil, family, camaraderie. New destinies awoke new feelings, or ancient ones that were frozen and faded.[100]

Above all, these hopes were linked to the wartime governments' and bureaucracies' observable expansion of authority in the area of social policy. This was interpreted as a decisive step away from state and society towards a more humane, "more feminine" form of organization, i.e. towards the form that the women's movement had repeatedly called for before the war. Because of its positive stance toward wartime society as a whole, it was natural for the women's movement to put aside its demands for political and social emancipation as petty and to submit itself entirely and almost unquestioningly to the requirements and discipline of the home front. This not only meant that the question of women's suffrage almost completely disappeared from public discussion. It meant, as well and above all, that the women's movement expressly renounced the possibility of deriving any moral-political rights from the activities and burdens confronting not only its members but the entire female population during the war. As Elisabeth Altmann-Gottheiner explained in January 1916, the areas of and opportunities for employment opened up for women by the war had not enticed the "responsible" women of the women's movement to a "cheap triumph:"

> That this was not so, is undoubtedly the greatest proof of the patriotic attitude and the deep feeling of responsibility on the part of the organized German women's movement. Every German woman who consciously considers these things is aware that she is, *during the war, just the substitute for the man* who held her position earlier, and that she must step down as soon as he returns home and reclaims his position. In wartime, a *truce [Burgfrieden] prevails between the sexes*, and German women emphatically reject the desire to extract a possible "war profit" from the war.[101]

This renunciation of a "war profit," as well as the competence that many representatives of the women's movement possessed in questions of female employment, social policy and administration, rendered the bourgeois women's movement a prime source of recruitment for the incipient administrative apparatus of the women's employment organization that was to be established within the War Office. Groener appointed Marie-Elisabeth Lüders as consultant in charge of female labor; her colleague was Agnes von Harnack.[102] One of the first meetings between Lüders and other representatives of women's organizations and the war minister and Groener occurred on 17 November 1916. Here, the orders read as follows: "Short and concise: 'To introduce, with the greatest speed, everything necessary to replace men with women in all areas of employment.'"[103] The organizational plan submitted by the women on the following day sought to meet this directive through a close connection between the labor procurement and labor welfare, "in order to awaken in women the necessary *willingness* to work, to train in them the indispensable *ability* to work, and to educate them in the essential *steadiness* of work."[104] It was, above all, in women's work in the family that Marie-Elisabeth Lüders perceived the greatest obstacle to successfully mobilizing them for the war industry. She was consequently also opposed to the extension of obligatory auxiliary service to women, preferring instead a strengthening of women- and family-oriented social policy as the functional equivalent of the former. As she said:

> The indissoluble closeness between woman's life and work, which is given by Nature, makes the ... attempt to recruit women, as ordered, in the case of an emergency seem hopeless ... The execution of compulsory recruitment must founder on the physiological, psychological and sociological limitations of female life. This forcing of naturally impossible demands avenges itself in the defeat of the one making the demands.

Lüders believed that ways and means had to be found that took these limitations of women's lives into account – and that this would lead directly to a social policy tailored specifically to the needs of women and families.[105]

The military authorities promised Lüders all necessary support and full freedom of action. But once again, it became obvious that Groener, in expecting the War Office to collaborate with knowledgeable civilians, had strongly overestimated the military bureaucracy's ability for innovation. Not only did he himself ultimately fail in his attempt to pursue a quasi class-neutral policy in the War Office between industrialists and workers' organizations,[106] but also Lüders, equally resolute in her own way, eventually had to resign in the face of the political and social prejudices, the "male pride" and the "self-centered animosity of several higher-ranking officers." She left the War Office of her own accord shortly after Groener's departure on 1 December 1917. The bitterest memories in her autobiography are connected with what she saw as the military's lack of expertise, which created an essential obstacle to working with it. Thus, regarding Major Henrici, who, after Groener's "promotion" to the army, became her immediate superior, Lüders wrote that he had

> no clue about the considerable differences between a subordinate soldier in the army and his entire life situation in family and profession. The legal problems pertaining to society, the economy and labor were so alien to Henrici that one was continually placed in the embarrassing situation of trying not to disgrace him too much in front of others and oneself ... At the beginning of his activity, Henrici, who, incidentally viewed me with the greatest suspicion, sent an orderly to me one day, with the request that I write down all "specifically female professions" for him. I truthfully could do nothing other than write him that there was only one specifically female profession and that was that of wet-nurse. All other professions

could be and were also practiced by men. He resented this communication.[107]

These were not, however, the only problems confronting the
women designated to organize female labor for the war industry.
In addition, before they could even begin working on their actual
task, they had to create the requisite, nation-wide organization
and then provide it with a suitable staff. Through this, the complex structure of the War Office and its subdivisions was rendered
even more confusing, and the sources of friction between this
new organization, the Deputy General Commands and the civil
authorities became even more numerous. Starting with the organizational premise of creating a link between official labor-market
policy and the welfare activities of individuals inside and outside
of the government, these women developed a nation-wide network of female consultants, parallel to working through the
official channels of the War Office. In the War Office itself, the
Women's Department (*Frauenreferat*) and the Headquarters for
Women's Labor were inaugurated, both under the direction of
Lüders. While the Women's Department was to lead the actual
mobilization, the FAZ was responsible for the accompanying
welfare policy. In June 1917, the two offices were merged. On
12 December 1916, Groener issued an appeal to women's organizations, trade unions and socio-political associations to send
representatives to the newly founded National Committee for
Women's War Work (*Nationaler Ausschuß für Frauenarbeit
im Kriege*), which was to harmonize the activity of the War
Office with that of the large socio-political organizations, particularly in terms of content and personnel. Lüders was appointed
managing director of this committee, which was composed of
thirty-six socio-political associations. Apart from the propaganda
benefits of its assemblage, this committee remained ineffective.
The contact between women's groups and welfare associations
occurred on the local level, and the flow of information between
the FAZ/Women's Department and the committee was extremely
poor.

A Women's Department and a Women's Labor Office (*Frauen-
arbeitshauptstelle*), both of which were headed by the same
woman, were established at each bureau of the War Office. Here,
as well, the Women's Department was responsible for the work
of mobilization in a narrower sense, the Women's Labor Office
for the accompanying welfare measures. In particularly industry-

rich areas or in those where the administrative areas of the Army Corps did not overlap with those of the civilian authorities and thus necessitated it, branch offices of the Women's Labor Office (*Frauenarbeitnebenstellen*) were established. As on the central level of the Women's Department and the FAZ, where the Committee for Women's War Work was designated as the umbrella organization for all non-official welfare efforts, honorary "welfare agencies," which were to function as the mediating authority between local socio-political activities and the respective Women's Department, were created on the local level. In the spring of 1918, in addition to the Women's Department or Women's Labor Office, 51 branches of the Women's Labor Office and 424 welfare offices were functioning in those areas administered by the Army Corps; at the beginning of January 1918, approximately 1,000 women were working in these offices.[108]

The following work program for the FAZ gives an impression of the almost unlimited number of tasks that this newly created organization was intended to tackle.

1. The Headquarters for Women's Labor has the task of initiating all measures that foster the ability and willingness to work of female workers of every sort, with the aim of the greatest possible increase in production. 2. The Headquarters for Women's Labor consequently must see to it that, if possible, all impediments to work are removed for women. The following belong to this task: a) protection of health, b) preparation of appropriate recuperation rooms, places to live and sleep, c) obtaining of suitable work clothing, d) improvement of conditions and means of transportation, e) improvement of foodstuff procurement and distribution. 3. In addition to providing for the enhancement of women's ability to work, the Headquarters for Women's Labor must create institutions that serve the well-being of the women's family members and that thereby contribute to increasing women's willingness to work: organizing nursing wards, day-nurseries, kindergartens, day-homes for school children in the afternoon, wet-nurseries, mothers', infants' and young children's advice centers, etc. Employment of house-, community- and country-nurses, district welfare agents, etc.

Additionally, the FAZ was to conduct crash courses to train female civil servants for the aforementioned work and to direct the welfare agencies.[109]

This description of the FAZ's activity gives apt evidence of the tall order facing Lüders and her colleagues. Under the aggravated personnel and material conditions of wartime and at rapid-fire tempo, they were supposed to create – and wanted to create – a socio-political infrastructure that would befit a well-developed welfare state of the second half of the twentieth century. And this was to be accomplished by an organization that, apart from the consideration of Groener and his closest coworkers, only existed as a tolerated alien element in its own official military environment for the entire duration of the war. This attitude was exhibited both on the personal and on the institutional level. The Weapons and Munitions Procurement Office (Wumba) of the War Office, for example, was responsible for the entirety of state-armaments production and employed a large number of female workers – in mid-1917, approximately 150,000 – in its artillery factories. Only at the end of July 1918 did Wumba agree to employ in the factories under its jurisdiction only those female laborers who had been sent by employment exchanges for women, which had been established at the instigation of the Women's Departments.[110] Further examples of this kind, i.e. of a government institution's internal cooperation problems, can be recounted at will. The Women's Departments, for example, only succeeded in November 1917, one year after their founding, in being allowed to participate in those factory inspections and meetings of the expert officers for the Auxiliary Service where the replacement of male labor with female labor came into question. And still in July 1918, the War-Replacement and Labor Department (*Kriegs-Ersatz und Arbeitsdepartement*) of the War Office had to point out that the files of the Women's Department in the War Office had to be processed by the Women's Departments in the War Office bureaus and that, in general, the Women's Departments should be involved in all matters concerning women.[111]

Although the women's organization was thus very poorly integrated into the overarching bureaucracy of the War Office, it nevertheless shared in its internal and external institutional conflicts. The external quarrels between the War Office, Groener and the civilian departments even intensified after the establishment of the women's organization because the latter's competencies overlapped so severely with the jurisdiction of the Factory Inspectorate that conflicts with the Prussian Ministry of Trade (*preußisches Handelsministerium*) and subordinate departments became almost unavoidable. Above all, however, the

Women's Departments shared the War Office bureaus' complicated relations with the Deputy General Commands. In February 1917, Groener subordinated the War Office bureaus to the Deputy General Commands, with which, heretofore, they had only been affiliated. They thus continued to receive their instructions directly from the War Office, but were required to inform the Deputy General Commands of all events of a "fundamental" nature, even when these were only tangential to their area of responsibility. The bureaus' areas of work were thus divided into those in which they acted as organs of the War Office (Auxiliary Service matters, female labor and female-labor welfare, the general stimulation of production and infrastructure questions) and those in which they acted as organs of the Deputy General Commands (deferment questions, rationing of raw materials, imports and exports, food provisions for workers in the armaments industry). The enumeration of these areas of responsibility points to the dilemma that might have been the cause for this "extraordinarily puzzling arrangement."[112] The commanding generals still had primary jurisdiction over those conscripted workers who had been sent back from the front because their skills were needed for the war industry. It was precisely this jurisdiction that the bureaus of the War Office required to fulfill their priority task, namely the "freeing up" of these "reclaimed" laborers for the front. The War Office and its subordinate divisions could only operate independently in those fields of work that had been newly created by the Auxiliary Service Law: The enlistment of individuals obligated for auxiliary service or female workers was thus legitimate territory; the conscription or deferment of those individuals liable for military service was not. Here, they were dependent upon the cooperation of the Deputy General Commands, whom Groener could not order, but only request to integrate their responsible departments into the structure of the War Office.[113] At this level of the relations between the War Office bureaus and the Deputy General Commands, just as on the centralized level of the War Ministry and the War Office, it was less that the anticipated, decisive "super"institution was created as that, in the long term, a "veritable chaos" was institutionalized.[114]

Let us now examine the effects the Auxiliary Service Law had on the mobilization of labor in the second half of the war.

The first consequence of the law was as uncontrolled as it

was undesired. Before a single individual who was obligated for auxiliary service could be recruited, even before the necessary organizational foundation of Auxiliary Service registration offices and draft boards could be laid, the War Office had to attempt to counter the war industry's tendency to fire female workers in the hope that it would "get strong, enduring and able help from the ranks of those men required to do auxiliary service."[115] This inclination resulted primarily from the acute shortage of skilled workers in the war industry, could only be alleviated in exceptional cases by female labor and was, already in the first half of the war, an essential reason for employers' lack of interest in hiring women.[116] A stop had to be put to such an interpretation of the Auxiliary Service Law by employers if the increased demand for war-industry workers – which Groener estimated to be between 2 and 3 million – was to be even approximately met. Employers soon abandoned the hopes they had placed on the Auxiliary Service Law, however, and returned to their old practice of "reclaiming" workers from the front – a practice that the Auxiliary Service Law was specifically targeted to curb.[117] The individuals designated for auxiliary service who appeared in war-industry concerns were significantly less numerous and also less capable than employers and the military bureaucracy had expected. Eventually almost all men obligated to do so reported for auxiliary service duty. However, the skilled workers previously not employed in the war industry – i.e. those who had been sought above all other laborers – revealed themselves to be:

> either sickly men, or such whom, owing to their laziness, could not be utilized, or such who, owing to their agitative activities, were discharged from the factory or whom, only with reluctance, would be rehired . . . According to the previous results of notifications for service, almost all individuals obligated for auxiliary service are critically ill, if one believes their personal testimony, the reports of majors' offices and the certificates from their doctors, although when one personally meets the individuals in question, one has the impression that they are indeed able to work very well, as long as they do not have to do auxiliary service.[118]

Those who could not provide a medical attestation – although the draft boards constantly complained about the over-cooperative attitude of doctors and local government offices – joined volunteer fire departments or other institutions where they could receive proof of working in activities important for the war effort. The number of remaining and actually employable individuals required to perform auxiliary service was estimated at a maximum of 25% of those theoretically obligated for service; and only a small fraction of those 25% could be used as skilled laborers.[119] In March 1917, the 1st Bavarian Army Corps Munich soberly summarized the situation as follows:

> If one were to infer the mood of the general public from voluntary enlistments for the Patriotic Auxiliary Service, one would have difficulty in classifying previous experiences as gratifying . . . The results up to now do not justify high expectations with regard to the Auxiliary Service Law. According to our War Office bureau, the voluntary enlistments are, for the time being, just burdensome work and a probably useless extension of the card files.[120]

The lack of enthusiasm on the part of individuals required to assume an activity central to the war effort was only one of the obstacles to the execution of the Auxiliary Service Law. Cases such as that in which eighty individuals were conscripted to put a gunpowder factory into operation and only eight came, four of whom left the worksite immediately,[121] were contrasted with examples like the one in Charlottenburg, where 278 draftees for auxiliary service reported for duty, but only 157 suitable positions could be found.[122] In any case, employers showed little interest in the majority of draftees because they were unfamiliar with factory work. An additional difficulty was that it was not often clear to the draft boards from the outset which of the individuals who were obligated for auxiliary service and who then reported for duty should actually be "conscripted." The problem here was that this action could not – and was not supposed to – occur on the basis of a general regulation, as, for instance, the calling up of men for the military according to their division into age groups, but had to be decided each time anew, according to the respective trade practiced by each obligated individual. In many cases, however, the requisite categorization of occupations and businesses as "integral" or "external" to the war effort – a task for which the diagnostic committees formed by the Auxiliary Service Law were responsible – had to first be carried out. In the middle of this total war, in which hardly any trade or activity was performed that was not directly or indirectly relevant for the needs of the army, this division proved to be surprisingly problematic. An enumeration of those occupations and branches of industry declared to be indisputably "external" to the war effort from July 1917 recorded, in addition to servants, elevator operators, waiters and hairdressers, only employees in such remote lines of business as the sale of stamps or toys, the manufacture of marble figures, amber goods or objects made of antlers, or the processing of ostrich plumes.[123] Tobacco firms, publishing companies and carpet firms, by comparison, were officially categorized as auxiliary service businesses.[124] In this way, the requirement for men to work that the Auxiliary Service Law introduced became, as well, a requirement for the responsible offices and committees to work, particularly in terms of their construction of a hierarchical reality through the classification of auxiliary-service-obligated individuals and the comparable hiring businesses and government authorities. This work of definition revealed that the majority of individuals required to do auxiliary service were already directly or indirectly active in the war economy – a fact which the government had often asserted in its fight against compulsory labor for the general population.[125]

The effects of the Auxiliary Service Law on the mobilization of labor were correspondingly short-lived. The number of suitable auxiliary-service draftees was and remained small. Ironically, it was the employment of those workers who did not at all fall under the letter of the Auxiliary Service Law – i.e. above all, women – that proceeded with the greatest speed and scope. The majority of the women mobilized by the Auxiliary Service Law, however, were neither taking a job for the first time, nor had they – like many of the men hired – previously been employed solely in positions declared "external" to the war effort, nor did this new workforce – be it male or female – primarily benefit the armaments industry. Here, it was rather an issue, in many cases, of men or women who had been employed as either low-level clerks or industrial workers and who now, attracted by the higher salaries and possibilities for advancement of white-collar work, transferred to military typing pools.[126] It was not work in the war industry *per se* that attracted these individuals, but rather that in the offices of war societies and military authorities, where an increased number of office soldiers were to be transferred to the front. Women, in particular, signed up voluntarily for these positions at the female-labor registration centers, which had been established at all auxiliary service registration sites. Office work practically developed into a synonym for auxiliary service in general. In August 1917, the War Office felt obliged to require military authorities "to counter emphatically the widespread opinion that auxiliary service equals office work for the military."[127] By the end of 1917, the military authorities had employed roughly 40,000 individuals obligated for auxiliary service throughout the Reich, a number that probably did not increase substantially during the rest of the war. The number of women employed during this same timeframe reached a good 88,000.[128] Women were particularly interested in those positions in occupied territories behind the front lines, jobs which the military itself wanted to fill with women in order to transfer male personnel from behind the lines to the front. Countless women, and above all younger women, applied to be "rear-echelon helpers" (*Etappenhelferinnen*) in the offices, laundries, etc. of occupied areas. That the women's demand for such positions was often greater than the supply was not due to any activity on the part of the Women's Departments, which were responsible for selecting and advising "rear-echelon helpers." The reason for this onslaught of women lay, among others, in the fact that these jobs, in addition to the relatively good pay and food, offered the possibility of leading an independent lifestyle, something which, in "civilian life," was only open to women of the middle and upper classes.[129] Additionally, employment as a "rear-echelon helper" offered young women the rare opportunity to travel and "to see something new."[130] Men, in comparison, were markedly less interested in jobs behind the lines. Consequently, from October 1917 until the end of the war, more women than men were employed in these areas – shortly before war's end, the number reached 17,000 – thus garnering those women working in Women's Departments one of the few official commendations they received for their efforts.[131] The military's ultimate objective here, i.e. to make the 200,000 military persons in the rear-echelon administration declared "replaceable" thereby available for the front, could not, however, even be approximately attained through the employment of women.

The Auxiliary Service Law was even less successful in terms of rectifying the labor shortage. The number of those conscripted workers "reclaimed" by the war industry, whom the Auxiliary Service Law, above all, was to "free up" for the front, continued to rise throughout the course of the war, as the following table shows.

The problem of the inadequacy of potential labor in light of the simultaneous needs of the army and the war economy was not solved by the Auxiliary Service Law; it was, rather, only shifted back and forth. Every month, as one shipment of labor reinforcements was sent back from the front to the war industry, another shipment of men, "freed up" from the war industry, was sent to the front. In September 1918, for example, 24,175 men transferred from the war industry to the army and 34,769 transferred from the army to the war industry.[132] The Auxiliary Service Law had no significant impact on the mobilization of new labor for the armaments industry. Nor did the law bring about a lasting, direct improvement in the army's supply of replacements through the "freeing up" of military persons. If we extrapolate the – most likely exaggerated – number of "freed-up" military persons throughout the Reich from the corresponding development in Bavaria, for which statistics exist until August 1918, then approximately 155,700 soldiers working in military positions on the home front would have been "freed up" for the military front. The 27,000 soldiers who were relieved of their duties by "rear-echelon helpers" would also need to be added to this number.[133] According to this projection, by the end of the war, the Auxiliary Service Law would thus have provided the army with roughly 183,000 replacement troops; this number, however, was not even two-thirds of the monthly military casualties in the battle of the Somme.

The regulations and execution of the Auxiliary Service Law were equally ineffective in solving the second central problem of wartime labor-market policy, the immense fluctuation in

Table 7. Number of "Reclaimed" Workers in Prussia, 1916–1918

Time	Total	Those fit for active duty
Middle of 1916	1.2 million	0.7 million
Beginning of 1917	1.4 million	0.8 million
Middle of 1917	1.9 million	1.0 million
Beginning of 1918	2.2 million	1.1 million
Middle of 1918	2.4 million	1.2 million

Source: E. von Wrisberg, *Heer und Heimat 1914–1918* (Leipzig, 1921), 90.

the workforce. The frequent changes of employment of skilled workers sent back from the front was not essentially reduced by the introduction of the so-called "Certificate of Employment Change." The Women's Departments, as well as women's employers, were supposed to counter the female workforce's "job restlessness," which was both extensive and extremely detrimental to the continuity of the production process, with an intensified welfare policy.[134] On closer consideration, however, we see that this restlessness was not a characteristic of the female workforce as a whole, but only of women working in unfamiliar locations or branches of industry.[135] After their first apprenticeship, these mostly young and unmarried women followed the best work offers made by companies in the armament industry, which competed for such labor to the industry's detriment. Female workers belonging to the permanent workforce of their companies were clearly less inclined to change their jobs. Thus, random sample surveys conducted by the War Office bureau in Munich from October to December 1918 revealed that 60% of the nearly 9,000 recorded female workers in its district had worked in the same company for longer than a year, and a good 15% longer than two years.[136] The enormously high rate of job change of the other women workers – a weekly turnover of one-third of the female workforce was not exceptional – more than made up for this, however.[137] The fluctuation rate of women employed in the war industry exceeded not only that of men, but also that of female workers before the war (see Table 8).

In December 1917, the shipyard Blohm and Voss reported to the War Office that 2,852 new appointments of female workers had been made between 23 December 1916 and 22 December 1917, with an average of 900 women on staff at any one time. Seeing, however, that 2,898 female workers left the firm during the same period of time, the female staff, despite the large number of hirings, was actually reduced by 46.[138] In spite of all efforts to the contrary – women were rewarded, for example, with prizes for constancy – the rate of fluctuation among female labor increased until the end of the war. The war industry, in turn, increasingly demanded the institution of a "Certificate of Employment Change" for women and adolescents or even their inclusion under the Auxiliary Service Law.[139]

Table 8. Fluctuation of Male and Female Workers, 1913 and 1917: Job-Placement Results of the Employment Exchanges of the Bavarian Association of Metal Industrialists

| | Per 100 Employees, Number of Filled Positions for | | | |
| | Men | | Women | |
	1.1.1913–31.12.1913	1.1.1917–31.8.1917	1.1.1913–31.12.1913	1.1.1917–31.8.1917
Skilled Workers	117.2	116.0	–	–
Unskilled over 21	109.8	120.3	–	–
Unskilled under 21	109.5	124.8	–	–
Total	115.0	120.4	128.9	148.0

Source: HStA/Kr, MKr 14200: Bavarian Association of Metal Industrialists to the Bavarian War Office, 2 October 1917.

The united efforts of the war industry and the Supreme Command were also unsuccessful in achieving either this or other proposed changes in the Auxiliary Service Law against the opposition of the civil government and the War Office, which, in this instance, maintained the same line. The imperial government recoiled from the possible domestic repercussions of a renewed discussion about the Auxiliary Service Law. And the War Office, also under Groener's successor Scheüch, did not want to increase the obligation workers had to their companies, if this did not, in turn, contain a comparable guarantee against employers' potential misuse of power in wage questions. In addition, the War Office still found compulsory labor for women to be superfluous.[140]

Aside from the ban on transferring out of the agricultural sector – which was not enforceable anyway – the Auxiliary Service Law did nothing to change the fact that the wartime female labor market remained a free labor market, in which women "mobilized" themselves according to the law of supply and demand. This meant that women took up jobs that were important for the war effort when – and only when – these were attractive in terms of the work conditions or the remuneration, not because of the intervention of a comprehensive mobilization policy. This pattern of female labor mobilization, typical for the first half of the war, also characterized the flood of women willing to do auxiliary service into the military typing pools on the home front and behind the lines.

The mobilization policy for women in the First World War did not succeed, therefore, in making the use of female labor in the war economy into a politically manageable variable, i.e. into one that could be altered to serve the interests, as defined by politicians and the military, of the war economy. If, when and how the use of female labor in the war industry increased was not due to the efforts of the responsible political and administrative authorities, but rather remained dependent, above all, upon two sets of factors.

The first of these was the general situation of the labor market. Women were predominantly employed in the war economy for those jobs for which and those periods of time during which "reclaimed" skilled workers – or foreigners or prisoners of war – could not be obtained. When such sources of labor were available, or when the general need for labor sank because of bottlenecks in production and transportation – which was sometimes the case in the second half of the war – then female employees were either dismissed or not hired at all.[141]

The second set of factors was the specific life situations of potential female war-industry employees. Women could not be mobilized for the war industry when they had children or other family members for whom they had to provide. These women preferred such jobs as housecleaning or homework, or they supported themselves and their dependants with government assistance for families and the unemployed.

The anonymous structural power of these two sets of factors proved to be more or less resistant to any political strategy that was organized and implemented. This was in part due, however, to problems specific to the political arena itself. In 1914, decision-makers had had no conception of a total war, of one that would drag on for more than four years, and consequently had formulated neither a strategy nor an organization for coping with such a war. Thus afterwards, organizations came into existence whose political and bureaucratic ability to act was determined much more by the extremely complex internal power and administrative structure of the belligerent German Reich than by their own ideas and planning. Within this configuration of the sometimes conflicting, sometimes parallel interests between the military and the civil government, within the military and civil bureaucracies themselves, between the military and business leaders, employers' and workers' organizations, government and

Reichstag, labor-market policy in general and that specifically concerned with women had no executive freedom.

However, an essential evaluation remains to be made. The sets of factors summarized above set the limits for the labor-market policy described here; simultaneously however, they also determined the limits of every other imaginable labor-market policy, i.e. the limits of the influence that governmental authorities could exert under wartime conditions. The labor shortage was and remained a shortage of skilled workers, not one of working hands in general, a fact which thus already set objective limits to the employment of women, who were, as a rule, not qualified. And the majority of those women who were available for mobilization were, and remained, not free-floating labor, but rather anchored to a pre-existent place of work, the family. The more women's work in the family and for survival intensified – a result, particularly since 1916, of the poor food situation and the collapse of the consumer-goods market – and the more the family economy and the money economy developed in opposite directions, the less interest they had in wage labor. Such a reading of the determining factors of wartime labor-market policy transcends the parameters of this particular policy and points to the changed conditions of life and survival the population experienced because of the war. These are the subject of chapter 4.

Patterns of Perception

Another level of the representation and analysis of women's wage labor in the First World War is still missing, however, without which the evaluation of this development during the war and its status after the war would remain superficial. In this book, I have sought to banish the dominant reading of the First World War – i.e. that it entailed an enormous increase in female employment and that countless women thus entered the workforce for the first time – to the realm of legend, and to correct it with the clearly different picture of the development of women's wage labor and the concomitant political efforts to influence it outlined above. Clearly, my reading severely undermines the traditional interpretation of the First World War as a pacesetter of women's "emancipation" or as a modernizing force with regard to women's economic and societal roles, at least on a quantitative level. In so far as emancipation or modernization is understood in this context as an increase in female employment (which, as a rule, is further understood to have implied or explicit consequences for women's societal role in general), then this emancipation or modernization did not occur. Traditional interpretations of the First World War cannot be so readily dismissed, however. Although their reading of emancipation and modernization is by no means compulsory, nor even the most convincing reading, it is the one with which most interpreters content themselves, probably because of its apparent self-evidence. This self-evidence must, from this point on, give way to the "veto power of the sources" (Koselleck), which, unfortunately, renders another not unimportant debate – namely what links there were between industrial work under the devastating conditions of war and "emancipation" – superfluous.[142]

We could, however, formulate a different interpretation by shifting the focus from the quantitative level to qualitative developments. Instead of basing it on the erroneous assumption of an above-average increase in women's employment during the war and the connected complications, we could look for proof of this reading in a change in the social acceptance of such work for women during and because of the war. To operationalize this question, we would need to examine how identifiable social actors – interest groups, governments and bureaucracies – and collective entities – the male workforce and, above all, the women concerned – evaluated women's wage labor in order to detect whether a change, brought on by the war and lasting beyond it, occurred in their attitudes. Such a change in attitude could be considered proven if we could show, through the statements of one or more of the named societal groups, that these did not perceive women's work in the war industry only as a passing phenomenon of the war situation, but that, as a result of women's much-debated contribution to the survival of the home front, these groups conferred a higher value upon women's wage labor as a whole, one that endured beyond the end of the war. The question of whether we can discover such a change in attitude will be explored in the following section. In this section, I will examine another question, which, while similar to the former, serves to illuminate the configuration of attitude changes from another perspective. Up to this point, female wage labor has been described on the structural and quantitative level, where I have analyzed its development in the form of fixed statistical data, and on the political level, where I have examined the possibilities and limits of political influence on its development. I have only mentioned the third level, that of the women in question, however, where the analysis of the other two levels rendered it necessary. The characterization of the four categories of wage-dependent women according to their economic behavior in wartime and the consequent policy pursued by the state, for instance, or the reference to women's specific patterns of behavior, such as their frequent changes of employment, have thus only been considered from the standpoint of the problem these posed for labor-market policy and of the subsequent efforts taken to solve it. They have not been examined, however, from the standpoint of the reasons for this said behavior – something that can only be analyzed from the perspective of the women themselves. This perspective has thus not received treatment in its own right, an omission I shall now correct. Without such a treatment, any description and analysis of female wage labor during the war would literally be left up in the air.

There are two primary reasons for introducing this level as the third under consideration. Firstly, in order to portray and analyze this level, we need thorough knowledge of the surrounding historical context, which greatly influences it. This necessary knowledge cannot, however, be gained on the third level itself. The level of the action, situation and self-definition of wage-working women cannot be examined by artificially narrowing our perspective to include only the perceptions of the women in question. The reconstruction of their patterns of perception has to occur as "authentically" as the sources permit – and that by no means to satisfy a postulate of completeness, but instead because societal groups' constructions of reality are historically crucial factors in and of themselves. They must always, however, be viewed in connection with political, economic and social developments. If this does not occur, then we relinquish the chance to develop relevant criteria for selecting certain aspects of the patterns of perception of the group or class under examination, aspects that cannot be established on the level of these patterns itself, but that require a "meta-level." Then we are confronted with the insolvable task of having to reconstruct a totality. This reconstruction, even if it were possible, would be hermetic and therefore meaningless because the totality's effects on the levels of the economy, politics, etc. would be just as unanalyzable as the latter's effects on the totality.

The second reason for placing the level of wage-working women's patterns of behavior and perception at the conclusion of this section is that a different approach is required for its treatment. In contrast to the other two levels, no clearly identifiable stock of contemporary sources exists. A satisfactory foundation of relevant and meaningful sources can also only be reproduced to a limited extent through the method of "oral history." The meaningfulness of interviews decreases not only because of the increasing distance from the past, but also because of the increasing complexity of the questions asked. By this, I do not mean to say that such interviews are completely meaningless. As Reinhard Sieder's interviews with working-class women about their lives during the First World War show, such sources can prove very informative about everyday behavior.[143] The search for these women's "authentic" patterns of perception via interviews often reveals more about the mental processes of dispersion over time, however, than it does interesting facts.[144] A functional equivalent for this missing, specific set of sources is available, however. If we consult sources normally used for different purposes, we can nevertheless create a body of sources – admittedly heterogeneous – of a "second order," the subject of which, while not directly concerned with the set of questions relevant here, can still yield interesting information for an analysis of these questions.

The following attempt to provide information about how wage-working women themselves perceived their wartime situation is based upon such a methodological approach. I will consult two groups of sources for this, the first of which is that concerned with the quasi "material parameters" of female wage labor during the war, i.e. women's wages, training opportunities and work conditions. Should a recognizable improvement for wage-working women be revealed here, this will be considered proof that at least a partial change in women's attitude towards their occupation (in the form of a greater identification with or a higher value placed on their job within a woman's life cycle, for example) cannot be excluded for the war and post-war periods. Secondly, I will consult sources that give information about how others evaluated wage-working women's wartime activity and how these women themselves esteemed their war work. Should these quasi "mental parameters" of wartime female wage labor reveal a change in attitude on behalf of co-workers, employers, workers' organizations, government bureaucracies and not least women themselves pertaining to female wage labor, this will be considered proof that a change in attitude of women regarding their own work, as well as a higher estimation of this work by society in general, can also not be disqualified for the period after the war. Thus, it should have become obvious that the aforementioned approach simultaneously helps answer the original question of whether the "emancipation" of women in and through the First World War and the modernizing effects of that war on women's situation can be proved by other than quantitative indicators.

It remains to be seen, however, how the analysis of attitudes to female wage labor during the war can be sensibly delimited and thus made manageable. A representative survey of publications by employers, labor organizations, etc. is prohibitive for reasons of methodology and space because it would go beyond the scope of this book. Furthermore, it is highly doubtful whether such a textual analysis would be meaningful, or whether it would simply reinforce the impression – gained from reading contemporary publications – that the description of the women's self-sacrificing work on the home front was merely a topos of the censured press between 1914 and 1918. Not surprisingly, it would be rather dubious to deduce a change in the societal acceptance of female wage labor or in the attitude of working women themselves from such data.

I would thus propose another point of departure for examining the problem of female wage labor, one that offers the guarantee that we can actually analyze attitudes instead of topoi, and that, additionally, also includes the evaluation of such labor for the period after the war. The discussion about the planning and execution of demobilization after the end of the war, which was begun shortly after it became obvious that the war was not an episode whose duration one could calculate in months, offers such a point of access. This discussion was hotly debated until the end of the war by a wide spectrum of society; participants ranged from employers' and labor organizations to women's organizations and socio-political associations to the Reichstag and the government. Against the majority of expectations, the end of the war descended upon the civilian arena like a catastrophe that scorned all planning; consequently, those preparations that had been made proved, in practice, to be obsolete. This discussion and the positions articulated within its scope are also interesting for a completely different reason. They elucidate the stances that various social groups took on the question of what lasting conclusions should be drawn from female wartime wage labor, and they also offer insights into the pertinent opinions of women themselves. It was not only the demobilization of the soldiers, whose repatriation into the Reich and civilian life had to be organized, that generated discussion, but also the demobilization of female workers from the war industry. And if the women in question did not actually themselves participate in the official debate, which spawned concrete preparatory measures, they certainly perceived and reacted to its occurrence and its effects.

I have thus considered first the "material parameters" of female wage labor during the war. With respect to women's work conditions in the war industry, it will suffice to mention what was previously addressed. The watering down of industrial health and safety regulations, which was tantamount to their repeal, led to a relapse into the nineteenth century, in terms both of general social policy and of women's actual work situation.

The development of women's wages as a further indicator for possible structural changes in female wage labor in the First World War is a story in its own right. In short,[145] the nominal wages of female industrial workers rose slightly more than those of their male counterparts; the gap between male and female absolute wages, however, only narrowed insignificantly. As the reports from 335 businesses about the average daily earnings of their male and female workers from 1914 to 1919 show,[146] these were 2.28 marks for women in March 1914 (equivalent to 44% of men's average daily wage) and 5.55 marks in September 1918 (equivalent to 47.7% of men's average daily wage). If we take the sum in March 1914 to be 100, then, in the same period, male wages rose to 240.9, and those of women to 261.0.

This slight improvement in female wages compared to those of men – which can be partially attributed to the fact that women were in greater demand and were increasingly employed in "male industries," where higher wages were the norm – would have already returned to the "normal" gender-specific wage margins by 1919. From the reports of these 335 companies, we can also see how much more marked the increase in nominal wages was in war industries than in peace industries. If we again set March 1914 wages at 100, then the average daily wage for female workers in the metal industry had risen to 326 by September 1918, to 278 in the chemical industry, 267 in the electrical industry and 265 in the machine industry. Whereas women's wages in the industries of leather and rubber (171), woven goods (186), mimeograph (199) and food and luxury goods (202) clearly remained behind.

At first glance, the percentage increase in women's wages during the war seems quite impressive. In reality, however, the increase in their actual average daily earnings was relatively modest. The high rate of increase refers less to a correspondingly high income than to the extremely low average wage women received before the war. Even a slight increase in this wage thus translated into an impressive rate of increase. In September 1918, however, the average daily wage of women in the metal industry, which exhibited the greatest rate of increase, and in the electrical industry, in which female workers achieved the highest average wage in absolute numbers, was still lower than the lowest wage for men, namely that of those working in the textile industry, although one should rather include this branch in the peace industry. Throughout the entire war, paying women inferior wages for homework, for overtime or even for jobs that men had performed before their conscription and where they had demonstrably earned more was taken for granted.[147]

The following table provides information about the change in wages for female homeworkers. In the cottage industry, the fluctuation in weekly wages according to the type of work, season, existing commissions, etc. was especially pronounced. Consequently, instead of using highly aggregated data, it seems prudent to employ a local comparison, organized according to the type of work, of the wages for male and female homeworkers before and during the war.

Here as well, we cannot speak of a radical change in the structure of women's wages. In some of the jobs listed above weekly wages clearly did increase – as in knitting or cigar-making – in others, however, they either changed insignificantly or not at all. This pattern was typical for all homework during the war.[148] After military administrators introduced a minimum wage and began to regulate work conditions better, the work and wage

Table 9. Wages for Male and Female Homeworkers before and during the War

Type of Work	Male Homeworkers		Female Homeworkers	
	Before the War	At War's End	Before the War	At War's End
	Weekly Earnings in Marks			
Pressing and other work on metal objects	–	–	5–15	6–18
Thread-spooling	–	–	3–10	3–10
Knitting (with machine)	10–22	9–40	3–20	4–40
Furniture-building (for sitting)	10–35	5–60	10	5
Chair-caning	–	–	4–10	4–12
Polishing work	20–25	30–45	20–25	30–45
Painting wooden toys	5–12	5–15	5–12	5–15
Cigar-making	9–23	11–45	6–29	8–40
Sewing gloves	3–40	3–40	3–40	2–40
Stitching and trimming shoes, removing nails from shoes	6–20	3–27	3–20	3–30

Source: Jahresberichte der Gewerbeaufsichtbeamten und Bergbehörden für die Jahre 1914–1918. Official publication (Berlin, 1919/1920), 2,3: 290 (Leipzig).

situation improved for those women who did sewing for the army. This, however, was an exception. The wartime cottage industry, which attracted numerous women who, for familial or other reasons, did not want to work in factories, was and remained one of starvation wages.

One essential point remains to be made regarding the development of wages during the war. In juxtaposition to the nominal increase in wages for both women and men in both the war and peace industries that has been described, there existed a clear decrease in real wages (see Table 10).

If we set March 1914 as 100, then men's average yearly real income had sunk to 63.4 by March 1918, and only slightly increased by September of that year to 65.7. The differentiation between war and peace industries reveals a lower loss of real income in the former (September 1918 = 77.4) as in the latter

Table 10. The Average Yearly Real Income of Workers in 370 Enterprises, 1914–1918 (March 1914= 100)

Date	War Industries		Joint Industries		Peace Industries		Total Average	
	Male	Female	Male	Female	Male	Female	Male	Female
March 1914	100	100	100	100	100	100	100	100
September 1914	90.8	76.4	92.3	86.3	83.5	79.2	88.9	80.6
March 1915	91.8	90.8	83.4	83.6	82.6	78.0	85.9	84.1
September 1915	89.8	95.3	81.6	77.7	77.5	71.9	83.0	81.6
March 1916	88.9	101.5	79.9	77.6	73.5	72.4	80.8	83.8
September 1916	78.4	92.0	68.3	67.1	57.9	59.3	68.2	72.8
March 1917	76.2	83.5	62.3	65.9	54.3	53.2	64.3	67.5
September 1917	78.8	86.7	62.8	64.8	52.7	57.8	64.8	69.8
March 1918	77.8	86.0	60.4	64.0	52.2	58.9	63.4	69.6
September 1918	77.4	87.9	64.2	71.1	55.5	61.9	65.7	73.6

Source: Kocka, J. *Klassengesellschaft im Krieg. Deutsche Sozialgeschichte 1914–1918*, 2nd expanded ed. (Göttingen, 1978), 18.

(September 1918 = 55.5), which is not surprising in light of the greater increase in nominal wages in war industries. The real average yearly income for female workers had decreased to 69.6 by March 1918, increasing once again to 73.6 by September 1918. The difference in loss of real income women experienced in war industries as opposed to that in peace industries is even more pronounced as that for men; by September 1918, women's incomes in war industries had sunk to 87.9, in peace industries to 61.9. As clearly emerges here, female workers suffered a relatively slight loss of real income in comparison to their male counterparts, a fact which refers to the most important reason for the minor qualification in the difference between men's and women's wages mentioned above. To the extent to which the general wage level approached that of subsistence, pre-war wage differences evened out, because the only point at which lower wages – i.e. women's wages in particular – stabilized was at the subsistence level: "Contrary to the impression that the reduction of wage differences was due to a real increase in female wages, one should note that an alignment occurred through the reduction in the wages of both groups to subsistence level."[149] The fall in real income, which was a consequence of the constant price increases between 1914 and 1918, was actually more extreme than can be reproduced by statistics. Its true scope can only be measured if the collapse of the money economy, which resulted in the prohibitive expense and extreme scarcity of consumer goods and food in the second half of the war, is also taken into account.

The third and last "material parameter" of female wage labor, namely that of a possible improvement in the vocational training and qualification of women workers, remains to be examined. In 1919, *Arbeitsnachweis in Westfalen* wrote that "During the war, skills training for women, which had gradually been advancing, fell into decline in every area,"[150] and I would concur with its assessment that the war exerted much more of a retarding influence here than a modernizing one. Despite the oft-repeated reminder of the War Office to train female apprentices properly,[151] and the corresponding efforts of associations that trained women as craftsmen or skilled industrial workers and of the Association of German Engineers (*Verein Deutscher Ingenieure*), the female apprentice, as all apprentices during the war,[152] was in poor shape. The normal vocational training female workers received during the war, which consisted of a short period of instruction and thereby a superficial teaching of skills, offers a picture of semi-qualification rather than of qualification.[153] The reason for this deterioration in the female qualifications scale despite the urgent shortage of skilled workers was that the War Office found no support for its efforts to push the issue of training female skilled workers. In the majority of cases, employers preferred to "reclaim" their conscripted workers from the front and, even though the possibility existed that women could continue to receive municipal aid during their apprenticeship – thus relieving employers of the need to pay them wages – the latter could not be moved to train women for jobs formerly performed by men.[154] As for the trade unions, they feared the potential competition of women and pressure on wages.[155]

As these attitudes were also typical of female apprentices' male coworkers, the training process, when it occurred at all, often proved to be of little value. As the War Office bureau in Nuremberg reported, the training of women in mechanical engineering by male skilled workers led to:

> differences, seeing that the women did not put their full attention to the matter, whereas the men showed no inclination to satisfactorily introduce the female workers to the details of their job . . .[156]
>
> As trainers, men frequently make no effort to teach female replacement labor, whose competition they fear in the coming time of peace, about the different processes of the machine and the tricks to use when operating it. While, on the other hand, the woman in training often has little trust in the man's instruction, since she knows his particular prejudices.[157]

Male workers' resistance to training female workers was only less when the apprentice in question was either the wife or the daughter of a conscripted worker.[158] In such cases, the familial ties guaranteed that the position would be returned to the conscripted worker once the war was over; consequently, his coworkers had no competition to fear.

The stance of male coworkers was not the only reason that women often prefered to change companies than to submit themselves to an apprenticeship program, an attitude of "passive resistance" that, as Marie-Elisabeth Lüders noted, always required "persuasion and not seldom a gentle pressure . . . to overcome."[159] In addition, the permanence of the discussion about demobilization undercut women's interest in vocational training. The

general view that their war activity, so long as it involved positions
that had formerly been held by men, was absolutely temporary
was made perfectly clear to female workers, and consequently
persuaded many of them to refuse to be trained for such jobs.[160]
For the same reason, many companies had little interest in any
longer-term vocational training for female labor.

The latter point leads to the next under discussion, that of
the "mental parameters" of female wage labor as they manifested
themselves in the discussion about demobilization. This debate
about the repatriation of soldiers and the regulation of the labor
market – which is to be understood as the reversal of all alter-
ations to this market that resulted from the war-necessitated
influx of women into jobs previously performed by men – after
the war had already begun in 1915 and was characterized by
the overwhelming homogeneity of opinion. All of the governmental authorities and interest groups, i.e. military and civil
bureaucracies, employers and labor organizations as well as the
women's movement, who participated in this discussion were,
independent of differences in *modus operandi*, united in their
efforts to re-establish the former status quo of female labor.
This meant that, by the end of the war, women were to have
vacated "men's jobs" so that they were free for the returning
combatants.[161] This was already the consensus of the meeting
that took place between the Imperial Office of the Interior,
several Prussian and other ministries, the General Staff, the
Imperial Naval Office (*Reichsmarineamt*), the German Congress
of Municipal Authorities (*Deutscher Städtetag*), welfare agency
associations, employers' associations and trade unions on 30
April 1915 at the Reichstag,[162] which was then reconfirmed in
the 1916 and 1917 negotiations of the Reichstag Committee for
Trade and Industry (*Reichstagsausschuß für Handel und
Gewerbe*). In October 1916, State Secretary of the Interior Helfferich inaugurated the work of this committee with the following
dictum about the "numerous women today who are employed
in occupations where men were previously employed and who
– of this we need to be aware – in the long term, are not suitable
for these occupations." Said Helfferich:

> The issue here is . . . not to free up jobs for the returning men, but
> also to recreate a balance in the division of labor for men and women,
> for adults and adolescents, which is beneficial for the people's health.
> I repeat that this will not occur without severity; women, who have

gotten used to the high wages and independent work, will not easily and voluntarily find their way back into the old circumstances.[163]

The representative of the Imperial Office of the Interior who addressed the same committee in March 1917 had a different problem with female labor in the war industry:

It cannot be denied that there is something disturbing about this entire development [of female labor in the war]. When one looks at women these days, how they are working in all of these difficult positions, the women in armaments factories, on the coachbox, cleaning the streets, one has to look closely in order to tell whether one is looking at a woman or a man. Through the employment of women in male occupations, the entire female organism and the entire female sensibility is being pushed down other paths, and that ultimately expresses itself on the outside. We must, with all serious-ness, take care to reverse this development. It will not always be easy. Women have found a very rewarding occupation in the various companies; they have, incidentally, often taken a great liking to this, and there will consequently be difficulties in removing them from these occupations. And yet this must be strived for in the interest of our common good, [and] simultaneously in the interest of the male worker as well. We must therefore proceed, on the one hand, with all advisable caution, but on the other, also with all the necessary energy.[164]

Further examples of such assessments of women's war-necessitated work can be cited at will. Not all, however, conveyed such a strong image as this, which is more reminiscent of the difficulties a pest controller has in ridding a house of vermin, than of the eulogies about women's self-sacrificing service for the Fatherland that were so frequently held.

Participants in the demobilization discussion also agreed on the means to be used to remove women from male positions, which consisted of reintroducing worker-protection laws, planned immediately for the end of the war, in such a strict form that women would be "protected" out of these jobs. If, contrary to expectations, this measure proved unsatisfactory, then it was recognized one would have "to intervene with force."[165]

As the end of the war approached, it became clear that demo-bilization would by no means proceed in its planned form, but, it was feared, would lead to social collapse, the potential dynamite of which, i.e. the soldiers returning from the front and the male and female workers fired from the war industry, would meet in the streets of the Empire's population centers. Consequently, further measures were taken. In the last weeks of the war, the introduction of general unemployment support, to be implemented by the municipalities, was prepared. Additionally, employers were to be required to continue to pay workers if necessary, even if there was no job for them,[166] and the Reich committed itself to the maintenance of army commissions.[167]

Independent of these plans, employers and trade unions resorted in many cases to preventative self-help. Within a single business, region or branch of industry, these two groups concluded agreements whereby returning soldiers would be guaranteed a right to their former job over the replacement labor that had been employed in the meantime.[168] Unlike in Great Britain, where the "dilution," i.e. the "stretching" of labor potential through the increased use of unskilled and female labor, was the subject of heated debate between employers and labor organizations, in Germany the assessment of women's work during the war was much more a factor that fostered unity between these two groups. It was the employers, and not the trade unions, as in Great Britain, that were identified by governmental labor authorities as the main source of resistance to extending female employment during the war.[169] Labor organizations, which feared women as competitors and as "gravediggers," i.e. as the cause of the "freeing up" of workers for the front,[170] backed up the employers' stance. Furthermore, in spite of the increasing number of organized women, in particular in the Free Trade Unions, which had social-democratic sympathies,[171] the wartime trade unions continued to act primarily as representatives of the interests of their male members. They tolerated the temporary employment of women in "men's jobs" because of their stance toward the war and its requirements, not because of any correspondingly positive stance toward female labor in general. As Gertrud Hanna, the chairwoman of the Trade Unions' Women's Office (*Frauensekretariat der Gewerkschaften*) argued in a *Vorwärts* article in February 1918, in the end, women had not taken up their wartime positions willingly, but rather had been forced to do so because of the breadwinner's absence.[172] The War Office ascertained "that the skilled workers' organizations think it important to remove unskilled workers, where possible, from companies."[173] If the trade unions raised demands such as equal pay for equal work, this occurred primarily in the interests of its male members, to protect them from unfair competition that drove down wages. For, as the commanding general of the 7th Army Corps Münster reported, it was ultimately "to be feared, that, after the war, the stronger women will remain in these positions and men will be forced out by cheaper wages."[174] As an article in *Metallarbeiterzeitung* explained with refined casuistry, the demand for equal pay for women, including the rate for piecework, was only to be welcomed if it were certain that women could produce the same output in the same amount of time. Otherwise, this demand would put women at a disadvantage, because no employer would hire them for the same wage without the same output, but would rather hire men from the outset. As the newspaper wrote, "There is no legitimate right for the preference of men over women. On the contrary, women also have the right to equality in this area."[175]

The women in question here were themselves cognizant of the general societal consensus concerning their war-necessitated labor. The public debate conducted about this issue gave them every opportunity to become aware of the general valuation of their activity. Additionally, society's assessment of female labor often found its way into the conditions of employment for female workers, so that those women who were hired could not fail to grasp its practical relevance. Upon their hiring, many women had to sign a declaration, consenting to their automatic dismissal at the end of war.[176] Other women were hired expressly under the stipulation that they would possibly be dismissed on short notice in order to make room for returning war-wounded.[177] For wives working for the companies of their conscripted husbands, the transfer of their position at the end of the war back to their husbands was already predetermined as a family matter. Women not only recognized the explicit provisionality of their wartime jobs, they also reacted to it. Just as the permanence of the demobilization debate strengthened employers' negative stance toward expanding female employment,[178] it reinforced women's avoidance of work in the war industry in general, and their oft-lamented low work motivation in particular. The inadequate commitment these working women had to their jobs found its most manifest expression in their frequent changes of employment, which was only logical in light of the constantly stressed provisionality of their activity.[179] Instead of orienting themselves to a value scale of work and advancement, which, under these conditions, would have been fairly irrational, these working women preferred to view their situation in correspondingly "rational" terms[180] and thus moved other criteria to the forefront. These criteria were, on the one hand, of a material nature. Women left positions in which they had just concluded a several-week training process in order to do those, just opened, which offered them the possibility of improving their work conditions and wages.[181]

On the other hand, these criteria were just as frequently of an emotional nature. Friendships among working women often proved to be the decisive factor why a woman chose to stay in a job or to indulge in the "infectious *Wanderlust*"[182] that so irritated labor-market policy makers. Frequently, women did not want to change positions when they were supposed to. As the Dräger-Werks in Lübeck reported:

> It turned out that women, when they work under the same conditions, develop a strong communal spirit . . .; the transfer of one woman from one workroom to another proved to be practically unfeasible, because, with her separation from the accustomed work group, the woman was put under such strong psychological pressure, that her ability to work and general condition were reduced.[183]

Or – and this was the main problem – women changed jobs when they were not supposed to, usually "without an clear reason and unconcerned that they thereby put the employer into a very awkward position."[184] The Headquarters for Women's Labor took the view that

> the reason for women's and girls' changes of employment, which is currently occurring with particular frequency in some districts, does not only lie in the lack of suitable welfare measures. It is often said that women and girls, . . . even independent of the better wages and working conditions that might be offered elsewhere, only change their job out of a desire "to change themselves."[185]

One Women's Department, which conducted an investigation into this issue, reported the following results.

> One fact, observed almost equally in all industries, is certain . . .. Younger female workers in particular are completely without any sense of professionalism and have no idea and consequently no pangs of conscience about the disturbances that they themselves cause in a company through their own fickleness. In general, they regard their work purely from a personal standpoint, are unusually prone to being persuaded by female work comrades to change [their job],

and normally move not as individuals but in small groups from one factory to another. Within a single company, such personal motives for the acceptance or refusal of this or that job play the main role.

[In some of the listed factories], for example, unpleasant jobs that can, however, be performed in a group and where coworkers can talk with one another are preferred to more pleasant and higher-paid jobs where one has to work alone.[186]

When given the choice of fulfilling either their personal emotional and material interests or the requirements of the war economy – a conduct alternative that included both was something that seldom existed for working-class women, as opposed to their middle-class counterparts – the majority of female workers acted according to their own interests. This was at the heart of their reputed lack of professionalism. The opposite conclusion therefore suggests itself. If possibilities of economic behavior had existed for working-class women in which their personal and economic benefit were united, then perhaps their individual behavior would not have proved to be such a disruptive factor for the entire economy. As was taken for granted in the planning of demobilization – and not without reason – these women would have been very interested in permanently retaining the better work opportunities that the war industry had opened up to them. The results of a questionnaire survey, conducted by the Leipzig War Office bureau in two Chemnitz firms in May 1918, unambiguously confirm this conclusion.[187]

Question	Engineering Works Sch. & S. 624 Interviewees	Textile Factory B. & L. 340 Interviewees
Would you like to continue working?	Yes: 78.7%, 83% of which in the same occupation No: 0.3% Undecided: 21%	Yes: 88%, 24.5% of which in the same occupation No: 1% Undecided: 11%
Were you employed before the war?	Yes: 90%, 15% of which in the same industry	Yes: 89%, 79% of which in the same industry
Marital Status	Married: 10% With Children: 16% Husband Drafted: 73%	Married: 10% With Children: 33.3% Husband Drafted: 62%

Of the women interviewed in the textile factory who wanted to continue doing industrial labor, only about one-fourth wanted this to be in the same occupation. Over 80% of the remaining three-fourths could not state a concrete alternative to their current occupation, however. Of the women in the engineering works who answered "yes" to this question, over three-fourths would have remained in the same occupation.

Thus, these women's preferences were exactly contrary to the traditional distribution of female labor in industry, as the answers to the second question also reflect. Of those women interviewed who were already employed before the war – which here, as in other cases, was the decisive majority – almost 80% of the textile workers had been working in the same field. Only 15% of the employees in the engineering works had been active in that industry before the war; of the other 85%, 10% came from the textile industry. The others had moved to the company during the war and clearly found their work there to be more attractive than what they had previously done. The ambitions female workers maintained for the future, however, were destined to founder on the powerful societal consensus to treat the wartime shift to female labor as a transitory phenomenon. And this, in turn, ensured the failure of women's effective mobilization for the war industry. The societal estimation that women were second-class wage laborers, who would only be allowed to advance to better positions when, literally, there was a shortage of men, proved, next to women's familial obligations, to be the greatest structural obstacle to procuring labor. Both obstacles could have been eliminated if an entirely new valuation of women's family and wage labor, and thereby of their role in society, had been advanced. Under the social, economic and political conditions of war, however, there were no efforts of note in this direction.

Notes to Chapter 3

1. F. Blei, *Erzählung eines Lebens* (Leipzig, 1930), 20.
2. M.-E. Lüders, "Die volkswirtschaftliche Bedeutung der qualifizierten Frauenarbeit für die gewerblichen Berufe," in *Frauenberufsfrage und Bevölkerungspolitik. Jahrbuch des BDF 1917* (Berlin and Leipzig, 1917), 7–8.

Women's Wage Labor in the First World War

3. S. Bajohr, *Die Hälfte der Fabrik. Geschichte der Frauenarbeit in Deutschland 1914 bis 1945* (Marburg/L., 1979), 101. See above, as well, in particular endnote 12 of the introduction.

4. The results of the 1916 occupational census for Bavaria, which were published after the war, will be discussed below.

5. W. Zimmermann, "Die Veränderungen der Einkommens- und Lebensverhältnisse der deutschen Arbeiter durch den Krieg," in R. Meerwarth et al., *Die Einwirkung des Krieges auf Bevölkerungsbewegung, Einkommen und Lebenshaltung in Deutschland* (Stuttgart et al., 1932), 350–351. See as well, J. Kocka, *Klassengesellschaft im Krieg. Deutsche Sozialgeschichte 1914–1918*, 2nd expanded ed. (Göttingen, 1978), 12.

6. In this book, I follow Gerhard Bry's classification of industries. The metal, mechanical engineering, electric and chemical industries belong to the war industry. Those of food, luxury items, confections, textiles and printing belong to the peace industry. Those industries involved in the processing of wood, paper, leather and stone, as well as those of building and construction and mining, count as "in-between" industries. G. Bry, *Wages in Germany, 1871–1945* (Princeton, 1960), 193–194.

7. See "Der Anteil der Frau an der Sozialversicherung," *Archiv für Frauenarbeit* 5 (1917), 143ff; A. Lauter, "Die deutsche Sozialversicherung vom Kriegsausbruch bis zum Frieden von Versailles," diss. (München, 1920/21), 52; "Die zahlenmäßige Gestaltung der Frauenarbeit während des Krieges," *RABl* 14 (1916), 986, 989.

8. Apart from the differences from the pre-war condition mentioned in the text, the bases for investigation by the health-insurance companies did not change during the war. Lauter, "Sozialversicherung," *passim*. On the basis of the available material, it is impossible to decide whether, and if so, to what extent, the increased fluctuation in the wartime labor force might have led to an underregistration of female wage laborers. The authorities responsible for labor allocation did not believe that this was the case. *Reichsarbeitsblatt* (1914–1918), *passim*. The general reliability of health-insurance company reports as indicators for the development of female employment can be deduced from correlating the increase in female labor, as shown in the three pre-war occupational censuses, with the corresponding numbers of female employees with health insurance:

	Employed Women*	Insured Women**
1882	7,794,000	983,033***
1895	8,219,000	1,690,326
1907	9,742,000	3,166,756

* *Source*: W. Müller et al., *Strukturwandel der Frauenarbeit 1880–1980* (Frankfurt and New York, 1983), 35.
** *Source*: *Statistik des Deutschen Reiches*, new series, vol. 289 (Berlin, 1921), 55*.
*** This number is for 1888; the corresponding data for 1892 is not available.

The calculation for these sequences of numbers results in a correlation coefficient of 0.99. Although a correlation coefficient of only three cases should not be overemphasized, it nevertheless points to a very close relation between the developmental trends of both sequences of numbers.

9. *Arbeitsnachweis in Deutschland* 7 (1919/20), 310.

10. Memorandum from the Trade and Industry Department of the General-Governor in Belgium: W. Asmis, ed., "Nutzbarmachung belgischer Arbeitskräfte für die deutsche Volkswirtschaft nach dem Kriege": ZStA Merseburg, Rep. 120 CVIII 1, Nr. 106, Bd. 14, Bl. 234ff.

11. Compare, for example, Bajohr, *Hälfte*, 102-129.

12. *RABl* 14 (1916), 736. "Der Anteil der Frau an der Sozialversicherung," *Archiv für Frauenarbeit* 5 (1917), 148.

13. Since the inclusion of service personnel and workers in the agrarian sector in compulsory insurance on 1 January 1914 dramatically increased membership numbers, this development has been excluded from the calculation of increase rates.

14. *Jahresberichte der Gewerbeaufsicht und Bergbehörden für die Jahre 1914/1918.* Amtliche Ausgabe, Statistisches Reichsamt, ed. (Berlin, 1920), Saxony, 2: 242.

15. The editors of the wartime census interpret the clearly visible decline of female labor in Bavaria between 1907 and 1916 by the fact that only the latter census was conducted in winter. Female laborers in the agrarian sector, primarily employed in summertime, would have been included as laborers in the 1907 census, whereas in 1916, they would have been counted among the non-working population, exclusively occupied with housework. *Die Kriegsvolkszählungen vom Jahre 1916 and 1917 in Bayern.* Beiträge zur Statistik Bayerns 89. Bayerisches Statistisches Landesamt, ed. (München, 1919), 128-134. The argument they use to buttress their case - that the number of female employees actually increased noticeably between 1907 and 1916 - is, however, not convincing. The stratification of the entire population into professions uses only two other categories on the level of "employed" (including work in the home), those of "dependants" and "jobless self-employed." Consequently, the women who had vanished - for whatever reason - from the category "employed" could only have reappeared as pensioners, asylum inhabitants, etc. in the category of the "jobless self-employed."

The editors of the wartime censuses in Bavaria, however, in rejecting the supposed decline of female labor in Bavaria between 1907 and 1916 as a statistical illusion, estimate a constant quota of female labor at most during this period. Ibid.

16. *Die Frauenarbeit in der Metallindustrie während des Krieges, dargestellt nach Erhebungen im August/September 1916 vom Vorstand des Deutschen Metallarbeiterverbandes* (Stuttgart, 1917), 12.

17. Calculated according to: Arbeitskräfteerhebung, Stand 15 February 1917: HStA/Kr, MKr 14198. In 1913, 5,557 women were employed in enterprises organized in the Association of Bavarian Metal Industries; by 1918, the number had almost quadrupled to 19,415. B. Adam, *Arbeitsbeziehungen in der bayerischen Großstadtmetallindustrie von 1914 bis 1932* (München, 1983), 153. Regarding female wage labor in Bavaria before 1914 compare E. Plössl, *Weibliche Arbeit in Familie und Betrieb: Bayerische Arbeiterfrauen 1870-1914* (München, 1983), 142-271.

18. *RABl* 16 (1918), 660.

19. The migration of women from the textile industry is also reflected in the

Women's Wage Labor in the First World War

decrease of female membership in the textile workers' association. Whereas 54,846 women were organized in the association in 1913 (the numbers always reflect the annual average membership), their numbers decreased continuously until 1916, when they amounted to only 35,889. In 1917–1918, many women obviously returned since their numbers first rose to 45,971 and then to 67,797 in 1918. Deutscher Textilarbeiterverband, *Jahrbuch 1918* (Berlin, 1919), 68–69.

20. *Die Frau in der bayerischen Kriegsindustrie nach einer amtlichen Erhebung aus dem Jahre 1917*, Beiträge zur Statistik Bayerns 92, Bayerisches Statistisches Landesamt, ed. (München, 1920), 12; rpt. in Ute Daniel, "Fiktionen, Friktionen und Fakten - Frauenlohnarbeit im Ersten Weltkrieg," in G. Mai, ed., *Arbeiterschaft 1914–1918 in Deutschland. Studien zu Arbeitskampf und Arbeitsmarkt im Ersten Weltkrieg* (Düsseldorf, 1985), 286–287. In some cities, the share of former servants among female wage labor in the war industries was even higher; in Munich and its surroundings, for example, it amounted to 28.7%, in Schweinfurt to 29.2% and in Ingolstadt to 43.1%. *Die Frau in der bayerischen Kriegsindustrie*, 18. The migration of former female servants into the war industries continued throughout the war, ibid., 68–69.

Out of all female employees in Bavaria recorded in the occupational census of 1 December 1916, the following had not been employed previously:

	1 Female Employees on 1.12.1916	2 Number of Female Employees not yet in this Profession or Position on 31.7.1914		3 Number of New Employees not Previously Employed	
		Absolute	% of Column 1	Absolute	% of Column 1
Total	1,458,289	158,039	10.8	101,041	6.9
Of these, the highest relative and absolute increases were in:					
Chemical Industry	31,596	17,436	55.2	7,143	22.6
Mining	1,436	495	34.5	241	16.8
Traffic Industries	9,315	2,357	25.3	1,806	19.4

Source: Kriegsvolkszählungen, 195–202, 208. The percentages are my own calculations.

Thus, in December 1916, only 7% of all female employees in Bavaria were "real" newcomers to the labor market, and many of those were probably adolescents now reaching the age where they could start work.

21. According to a later statistic, whose bases and instances of investigation were not identical to those of the 1917 inquiry about women in the Bavarian war industry, thus rendering a comparison between absolute numbers impossible, the Bavarian war industry employed, on the following dates the following numbers of female wage-laborers:

109

1.12.1917	107,909	15.4.1918	101,105
15.12.1917	100,135	1.5.1918	108,166
1.1.1918	119,823	15.5.1918	97,025
15.1.1918	111,575	15.6.1918	109,193
1.2.1918	118,158	1.7.1918	111,219
15.2.1918	102,875	15.7.1918	105,686
1.3.1918	113,457	August 1918	122,246
15.3.1918	105,747	September 1918	118,050
1.4.1918	109,203	October 1918	110,203

(*Source*: "Bestand/Bedarf an Arbeitskräften im Königreich Bayern 1918:"
HStA/Kr MKr 14391, Anlagen 11e and 12f zu 38732 K/F.)

My own calculations resulted in the finding that, between 1 December 1917 and October 1918, the number of women employed in the Bavarian war industries rose by 2.1%.

The number of "war wives" recorded in the 1917 investigation about women in the Bavarian war industry was 18,469, or 20.3% of all the women included. The number of married women was 26,239, or 28.9% of the total. 61,279 women (67.4%) stated that they had no children under 19 years of age. *Die Frau in der bayerischen Kriegsindustrie*, 12, rpt. in Daniel, "Fiktionen," 286-287. The percentage of single and childless women increased up until the end of the war. (In 1917, this figure was 65.2%; ibid.) Kriegsamtstelle München to Ministerium für militärische Angelegenheiten, 23 January 1919: HStA/Kr, MKr 14391, 3.

22. *Arbeitsnachweis in Deutschland* 3 (1915/16), 98.

23. *Jahresberichte der Gewerbeaufsicht 1914–1918*, 1: 280.

24. *Arbeitsverhältnisse und Organisation der häuslichen Dienstboten in Bayern*. Beiträge zur Statistik Bayerns 94, Bayerisches Statistisches Landesamt, ed. (München, 1921), 14. Regarding servants during the war, consult also Th. Justus, "Die weiblichen Hausangestellten in Frankfurt/Main. Ergebnisse einer privaten Erhebung vom Jahre 1920. Diss. (n.p., n.d. [1924]), 118ff., and R. Berger, *Die häuslichen Dienstboten nach dem Kriege* (M.-Gladbach, n.d.).

25. Memorandum of conversation, led by General Groener, re. the establishment of War Industry Offices, 18 January 1917, 17ff.: BA/MA RM31/1003.

26. Notes from the Bavarian War Ministry, 7 June 1918: Testimony of an official of the Munich Employment Office, 25 January 1918: HStA/Kr, MKr 14203.

27. Kgl. Staatsministerium des Inneren to the Distriktpolizeibehörden, 27 February 1918: HStA/Kr, MKr 14201.

28.This also becomes very clear from the reports of the Bavarian Factory Inspectorate about the level of female labor in the middle of 1915: HStA München, MH 15956, *passim*.

29. Here, see M. Hoffmann's detailed report about the employment, life situations and Family Aid of Berlin "war wives." M. Hoffmann, "Das Gesetz betreffend die Unterstützung von Familien in den Dienst eingetretener Mannschaften vom 28.2.1888/4.8.1914 und seine Anwendung," diss. (Berlin, 1918), 122-342.

30. Kriegsamtsstelle München to Bayerisches Ministerium für militärische Angelegenheiten, 23 January 1919: Report about the sample survey "Frauen in der Kriegswirtschaft" from November and December 1918: HStA/Kr, MKr 14391.

31. *Vorwärts*, 1 August 1915 and 21 October 1916.

32. Scheidemann to Reichsamt des Innern, 25 June 1915: ZStA Potsdam, Reichsministerium des Innern 12092, B. 121; Staatssekretär des Innern to Scheidemann, 9 August 1915: ibid., Bl. 332; Preußischer Innenminister to Reichskanzler, 25 August 1916: ZStA Potsdam, Reichsministerium des Innern 12097, Bl. 284.

33. See, for example, the Imperial Naval Office's reaction to the 18 November 1916 survey conducted by the Prussian War Ministry, re. "war wives" who refused to work: BA/MA, RM31/1003, as well as the survey the Munich Deputy General Command conducted the end of 1916 about the same subject: HStA/ Kr, Stellv. Gen.kdo. I. Bayerisches AK München 980. The Munich survey revealed that a good half of the 42 district authorities that filed reports did not have any complaints of such a nature. For the other districts, when cases of this problem surfaced, the authorities either threatened "war wives" with cutting their Family Aid, or had indeed already cut it.

34. Reichskanzler/Reichsamt des Innern, 6 March 1917: HStA/Kr, Stellv. Gen.kdo. I. Bayerisches AK München 882; rpt. in: *Norddeutsche Allgemeine Zeitung*, 8 March 1917.

35. Kriegsamt to Reichskanzler, 31 January 1917: GLA Karlsruhe, 456 EV 8/ 111 Kriegsamtsstelle Karlsruhe, Bl. 17.

36. They constituted, for example, an ever-surfacing component of the feared "letters of lament" that women sent to the front. See Monatsberichte, 3 August 1917, 8: BA/MA, RM3/4670, as well as the comments of the Prussian Minister of the Interior in *Ministerialblatt für die Preußische Innere Verwaltung* 79.5 (31.5.1918).

37. Gewerbeinspektion Mönchengladbach to Regierungspräsident Düsseldorf, 2 December 1914: HStA Düsseldorf, Regierung Düsseldorf 15058. Similar cases are described in Hoffmann, "Gesetz," 324, 338-339.

38. Reichskanzler/Reichsamt des Innern, 6 March 1917: HStA/Kr, Stellv. Gen.kdo. I. Bayerisches AK München 882; Reichskanzler/Reichsamt des Innern, 14.8.1917: ibid.

39. Ibid., as well as Kriegsersatz- und Arbeitsdepartement to Bundesregierungen, 13 July 1918: HStA/Kr, Stellv. Gen.kdo. I. Bayerisches AK München 882; O. Most, "Kriegsfürsorge," in J. Brixen et al., eds., *Handwörterbuch der Kommunalwissenschaften* (Jena, 1924), 3: 175; P. Hirsch, "Die Kriegsfürsorge der deutschen Gemeinden," *Annalen für soziale Politik und Gesetzgebung* 4 (1916), 269.

40. Monatsberichte, 3 September 1917, 21: BA/MA, RM3/4670.

41. Report from Agnes von Harnack about her trip to Warsaw from 25 March to 5 April 1918 at the behest of the War Press Office: BA, NL 151/165.

42. M.-E. Lüders, *Die Entwicklung der gewerblichen Frauenarbeit im Kriege* (München and Leipzig, 1920), 23.

43. For this, see Hoffmann, "Gesetz," 208-209; M.-E. Lüders, *Das unbekannte Heer. Frauen kämpfen für Deutschland 1914-1918* (Berlin, 1937), 86; M. Sogemeier, *Die Entwicklung und Regelung des Arbeitsmarktes im rheinisch-westfälischen Industriegebiet im Kriege und in der Nachkriegszeit* (Jena, 1922), 22, 30; *Archiv für Frauenarbeit* 4 (1916), 17; *Archiv für Frauenarbeit* 7 (1919), 33ff.; *Archiv für Frauenarbeit* 10 (1922), 73; Middle of 1915 report from the Bavarian Factory Inspectorate on the development of female labor: HStA München, MH 15956, *passim*.

The War from Within

44. Lüders, *Heer*, 205-206.

45. H. Fürth, *Die deutsche Frau im Kriege* (Tübingen, 1917), 13-14. Many wives of consripted railway white-collar employees and railway laborers also worked in their husbands' positions. Sogemeier, *Entwicklung*, 17.

46. From the large amount of relevant evidence, see: G. Hanna, *Die Arbeiterinnen und der Krieg* (Berlin, 1916), 11ff.; H. Horst, "Maßnahmen zur Behebung der durch den Krieg entstandenen Arbeitslosigkeit in Krefeld," *Arbeitsnachweis in Deutschland* 2 (1914/15), 205ff.; L. Schraut, "Verteilung der Heimat im Ghzgt. Hessen durch die öffentlichen Arbeitsnachweise," *Arbeitsnachweis in Deutschland* 3 (1915/16), 261; K. Blaum, "Heimarbeit und Arbeitsmarkt," *Arbeitsnachweis in Deutschland* 4 (1916/17), 67; Report about a meeting in the War Ministry, re. the possibility of further expanding homework for war deliveries, 11 December 1915, 1: StA Münster, Oberpräsidium 4123, Bl. 344.

47. The reports of the Factory Inspectorate give a very vivid picture of wartime homework. They clearly show the different development homework took in different regions. In some rural areas, homework declined between 1914 and 1918, because women, after the conscription of their husbands, had to perform the agricultural work alone or because the raw materials for certain traditional branches of homework were now lacking. A portion of the male and female homeworkers in these areas moved, where possible, into the war industry. In other areas, homework experienced an economic boom as a result of military commissions. In spite of the decline in traditional homework in certain regions, homework as a whole increased during the war, primarily because of these commissions. The statistics that companies commissioning homework provided about the number of male and female homeworkers they employed understate the actual number of individuals working in this field, since company reporting was very incomplete during the war. *Jahresberichte der Gewerbeaufsicht 1914–1918*, 3: 18, and 1-4: *passim*.

48. *Jahresberichte der Gewerbeaufsicht 1914–1918*, 3: 18.

49. Ibid., 1: 871, 873. Of the total number of female homeworkers in September 1918 approximately 5,000 were sewing for the army. The rest were doing textile piecework for companies that also served the needs of the army.

50. Schrauth, "Verteilung von Heimarbeit," 261-265; E. Schindler, "Bekämpfung der Arbeitslosigkeit des weiblichen Geschlechts in Schlesien durch Vermittlung von Heeresnäharbeiten," *Arbeitsnachweis in Deutschland* 4 (1916/17): 48-53.

51. Preußischer Kriegsminister to Preußisches Ministerium für Handel und Gewerbe, 30 August 1915: StA Münster, Oberpräsidium 4123, Bl. 306; Prussian Kriegsminister to Stellv. Gen.kdo.s et. al., 5 January 1916: Report about a meeting in the War Ministry, re. the possibility of further expanding homework for war deliveries, 11 December 1915: ibid., Bl. 344.

52. The most important principles for this regulation are in: Verfügung des preußischen Kriegsministeriums, betr. Grundsätze für die Vergabe der Heeresnäharbeiten, 14 September 1916: BA/MA, RM31/1003. Regarding wartime sewing for the army, see Ch. Lorenz, "Die gewerbliche Frauenarbeit während des Krieges," in P. Umbreit and Ch. Lorenz, *Der Krieg und die Arbeitsverhältnisse* (Stuttgart et al., 1928), 351-356. In terms of wartime homework in general, see the relevant sections in the *Jahresberichte der Gewerbeaufsicht*

112

Women's Wage Labor in the First World War

1914–1918, part of which are reprinted in: "Kriegsverdienste in der Hausindustrie nach den Jahresberichten der Gewerbeaufsichtsbeamten," *RABl* 18 (1920): 144-149, and *Archiv für Frauenarbeit* 7 (1919): 152-157. In spite of all the efforts to "weed" all those women who were neither prevented for health nor family reasons from working in a factory out of the cottage industry (see, for example, Erlaß des Oberkommandos in den Marken, 23 April 1918, rpt. in *Arbeitsnachweis in Deutschland* 5 (1917/18): 191), the number of army seamstresses rose throughout the war. See, for example, Nachweisungen betr. Heeresnäharbeiten: HStA/Kr, MKr 13594 and 13595.

53. There was already a precedent for the military administration's intervention in the wage structure of private industries in the first weeks of the war. At that time, many companies had used the high unemployment and the widespread patriotic willingess to make sacrifices as an opportunity to cut their employees' salaries. Several military commanders took action against this; the military governor of Metz was particularly emphatic in countermeasures and immediately closed the companies concerned until they paid back the salaries still owed. Although the Imperial Office of the Interior did not consider such drastic action permissible, it did reject the complaints of the war committee of German industry, among others, with the remark that military commanders' intervention was, after all, only directed against unjustified wage cuts. ZStA Potsdam, Reichsministerium des Innern 6697, Bl. 49-52, 124, 127-130, 151, 207; Minutes of a meeting in the State House of Münster, re. support of commercial activities in the area of the 7th Army Corps, 16 October 1914, 14: StA Münster, Oberpräsidium 4123, Bl. 126-133. Also see G. Mai, "Burgfrieden und Sozialpolitik in Deutschland in der Anfangsphase des Ersten Weltkriegs (1914/15)," *MGM* 20 (1976): 29-36, and W. Deist, "Armee und Arbeiterschaft 1905-1918," *Francia* 2 (1974): 458-481, *passim*.

54. Polizeipräsident Berlin to Preußischer Minister für Handel und Gewerbe, 12 September 1914: StA Potsdam, Pr. Br. Rep. 30 Berlin C Pol. Präs. 1459, Bl. 116-117.

55. L. Preller, *Sozialpolitik in der Weimarer Republik* (Kronberg/Ts. and Düsseldorf, 1978), 3.

56. H. Schäfer, *Regionale Wirtschaftspolitik in der Kriegszeit. Staat, Industrie und Verbände während des Ersten Weltkriegs in Baden* (Stuttgart, 1983), 91ff. Regarding the development of the textile industry between 1914 and 1918, see W. Niecz, "Untersuchung der Lage der weiblichen Arbeitskräfte in der Textilindustrie während der Kriegs- und Übergangszeit," diss. (Frankfurt/M., 1924/25).

57. Preußischer Innenminister to Regierungspräsident, 4 February 1916: StA Detmold, M1IE/2803. Also see "Die Erwerbslosenfürsorge für Webstoff- und Bekleidungsarbeiter," *RABl* 14 (1916): 318-322, and M. Niehuss, "Textilarbeiter im Ersten Weltkrieg. Beschäftigungslage und Fürsorgemaßnahmen am Beispiel Augsburg," in Mai, ed., *Arbeiterschaft*, 249-276.

58. According to: Association of Westphalian Employment Exchanges to the members of the Committe for Combatting the Consequences of Unemployment in the Westphalian Textile Industry, 4 December 1915: Report about the survey on unemployment in the Westphalian textile industry, conducted in October 1915 by the Association of Westphalian Employment Exchanges: StA Münster, Oberpräsidium 4124, and Association of Westphalian Exmployment Exchanges:

Memorandum about a meeting in the State House of Münster, re. unemployment in the textile industry, 31 August 1915: ibid.

59. *Arbeitsnachweis in Deutschland* 4 (1916/17): 84.

60. *Arbeitsnachweis in Deutschland* 3 (1915/16): 80.

61. According to: Kgl. Sächsisches Ministerium für Äußere Angelegenheiten to Reichsschatzamt, 7 October 1915: ZStA Potsdam, Reichsministerium des Innern 1055.

62. Compare this with the statistics about the number of employees in the textile and clothing industry in Saxony from 1913 to 1918 in *Jahresberichte der Gewerbeaufsicht 1914–1918*, 2: 19, 31. They confirm these figures.

63. Kriegsersatz- und Arbeitsdepartement to Kriegsamtsstelle Karlsruhe, 17 February 1917: GLA Karlsruhe, 456 EV 8/111.

64. See, for example, stellv. Gen.kdo. IV. AK Breslau to Preußisches Kriegsministerium, 28 October 1916: HStA/Kr, MKr 12689: Regierungspräsident Minden to Oberpräsident Münster, 20 December 1915: StA Münster, Oberpräsidium 4124; Association of Westphalian Employment Exchanges, 4 December 1915: Report about the survey, conducted in October, re. unemployment in the Westphalian textile industry: ibid.; *Jahresberichte der Gewerbeaufsicht 1914–1918, passim*.

65. See, for example, Horst, "Maßnahmen," 206. During the war, the same problem arose for unemployed tobacco workers, who likewise received financial assistance. They were tied to their place of residence not only because of their family, but also because they owned a small piece of property. See, for example, Regierungspräsident Minden to Preußischer Minister für Handel und Gewerbe, 27 August 1918: ZStA Potsdam, Reichsarbeitsministerium 33998/2814; Bayerisches Konsulat Karlsruhe to Bayerisches Außenministerium, 10 October 1918, re. industry's position on expanding female employment: HStA München, MH 15956.

66. Preußisches Ministerium für Handel und Gewerbe 5 December 1916: StA Münster, Oberpräsidium 4124, rpt. in *Arbeitsnachweis in Deutschland* 4 (1916/17): 74–75.

67. R. Zesch, "Was ist geschehen zur Ermöglichung der Arbeit von Ungelernten und Frauen in der gesamten Schwer-, Maschinen- und chemischen Industrie und im Handwerk? . . ." (Unpublished manusript, Berlin, 1933), 55, note 23: BA/MA, MSG 779/80. Zesch does not give proof of this estimate.

68. Rpt. in I. Jastrow, *Im Kriegszustand. Die Umformung des öffentlichen Lebens in den ersten Kriegswochen* (Berlin, 1914), 150. For an overview of the health and safety regulations for female workers at the beginning of the war and the most important changes they underwent during the war, see H. Oppenheimer and H. Radomski, *Die Probleme der Frauenarbeit in der Übergangswirtschaft* (Mannheim et al., 1918), 77–83. In 1915 and 1916, numerous companies assumed that all restrictions on the employment of women and adolescents had been abolished, and thus used this labor accordingly. *Jahresberichte der Gewerbeaufsicht 1914–1918, passim*.

69. Wumba to Regierungspräsident Aachen, 24 October 1916: HStA Düsseldorf, Regierung Aachen 8067. For a similar official view, see Reichsamt des Innern to Bundesregierungen, 11 December 1916: ibid.

70. M.-E. Lüders, *Fürchte dich nicht. Persönliches und Politisches aus mehr als 80 Jahren* (Köln, 1963), 68; Frauenreferat des bayerischen Kriegsamts, Report

to Kriegsamtsstellen, 14 December 1917 (Anlage 18 to 38732 K/F): HStA/Kr, MKr 14391.

71. See, for example, the description of the explosion in the Hamburg-Quickborn gunpowder factory in V. Ullrich, *Kriegsalltag. Hamburg im Ersten Weltkrieg* (Köln, 1982), 73–77, and G. Meyer, *Die Frau mit den grünen Haaren. Erinnerungen*, M. C. Wiessing, ed. (Hamburg, 1978), 30–37.

72. Kreisgesundheitsamt Offenbach to Hessisches Innenministerium, 10 March 1918: StA Münster, Oberpräsidium 6575. In the same letter, the health office advised that, where possible, such work should be performed by soldiers.

73. Reichswirtschaftsamt to Bundesregierungen, 13 February 1918 StA Potsdam, Pr. Br. Rep. 30 Berlin C Pol. Präs. 1433, Bl. 274; emphasis in the original. The factory doctors took the same position.

74. Preußisches Handelsministerium to Regierungspräsidenten, 29 October 1915 StA Potsdam, Pr. Br. Rep. 30 Berlin C. Pol. Präs. 1958, Bl. 46. The reports of Factory Inspectorate officials, which were ultimately published in 1920, did indeed contain very detailed descriptions of accidents and health risks that women suffered because of their employment in explosives and armaments industries. *Jahresberichte der Gewerbeaufsicht 1914–1918, passim.*

75. See, for example, Röchling at the meeting of the Wumba Advisory Council in Berlin, 26 January 1917, p. 2 of the minutes: HStA/Kr, MKr 14364; Lüders, *Heer*, 152. P. Umbreit's statement that no women worked underground during the First World War needs to be revised. P. Umbreit, "Die deutschen Gewerkschaften im Kriege," in P. Umbreit and Ch. Lorenz, *Der Krieg und die Arbeitsverhältnisse* (Stuttgart et al., 1928), 87.

76. Reichsamt des Innern to Bundesregierungen, 11 August 1917: HStA/Kr, MKr 14385.

77. Kriegsamt to Preußischer Minister für Handel und Gewerbe, 14 July 1917: HStA Düsseldorf, Regierung Aachen 8067, Bl. 80, as well as note 76.

78. Reichswirtschaftsamt to Bundesregierungen, 9 January 1918: StA Münster, Oberpräsidium 4123; rpt. in *Ministerialblatt der Handels- und Gewerbeverwaltung 1918.*

79. Arbeiterbeschaffung und Menschenökonomie während des Krieges. Denkschrift der wissenschaftlichen Kommission zur Untersuchung der Kriegswirtschaft, vorgelegt in Zusammenhang mit der Einführung des Hilfsdienstgesetzes, 8–11: BA/MA, N46/121.

80. This number is somewhat lower the estimation of a good 10 million cited elsewhere; see the section in chapter 4 entitled "The Demographic Development."

81. Arbeiterbeschaffung und Menschenökonomie während des Krieges. Denkschrift der wissenschaftlichen Kommission zur Untersuchung der Kriegswirtschaft, vorgelegt in Zusammenhang mit der Einführung des Hilfsdienstgesetzes, 8–11: BA/MA, N46/121.

82. File notes of Department K5 of the Bavarian War Ministry, 16 August 1918: HStA/Kr, MKr 14204. Women who were not from Bavaria also resorted to similar strategies. It was reported from the police administrative district of the state of Berlin that many housewives had supposedly applied for their husbands' conscription "because many of these, who had very high salaries, had taken to a dissolute way of life and did not provide for wife and children. If their husbands were at the front, such women were fundamentally better off with the income

for war wives and children." *Jahresbericht der Gewerbeaufsicht 1914-1918*, 1: 213.

83. An unnamed representative in the Reichstag, as quoted in: W. Groener, *Lebenserinnerungen* (Göttingen, 1957), 348.

84. G. Ritter, *Die Tragödie der Staatskunst. Bethmann Hollweg als Kriegs-kanzler (1914-1917)*, Staatskunst und Kriegshandwerk 3 (München, 1964), 426.

85. Generalstabschef to Preußischer Kriegsminister, 31 August 1916: BA/MA, N46/128, Bl. 46-49.

86. Ibid., Bl. 24a-29.

87. Comments on the letter from Generalstabschef des Feldheeres to Reichs-kanzler: HStA Potsdam, 13 September 1916: Reichskanzlei 2398/7, Bl. 254ff.; Reichskanzler to Generalstabschef des Feldheeres, 30 September 1916: ibid., 2398/8, Bl. 56-65. In reality, female unemployment was still quite considerable in 1916. Of the female members of the German Textile Workers' Association, for example, a good 20% were unemployed in July 1916. Deutscher Textil-arbeiterverband, *Jahrbuch 1918* (Berlin, 1919), 72. Regarding unemployment in the textile industry, see pp. 58-62.

88. Preußischer Kriegsminister to Generalstabschef, 14 October 1916, rpt. in: R. Sichler and J. Tiburtius, *Die Arbeiterfrage, eine Kernfrage des Weltkrieges. Ein Beitrag zur Erklärung des Kriegsausgangs* (Berlin, n.d. [1925]), enclosure 5, 112-113.

89. Conclusion of the commissary meeting between the Imperial and Prussian departments in the Imperial Office of the Interior, re. provision of the war industry with labor, 17 October 1916: ZStA Potsdam, Reichskanzlei 2398/7, Bl. 139ff.

90. Generalstabschef to Reichskanzler, 23 October 1916, rpt. in: Sichler and Tiburtius, *Arbeiterfrage*, 138-143; emphasis in the original.

91. On the War Office, see G. D. Feldman, *Army, Industry and Labor in Germany, 1914-1918* (Princeton, NY, 1966), 149-404, and Groener, *Lebens-erinnerungen*, 334-373.

92. Like the Supreme Command, public opinion and many interest groups were in favor of mandatory labor for women. Around the New Year of 1916-1917, its introduction was called for, for the most disparate reasons, in many newspaper articles. Big landowners east of the Elbe and the deputy general commands there hoped that such a measure would remedy the shortage of agricultural labor. Within the bourgeois women's movement, mandatory service for women was discussed, above all, within the context of a female "year of service," during which women and girls were to learn house-, agricultural and nursing work. Compare A. von Harnack, *Der Krieg und die Frauen* (Berlin, 1915); E. Gnauck-Kühne, *Dienstpflicht und Dienstjahr des weiblichen Geschlechts* (Tübingen, 1915); L. A. Hohmann and E. Reichel, *Die Dienstpflicht der deutschen Frauen* (Berlin, 1917); K. Schirmacher, *Frauendienstpflicht* (Bonn, 1918). For a devastating critique of such a service year for women, see R. Kempf, "Das weibliche Dienstjahr," *Archiv für Sozialwissenschaft und Sozialpolitik* 41 (1916): 422-437. Compare this to S. Dammer, *Mütterlichkeit und Frauendienstpflicht. Versuch der Vergesellschaftung "weiblicher Fähig-keiten" durch eine Dienstverpflichtung. Deutschland 1890-1918* (Weinheim, 1988).

I follow Gerald Feldman in his opinion that it was Groener who dissuaded the Supreme Command from its plans to institute compulsory labor for women. Feldman, *Army*, 198.

93. The text of the Auxiliary Service Law is printed in: Umbreit and Lorenz, *Krieg*, 239–245.

94. This reason was given by the representative of the Imperial Office of the Interior at the first meeting of the temporary consultation about regulations for implementing the Auxiliary Service Law, 16 December 1916: HStA/Kr, MKr 17312.

95. Ritter, *Tragödie*, 426.

96. Wrote Marie-Elisabeth Lüders, "'The mobilization of women by women,' that was the first task that the [War Office] plan required." Lüders, *Heer*, 119.

97. Groener, *Lebenserinnerungen*, 355. Regarding the role of women's movements in wartime social and labor-market policy, see C. E. Boyd, *Nationaler Frauendienst: German Middle Class Women in Service to the Fatherland, 1914–1918* (Athens, Ga., 1979); Ch. Sachße, *Mütterlichkeit als Beruf. Sozialarbeit, Sozialreform und Frauenbewegung 1871–1929* (Frankfurt/M., 1986), 151–173; B. Guttmann, *Weibliche Heimarmee. Frauen in Deutschland 1914–1918* (Weinheim, 1989); S. Hering, *Die Kriegsgewinnlerinnen. Praxis und Ideologie der deutschen Frauenbewegung im Ersten Weltkrieg* (Pfaffenweiler, 1990). The "left" wing of the women's movement in Germany was more critical of the First World War than the BDF majority. For this, see L.G. Heymann and A. Augspurg, *Erlebtes – Erschautes. Deutsche Frauen kämpfen für Freiheit, Recht und Frieden 1850–1940* (Meisenheim am Glan, 1977).

98. On Patriotic Women's Associations, see U. Daniel, "Vaterländische Frauenvereine in Westfalen," *Westfälische Forschungen* 39 (1989), 158–179.

99. G. Bäumer, "Weiblicher Aktivismus," *Die Frau* 30 (1922/23): 165, as cited in: B. Greven-Aschoff, *Die bürgerliche Frauenbewegung in Deutschland 1894–1933* (Göttingen, 1981), 41.

100. G. Bäumer, *Lebensweg durch eine Zeitenwende* (Tübingen, 1933), 280; emphasis in the original.

101. Lecture held by Elisabeth Altmann-Gottheiner for the Association of Women's Interests, as cited in: *Münchener Neueste Nachrichten*, 30 January 1916; emphasis in the original. Altmann-Gottheiner was a member of the select executive board of the BDF.

102. On Marie-Elisabeth Lüders (1878–1966) and Agnes von Zahn-Harnack (1884–1950), see U. Daniel, *Arbeiterfrauen in der Kriegsgesellschaft. Beruf, Familie und Politik im Ersten Weltkrieg* (Göttingen, 1989), 301–302, note 198 and the literature cited there.

103. Lüders, *Heer*, 120.

104. Ibid.; emphasis in the original.

105. M.-E. Lüders, *Volksdienst der Frau* (Berlin, 1937), 100. Also see Lüders, *Heer*, 180–183.

106. Compare this with Feldman, *Army*, 349–404.

107. Lüders, *Fürchte dich nicht*, 71–72.

108. Lüders, *Heer*, 122ff. Regarding the organizational structure of these institutions, also see U. von Gersdorff, *Frauen im Kriegsdienst 1914–1945* (Stuttgart, 1969), 22–25 and the relevant printed documents; Reports about the work of the women's group in the War Replacement and Labor Department,

rendered at the third convention of the National Committee for Women's War Work on 22-23 April 1918, 3: HStA/Kr, MKr 14389; and Erster Vierteljahresbericht der Frauenarbeitszentrale for the Kriegsamt/Stab, 1 February-1 May 1917: HStA/Kr, MKr 17309. A listing of the existent Women's Labor Offices, Women's Labor Office branches and welfare offices can be found in *Jahrbuch des BDF 1918* (Berlin, 1918), 13ff.

109. The work plan for the Headquarters for Women's Labor from 16 January 1917 is printed in: Gersdorff, *Frauen im Kriegsdienst*, 129-130.

110. Lüders, *Heer*, 137. The figures for women working in Wumba factories are taken from: Minutes of a meeting of the National Committee for Women's War Work, 22-24 August 1917, 10: HStA/Kr, MKr 14385.

111. Lüders, *Entwicklung*, 12, and Kriegsministerium/Kriegsamt to Kriegsamtsstellen, 8 June 1918: BA, NL 151/158.

112. Feldman, *Army*, 295.

113. Groener to Stellv. Gen.kdo.s, 9 February 1917: BA/MA, RM31/1007; Feldman, *Army*, 290-297.

114. Feldman, *Army*, 294. A definite clarification of authority was only effected immediately before the end of the war. W. Deist, ed., *Militär und Innenpolitik im Weltkrieg 1914-1918* (Düsseldorf, 1970), 1: XLVII-XLVIII and the documents cited there.

115. Kriegsministerium/Kriegsersatz- und Arbeitsdepartement to Stellv. Gen.kdo.s, 12 December 1916: HStA/Kr, MKr 14197; Kriegsamt to Wumba, 5 February 1917: ibid., MKr 14383.

116. For this, see Daniel, *Arbeiterfrauen*, 51-61.

117. See, for example, Kriegsersatz- und Arbeitsdepartement to Stellv. Gen.kdo.s, 15 January 1917: HStA/Kr, MKr 14197.

118. Einberufungsausschuß Kaiersläutern, sent from Kriegsamtsstelle Würzburg to Bayerisches Kriegsministerium, 21 October 1917: HStA/Kr, MKr 14368.

119. Einberufungsausschüsse Landau and Neustadt A.H., sent from Kriegsamtsstelle Würzburg to Bayerisches Kriegsministerium, 21 October 1917: ibid.

120. Monatsbericht des stellv. Gen.kdo.s I. Bayerisches AK München für Februar 1917, 3: HStA/Kr, MKr 12843. There are countless similar reports about individuals obligated for auxiliary service who either never appeared at their assigned place of work, immediately left it or were, for other reasons, not very useful. See *Jahresberichte der Gewerbeaufsicht 1914-1918, passim*.

121. Zesch, "Was ist geschehen," 58.

122. "Kriegswirtschaftliche Erfahrungen des städtischen Arbeitsnachweises Charlottenburg," *Arbeitsnachweis in Deutschland* 4 (1916/17): 230.

123. Preußisches Kriegsamt to Stellv. Gen.kdo.s, 21 July 1917: HStA/Kr, MKr 14367.

124. Meeting of the Diagnostic Committee for the High Command in the Marches, 27 April 1917 (List of recognized auxiliary service businesses): StA Potsdam, Pr. Br. Rep. 30 Berlin C Pol. Präs. 1915, Bl. 105-110.

125. Also see H.-J. Bieber, *Gewerkschaften in Krieg und Revolution. Arbeiterbewegung, Industrie, Staat und Militär in Deutschland 1914-1920* (Hamburg, 1981), 303.

126. See, for example, Monatsberichte, 3 February 1917, 7: BA/MA, RM3/4670, and Monatsberichte, 3 September 1917, 21: ibid.

127. Preußisches Kriegsamt to stellv. Gen.kdo.s, re. increased enlistment

of female labor, 14 August 1917: HStA Düsseldorf, Regierung Aachen 8067, Bl. 95.

128. See the detailed statistics and calculations in Daniel, *Arbeiterfrauen*, 90-93.

129. The "rear-echelon helpers'" great interest in finding private accommodation, instead of living in one of the hostels established for them, is a clear indication of this; A. von Harnack at the meeting in the War Office, 22 December 1917: BA, NL 151/158.

130. The Head of the Women's Department at the Bavarian War Ministry, Wolf, at the meeting of the Bavarian Committee for Women's Labor in the War, 12 July 1917, 4 of the minutes: HStA/Kr, MKr 14384.

131. Kriegsamt to Kriegsamtsstellen, 15 October 1917: HStA/Kr, MKr 17310. Compare this with the list about the number of "rear-echelon helpers" 1917–1918 in Daniel, *Arbeiterfrauen*, 92.

132. E. von Wrisberg, *Heer and Heimat 1914-1918* (Leipzig, 1921), 92.

133. In Bavaria, the rate of increase in the replacement of military persons was approximately 22% from the beginning of September 1917 to the beginning of August 1918; calculated according to the table in Daniel, *Arbeiterfrauen*, 92.

134. The unanimous opinion of the authorities responsible for labor allocation was that women more frequently changed jobs than men. See, for example, Notes for the meeting with the Chancellor on 1 July 1918 (from the Prussian War Ministry): ZStA Potsdam, Reichskanzlei 2398/11, Bl. 321-322.

135. Zesch, "Was ist geschehen," 50–51.

136. *Die Frau in der bayerischen Kriegsindustrie*, 78–79.

137. A. Seidel, *Frauenarbeit im Ersten Weltkrieg als Problem der staatlichen Sozialpolitik. Dargestellt am Beispiel Bayerns* (Frankfurt/M., 1979), 190.

138. Gersdorff, "Frauen im Kriegsdienst," doc. no. 59.

139. The Supreme Command also returned to its old demand of mandatory labor for women. See Hindenburg to Reichskanzler, 15 May 1917: ZStA Potsdam, Reichskanzlei 2398/10, Bl. 288-289, and Hindenburg to Reichskanzler, 18 June 1918: ibid., 2398/11.

140. Meeting about Hindenburg's letter of 18 June 1918: ZStA Potsdam, Reichskanzlei 2398/11, Bl. 312-320. Regarding the discussions about an amendment to the Auxiliary Service Law, also see Feldman, *Army*, 301-458.

141. On the employment of foreigners and prisoners of war, see Daniel, *Arbeiterfrauen*, 56-61 and the literature cited there.

142. Theoretical approaches of modernization have it easier here, since they can establish a "debit account" for the costs of modernization, without having to alter the entire invoice. An advocate of the emancipation approach such as S. Bajohr, however, has to leave open the contradiction between his abstract, general assumption of the "emancipatory" effect that the generalization of wage work had and his concrete descriptions of the obviously less "emancipatory" working conditions, without mentioning it. Bajohr, *Hälfte*, 101-167 and *passim*.

143. See R. Sieder, "Behind the Lines: Working-Class Family Life in Wartime Vienna," in R. Wall and J. Winter, eds., *The Upheaval of War: Family, Work and Welfare in Europe, 1914-1918* (Cambridge, 1988), 109-138.

144. In terms of the methodology of oral history, see L. Niethammer, ed., *Lebenserfahrung und kollektives Gedächtnis. Die Praxis der "Oral History"* (Frankfurt/M., 1980), and F. J. Brüggemeier, "Traue keinem über sechzig?

Entwicklungen und Möglichkeiten der Oral History in Deutschland," *Gd* 9 (1984): 199-210.

145. The development of wages between 1914 and 1918 has been thoroughly examined on several occasions. See here A. Karbe, *Die Frauenlohnfrage und ihre Entwicklung in der Kriegs- und Nachkriegszeit* (Rostock, 1928), 73-95; W. Zimmermann, "Die Veränderungen der Einkommens- und Lebensverhältnisse der deutschen Arbeiter durch den Krieg," in Meerwarth et al., *Einwirkung*, 368-412; Bry, *Wages*, 191-214; Kocka, *Klassengesellschaft*, 13-19; Bajohr, *Hälfte*, 31-41; U. Malich, "Zur Entwicklung des Reallohns im Ersten Weltkrieg," *JbWG* 2 (1980): 2: 60-61.

146. "Berichterstattung von 335 Betrieben ab März 1914," *RABl* 18 (1920): 64. The averages concerned here are relatively broad; they do not take the difference between skilled and unskilled workers (male or female) into consideration, nor the amount of overtime worked. The tables of these figures are reprinted in full in Daniel, *Arbeiterfrauen*, 112-113.

147. Also see Eingabe der Zentralkommission der Berufsorganisationen im Verbande Katholischer Vereine erwerbstätiger Frauen und Mädchen Deutschlands, betr. Arbeiterinnenschutz, to the Bundesrat, 1 December 1916: HStA/Kr, MKr 14383; concrete cases are given here. Marie-Elisabeth Lüders complained, in retrospect, about one of the large companies' "summarily" practiced wage policies; here, women's wages were fixed at two-thirds of the usual piece-rate that men received for the same work. Lüders, *Entwicklung*, 46.

148. See here *Jahresberichte der Gewerbeaufsicht 1914-1918, passim*. The relevant sections are summarized in "Kriegsverdienste in der Hausindustrie nach den Jahresberichten der Gewerbeaufsicht," *RABl* 18 (1920): 144-149.

149. Karbe, *Frauenlohnfrage*, 88. Bajohr, with reference to J. Kuczynski, argues this point the same way. See Bajohr, *Hälfte*, 35.

150. *Arbeitsnachweis in Westfalen* 3 (1919): 8 (15.8.1919): 90. Also see Oppenheimer and Radomski, *Probleme*, 31ff.

151. Kriegsersatz- und Arbeitsdepartement, 29 January 1917; Kriegsamt, 5 February 1917; and Kriegsamt, 21 February 1917, all rpt. in: Zesch, "Was ist geschehen," doc. nos. IIa, IIb, X.

152. On the training of apprentices during the First World War, see H. Böhme, "Die Entwicklung des gewerblichen Lehrlingswesens in Preußen während und nach dem Kriege," diss. (Hamburg, 1923); *Jahresberichte der Gewerbeaufsicht 1914-1918, passim*; Oppenheimer and Radomski, *Probleme*, 31ff.; and Bieber, *Gewerkschaften*, 210ff. H. Oppenheimer and H. Radomski attribute the fall in apprenticeships during the war primarily to the fact that many families had to let their adolescent children contribute to the family income by working in the war industry. This is confirmed by contemporary reports about adolescents from "war families" working as unskilled laborers to contribute to the family's livelihood. See, for example, Landrat Düsseldorf to Regierungspräsident Düsseldorf, 2 April 1915: HStA Düsseldorf, Regierung Düsseldorf 33120. Furthermore, master craftsmen often refused, because of the high cost of living, to provide apprentices with room and board. Minutes of a meeting in the Reichstag, re. demobilization of women and adolescents, 15 January 1918: BA Koblenz, NL 151/159, 8.

153. See, among others, Lüders, *Entwicklung*, 33-46; Adam, *Arbeitsbeziehungen*, 158-169; Städtisches Arbeitsamt Frankfurt/M. to Verband für

handwerksmäßige fachgewerbliche Ausbildung der Frau, 2 March 1918: BA Koblenz, NL 151/166; and Kriegsamt Magdeburg to Kriegsersatz- und Arbeitsdepartement, 7 July 1917, rpt. in: Zesch, "Was ist geschehen," doc. no. XII.

When certain authors (see, for example, G. Wellner, "Industriearbeiterinnen in der Weimarer Republik: Arbeitsmarkt, Arbeit und Privatleben 1919–1933," *GG* 7 (1981): 542, and Bajohr, *Hälfte*, 33) assert that the First World War had a positive effect on the qualifications scale for female labor, this is usually based upon a misunderstanding. The increased vocational training that women in war-industry jobs received – which really was observable in the war and which is the basis for such interpretations – was production- and not skills-oriented. Especially when considered together with the simultaneous decline in apprenticeships, this increase provides no grounds on which to argue that women had more opportunities to improve their qualifications. Such vocational training adhered, so to speak, to the job, not to the person who filled it. When women, trained in this manner, left the position where they had been trained, they generally were not entitled to a higher step on the qualifications scale – and thereby more money – with regard to another job.

154. Horst, "Maßnahmen," 207.

155. On trade unions, also see pp. 100–103. R. Zesch documents one case of trade-union resistance to training women in the printing trade. See Zesch, "Was ist geschehen," 60.

156. Kriegsamtsstelle Nürnberg to Bayerisches Kriegsamt, 28 April 1918: HStA/Kr, MKr 14204.

157. Kriegsamtsstelle Nürnberg to Bayerisches Kriegsamt, 27 September 1917: HStA/Kr, MKr 14200.

158. Zesch, "Was ist geschehen," 52.

159. Marie-Elisabeth Lüders about the implementation of war welfare in Charlottenburg, 9 June 1915: BA Koblenz, NL 151/165.

160. Kriegsamtschef Scheüch to Staatssekretär des Reichswirtschaftsamts, 18 April 1918: ZStA Potsdam, Reichsarbeitsministerium 1734, Bl. 30; "Jahresberichte der Gewerbeaufsicht Baden 1914–1918," in *Jahresberichte der Gewerbeaufsicht 1914–1918*, 2: 42.

161. There is an abundance of material about the planning of demobilization and the respective positions of various interest groups in the five Teilberichte des Ausschusses für Handel und Gewerbe des Reichstag betreffend Überführung der Kriegs- in die Friedenswirtschaft 1916/17 (Reichstagsdrucksachen 13. Legislaturperiode II. Session Nr. 504, 740, 749, 805, and 875; also see the numerous petitions concerning this), cited as Teilberichte in what follows; Minutes of the meeting in War Office/War Replacement and Labor Department, re. planning women's demobilization, 12 January 1918 (BA Koblenz, NL 151/157); and Memoranda about the meeting of the Labor Committee of the Commission for the Demobilization of the Workforce and the Commission itself in October and November 1918 (BA/MA, RM20/627).

Beyond this, on the trade unions' plans for demobilization, see Generalkommission der Gewerkschaften Deutschlands, *Sozialpolitische Arbeiterforderungen der deutschen Gewerkschaften* (Berlin, 1918); H. Jäckel, *Übergangswirtschaft und Textilarbeiter. Denkschrift des Deutschen Textilarbeiterverbandes*, Kommission für Übergangswirtschaft, Textilarbeiterverband,

The War from Within

ed. (Berlin, 1918); Petition of the General Commission of the Trade Unions of Germany, etc., re. "Gewerkschaftliche Forderungen für den Übergang von der Kriegs- zur Friedenswirtschaft," 30 June 1917 (BA Koblenz, NL 151/157). For one of the few instances in which the trade unions did not decide the question of who was entitled to the positions – i.e. the returning soldiers or the (female) replacement labor – in favor of the soldiers, but left it open, see *Die Frauenarbeit in der Metallindustrie während des Krieges, dargestellt nach Erhebungen im August/September vom Vorstand des Deutschen Metallarbeiterverbandes* (Stuttgart, 1917), esp. 53ff.

On the demobilization planning of the German National Association of Commercial Clerks (DNHV), see *Wenn der Friede kommt. Sozialpolitische und wirtschaftliche Forderungen der deutschen Handlungsgehilfen für die Überleitung der Kriegs- in die Friedenswirtschaft. Eine Denkschrift an die deutschen Gesetzgeber* (Hamburg, 1916).

On the demobilization planning of employers' associations, see the Memorandum of the Union of German Employers' Associations on the transition economy, partially summarized in: *Arbeitsnachweis in Deutschland* 5 (1917/18), 187, and Arbeitgeberverband der Eisen- und Stahlindustriellen, petition to the Reichsamt etc., 28 October 1918: BA Koblenz, NL 151/161.

On the demobilization planning of the BDF, see "Sozialpolitische Aufgaben der Übergangswirtschaft mit Bezug auf die Probleme der Frauenarbeit. Denkschrift des BDF und des Ständigen Ausschusses zur Förderung der Arbeiterinneninteressen," Berlin, February 1918 (BA Koblenz, NL 151/157); as well as Marie-Elisabeth Lüders' articles "Arbeitslose Frauen," *Norddeutsche Allgemeine Zeitung,* 26 October 1918 and 17 January 1918, and Oppenheimer and Radomski, *Probleme, passim.*

Further planning for demobilization came out of the area of social policy. For this, see G. Albrecht, *Übergangswirtschaft und Arbeiterfrage* (Berlin, 1917), and "Eingabe der Gesellschaft für soziale Reform an Bundesrat und Reichstag," rpt. in: *Archiv für Frauenarbeit* (1918): 49-64. The labor authorities also expressed an opinion about this problem. See, for example, "Gesichtspunkte für die Entlassung der Kriegsteilnehmer nach Friedensschluß," rpt. in: *Arbeitsnachweis in Deutschland* 3 (1915/16): 182-183.

The Social Democrats were no exception in their stance toward female labor with regard to demobilization. Luise Zietz, who did adopt a position on this question, only distinguished herself from other demobilization planners in her belief that female labor would continue to be in greater demand after the war as before because of the military losses. She consequently asserted that the problem of female unemployment would not materialize. L. Zietz, *Zur Frage der Frauenerwerbsarbeit während des Krieges und nachher*, Parteivorstand der SPD, ed. (Berlin, 1916), esp. 10ff.

On general demobilization planning, also see F. Zunkel, *Industrie und Staatssozialismus. Der Kampf um die Wirtschaftsordnung in Deutschland 1914-1918* (Düsseldorf, 1974), 116-129, and Bieber, *Gewerkschaften*, 369-383.

162. Notes re. the meeting on 30 April 1915 about procuring employment for returning participants in the war and regulating the labor market after the conclusion of peace: BA/MA, RM3/5163.

163. 1. Teilbericht (Reichstagdrucksache 504), 7.

164. Unterstaatssekretär in Reichsamt des Innern, 29 March 1917; 3. Teilbericht (Reichstagsdrucksache 749), 6.

165. Memorandum about the 11th meeting of the Labor Committee of the Commission for the Demobilization of the Workforce, 7 November 1918, 5: BA/MA, RM20/627.

166. The Labor Committee of the Commission for the Demobilization of the Workforce "did not deny that a payment of wages without any output in labor was unpleasant. It believed, however, that, in the interest of public order, unemployed individuals with money were preferable to those without any money." Memorandum about the 3rd meeting of the Labor Committee of the Commission for the Demobilization of the Workforce, 24 October 1918: BA/MA, RM20/627, 5. On women's unemployment benefits in the immediate postwar period, also consult the appropriate sources in HStA Düsseldorf, Regierung Düsseldorf 15133, as well as S. Rouette, "Die Erwerbslosenfürsorge für Frauen in Berlin nach 1918," *IWK* 21 (1985): 295–308.

167. Employers in the iron and steel industry, in consultation with Marie-Elisabeth Lüders, had petitioned for this stipulation from the Imperial Employment Office in order to avoid the "unavoidable, sudden mass dismissals of female labor" that would occur with a transitionless conversion to a peacetime economy. Wrote the employers, "As the food riots in the summer of last year showed, with women, there only needs to be a slight, external influence in order to induce them to impulsive and rash behavior. The introduction of extensive or general dismissals would give cause for great revolts." Petition of the Employers' Association of the Iron and Steel Industries to the Imperial Employment Office etc., 28 October 1918: BA Koblenz, NL 151/161. Arbeitgeberverband der Eisen- und Stahlindustriellen to Marie-Elisabeth Lüders, 6.11.1918: ibid.

168. See, for example, *Arbeitsnachweis in Deutschland* 3 (1915/16): 239 for the shoe industry, 280 for the leather industry, 228 for the wage-rate valid in Stuttgart, Leipzig and Berlin; "Frauenarbeit im deutschen Steindruckgewerbe," *Arbeitsnachweis in Deutschland* 4 (1916/17): 186–187; "Arbeitsgemeinschaft zur Wiedereinstellung der Kriegsteilnehmer in der Berliner Herrenkonfektion," ibid., 22ff; corresponding agreements in the baking and pastry trade and in the Berlin laundry industry can also be found here.

169. In addition to the sources cited above, see Kriegsersatz- und Arbeitsdepartement to Stellv. Gen.kdo.s, 1 December 1917: HStA/Kr, MKr 14386; Preußisches Kriegsamt to Kriegsamtsstellen, 16 July 1917: HStA/Kr, MKr 14199; Kriegsersatz- und Arbeitsdepartement to Kriegsamtsstellen et al., 2 August 1917: ibid.; Lüders, *Fürchte dich nicht,* 68; Lüders, *Heer,* 95.

170. Lüders, *Heer,* 137. Behind the lines, the term "gravedigger" was adopted for female and male individuals doing auxiliary service, since their employment in the rear was the reason for soldiers hitherto working there to be sent to the front. Preußisches Kriegsamt to Ludendorff, July 1917: HStA/Kr, MKr 14366. The soldiers who were affected by this considered female labor a "war ill;" Bieber, *Gewerkschaften,* 207, 208ff.

171. In 1910, there were over 2 million members of the Free Trade Unions, 161,512 of whom were women; in 1918, 422,957 were of the almost 1.7 million members were women. There were roughly 300,000 members of the Christian Trade Unions in 1910, 21,833 of whom were women. In 1918, these figures

were over 400,000 and 72,409, respectively. In the Hirsch-Duncker Trade Unions, the total number of members was over 100,000 in 1913, 5,937 of whom were women; in 1918, of the almost 114,000 members, 11,684 were women. See the statistics regarding female membership in trade unions in Daniel, *Arbeiterfrauen*, 314.

172. ZStA Potsdam, 61Re1/6971, Bl. 110. The trade unions' and Social Democrats' stance towards wartime female labor was in keeping with the cliché-ridden image of women that had already been cultivated before the war. For this, see W. Albrecht et al., "Frauenfrage und deutsche Sozialdemokratie vom Ende des 19. Jahrhunderts bis zum Beginn der 20er Jahre," *AfS* 19 (1979): 477–478, 494–495.

173. Kriegsersatz- und Arbeitsdepartement to Stellv. Gen.kdo.s, 15 January 1917: HStA/Kr, MKr 14197.

174. Bericht des Kommandierenden Generals des VII. AK Münster, 26 May 1915: StA Münster, Oberpräsidium 4123, Bl. 213.

175. *Metallarbeiterzeitung* 46, 13 November 1915. The newspaper also wrote that, due to the danger of unfair competition, lower wages for women should not be approved; ibid. On the trade unions' attitude toward female labor in general, see W. Thönnessen, *Frauenemanzipation. Politik und Literatur der deutschen Sozialdemokratie zur Frauenbewegung 1863–1933* (Frankfurt/ M., 1976); G. Losseff-Tillmanns, *Frauenemanzipation und Gewerkschaften* (Wuppertal, 1978); H. Niggemann, *Emanzipation zwischen Sozialismus und Feminismus. Die sozialdemokratische Frauenbewegung im Kaiserreich* (Wuppertal, 1981); H. Niggemann, ed., *Frauenemanzipation und Sozialdemokratie* (Frankfurt/M., 1981); R. J. Evans, *Sozialdemokratie und Frauenemanzipation im deutschen Kaiserreich* (Berlin and Bonn, 1984).

The associations of white-collar workers, in particular the German National Association of Commercial Clerks (DNHV), were especially emphatic about bringing their demand that all female labor be dismissed immediately after the war to the public eye. In the memorandum "Die Regelung des kaufmännischen Arbeitsmarktes bei Friedensschluß," which the DNHV submitted to the Bundesrat in 1915, the association asserted that all employed female white-collar workers should be fired at the end of the war:

> On principle, the view must be supported that men's war service not be permitted to become an opportunity for women, during this time where men are giving up their lives for the Fatherland, to seize all employment opportunities heretofore denied them. The war, in particular, made the dividing line between the tasks of both sexes clear and unambiguous. The man as protector and guardian of the Fatherland and the family, as fighter and warrior; the woman as housewife and mother, who in this capacity often has great and more pleasant tasks to fulfill.

The DNHV felt that housewives and mothers were especially needed in the present situation, and that this was more important than the "small fleeting wishes of the women's movement." ZStA Potsdam, Reichsministerium des Inneren 6697, Bl.274–306. Reactions to an October 1915 petition by the DNHV and the Social Cooperative Community of the commercial associations to state governments, chambers of commerce et al. proved that public and private employers shared this attitude of employee associations toward female labor, i.e. they also

Women's Wage Labor in the First World War

considered women as temporary replacements for drafted male labor. Compare the rendition of opinion polls in *Archiv für Frauenarbeit* (1916): 1ff.

In 1916, a new petition, in which the DNHV pleaded for protection from female competition in the transition economy before the Prussian House of Lords, also contained the request for a regulation which would prevent the subordination of male to female civil servants in general. On 8 December 1916, *Vorwärts* reported on the small amount of understanding that this petition received in the House of Lords:

> The German National Association of Commercial Clerks . . . now has formal proof that it wants to prevent development, and it is very delightful that it received this proof from the Prussian House of Lords of all places. If one really wanted to establish by law that men could only be the superiors of women, women, however, never the superiors of men, then one would first of all have to oblige men by law to be brighter than women. Such an obligation, however, should never have to be fulfilled by the chairmen of the DNHV because it would violate the legal maxim that no one must fulfill an obligation beyond one's capacities.

176. Marie-Elisabeth Lüders, "Demobilmachung der Frauen," draft, ca. 1917: BA Koblenz, NL 151/158; E. Buß, "Die Frauenarbeit im Dienst der preußisch-hessischen Staatseisenbahnen und ihre Entwicklung während des Krieges," diss. (Göttingen, 1919), 68.
177. The Prussian Minister for Public Works arranged this for the Prussian-Hessian Railway, which employed a large number of women for the first time during the war, with a decree issued on 5 May 1915. The decree is printed in: *Arbeitsnachweis in Deutschland* 2 (1914/15): 229–230. Regarding women's work on the railway during the war, also consult Buß, "Frauenarbeit," *passim*.
178. "Mitteilung der IHK Zittau," rpt. in: *Archiv für Frauenarbeit* 3 (1915): 215–216. Also see Preußisches Kriegsamt to Staatssekretär des Reichswirtschaftsamts, 18 July 1918: ZStA Potsdam, Reichsarbeitsministerium 1734, Bl. 30. The yearly reports of the Factory Inspectorate also confirm that the majority of employers regarded the war-necessitated employment of women as a transitory phenomenon. See *Jahresberichte der Gewerbeaufsicht 1914–1918*, *passim*.
179. Lüders, *Entwicklung*, 36–37. Shortly before his fall, Groener had envisioned extending the Auxiliary Service Law's restrictions on changes of employment (Paragraph 9) to include women, in addition to other amendments to the law. This change was not enacted, however. Here, see Feldman, *Army*, 384–385.
180. The rationality of this practical expectation was confirmed by the actual process of demobilization after the war. Working women were dismissed from their places of wartime work with the well-meant advice "Be frugal, take care of honor and health" (Merkblatt des Demobilmachungsamts für Arbeiterinnen und weibliche Angestellte, November 1918. BA Koblenz, NL 151/157). Compare W. D. Dazur, "Der Deutsche Arbeitsmarkt seit Kriegsbeginn und die Bekämpfung der Arbeitslosigkeit durch das Reich," diss. (Würzburg), *passim*.; L. Marx, "Die wirtschaftliche und soziale Lage der berufstätigen Frau bei Kriegsende in Mannheim," diss. (Heidelberg, n.d. [1920]); P. Prange, "Die Demobilmachung des Arbeitsmarktes im deutschen Reich nach Beendigung des Weltkrieges 1914/1918," diss. (Würzburg, 1923); E. M. Gravert, "Der Einfluß der wirtschaftlichen

The War from Within

Demobilmachung auf die Entwicklung der Frauenarbeit," diss. (Hamburg, 1924/ 25); E. Kinzinger, "Der Einfluß der Sozialpolitik der Nachkriegszeit auf die Arbeitsmarktlage insbesondere in Ludwigshafen a. Rh.," diss. (Heidelberg, 1926); R. Bessel, "'Eine nicht allzu große Beunruhigung des Arbeitsmarktes:' Frauenarbeit und Demobilmachung in Deutschland nach dem Ersten Weltkrieg," *GG* 9 (1983): 211–229. The first large demobilization of women at the end of the war was followed by another wave from 1919 to 1921. During the course of this second demobilization, those women who had received unemployment benefits up until then were no longer eligible for these benefits. It should be noted, however, that already previously women were automatically ineligible for unemployment benefits whose wartime occupation "had simply been conditioned and made possible by the war, so that, from the beginning, it had to be considered temporary," Innenminster to Regierungspräsident Köslin, re. unemployment benefits for war widows, 13 October 1919: ZStA Potsdam, Reichsarbeitsministerium 1170, Bl. 4. The loss of unemployment benefits in the second demobilization wave was primarily due to the fact that unemployed women were counseled to take up work in housekeeping, where a large number of positions were available. If they turned down such positions, their unemployment benefits were cut. Verband Badischer Arbeitsnachweise to Badisches Arbeitsministerium, 30 August 1920: ZStA Potsdam, Reichsministerium des Innern 1170, Bl. 35; Stellv. Gen.kdo. Karlsruhe, Minutes of the meeting of the Karlsruhe Demobilization Committee, 18 December 1918: GLA Karlsruhe, 456 EV8/102. Also see Rouette, "Erwerbslosenfürsorge," *passim*; S. Rouette, *Sozialpolitik als Geschlechterpolitik. Die Regulierung der Frauenarbeit nach dem Ersten Weltkrieg* (Frankfurt/M. and New York, 1993), *passim*.

181. Report of the Bavarian Women's Department to the War Office bureaus, re. survey about women in the war industry, 14 December 1917: HStA/Kr, MKr 14391.

182. Kriegsamtsstelle Nürnberg to Bayerisches Kriegsministerium, 30 August 1918, 12: HStA/Kr, MKr 14205.

183. "Bericht des Dräger-Werks in Lübeck," rpt. in: *Archiv für Frauenarbeit* 5 (1917): 5ff. The editorial staff described the report as "almost typical."

184. "Gewerbeaufsichtsbericht des Regierungsbezirks Wiesbaden 1914–1918," *Jahresberichte der Gewerbeaufsicht 1914–1918*, 1: 899. The report about the administrative district of Potsdam ascertained that female workers changed employment more frequently than before the war and more frequently than men. Ibid., 90.

185. FAZ, 7 March 1917, rpt. in: Zesch, "Was ist geschehen," doc. no. VIc.

186. "Wochenbericht des Frauenreferats einer Kriegsamtstelle, 20.3.-26.3.1917," rpt. in: Zesch, "Was ist geschehen," doc. no. XI.

187. Kriegsamtstelle Leipzig to Marie-Elisabeth Lüders: BA Koblenz, NL 151/ 159.

126

4

The Family in the First World War

At lunchtime, [in the mental hospital], when the plates were placed on the table, another [patient] came along, put little scraps of paper on them and said to everyone: "So, there you have your bread and meat coupons, your ration of fat, and now, eat up! Eat up!"

Oskar Maria Graf, *Wir sind Gefangene*[1]

In the First World War, the family, as the "decisive social institution for managing everyday life,"[2] played an even more central role in the population's physical and psychological coping with existence than previously, and this affected women in particular. Managing everyday life had already been a priority of female family members, and especially wives, before the war. The change that the war induced here consisted "only" in accentuating this traditional gender-specific division of labor, caused by the often years-long absence of numerous husbands, to a completely new degree under very aggravated circumstances.

The decisive transformations that the First World War held for the family resulted from the altered structure of everyday life. In order to understand what impact the changed everyday life of wartime had on the family, it is first necessary to break down the functions of the family according to type. Following a suggestion from Karin Hausen,[3] I shall use two types of familial functions as a starting point.

The first of these is the family's function in the physical, psychological and societal reproduction of people. The tasks here include the raising and socialization of children and the reproduction of adults in terms of their psychological and physical components (material support, psychological stabilization, sexuality, etc.).

The second type concerns the family's function in the production and consumption of goods. Next to the production of goods for personal use or the market, activities include the obtaining, conservation, care and preparation of consumer goods and the consumption of goods.

The following four hypotheses lend structure to the narrative of this chapter; they will, in turn, be substantiated by its analysis.

1 In the war and through the war and its consequences, the family's function of physically, psychologically and socially reproducing people diminished. The frequent and long-lasting separation of spouses through either the husband's conscription or the demands of an extended workday and intensified house-work (e.g. waiting in line at stores or for food rations) reduced the family's physical and psychological reproductive performance to the bare minimum. The most fundamental expression of the family's diminishing reproductive performance was the decline in the birthrate during the war.

2 In contrast, the other function of the family, namely the production and consumption of goods, became so important during this same period that the family's entire life was shaped by its economic function. The home-production of food once again became an activity in urban households, from which it had increasingly disappeared over the course of the nineteenth century. And obtaining consumer goods, particularly in the second half of the war, developed into an extremely energy- and time-intensive task, the burden of which fell mostly on women. Additionally, as a result of the collapse of the money and con-sumer goods market, the family was increasingly forced to resort to semi-legal or illegal means (e.g. foraging trips to the country, stealing crops) to provide for its existence, which further inten-sified the predominance of its economic function.

3 Each of these, the decline in the family's reproductive function on the one hand and the dominance of its economic function on the other, developed into a political issue. By this I mean that decision makers came to view them as factors that affected the stability of wartime society and thus introduced political and bureaucratic measures, such as a strongly pro-natal population policy, to counter what they considered to be negative trends – in this instance, the decline in the birthrate. Sexuality, for example, which was practically removed from the familial arena due to the separation of numerous spouses, was realized in forms that slipped out of the grasp of social regulation; the key words here are, above all, so-called "secret prostitution" and German women's relationships with prisoners of war.

Furthermore, the rudiments of the family's emotional connection to conscripted soldiers, especially that of wives to their husbands on the front, became, with the increasing deterioration of the civilian population's life situation, a subversive element. Here, the watchword is the "letters of lament" sent from Germany to the front. On the other hand, the fact that the wartime family was overtaxed by having to provide for itself led to familial strategies of survival that not only circumvented state rationing measures, but also obstructed them, thereby calling the rationality of the institutional state (M. Weber) as well as its legitimizing and reality-managing aspects into question. This concerned both semi-legal and illegal means of family survival as well as the pattern of behavior, accepted since 1916 and exhibited especially by women, of forcing the state to improve its food provision through spontaneous collective action such as hunger demonstrations and looting.

4 The political and bureaucratic efforts to counter the structural subversity of the family's altered functions and of their perception, especially by women, proved to be unsuccessful for various reasons. The causes for this failure primarily lay in the state's inability to integrate working-class women and families into the framework of its domestic policy of behavioral control.

The Family in War I: Reproduction

In order to outline and analyze the changes in the family's reproductive performance during the war, there are two ways for us to proceed. The first is predominantly descriptive and relies upon the use of familial basic data, i.e. the separation of spouses caused by the war and the consequent changes in demographics and household statistics. The second method is more problem-oriented and analytical; here we will attempt to determine the nature of the family's wartime reproduction through a general analysis of its transformations during and through the war and the specific problems these entailed for wartime society. This analysis of the whole will then be supplemented by several examples.

The Demographic Development

The most important point of departure for examining the wartime changes in the structure of the family is the number of conscripted (married) men, from which the extent of marital and familial separation arises. At the outset of the war, the number of men required to do military service (*Wehrpflichtige*), i.e. men between 17 and 45 years of age, was almost 10.5 million. In other words, almost one-third of the entire male population of 32 million fell under the draft.[4] In August 1914, there were 2.8 million men serving; in December 1914, the number was 5 million.[5] For 1 December 1916, it was reported that the number of men conscripted in Prussia was 6,104,000, in Bavaria 1,035,000, in Saxony 760,000 and in the entire German Reich 10,090,000. The percentage of the total male population was 28.9% for Prussia, 29.2% for Bavaria, 31.9% for Saxony and 29.8% for the entire Reich.[6] On the basis of the number of conscripted trade-union members,[7] we arrive at a figure for the end of 1915 of 1.2 million conscripted union members and of 1.8 million members obligated to do military service. In other words, at this point in time, approximately 67% of those organized individuals who were required to do military service had been drafted. If, when calculating the total number of conscripted men, we take the total number of those from the trade unions to be between 60 and 65% – assuming that the unions consisted of better-paid and thereby healthier workers – then we arrive at a total number of approximately 9 million at the end of 1915, which coincides with the figure cited above. On average, about 172,500 men were sent to the front a month (between 1915 and 1917, slightly more; in 1918, slightly fewer), of whom approximately 64,000 were wounded soldiers who had recovered and 108,500 were new conscripts.[8] In total, 13.3 million men were mobilized during the First World War. On 11 November 1918, 5.3 million of these were stationed at the front and in occupied territories and 2.7 million in the homelands.[9] Of those trade-union members conscripted in the middle of 1915, roughly 66% were married; of the 9 to 10 million men drafted that same year, 5 million, or half, were married. With over 12 million married men – the 1913 figure for the German Empire was 12,108,000[10] – this meant that, by the end of 1915, well over one-third of all husbands were serving at the front or in the garrison and that, consequently the majority of these marriages were lived out separately for the length of the war.[11] The long duration of this separation became a kind of "war normality" for those families concerned. As one women from Allgäu wrote to her brother in March 1917: "One gets used to the misery, one thinks, it has to be this way, the man belongs on the front, the woman has to struggle and slave away, has to raise the kids alone, and is only allowed to write her husband and send him packages."[12] The impact of conscription on individual families becomes much more extensive if we also consider the conscription of male family members in general, not only that of husbands and fathers. The results of a survey conducted in November 1916 among 623 shophelpers gives an indication of this. The results showed that a good one-fourth of the women questioned had either a father, husband, or one or more brothers "in the field." For 11.4%, it was the father who had been drafted, for 1.3% the husband – a statistic that is not generalizable, since an above-average number of the shop helpers were not married – for 37.4% one brother, for 17% two brothers, for 6.9% three or more brothers. Twenty-six per cent of the women had no male family member at the front.[13]

In the statistics about the demographic development between 1914 and 1918, we find information regarding the conscription of men required to do military service and their high rate of mortality – 1.9 million military persons died in the war[14] (see Table 11).[15]

A direct consequence of male conscription was the clear drop in the number of people getting married. The pre-war marriage rate was approximately 8 per 1,000 inhabitants for a single year. This rate dropped roughly 50% during the war and only rose again in 1919 and 1920, but then well over the pre-war rate.[16] It is estimated that, including Alsace-Lorraine, 870,000 fewer marriages were performed because of the war; 82% of this loss, however, was made up in the first two years after the end of casualties. In August 1914, there were 80,226 marriage ceremonies. This represented a rather large increase in comparison to the 32,978 performed in the August of the previous year and was due to the fact that many conscripts chose to marry earlier than planned in light of their pending military service. The number of marriages began to fall conclusively in September 1914, sinking to half the number that had previously been performed in this month. These developments ran parallel in the German states and in the German Empire as a whole; the only differences that were revealed were between agricultural areas on the one hand and city and industrial areas on the other. In cities and industrial regions, the marriage rate reached its lowest point somewhat later than in agricultural areas, but was still

Table 11. Population Growth in the German
Empire, 1913–1919

a = Sum total   b = per 1,000 inhabitants

Year	Marriages 1		Births* 2	
	a	b	a	b
1913	513,283	7.7	1,894,598	28.3
1914	460,608	6.8	1,874,389	27.7
1915	278,208	4.1	1,425,596	21.0
1916	279,076	4.1	1,062,287	15.7
1917**	308,446	4.7	939,938	14.4
1918**	352,543	5.4	956,251	14.7
1919***	844,339	13.4	1,299,404	20.7

Year	Deaths* 3		Surplus of 2 compared to 3 4	
	a	b	a	b
1913	1,060,798	15.8	833,800	12.5
1914	1,347,103	19.9	527,286	7.8
1915	1,493,470	22.0	-67,874	-1.0
1916	1,330,857	19.7	-268,570	-4.0
1917**	1,373,253	21.0	-433,315	-6.6
1918**	1,635,913	25.2	-679,662	-10.5
1919***	1,017,284	16.2	282,120	4.5

* Including stillborns.
** Excluding Alsace-Lorraine.
*** Excluding the section of the Posen province that was ceded to Poland.
Source: *Bewegung der Bevölkerung in den Jahren 1914–1919*, Statistik des Deutschen Reiches 276 (Berlin, 1922), III.

somewhat higher than the lowest point that was reached there. This was connected to the fact that, of the draftees who were "reclaimed" to work in the war industry, more lived in industrial and urban areas than in the country.

The fall in the number of marriages was actually much more pronounced than we can discern from the marriage rate. If we apply the number of weddings per year to those individuals over 15 who were unmarried instead of to the entire population, then the fall in the number of marriages proves to be more distinct, and its incipient increase from 1917 less so. Whereas, in 1913, there were 76.6 marriages per 10,000 of the total population (index = 100), the corresponding number for 1915 sank to 41.0 (index = 53.5), increasing again by 1918 to 54.2 (index = 70.8). Calculated per 10,000 of unmarried individuals, the number of marriages thus came to 252.2 in 1913 (index = 100), dropped to 127.0 in 1916 (index = 50.4) and then reached 156.2 in 1918 (index = 61.5).

Statistics regarding the number of war weddings, i.e. those marriage ceremonies that were concluded either earlier than the public wedding announcement required by law or completely without it because of the war, are not available for the entire Reich. Such statistics do exist for Hamburg, however. There, war weddings made up 77% of all marriages performed in August 1914, 43% of those in September 1914, 40% of those in October 1914, 44% of those in November 1914, 49.5% of those in December 1914, 55% of those in 1915, 46% of those in 1916, 39% of those in 1917 and 34% of those in 1918.[17] The fall in the number of marriages is most highly reflected in the female population, since the number of younger unmarried men was starkly reduced through casualties at the front. If we compare the proportion of married to single women in 1913 and 1918, we discover a great increase in the number of single women for 1918 in comparison to an equally marked reduction in that of married women. In 1913, there were 7.9 million single women, or 347 per 1,000 of the female population over 15; whereas, in 1918, that figure came to 9.2 million, or 386 per 1,000 of the female population over 15. In contrast, the number of married women stood at 12.1 million in 1913 (533 per 1,000 of the female population over 15) and had sunk to 11.4 million by 1918 (479 per 1,000 of the female population over 15).

Closely connected to these transformations was the change in the proportional relationship of the sexes. In 1910, the number of women had only slightly exceeded that of men by 52,000. In 1919, there were close on 2.2 million more women than men, whereby the numerical difference in the age groups between 20 and 30 was especially pronounced. It would be correct if we called this altered proportion of the sexes a "decimation of men;" it has been and continues to be discussed primarily as a "surplus of women," however. In some respects, this term must have corresponded fairly closely to how women themselves perceived the situation. As one Munich woman formulated it in a letter she wrote at the beginning of 1917: "Maybe they are going to strangle us, so we don't need absolutely anything [to eat]. There are too many women, even if it's only a few thousand."[18]

Another important consequence of the war for marriages was the increase in the average marriage age. Commented another female letter-writer from Munich in March 1917, "Think, dear Mini, now I'm going into my 28th year of life. Thus, soon an old maid. One has the war to thank for that, too."[19]

Before the onset of the war, the average marriage age had remained relatively constant since 1901, when statistics began to be kept. For men, it was 28.9 in 1901 and 29.0 in 1913, and for women, 25.8 and 25.7, respectively. From 1914 to 1918, the average marriage age increased by 2.2 years for men and 1.4 for women. This meant that the age difference in marriages increased as well. Before the war, the difference was, on average, 3.3 years; whereas, in 1918, it was 4.1 If the rise in the average marriage age refers to a war-necessitated postponement of marriages, then men's increased age at the time of their marriage points to the fact that older men replaced the fallen young. In this, the age of men and women marrying for the first time increased less dramatically than the age at the time of marriage *per se*. In 1918, single men engaged to be married were, with 28.7 years, on average 1.2 year older than those in 1913 and the single women, with 25.8 years, 1.4 years older. That the marriage age *per se* rose even more can be explained by the fact that widows and widowers remarried in increasing numbers.

Not unexpectedly, the number of newborns receded considerably between 1914 and 1918 (see Table 11). The decline by roughly 20,000 between 1913 and 1914 still corresponded to the "normal" peacetime development since 1900. In 1915, however, already 450,000 fewer newborns were recorded, in 1916 another 363,000 fewer than in 1915, and in 1917 still approximately 100,000 fewer than in 1916. Only from 1917 to 1918 did the numbers increase slightly again by 17,000. And in 1919, 400,000 more babies were born than in the last year of the war. In summary, the drop between 1914 and 1918 amounted to a statistical loss of 2.2 million newborns.[20] Corresponding to the first wave of draft calls, the first indications of a decline in the birthrate came in April and May 1915: Compared to the April of the previous year, there were 12,000 fewer babies born in this month and in May already 50,000 fewer. As we have seen with marriages, developments in the various German states paralleled those in the Empire as a whole; there was also a noticeable difference between the cities and the countryside, but this time the other way round: In industrial centers, the birth rate dropped faster than in rural areas – reaching its lowest point in 1917, whereas this occurred one year later in the countryside – and the minimum was mostly lower than in rural areas. In Berlin, for example, the lowest birthrate in 1917 was 46% of the rate in 1913, in Saxonia 41% and in Hamburg 43%. In the rural areas of Eastern Prussia, on the other hand, the lowest point was reached in 1918 with 56% of the rate in 1913, in Western Prussia 52.5%, in Pomerania 51% and in Mecklenburg-Schwerin 62%. The fact that more marriages but fewer births occurred in the cities in comparison to the countryside might be explained by the widespread use of birth control or abortion in urban areas.[21]

The rise in the number of illegitimate children during the war (10% of all newborns before the war, 13% during the war)[22] must, however, be qualified. This figure corresponded to the altered proportion of married to unmarried women, which changed from 100:85 in 1913, to 100:106 in 1917 and even 100:113 in 1918. If we relate the number of legitimate children to that of married women and the number of illegitimate children to that of unmarried women of between 15 and 50 years and thereby calculate the marital and nonmarital fertility rates (i.e. the number of newborns allotted to every 1,000 women between 15 and 50; see Table 12), then we can observe that the number of illegitimate children dropped more dramatically than that of legitimate children. This development, too, especially considering the relative frequency of non- and extramarital relationships, may be attributed to the increasing ability and willingness to use birth control or to get an abortion. The index of marital fertility (1913 = 100) reached its wartime lowpoint in 1917 with 52.4, while that of nonmarital fertility (1913 = 100) dropped to 50.9 in the same year. In 1918, the rate of nonmarital fertility surpassed that of marital fertility.

The changed proportion of married to unmarried women is also the reason why the overall fertility rate in the war dropped more than both the marital and nonmarital fertility rate. If the aforementioned proportion had remained the same throughout

Table 12. General, Marital and Nonmarital Fertility Rates in
the German Empire, 1913–1918

General Fertility Rates

Year	Women between 15 and 50 years of age	Total number of births	General fertility rate	Rate of measure-ment
1913	17,143,045	1,894,598	110.5	100.0
1914	17,411,280	1,874,389	107.7	97.4
1915	17,684,226	1,425,596	80.6	72.9
1916	17,962,584	1,062,287	59.1	53.5
1917*	17,722,633	939,938	53.0	48.0
1918*	17,937,140	956,251	53.3	48.2

Marital Fertility Rates

Year	Married women between 15 and 50 years of age	Number of legitimate births	Marital fertility rate	Rate of measure-ment
1913	9,265,913	1,710,621	184.6	100.0
1914	9,340,953	1,690,475	181.0	98.0
1915	9,231,342	1,266,174	137.2	74.3
1916	9,024,061	944,610	104.7	56.7
1917*	8,600,876	831,605	96.7	52.4
1918*	8,427,125	830,998	98.6	53.4

Nonmarital Fertility Rates

Year	Unmarried women between 15 and 50 years of age	Number of illegitimate births	Nonmarital fertility rate	Rate of measure-ment
1913	7,877,132	183,977	23.4	100.0
1914	8,070,327	183,914	22.8	97.6
1915	8,452,884	159,422	18.9	80.7
1916	8,938,523	117,677	13.2	56.4
1917*	9,121,757	108,333	11.9	50.9
1918*	9,510,015	125,253	13.2	56.4

* German Reich excluding Alsace-Lorraine.
Source: Same as Table 11, page XXXV.

the war, the overall fertility rate would have lain between the marital and nonmarital fertility rates.

Via statistics, we can also apprehend the changes that the war induced in family structures by analyzing wartime family households and their composition. The 1916 census for Bavaria provides relevant information for such an endeavor.[23] The Bavarian statistics reveal an increase in the number of households in comparison to 1910, with a simultaneous decrease in the number of persons belonging to a household who actually lived there. The reason for this lies in the growth in single households, i.e. single persons with their own apartment and household budget. What is particularly conspicuous here is the increase in the number of women living alone. For every 1,000 women in Bavaria in 1910, 960.0 lived in family households, 22.8 in institutional households and 17.2 in single households. In 1916, the number of women living in family households had dropped to 950.6, whereas the number of women living in institutional households had increased slightly to 23.3 and of those in single households markedly to 26.1. In the majority of cases, this rise pertained to childless "war wives" or widows whose sons had been conscripted. A certain portion of women living alone was also probably made up of female war workers. As another investigation in Bavaria revealed, of the almost 91,000 women working in the Bavarian war industry, 32% lived in 1917 in their own apartments and about 16% as subletters. Roughly 50% lived with parents and relatives.[24]

Taken in its entirety, the demographic data about the change in the family during the war reveals a picture of deficit. Many families were separated for the duration of the war, fewer marriages were entered into and fewer children were brought into the world. Although this picture conveys essential information about the situation of the family in the war, it remains incomplete. It leaves unanswered the question of whether or not changes in the separate areas of familial reproduction occurred, in spite of, or perhaps because of, the decline in its overall performance – changes that provide important information for an examination of wartime family life and those aspects of human coexistence that, due to the war situation, were no longer realizable within the framework of the family. It is clear that such an inquiry into the changes in child-rearing, sexuality, the emotional relationship between family members, etc. rapidly pushes to the limits what can be ascertained from sources. The questions are, however, too central to women's and families' situation during the war for us not at least to try to find an answer to them, however fragmentary. In what follows, I will therefore attempt to determine what changes occurred in the areas of sexuality, the emotional relationship of separated spouses, child-rearing and adolescent socialization, as well as in the pertinent direct or indirect social-policy efforts to regulate these areas. It is my contention that it was exactly this decline in the reproductive functions of the family caused by the war, in other words the separation of many families, the decline in the birth and marriage rates and the increase in the number of women who no longer lived either with a husband or other family members outlined above, that moved those aspects of human coexistence previously situated in the context of the family into the arena of public interest, where they were then defined as symptoms of a crisis affecting the entire society.

All three problem areas of the family's wartime reproduction had one thing in common. In each, actual structural changes caused by the war situation intersected with how these changes were perceived by the authorities, social politicians and others, on the one hand, and by the women and men living through them, on the other. And it was especially the contradictory and even irreconcilable nature of these clashing perceptions that turned the realm of the family in the First World War into a problem.

Sexuality

The removal of sexuality from the separated marriages of conscripted soldiers represented, in terms both of its extent and of its duration, a mass phenomenon heretofore unknown. The consequence of extramarital sexuality was dramatized by its close relationship to the idiosyncracies of a belligerent society. In various regards, these idiosyncracies turned the sexual conduct of military and civilian persons into a matter of national importance: The sexual conduct of an army of millions of soldiers currently single because of the war and its possible health consequences were inseparable from the problem of "toughening up the army," or of its "being undermined." On the other hand, the sexuality of the female civilian population was a subject of particular interest due to the feared repercussions it would have on morale at the front. This was especially true for "war wives," i.e. the wives of conscripted soldiers, and for German women who had relationships with prisoners of war or foreign workers.[25] In addition, there was an increased attentiveness, fed by population-policy considerations, in political, public health and journalistic circles: It was feared that the decimating effect, which high losses on the front and the decline in the birthrate had already wrought on the next generation of potential soldiers, would be increased even further by the spread of venereal disease, due to the changed sexual conduct of the population during the war.

Because of how they were perceived by authorities and social hygienists, the forms sexuality took during the war initiated a discussion about how these changes in behavior, understood as aberrations, and their consequences could be regulated. Both the connotation of moral indecency and the treatment of the subject under the guise of regulation were at the same time cause and consequence of the fact that the discussion, while addressing the overall manifestations of wartime sexuality, was summarized under the term "prostitution." What was taken to be characteristic of "prostitution" under the conditions of war was that the so-called "secret" or "wild prostitution" increased in comparison to the controlled, legal prostitution of women registered with the vice squad (*Sittenpolizei*).[26] This official interpretation of the development should be used with care, however, since it would be more correct to view the relative drop in controlled prostitution – the clientele of which had, for the most part, been conscripted – as its export to occupied territories. Such prostitution was very prevalent behind the lines of the Western and Eastern Fronts, where it partly occurred in regulated form, in separate bordellos for officers and soldiers. The military administration declared that it could not determine the location of "these institutions;" as it said on record, "This institution exists against the intention of the highest military authority. Remedial action would be taken immediately, if the army administration learned of exact details."[27] However, every participant in the war knew "that prostitution behind the lines had not only blossomed, but was extensively tolerated, even supported, by the military authorities, in order to relax the troops in sexual respects and thereby to boost their morale after all the depressing impressions in the trenches."[28]

Brussels was the center of prostitution in the rear of the Western Front. Alice Salomon, who, as an employee of the War Office, worked for a time in Brussels, gave this report of Brussels prostitution in her autobiography: "There were also brothels under German control and pressure was put on local women to keep them operating. The best hotels, where the officers stayed, were not dissimilar to those institutions."[29]

Prostitutes were recruited either from women in occupied foreign countries or from German women who had followed their clients.[30] This fact, as well as sexuality, was not problematized as such, but rather for the threat it posed to army and population policies. Infection with venereal disease, which was carried by prostitutes, could render numerous men unfit for military service and for fathering children. The military administration tried to counteract the spread of venereal disease in the army[31] and its subsequent transfer to the German civilian population by instructing soldiers accordingly and then providing them with prophylactics. Efforts were made to reduce the number of prostitutes in occupied territories. For example, Belgian women were given contracts, financed by state insurance agencies and the Wartime Committee for Warm Underclothes in Berlin (*Kriegs-ausschuß für warme Unterkleidung in Berlin*), to manufacture wool articles for German troops on the Western Front, through which, one hoped "to keep some women away from prostitution, into whose arms hunger and misery had often pushed them."[32] These efforts, however, could not have any widespread impact as long as the overall distress of the resident population persisted. Therefore, appropriate instruction for soldiers, as a drafted carpenter on the Eastern Front described in a letter to his wife:

> Once again, some of us contracted venereal disease and were punished for it. Now, we got instructions on behavior from the doctor. He counseled abstinence as the only safe remedy, because supposedly all the women are infected here. Anyone who wants to have sexual intercourse anyway has to go to the typing pool or guard post and get a free carton with ointment and a vial for injections. He has to use this before he has sex. As soon as he returns, he has to report immediately to the guard office at any time of day or night for treatment after the fact. Those who don't do this will be punished. He also told us that the medication costs 2.50 marks for each individual case, in order to show us what value the state puts on these matters.[33]

The showing of an anti-venereal disease film, made during the war to educate lower-ranking members of the army, was later banned because the authorities believed that its portrayal of the sexual corruptness of the upper classes would incite class hatred. The general implementation of prophylactic measures came up against specific difficulties, however. For one, women were often disgruntled about the way in which men were advised. As the representative of the Imperial Insurance Agency for White-Collar Employees (*Reichsversicherungsanstalt für Angestellte*) commented at a meeting about venereal disease called by the Imperial Insurance Office (*Reichsversicherungsamt*) in November 1915, many women had "taken it badly that the soldiers were supplied with prophylactics from the military administration. They perceived it as an invitation to adultery."[34] Additionally, in its provision of soldiers with prophylactics, the military, as a rule, expressly avoided the more effective, mechanical prophylactics, above all condoms, and relied entirely on chemical means. "The precise reasons, not to be discussed here," that one representative of the War Ministry put down as the cause of this decision[35] are probably to be found in population-policy considerations: Condoms and other mechanical prophylactics against venereal disease were normally condemned by the state, church and population policy makers because of their contraceptive effect, which is clearly why the military bureaucracy did not want to allow their use to spread throughout the entire German army.[36] A clear impediment to the prevention of venereal disease was that the identity of interest between soldiers and military administration, requisite for attaining this goal, in this instance often did not exist. Again and again, soldiers and conscripts preferred to contract an illness in the "house of shame" than to die on the "field of honor."[37] This particular aspect of prostitutes' work was considered subversive to the fighting capability of the army and earned these women, who complied with the specific increase in demand and were already waiting at the station for army trains transporting soldiers on leave,[38] the suspicion that they were "possibly, female persons working for enemy agents" who were "contriving to damage our soldier material in such a way."[39]

The military and civil authorities awaited demobilization with particular apprehension, since it entailed the return of countless infected soldiers to the homeland. Already in the first half of 1915, they began to consider how this social ill could be managed. Among other considerations, it was planned that all military personnel to be discharged would be examined for venereal disease at the end of the war. In 1918, however, as demobilization, against all expectation, took an uncontrolled course and the majority of soldiers discharged themselves, such plans could not be put into practice. The spread of venereal disease was, however, by no means a problem that only concerned the military. Since the beginning of the war, venereal disease had been increasing throughout the Reich as well, making inroads into rural areas and social classes that had previously proved less susceptible to the illness.[40] Its prevalence among the civilian population and soldiers remaining in the German homeland was so high that some political, military and medical observers were inclined to think that the homeland was more dangerous for these soldiers than they were to it.[41] According to the unanimous opinion of all observers, the rise in venereal disease infection was caused by the increase in extramarital sexual intercourse. This was acknowledged, for one, for the soldiers stationed in the German homeland: "During the war, a number of General Commands maintained that, in order to improve morale among the soldiers, the laxest attention to the necessary demands of morality and hygiene was permitted."[42]

The relationships that were often formed between military men in the German homeland and the female population were not only highly unwelcome for moral or prophylactic reasons, but also for political ones. In the course of the war, these relationships contributed to the fact that soldiers sympathized with the demonstrations and unrest they were deployed to combat and in which primarily women took part.[43] The greatest source of venereal disease proved to be the increase in so-called "secret prostitution," however. The number of women who were apprehended as "secret prostitutes" and subsequently found to be infected with venereal disease grew throughout the war.[44] In 1914 in the cities of Barmen, Elberfeld and Düsseldorf, of the 506 women arrested for being prostitutes, 133 had venereal disease, whereas, of the 1,020 women apprehended in the same cities in 1918, 315 were infected.[45]

As we have seen, the sources that assert a wartime decline in controlled prostitution need to be qualified, since this decrease was most likely due to the transfer of this activity from regional centers in Germany to areas behind the lines. Similarly, we also need to interpret the source findings about an increase in "secret prostitution" with care. When the sources speak of a rise in "secret prostitution," we find, upon closer analysis, that they actually mean two completely heterogeneous things. Firstly, they refer to the increase in the number of women who, because of their material distress as unemployed workers or as wives or daughters of conscripted soldiers, earned their living totally or in part as prostitutes, but evaded vice-squad registration in the process.[46] Secondly, these words were frequently used to describe the generally criticized increase in nonmarital relationships between men and women. For the most part, as reported from Aachen, "foolishness in connection with the general loosening of morals [was] the cause of the scope of secret prostitution, facts that fill us with horror for the future."[47] Wives of conscripted soldiers, "who, through intercourse with other men, seek to satisfy their yearning for pleasure and entertainment"[48] and who "keep a lover"[49] were thus regarded as "secret prostitutes" in this sense.

Contrary to the usual definition of prostitution as "a sexual offense of commercial nature," here the commercial aspect was often missing. As the Essen police headquarters wrote to the chairman of the Düsseldorf Regional Council (*Regierungspräsident*): "For the most part, the decisive factor here certainly seems to be pure foolishness and hedonism, so that the sexual offense was pursued more for its own sake than as a means to an end."[50]

The sexual behavior of the entire civilian population became the object of police intervention and surveillance. Proceeding from the principle that "almost all women who abandon themselves to extramarital sexual intercourse are infected with venereal disease,"[51] which practically postulated that every relationship between men and women not sanctioned by law could lead to an offense against epidemic laws, authorities developed a comprehensive catalogue of measures for observing sexual behavior. The intensification of vice-squad surveillance not only extended to women registered with the police but also to those women whose "commercial sexual offense" could not be proven.[52] In Dresden, the vice squad was instructed to "proceed in a ruthless manner against all female persons who are in any way suspected of commercial sexual offense, and against all men who become a nuisance because they pursue and speak to women in the evening and at night." All persons apprehended in accordance with these stipulations were held in custody overnight.[53] Similarly, the Deputy General Command of the 20th Army Corps Allenstein decreed on 12 May 1916: "Female persons having sexual intercourse with a number of men in the course of one month – be it for compensation of any kind or not – are to be placed under the supervision of the vice squad after two unsuccessful warnings from the police."[54]

The authorities paid special attention to the moral conduct of "war wives."[55] Although the authorities avoided such comprehensive measures as subjecting "wives" to vice-squad surveillance,[56] they nevertheless attempted to influence these women's willingness and opportunities for marital infidelity. The Prussian War Ministry, for example, encouraged the dissemination of appropriate propaganda pamphlets:

> There are war wives who have forgotten about love, loyalty, discipline and morals and throw themselves at strange men, while their own husbands are starving and bleeding on the front; war wives who run to the dance and toward pleasure, who spend the money their husbands send them, dress up like prostitutes or eat like gourmets while their own unkempt children are roaming the streets with torn socks and clothes.[57]

For these reasons, boarding houses were also to be placed under greater supervision.[58] The actual boarding of young, primarily single workers diminished of its own accord because of conscription, which fell particularly hard on men in this age group. Concomitantly, the demand for such accommodation rose, especially in centers of war-industry production, due to the influx of armaments workers. This conjunction of availability and demand, in addition to the increased number of women who, because of the war, lived alone, gave the authorities cause for concern.

Vigorous action was certain in all cases where it became known that a relationship existed between a German woman, whether married or not, and a prisoner of war. Corresponding to the high number of imprisoned foreign soldiers working in industry and agriculture, such relationships were very common, in spite of their prosecution by the authorities and their ostracism in published opinion.[59] As one woman from the region of Lauf in Bavaria wrote to her husband, also a prisoner of war, in the middle of 1918:

> if the war isn't over soon, [so] that the men come home, then the women of Röthenbach will be going crazy with the imprisoned French frogs[60] and Belgian Russians everyday one hears more fooling around, the pri[soners] come into the wo[men's] apartment at night so that one hears things going on, maybe you all do it the same way. . .

The gendarmerie station of Röthenbach confirmed this woman's observations. As it reported on 23 August 1918: "the prisoners of war and Belgians in the Grünthal factory, in spite of the ban, frequently find the opportunity to make contact with the female workers employed there, usually outside of the factory after work, and there have already been several female workers who have been indicted and judicially punished because of this."[61]

Relationships between prisoners of war deployed as agricultural labor and the female farmers who hired them or their female agricultural workers were particularly widespread and, in individual cases, less conspicuous. As the District Office (*Bezirksamt*) of Aichach wrote to the Munich Regional Council (*Regierungspräsidium*) in August 1918:

> With regards to the forbidden contact between female persons and prisoners, it must unfortunately be said that this is increasing rather than decreasing, although many female persons have already been punished because of this, and it is also well known among the population in the country. Almost every week one or two persons (farm girls, farmers' daughters, as well as farmers' wives) are indicted because of illegal sexual intercourse with prisoners. But this usually concerns cases in which the sexual intercourse has not gone unpunished. The remaining cases frequently do not become known.

The authorities believed that, because of their often longer-term accommodation on individual farms and because of their invaluable contribution to running them, prisoners of war carried an uncontrollable emotional weight with rural women.[62]

> [F]emale persons who resisted the temptation for a long time [have], as a result of the long, continual coexistence with the same prisoners, ultimately given in [to it].[63]

> Because of their indispensability, prisoners of war gradually develop into a serious danger. In many cases, they not only have control over

the family, in whose service they are, but also, to a certain extent, over the community . . ., and one can hardly write anymore about the reception they often receive from women and girls.[64]

Where possible, prisoners of war who had been assigned to women's farms as labor were removed from the employ of these women, who showed so "little feeling for national consciousness" and "often absolutely no feeling of shame."[65]

In order to end these relationships in cities and the country, which were as frequent as they were undesired, military and civil authorities also called in the media. Under such head-lines as "In the Stocks" or "Dishonored Women," the authorities allowed articles to be inserted into regional and national daily newspapers in which the full name and place of residence of women who had exchanged letters with prisoners of war, blown them kisses or otherwise "shown an unpatriotic cast of mind" by "dragging their national dignity through the dirt" with prisoners of war were printed.[66] Even the names and places of residence of women who had committed suicide after their relationship to a prisoner of war had become known were made public in this way.[67] Women who were brought to trial because of such a relationship were dealt with in a similar fashion. The formal legal grounds for such trials was the law concerning the state of siege. This law granted military commanders extensive authority in domestic areas, which they could then use to issue corresponding ordinances. The Supreme Command's December 1916 edict in the Marches, for example, was summarized in the *Deutsche Tageszeitung* as follows: "The population has to restrict its intercourse with prisoners of war to those absolutely necessary tasks that arise from their work, accommodation and feeding. Every other overture beyond this, in particular such intercourse of female persons with prisoners of war that offends good morals, is forbidden."[68] On this legal basis, women were sentenced to fines and prison terms because of their sexual relations with prisoners of war, but also because of their letter-writing and "coquetterie." These women, as well, had to reckon with their names being published by the media.

There were also other voices raised about this issue, voices which expressed their doubts about the denunciation of women. In January 1915, "one German woman" wrote the following to the Munich Deputy General Command:

Whoever has the opportunity occasionally to read letters from the military forces gets the impression that our soldiers in France have made friends more than is necessary with the local population – in particular with the female population – and that, in the German-occupied territories, they are having a great time. Couldn't it be changed here? When a pair of geese tried to get closer to prisoners, the newspapers devoted column-long reports to them, so that one was led to believe that there was a danger of it spreading. Every reasonable woman condemns the tasteless conduct of these individuals, but one would also expect somewhat more national pride from our warriors, because, first of all, the scope and the consequences of possible alliances are much more serious in enemy territory and, secondly, there is the just demand that, what is said for one half of the German nation, should also be law for the other.[69]

A number of sources suggest that the different degree of sexual permissiveness granted to men and women began to garner general attention primarily in connection with the constantly circulating rumors about the dissolute life behind the lines. In November 1916, a postmaster's widow sent a newspaper article about women who were sentenced because of their relationships with prisoners of war, to the Munich Deputy General Command, to which she added the following comments: "From uneducated women [In both cases, the convicted women were maids who were working in a brickworks.], one demands dignified behavior with respect to the enemy, while behind the front, many officers amuse themselves with French whores and champagne and the privates are angry about it."[70]

Published opinion, however, remained uncompromising on the question of "unpatriotic women" throughout the entire war. Even in October 1918, as some German states granted partial amnesty to "war wives" and widows for small offenses, the *Berliner Tageblatt* proposed that "war wives'" illegal intercourse with prisoners of war be exempt from this action.[71]

Emotional Relationships

The emotional relationships of family members represents one of the most interesting areas concerning the war-induced changes in the family. It is also, however, one of the most difficult to grasp from existing material. Socio-historical sources and literary treatments of the First World War provide only a few clues about this aspect of wartime family life, but they are, fortunately, quite informative.

The war's most manifest and severe intrusion into familial relationships existed in the gaps it ripped open. There was hardly any family that was spared the grief of the death of one, if not more, of its male members on the front,[72] and the harsh conditions of life during the war ensured that the civilian population's encounters with suffering and death also multiplied. Public discourse only permitted coping with this mass dying in the patriotic, stylized form of the rolls of the fallen ("They died for the Fatherland", "They fell on the field of honor") and grieving only with the attribute "proud." Consequently, women and families were more or less left to work through this experience themselves. In terms of the "work of grieving," there was also, as it were, a division of labor for society as a whole: If the killing was socially organized, then the dying and the survivors' processing of death remained "private affairs." The churches, as traditional and – as a result of the war – reinvigorated sites for coping with death in an institutionalized form, did offer a certain refuge. The number of people leaving the church in Berlin, for instance, receded at the end of 1914, and that of people rejoining the church and participating in the services actually increased. Obviously, some of those immediately affected by death found comfort in religion.[73] It was exactly these representatives of the church, however, who often functioned as "messengers of death."[74] The longer the war lasted and the higher the losses climbed, the less receptive women and families became to religious messages. In his autobiographically inspired novel *Jahrgang 1902*, Ernst Glaeser – through the eyes of a 13- to 14-year-old boy – reflects on the changing ability to accept announcements of death:

> In those days, the pastors were the messengers of death, and when one of them turned a corner with his pastoral steps, the heartbeat of the street stood still for a few minutes just to restart forcefully and with relief if one saw the pastor vanish behind the neighbor's door. I had observed this often and then pressed myself with friends against the door which the pastor had entered, listened breathlessly until my lips were dry and then always heard the same: an outcry, a rumble as if a table or a picture from a wall were falling, then a wimper, interrupted by the monotonous words of the pastor that sounded like a leaking oil drum.

Recently, however, we had heard laughter instead of the outcry, sometimes a curse, and had then seen the pastor leaving the house in a hurry and biting his lips. Once even, in a workers' neighborhood, a mother, shortly after the visit of the pastor announcing the death of her only son, had doused the hardwood floors with petroleum and had set fire to her small house, whose ash-white smoke stood in the October afternoon like pieces of cotton saturated with carbolic acid in a suddenly open wound. The woman was saved against her will and after a heavy struggle by a handful of 60-year-old men. She bit and struck out at them. Since, with unsuspected strength, she had kicked an old country policeman in the stomach after he had carried her by force out of her burning living room, she was sentenced, four weeks after her forced rescue, by a court of law, whose jurors and judges had a combined age of two hundred, to five months in prison because she had resisted government authority. There, she finally managed to hang herself. Her neighbors said that she was crazy, since she could have had a nice pension now that her son was dead.

All of this happened in 1916, as a German army was fighting at Verdun, as the list of losses grew overnight . . ."[75]

The authorities had to acknowledge that – in addition to the population's difficulties in feeding itself – it was the death announcements that exacerbated its mood.[76] At the same time, the population resented the further draft calls.[77] This was also true of the draftees themselves, who were reinforced in their dissatisfaction by their wives, as the senior member of the Garrison Kaufbeuren observed: "Furthermore, it is women who are encouraging their husbands in those ideas [of not wanting to be drafted]. Women go as far as visiting the head of the office to remonstrate with him forcefully. It is also they who complain the loudest! Hence, all the letters that they write and about which others complain."[78]

"All the letters" that women wrote to the conscripted members of their families and especially the letters that wives wrote to their husbands refer to the residue to which the marital and familial emotional relationships of spouses and families separated by the war had been distilled, namely the exchange of letters. In many cases this correspondence became, sometimes for months and years, the almost exclusive medium for what Peter L. Berger and others have defined as the essential socio-psychological aspect of the family's reproductive functions: the "hardening and stabilization of common objective reality," i.e. the construction of reality through marital communication.[79] This correspondence simultaneously became a source, feared by the authorities, of subversive constructions of reality. The reason for this was that the accounts of their life situations that soldiers sent home, as well as those that "war wives" wrote to their husbands, were, in the great majority, distinguished by bitter criticism of the conditions that had been created by the war. As the 11th Bavarian Infantry Division wrote to the Bavarian War Ministry in December 1915:

> From numerous letters of women to their husbands on the battlefield . . . I gather that, many times, a totally unrestrained yearning for peace and the men's return home is expressed in these letters and that the families' domestic conditions are surely often described in a very exaggerated manner in the blackest colors, so that, through this, an ardent desire for the conclusion of the war and homecoming is also awakened in the men on the battlefield.[80]

In this case, we can exclude a possible exaggeration on the part of the observers. The authorities selected a sample of letters, based on their representivity, from the correspondence between German prisoners of war in France and Italy and the populations of the German states of Bavaria, Saxony and Silesia that passed through Railroad Post Office I in Munich. These letters were filled with exceedingly drastic descriptions of the civilian population's everyday life under the conditions of war, descriptions which could no longer be brought into accord with the authorities' exhortations to "hold out."[81] As one woman from Saxony, for example, wrote to her imprisoned husband on 5 March 1917:

> The want keeps growing because we don't have anything anymore. Now I want to describe my distress to you, the prospects for me and my family. It looks bad for us because we don't have anything to eat, no turnips, no carrots and we can get absolutely nothing more . . . For fourteen days, I have gotten lunch from the soup kitchen and only two portions and then five people are fed from it. For me, I feel really shitty because I'm so hungry the whole day. Should this nonsense not come to an end soon, or one has to pick up a gun oneself, so that at least the children may escape from the world, because I can't bear this misery any longer. I really feel sorry for the poor children, they look at me nonstop and I can't do anything to help them.[82]

Such "letters of lament" from women did not remain, as official observers ascertained, "without affect on the men."[83] By putting massive pressure on women ("Learn to control yourselves!"), the civil and, above all, military authorities went to great lengths to eliminate the negative influence they had on their male relatives at the front. Despite these efforts, however, the reality that family members constructed among themselves through letters, together with other unofficial channels of communication, proved to be stronger; the picture of war communicated through this correspondence gained more and more acceptance.

The above description, of course, portrays only one aspect of marital-familial relationships under the conditions of war. Another facet was the mutual alienation caused by the long separation and the different life situations. The correspondence also provides us with information about this. As one married man wrote in March 1917, for example:

I can't be like so many fathers of families that we've got here. Only yesterday we had a case where one gambled away 160 marks in an evening, when his wife had just written to him that she and their children were starving and freezing – and he even had the gall to read that letter to us . . . with the comment that he was freezing as well. There are more who commit similar mockeries but, fortunately, the majority is of another mind. And even though the war creates a state of brutalization, a man's heart should not be alienated from his family, and he should not mock his family in front of his comrades. God prevent me from such meanness.[84]

Another example can be found in Bernard von Brentano's novel *Theodor Chindler*, where he has an officer on leave tell his wife:

When you see me spending my vacation with you, you really see a man on vacation, meaning a man who is not where he belongs when he is with you but a man who is where he doesn't belong. In general, no one pays enough attention to this fact! Furthermore, you are seeing a man who is only in charge of the REST of his energy that has remained for what we call private life (or called once, to be more exact). To put it more simply, one could say that I am a good officer (*entre nous:* one should not refer to "officers" anymore, but to "civil servants of defense and attack"), but a bad husband, and this is the truth. In the official propaganda aimed at the people, this truth does not exist. But if you look at me and all my friends, all men, really, whom you can look at a little more closely, you will see that this truth does indeed exist . . . [85]

We also find evidence of this alienation from the female perspective. A grocer from Hamburg, for example, described the same problem in a letter she wrote to her drafted husband in October 1914. As she wrote: "Tell me, whom are you going to fight with when you return home? All of you will be so used to the belligerent life that you won't be able to appreciate the peace at home anymore."[86]

The alienation between wife and husband mirrored, on the familial level, the division of belligerent society as a whole into the irreconcilable, everyday and relevant structures of the "front" on the one hand and the "home front" on the other. Furthermore, this alienation probably represented the most crucial consequence of the war in terms of the change it wrought on marital and familial relationships, the influence of which was felt long after the war had ended. During the war, however, and considered from a "bird's-eye perspective," it was precisely the effort to keep the marital-familial communication nexus "functioning" that represented a crucial aspect of the interrelation of the family and society as a whole, an interrelation that, not only in this instance, was increasingly characterized by collisions of interest and perception as the war progressed.

Child-Rearing and Adolescent Socialization

Of all the reproductive functions of the family, it was those that concerned children and adolescents that received the greatest amount of public attention. Public discussion and political and bureaucratic regulatory efforts concentrated primarily on two problem areas connected with this issue: the sinking birthrate, on the one hand, and the difficulty of socializing adolescents in incomplete families, on the other. There were several reasons for the increased attention that the various governments, civil authorities, the military, socio-political organizations and social hygienists devoted to these questions. First of all, both the declining birthrate and the incompleteness of numerous families were, in the end, direct consequences of the separation of spouses decreed by the state through military conscription. Thus, the assertion of the state's responsibility for these areas, just as for the material provision of war families, was obvious. In addition, regarding these two questions, a context of problematization had already developed before the war. Questions concerning the decline in the birthrate had constituted a central theme in the German Empire's discourse on population policy, and the creation of a state youth policy had also sparked lively debate. During the war, these two contexts of discussion gained an entirely new relevance. The high losses on the front and the drastic decline in the birthrate bestowed population-policy considerations and pro-natal strategies with an incomparably high urgency and thereby rendered the First World War the decisive impetus for the state's expanding its catalogue of functions to permanently include population-policy measures. Simultaneously, those aspects of adolescents' wartime political, moral and economic behavior that were considered problematic were taken by civil and military bureaucracies as an opportunity to formulate, via decrees, a state youth policy, which was to compensate for the family's deficits in socialization. Common to both the generative and the socializing aspects of wartime familial reproduction was the increased tendency of the state to try and exert control here. Differences revealed themselves, however, in terms of the measures through which this goal of increased state control was to be achieved. The adolescent policy, under the authority of the military governments and perhaps not altogether independent of the military's greater willingness to intervene administratively, was primarily put into practice through measures of direct control, including forced savings, curfews and a ban on going to the cinema. By comparison, the pro-natal population policy, in so far as it left the level of public or bureaucratic problem-solving and was translated into concrete measures, was based mainly on socio-political regulations and institutions. Communities, not the military governments, were the implementing organs in this instance. By initially taking on this task as a patriotic duty of honor, they further extended their functions in the socio-political realm, a development that had already started before the war.

Already in the pre-First World War German Empire, working-class families had frequently limited the number of children they had through contraception or abortion. An investigation of 100 of his married female patients who stemmed from working-class circles conducted between 1911 and 1913[87] by the dermatologist Max Marcuse revealed that 41 of these women had had one or more abortions; the highest number given was 10. Of the 59 women who reported that they had not had an abortion, a good

30 used contraceptive methods of the most varied nature. Of all the study participants, roughly 65 used birth control. As Marcuse ascertained, the women who had had an abortion lacked, without exception, any sense of their wrongdoing: "The 'women of the people' do not comprehend that [their abortion] is a punishable offense. They know it as something everyday, 'necessary', and thus do not even remotely see it as something immoral. [The men] apparently also found 'nothing wrong with it,' . . . but [were] aware, in comparison to their wives, of the punishability and illegality."[88]

The difficult material and emotional conditions of life during the war reinforced this trend to use birth control. As the chairman of the Düsseldorf Regional Council acknowledged in 1917, the wartime decline in the birthrate resulted "not only in natural ways from the disruption of familial circumstances through the war . . ., but also [because] . . . the artificial prevention of birth, carried over from peacetime, [is being] continued, if not partially increasing, in marriages, despite the gravity of the time and the extensive war losses."[89]

The absolute number of criminal convictions because of abortion did indeed fall during the war. The trend of this development, however, remained far behind the decline in the birthrate and thus points to a relative increase in the number of abortions.[90] Married women in particular were more frequently convicted because of abortion than previously. In 1910, for every 100,000 single women, 4.0 were sentenced due to abortion; in 1916, the number was also 4.0. For every 100,000 married women, 2.7 were convicted in 1910; in 1916, by comparison, the number was 4.5.[91] Population statistics, as well, indicate an increase in the use of contraceptives. These reveal, for one, the specific city–country contrast in the development of the population: In cities, there were more marriages but fewer births than in the country, which allows one to assume that birth control was practiced more frequently in urban than in rural regions.[92] Secondly, the change in the birth order provides a clue here: In 1917, the number of first-borns no longer fell at the same rate as that of second-borns, third-borns, etc., whereas, between 1914 and 1916, the number of first-borns in particular dropped off.[93] The population's growing rejection of the war gave this widespread willingness to use birth control, already existing before the war, a thoroughly political component. As one inhabitant of Lower

Bavaria counseled another individual, of unknown identity, in March 1917: "Also with kids, you should leave yourselves time, because, now, child-rearing isn't so brilliant anymore. These days, people aren't as dumb as before. Otherwise, they could immediately start a war again and then there would be plenty of people to shoot."[94]

The historian Karl Alexander von Müller, in his capacity as an observer of the people, summarized the feelings of resentment that were widespread in Bavaria in 1916 as follows:

> The entire war is a swindle. The people are being made to believe something. The top brass has agreed among itself that the ordinary people have to die. Therefore, we will think hard about bringing children into this world in the future and raising them with care only so that the top brass can slaughter them for no reason . . .. The people are too much for them, that's why they have started the war. We already know this, and we are going to lose it in any case.[95]

The will to limit the number of births was not only notorious on the "home front," but also among the soldiers. During their home leave, which had in part been granted out of population-policy motives, soliders paid the most attention to not fulfilling the state's pro-natal intentions for their leave.[96] The conditions of the war also did their part in raising the population's level of knowledge about this issue. The intensification of unofficial structures of communication – for men, the conversations in the trenches and in the compartments of leave-bound trains, and for women, the frequent and long waiting in line at shops and at public offices – provided individuals with the opportunity to trade information about contraceptives and abortion.[97]

Against the background of the massive loss of human life caused by the war, politicians and specialists found the population's inadequate willingness to propagate so alarming that the discussion about countermeasures was already institutionally established by the end of 1915.[98] Representatives of the Prussian ministries and population-policy experts met fifteen times in the Prussian Ministry of the Interior (*preußisches Innenministerium*) between 1915 and 1917 to discuss ways to raise the birthrate. The catalogue of measures considered ran the gamut from restricting prostitution and combating venereal disease to improving the legal protection of mothers and infants to introducing a special tax on single and childless women.[99] No practical results came of these comprehensive deliberations during the war, however, partly because of the Prussian Finance Ministry's (*preußisches Finanzministerium*) stubborn resistance to any measure that would lead to increased costs.[100] Various drafts of a law to combat venereal disease and the "prevention of birth" were laid before the Reichstag in February 1918, but none was passed during the war. Far-reaching effects were not to be expected, however, either from these proposals or from other instruments of population policy. As long as the drop in the birthrate was a consequence of marital separation, then, apart from the introduction of home leave for front soldiers, it would have evaded the grasp of pro-natal policies anyway. And in so far as this decline was a result of a change in opinion on the part of ever larger segments of the population, which increasingly considered themselves as actors instead of passive factors in the decision of how many children were born, then pro-natal deliberations were bound to fail because they only targeted quasi-automatic obstacles to population increases, such as venereal disease and infant mortality, instead of focusing on the much more important changes in attitudes.

In terms of the "racial hygienic" variation of contemporary population policy, which did not seek to foster all births, but only those that were "racially" valuable, the attitude of the authorities was somewhat contradictory. Where "racial hygienic" proposals collided with general pro-natal policies, as with the question of eugenically indicated abortion, then the authorities unambiguously decided against the "race" and in favor of the greater number, in that they stood, on principle, by their rejection of pregnancy terminations. But the German authorities rejected eugenic ideas no more than other countries' governments and authorities[101] did. When a petition in the Bundesrat demanded that certificates of "fitness for marriage" be introduced, the Imperial Office of the Interior (*Reichsamt des Inneren*) did indeed reject it. This, however, was not decided on principle, but only because, to the Imperial Office of the Interior, "it still seems too early to introduce certificates of fitness for marriage in light of the population's underdeveloped comprehension of the need for racial hygiene." It also counseled rejection because the measure would be very costly. The Imperial Office of the Interior stated, however, that the petition's intention "to educate the population to take health aspects into greater consideration when marrying should be recognized and supported where possible."[102]

Because of the state's tight resources, wartime pro-natal considerations were only put into socio-political practice when other institutions were willing to finance them. Health-insurance companies and communities took over this task. The Prussian minister of the interior (*preußischer Innenminister*) reconfirmed in May 1918 that "infant welfare," for example, "just like other charitable efforts, does not belong to the tasks of the state, but rather to the realm of communal associations, in so far as one is unsuccessful in soliciting the preferable private labor of love in the form of endowments and associational work." At the most, he said, the state could be involved in paying subsidies for the maintenance of infant welfare institutions, and then only with the provision that municipalities and districts contribute "in appropriate amounts" to these costs.[103] Consequently, the actual expansion of a social policy motivated by population-policy objectives occurred on the administrative level of the municipality, the district and the region, in so far as these entities, under the difficult financial and staff conditions of war, could afford it. This concentration on matters of population policy – above all, mother and infant welfare, the supervision of infant nutrition, nursery schools and household and child-care courses for women and girls were augmented – became a defining characteristic of local and regional social policy during the war. Wartime social policy was characterized furthermore by a close interrelation of official and private charitable endeavors. Even before the war, efforts had been made to centralize and unify the often uncoordinated, simultaneous social welfare activities of the government and organizations on the district and municipal level. Because of the increase in social work activities during the war, the task of coordinating them became particularly urgent, a task which was primarily tackled under the leadership of women's organizations of various sympathies. A centralization and coordination of private and official social policy was not achieved during the war, however. In the first half of the war, this was obstructed by the founding of numerous relief organizations, whose work was uncoordinated and consequently overlapping; in the second half, as a result of a shortage of money and personnel, private welfare efforts dwindled in comparison to the increasingly bureaucratized social work of the communities.[104] These socio-political measures were primarily financed through municipal monies, donation drives and subsidies from state insurance agencies and the imperial government.

The Reich, communities and health-insurance companies[105] also bore the costs of the most well-known population- and family-policy measure of the war, the so-called Imperial Maternity Benefit (*Reichswochenhilfe*). This was the practical application of the state's mother- and infant-welfare efforts in the First World War. The state's protection of women who had just given birth had started with the implementation of health insurance for workers in 1883.[106] Since the amount of such aid was limited to only half, at the most three-quarters, of the average daily wage, however, it never proved to be a source of financial security for women who had recently given birth. The amendment to the health insurance law of 1903 increased the lying-in benefit to seven weeks; the imperial insurance order of 1913 eventually extended this to eight weeks, in addition to passing a series of optional benefits for women before and after childbirth. These included, among other benefits, free midwife services and obstetrics, and a monetary allowance for women who nursed their own children, equaling up to half the amount of sickpay and lasting until the end of the twelfth week after the delivery. The majority of health-insurance companies, however, proceeded very hesitantly with these optional benefits. Consequently, up to the beginning of the war, the material provision for such women was not even approximately sufficient, a state of affairs which led the social hygienist Alfons Fischer to pose the following rhetorical question: "No horse and cattle breeder works a pregnant mare or cow, he leads it to the best place in the pasture and offers it plenty of feed. But how do things stand for women during pregnancy and shortly after delivery?"[107]

On 3 December 1914, the Bundesrat passed an ordinance that granted women who had just given birth and whose husbands had been conscripted and, prior to conscription, health-insured a maternity benefit from imperial funds. This benefit consisted of 25 marks towards the cost of delivery, 1 mark of maternity pay a day for eight weeks, a contribution to midwife and doctor's services and an allowance of 50 pfennigs a day for mothers who nursed their own children, to continue until the end of the twelfth week. This decree obligated health-insurance companies to reimburse women for these services who were themselves members of a health-insurance program. At the insistence of social politicians, the municipalities and the Congress of German Cities (*Deutscher Städtetag*),[108] the circle of women entitled to assistance was extended, via the Bundesrat decree of 23 April 1915 and based on need, to include "war wives" whose husbands had not been insured prior to their conscription, as well as the illegitimate children of soldiers who received Family Aid. In Bavaria, for example, by 1 August 1917, the Reich and the health-insurance companies had paid 4,855,557 marks in maternity pay, 2,413,797 marks in nursing mothers' allowances, 1,929,097 marks in contributions to delivery costs and 46,062 marks in subsidies for difficult pregnancies. The Reich bore 6,610,160 of the total 9,244,513 marks, and the health-insurance companies the rest.[109]

As we have seen, pro-natal social policy was both expanded and intensified during the war. There were, however, also factors that hindered this consolidation. The above-mentioned lack of resources on the part of the Reich, which reserved its tight funds for the direct costs of the war, was only one of the many effective countertendencies. The shortage of doctors, which assumed alarming proportions during the war, was another far-reaching obstacle to social policy because it led in some instances to acutely insufficient medical care for newborns and small children and because it hindered the expansion of personnel in welfare departments and similar institutions. In this context, the consequences of the Imperial Maternity Benefit, the showpiece of the social policy aimed at increasing the birthrate and ameliorating the care for mothers and newborns, should not be overestimated. The financial support women received through the Imperial Maternity Benefit did tangibly alleviate their material situation. But the efficiency of these benefits can be questioned when we consider the nursing premium, which was the pro-natal centerpiece of the maternity benefit and which was supposed to bring about a socio-political breakthrough in terms of encouraging more women to nurse their children themselves.[110] Apart from the shortage of cow's milk, it was the financial incentive of the nursing premium that observers credited for women's increased tendency to nurse their own children.[111] Furthermore, the intensified supervision of women who received the nursing premium – effected by regular visits to their homes and by their obligation to keep in close contact with welfare agencies – was welcomed as a very positive side-effect. But, on the whole, this "divining rod . . ., which lured much more (mother's) milk than all appeals to the love of the Fatherland,"[112] failed: because of their malnutrition during the war, mothers could not produce their own milk.[113]

The authorities also deemed the family's role in adolescent socialization to be a "problem area," a characterization which was not new, but which received new emphasis during the war. As before the war,[114] bureaucrats, the military and social reformers did not focus their attention on adolescents *per se*, but on male, working-class adolescents. Neither adolescent males of other social classes nor adolescent (working-class) females[115] were defined to any similar extent as problematic groups of the population. This fixation of youth policy on the target group of male working-class adolescents only increased during the war, particularly since the specific conditions of wartime society led to the fact that it was precisely this social group that occupied two neuralgic positions in society. Firstly, it was with recruits from their ranks that the insatiable need for men on the front was to be met. Secondly, these youths simultaneously represented, on the economic level, an important source of labor for the war industry and an important source of income for the family. It was in these two specific capacities that working-class youths attracted special attention, especially from the military governments, during the war. The military governments were the driving force behind contemporary youth policy, which was a policy of control. Somewhat overstated, under their aegis, youth policy lost its component of protecting male adolescents – worker-protection regulations for adolescents, for example, which had constituted an essential part of state youth welfare before the war, were *de facto* repealed, as those for female workers had been – and became instead a policy of protecting society from male working-class youths. Many military commanders, youth welfare officers and a section of the civil bureaucracy considered these individuals, particularly those in larger cities, to be "wayward" (*verwahrlost*),[116] a diagnosis for which there seemed to be more than enough proof. Especially conspicuous was the rise in adolescent criminality. In 1913, a total of 54,155 adolescents were convicted under the law in the German Empire, 46,034 of whom were male. By 1918, this figure had risen to 99,493, of whom 84,840 were male (see Table 13).

As was the case with general wartime criminality, the largest share of these offenses were those against property (see Table 14). In comparison to the statistics of 1913, crimes against property committed by adolescents between the years of 15 and 18 had climbed by 57.4%. This rise was less than the enormous 82.2% increase in the property crimes committed by 18- to 50-year-old women during the war, but was clearly higher than the 14.6% increase in such crimes among men over 50 – a group which offers itself for comparison because its ranks were not thinned by conscription. Although this aspect of the "waywardness" (*Verwahrlosung*) of male adolescents was clearly related to the overall material impoverishment during the war, the "waywardness" debate primarily revolved around the perception of youths as the "noveaux riches" of wartime society.

The frequent complaints about the "unruliness" of adolescent workers, which was generally attributed to their high wages, their indispensability as workers and the absence of any disciplining institutions, such as fathers, teachers or policemen, all point more or less explicitly in one direction, namely to the fact that contemporary observers believed that the war had brought a dangerous shift in the power relationship between the generations. Corresponding objections to a changed power relationship between the sexes never even approximately reached the same

Table 13. Adolescent Convictions in the German Empire, 1913–1920

Year	Total		Male		Female	
	Absolute	Index	Absolute	Index	Absolute	Index
1913	54,155	100.0	46,034	100.0	8,121	100.0
1914	46,940	84.6	39,734	86.3	7,206	88.7
1915	63,126	116.6	54,108	117.5	9,018	111.0
1916	80,399	148.5	69,463	150.9	10,936	134.7
1917	95,651	176.6	82,047	178.2	13,604	168.0
1918	99,493	183.7	84,840	184.3	14,653	180.4
1919	64,619	119.3	55,447	120.4	9,172	113.0
1920	91,170	168.4	78,621	170.8	12,549	154.5

Source: Liepmann, M. *Krieg und Kriminalität in Deutschland*, Wirtschafts- und Sozialgeschichte des Weltkriegs, German series (Stuttgart et al., 1930), 98.

intensity. During the war, countless representatives of the older generation were convinced that the conflict between the generations was now being waged in the open:

> The adolescent workers had obviously realized that, despite forming a minority, they were crucial to the continued functioning of the factories. This led to a self-consciousness on the part of male adolescents which, on the one hand, positively influenced their behavior and raised their feeling of responsibility, but which, on the other hand, degenerated into unruliness and recalcitrance, tolerated no reprimands and finally led to the break or dissolution of the work contract for insignificant reasons. Where domestic discipline, which the mother could often not sustain in the father's absence, was lacking, adolescents began, in time, to run wild. This state of affairs led to many serious and miserable excesses. The high wartime wages, which had risen to twice the peacetime levels, tempted adolescents to make wasteful and worrisome expenditure.[117]

Adolescents' high earnings supposedly "found their way into bars and tobacco stores, or they were wasted in the company of female colleagues."[118] Many complaints about the "waywardness" of adolescents were more or less explicitly related to their sexual behavior: Closer attention was paid to the function of male adolescents as customers of prostitutes. Furthermore, male adolescents seemed to be spending more time with female acquaintances in such places as bars and cinemas. They could only afford to visit such places because of their wartime earnings, but it was precisely this behavior that attracted more public

Table 14. Criminality on the Home Front, 1913 and 1917

Crimes and Misdemeanors against:	Adolescents 15–18 years old		Women 18–50 years old		Men over 50	
	1913	1917	1913	1917	1913	1917
The State and Public Order	1,981	2,625	12,528	5,504	7,926	2,665
War Ordinances	–	89	–	22,672	–	13,627
Property	26,572	41,833	28,836	54,362	12,414	14,277
Rate of Increase for Crimes Against Property	57.4%		82.2%		14.6%	

Source: Same as Table 13, p. 100.

attention than if they had frequented places with their respective partners that were free of charge.[119]

A further problem, which also entered into the contemporary "waywardness" debate, was the fact that schools could only partially perform their function of socialization during the war. One contributing factor was the cancellation of classes, which resulted from the conscription of many teachers and the army administration's frequent use of classrooms. Secondly, "absenteeism" from school, especially among juvenile males, was very pronounced during the war. In elementary schools in Cologne, for example, unexcused absences represented 15% of all the absences of schoolboys in 1914; by 1917, this figure had increased to 48%. In 1918, unexcused absences, which made up 41% of the cases, lay somewhat below the highest rate. For those Cologne schoolgirls who missed school in 1914, 12% of the absences were unexcused; in 1917, 31% were.[120]

Without a doubt, these problems of the life situation and behavior of (male) adolescents, especially from the working class, reflect aspects of the social reality of war. Both the increase in juvenile delinquency and the employment of adolescents in, at least nominally, better-paid jobs were indeed facts of wartime, as was the declining importance of schools as sites of socialization. How far these observations reflected real changes of wartime as opposed to the pre-war period, or signalized an alteration in the perception of observers, is a question that cannot be conclusively answered within the scope of this study. There is evidence, however, that the contemporary assessments of adolescent conspicuousness were, on the one hand, prompted by war-related phenomena, but that, on the other, these judgments stemmed largely from problems in perception. Firstly, an above-average increase in adolescent criminality could already be observed before the war.[121] Secondly, although male adolescents' high wartime wages represented one of the most-cited reasons for the diagnosis of "waywardness" and provided the opportunity for introducing the most radical measure in this area, namely forced savings for adolescents, the number of male adolescents who left school to become wage-earners clearly dropped among pupils receiving state assistance in several regions.[122] It is questionable, therefore, to what extent the above-mentioned indicators of deviant juvenile behavior permit us to accept the diagnosis of contemporary observers that working-class youths' "waywardness" was increasing during the war. In view of the notorious lack of conceptual clarity, which, apart from its negative connotations, is the only thing that characterizes the term "waywardness," its use – both during the First World War and today – seems to be determined much more by the *valuation* of social conditions than by their concrete manifest-ation.[123] The essential significance of the term "waywardness," therefore, lies less in its power of definition than in its power to direct action. The characterization of societal groups or social structures as "wayward" delimits them as the objects of bureaucratic and socio-political measures.

How much this characterization is determined by judgment and perception instead of by empiricism, can be seen, in the case of the First World War, in the fact that the family was made the center, i.e. the cause as well as the main arena, of the "way-wardness" of working-class youths. In other words, the authorities singled out exactly that social arena that exhibited no direct connection with the documented phenomena of juvenile behavior that were considered proof of this "waywardness." The military and civil authorities' identification of the family, or more exactly, its deficiency in socialization resulting from the father's conscription, as both the cause of adolescent "waywardness" and its principle victim, could not have been based on any knowledge of the internal conditions of these incomplete, working-class families: Neither they nor the social politicians had any insight into the family's socialization processes. Nor, for that matter, do we; in this instance, therefore, we only have the exterior view of familial socialization to use as a material basis for our socio-historical analysis.

What seems to have been even more crucial to this con-temporary discussion, however, were the perceptions and fears that resulted from the war-induced dissolution of count-less families. The erosion of the patriarchal model of the family through the conscription of men and the consequent anxiety this development generated appear to have contributed significantly to the perception that juvenile behavior was in a state of crisis. Consequently, the worsening of the "generation gap" between 1914 and 1918 simultaneously constituted a weakening of the societal paradigm "family." Because, as it was said, "the strict hand of the father, as well as the influence of any elder male persons, is lacking to preserve in them [adolescents] a modesty appropriate for their age,"[124] and mothers were deemed "too weak and without sufficient influence" to intervene in their children's lifestyle,[125] the military and civil bureaucracies sought for means by which they could officially take over the "paternal" socialization functions in the family. In this context, they developed an exceedingly patriarchal model of the family, which painted a shocking picture of the fatherless working-class family as a combat zone between delinquent juvenile tyrants and their weak, if not slovenly, mothers.

The youth policy of the civil authorities that developed out of this authoritarian perception of working-class adolescents and families in the war consisted primarily of building up socio-political institutions. Their efforts included, for example, placing youth-welfare workers in each administrative district and establishing government youth offices (*Jugendämter*). The youth policy of the military bureaucracy, which was primarily pushed forward by the Deputy General Commands, followed another path. The military, with the backing of the civil authorities of the Reich as well as lower offices, favored direct access to the lifestyles of male adolescents. This end was served by the "youth army" (*Jugendwehr*), a paramilitary organization that had already been established before the war and was to make adolescents who were not yet obligated for military service physically and mentally fit for later duty. Immediately after the outbreak of the war, military authorities strove to expand the "youth army;" at the beginning of 1915, it recruited approximately 600,000 youths on a voluntary basis, half of whom were in the targeted age group.[126] At the beginning of the war, participation in the activities of the "youth army" was more active. Once, however, the population recognized that what it had believed was the obligatory character of this institution was, in fact, a mistake, participation, much to the regret of the authorities, dropped off.[127] As the Landrat of the district of Soligen ascertained at the beginning of 1916: "Unfortunately, a share of our adolescents are deliberately staying away from these organizations, and, in many cases, it is precisely those individuals who need such supervision the most."[128]

The population reacted to this state-military intervention in the socialization of male adolescents, in part, with a lack of interest, but also with a certain mistrust. Evidence of this can be found in the rumors, which constantly resurfaced during the second half of the war, about the deployment of the "youth army" to combat food riots, where it was said that "youth army" members had shot at their own parents.[129]

In addition to the "youth army," numerous general commands issued announcements – the so-called "youth decrees" (*Jugenderlasse*) – in which adolescents were forbidden to smoke in public places, frequent bars after 9 p.m. and to go to the movies, among other things, and had to adhere to an evening curfew.

The High Command in the Marches (*Oberkommando in den Marken*) pursued another, much more radical path in order to control adolescents' consumption. The decree about mandatory savings for adolescents, issued on 18 March 1916, stipulated that all male and female juveniles, until the end of their eighteenth year, could spend only 18 marks from their weekly wages and a third of their remaining earnings. The employer was to deposit the rest of the wages in the bank, to which adolescents, or their families, only had access if they obtained the consent of the aldermen (*Gemeindevorstand*) of their place of residence.[130] Communities were only supposed to permit such withdrawals if the adolescents in question could prove that they had concrete support obligations to pay. This obvious transference of parental authority for child-rearing was intentional. As the High Command explained, it had consciously ignored parents in the forced-savings regulation because the fathers had usually been drafted and the mothers "[are], in all too many cases, now completely dependent on their adolescent children economically; they consequently would not dare, even if the wages were paid to them directly, to withhold something from the adolescents, otherwise these would leave the family and move out of town."[131]

The resulting administrative time and energy this regulation cost communities was considerable, even after each such "permission to pay" (*Auszahlungserlaubnis*) had been granted for two to three months. The Guardianship Office (*Vormundschaftsamt*) of the city of Berlin had approximately 1,000 applications for the release of savings a week to process; after roughly half a year, the rate of such withdrawals lay between 13% and 15%. The High Command deemed its savings measure a success: Adolescents' migration to areas that did not have forced savings could only be observed in a few cases and complaints about juvenile "lack of discipline" had decreased since the ordinance's inception.

Neither this positive assessment of the forced-savings policy nor the definition of the situation that the High Command had used to justify its introduction found much resonance in its administrative region. A "storm of indignation" swept through the ranks of Berlin adolescents affected by the measure and of their parents. As the War Administration of Neukölln, an administrative district of Berlin, reported:

They could not or did not want to understand the good intentions of the ordinance. A large number believed that they could only vent their feelings by applying to the responsible municipal department for the payment of the saved share of their wages belligerently and with all sorts of excuses, and frequently adopting a tone of voice that tested the level-headedness of the civil servants and the assistant workers entrusted with this work. Because of the deduction from their wages, many young people refused to work in order to then demand the payment of this saved sum; some also moved to regions where such a restriction did not exist. In any case, every way was attempted to oppose the effects of this ordinance.[132]

By 1 April 1918, 104,000 forced-savings accounts had been established in the city of Berlin, in which 8¾ million marks had been deposited and approximately 3½ million marks later withdrawn. Thirty-three thousand "savers" filed claims for the release of their funds and 23,000 accounts were consequently closed. The payment of the rest of these saved wages occurred after the end of the war.[133]

The repetition of this experiment in other areas of the German Empire likewise led to unrest among the population and to the migration of adolescents to other regions.[134] The Deputy General Command of the Army Corps Hannover had to repeal its own forced-savings decree after, in Braunschweig in May 1916, organized adolescents of the Left, with the benevolent support of wide circles of the population and, not least, of demonstrating women, violently agitated against the decree for several days, thereby rendering the city ungovernable.[135] In several army-corps-governed areas, the policy of forced savings never proceeded beyond the planning stages. In the Deputy General Command Altona's region, compulsory savings were never introduced because, according to the reports of the Factory Inspectorate, extremely high wages for adolescents had proved to be the exception and not the rule, and the reputation of juveniles was consequently not deemed to be so bad.[136] As the Factory

Inspectorate of the Koblenz administrative region explained in retrospect, forced savings, "for which, in the last two years of the war, there would have been more than sufficient grounds, but which, because of the general recalcitrance of the younger workers, could not have been implemented,"[137] were not introduced in the Army Corps Koblenz's sector.

The Deputy General Command Münster had originally preferred another variation for its sector, which also included the Rhineland-Westphalia industrial region. At the end of 1915, it suggested that the area's civil administrations, which were subordinate to it, adopt procedures in spirit with Paragraph 119a of the Imperial Trade Regulations (*Reichsgewerbeordnung*). This paragraph provided for the possibility of paying the wages of individuals under 21 years of age to their parents instead of to them. Corresponding local statutes were consequently introduced in several communities and districts, but hardly ever used. Neither the respective civil administrations nor employers approved of such action. They objected that the execution of these measures was complicated or even impossible, that adolescents living outside their parents' home were in need of their full wages, that their work morale would be endangered, that their migration into other areas would be encouraged, and that it was simply unavoidable that irresponsible or unscrupulous parents might also squander these wages. Furthermore, the administrations and employers emphasized that the measures concerned essentially qualified as an extraordinary law for industrial workers, which was not desirable for the current *Burgfrieden*.

After the High Command in the Marches, the Army Corps Hannover and the Army Corps Kassel had, in the meantime, enacted forced-savings decrees, the Army Corps Münster followed suit and sent the draft of a similar decree – combined with a ban on adolescent migration – to the chairmen of the respective regional councils. Forced savings were supposed to begin on 1 June 1916. But the majority of the civil administrations objected to this plan. The chief chairman of the Regional Council (*Oberpräsident*) of Westphalia pointed out "that the undeniably strong excitability of the working-class population of the industrial area will be increased in the most undesirable manner by this measure, which deeply intrudes not only into the legal sphere of adolescents, but also into that of their relatives."[138]

Only ten days later, the Deputy General Command Münster communicated to the Prussian War Ministry that it would not enact any forced-savings measures. It justified its refusal by citing the difficulties involved in executing such a measure and by pointing to contemporary inflationary conditions. But since the Deputy General Command must have been aware of both these conditions well before the aforesaid ten days, we can assume that the riots in Braunschweig about the imminent forced-savings decree had contributed to its change of opinion.

The next initiative was generated by the Prussian War Ministry, which recommended in September 1916 that, to prevent adolescents from migrating, the same or similar measures to the ones in Berlin should be enacted everywhere. This prompted another discussion about forced savings in the area of the Army Corps Münster. The reactions of the trade-union representatives who participated in this last round of discussions justified earlier fears that labor organizations would consider the introduction of compulsory savings for adolescents as a violation of the *Burgfrieden*. In the first place, the trade-union representatives rejected the definition of the situation that lay at the heart of forced-savings plans. Instead, they insisted that wages were not as high as commonly assumed, that adolescents were not unruly and that their families were not helpless against them. Furthermore, they pointed out that, because of the overall increase in food prices, families were dependent on their adolescents' income. Secondly, the trade unionists also rejected the patriarchal social philosophy that informed the forced-savings idea. This was not only true for the Social-Democratic, but also for the Christian and Hirsch-Duncker trade-union representatives. In the discussion about this question that the chairman of the Düsseldorf Regional Council held with trade unionists on 20 October 1916, the representative of the Christian trade unions declared that forced savings interfered "too roughly with internal family relations." The Hirsch-Duncker trade unionist recommended that: "One should stop giving less-well-off circles the feeling that they always have to be taken by the hand and led and guided. One should leave the workforce in peace."[139]

A speaker for the Free Trade Unions expressed the suspicion that the state wanted to obtain additional money in this way – which was not altogether unfounded, after the High Command in the Marches had suggested that the adolescents' savings be used for war bonds. As he explained, he certainly believed "that the state needed money, but that one should not take the money from the families that live in the most dire want and misery."[140] Thereupon, the Deputy General Command Münster informed the Prussian War Ministry at the beginning of 1917 that, in the industrial region of Rhineland-Westphalia, there was no need for mandatory savings and that, instead, serious objections had been raised to it. Forced savings were consequently not introduced in this area.[141]

In order fully to understand the state's and the military's wartime youth policy, we need to consider this policy in connection with the image of the family that became virulent during the war. The authorities proceeded from an authoritarian, patriarchal view of the family, which allowed them to perceive working-class families as a deficient leftover group that was no longer able to perform its task of socialization. In these families, the authorities saw the conflict between adolescents and adults, which was no longer suppressed by paternal discipline, erupt, and believed that only state intervention could regulate it. Implicit in the contrary position taken by the trade unions was an image of the family that diverged from that held by the state, which emphasized intrafamilial harmony, analogous to class solidarity. For the following description of the production and consumption aspects of wartime family life, I have used a different conception of the working-class family in the First World War. It presents an antithesis to both images of the family described above and unites them in a synthesis of a completely different nature. In it, the authoritarian image of the family is negated in favor of a working unity of solidarity, and the trade union image in favor of a working unity of subversion. This vision of the wartime family found literary expression in Ernst Glaeser's novel *Jahrgang 1902*:

> Soon the women, waiting in gray lines in front of the stores, were talking more about the hunger of their children than about the death of their husbands. The war changed its sensations. A new front developed. It was held by the women. Against the entente of the military police and engaged inspectors. Every pound of butter obtained, every sack of potatoes happily salvaged in the night was celebrated in the family with the same enthusiasm as the victories of the armies two years ago . . . Actually, we [children] liked this change because it awakened our impulse for adventure. It was lovely and dangerous to sneak away from the farms with forbidden eggs, to dive

into the grass when a gendarme appeared, and to count the minutes by the beats of one's heart. It was wonderful and sublime to dupe this gendarme and, after a lucky run to victory, to be celebrated by one's mother as a hero . . .. Soon a conquered ham shook us more than the fall of Bucharest. And a *Malter*[142] of potatoes seemed more important to us than the capture of an English army in Meso-potamia.[143]

The Family in War II: Production and Consumption

In the previous description of the reproduction of working-class families during the First World War, we have seen the impact that the decline in the family's reproductive functions caused by the war had on both the individual family and the societal perception and treatment of the institution of the family. By way of analogy, in this section we will explore the changes in the family's functions with regard to the production and consumption of goods, and the consequences that the war-induced increase in the family's work to provide for itself had on both the individual family and society as a whole. We will examine the following questions within these parameters:

1 State policy with regard to the material provision of the family, in particular, that of monetary assistance for families.
2 The situation and activity of working women and families in procuring consumer goods (buying, trading, foraging and demonstrating); in conserving, caring for and preparing consumer goods (housework in a narrower sense); and in producing goods for personal use (raising small animals, growing food).
3 The interaction between the state's rationing and social policy and the "private" efforts women and families made to provide for themselves.

It is my contention that this interrelationship gained a mom-entum during the war of a completely new nature. On the one hand, the shortage of essential consumer goods led, particularly in the second half of the war, to a new role for the state and communities in ensuring the existence of individual families.[144] On the other, this shortage brought about a change in the means by which single women and families provided for their existence. These were, to a large degree, illegal and consequently riddled these women's and families' relationship to the state, as the specific authority responsible for the conditions of familial subsistence during the war, with conflict. As a result of the conflicting strategies adopted by the state and the communities, on one side, and by women and families, on the other, to combat it, this objective shortage of food led to chaos, which in turn shaped the attitude of a large section of the population and especially of women to authority. The system of food rationing implemented by the state and the communities allotted rations to the "normal consumer" that were under subsistence level; these rations did not, however, represent a guarantee for the receipt of this food, but rather, a ban on acquiring more than the allotted amount. The state system of distribution was consequently rendered ridiculous and led to the spectacle that the state, in its central aspects, was transformed in the eyes of its citizens from a rational institution into an insane one. An essential characteristic of the rational state, namely legality, which it standardizes and guarantees, no longer held true for the German Empire in the second half of the war.[145] The communities cheated the state, in that they invented phantom inhabitants in order to increase their share of the state's total distribution of rations. The state cheated the communities, in that it fixed maximum prices, which it then itself exceeded, and, particularly when buying for the army, competed against the communities for food, to their ultimate detriment. The farmers cheated the cities and state rationing, in that they kept their products for themselves or sold them on the black market. The urban population black-mailed city administrations, once they "learned" that hunger riots could produce sudden increases in food supplies (which the intimidated city administrations themselves often obtained through illicit trading). Larger companies provided their work-force with products from the black market. The state rationing program "forbade" these companies to do so, in that it promised to allot to them legally the food which they would otherwise obtain illegally. And the entire population, and especially women and children, poured into the countryside – supported by the Imperial Railway (*Reichsbahn*) through its helpful provision of "foraging trains" – in order to illegally buy food, to exchange it or, doubly illegally, to steal it. The carousel was perfect. The more extensive the illicit trading, the fewer the rations alloted by the state; the more deficient the state provisions, the more extensive the illicit trading. This reciprocal relationship was carried to extremes by the government's unwillingness to enforce its own laws and ordinances against illegal food procurement. Had the government enforced these laws and decrees, however, the provision of the population would have become a total catastrophe. Additionally, those "from below" denied the legitimacy of such government action so emphatically that the authorities considered the danger of popular resistance to such measures as too probable to dare their implementation. The state, in turn, gave in *de facto* to this way of looking at things in that it postulated norms that it claimed to uphold, while simultaneously neglecting to fully furnish a corresponding apparatus for their enforcement. The state thus abdicated at least the part of its claim to power that is legitimized by rationality – and this can be established not only analytically, but also empirically, namely in the eyes of contemporaries.

In the following section, I shall analyze the changed role of the state, on the one hand, and the behavior and strategies of women and families, on the other, with regard to the material provision of existence in war, as well as the pertinent patterns of perception "from above and below." I shall use two examples, which concern the two socio-economic realms of policy and behavior that constituted the most important parameters for the life of wage-earning families during the war: provision with money and provision with consumer goods.

Provision with Money: Family Aid and "War Wives"

The idea that it was "a self-evident duty of honor and an unconditional social requirement" as well as "military necessity"[146] to establish state provision for the families of conscripted soldiers beyond that of poor aid (*Armenunterstützung*) was an inheritance from the nineteenth century. This meant that its actualization and execution in the years 1914–1918 could be based on previous discussions, experiences and codifications. It meant, as well, that this family assistance, which unmistakably originated out of the political, economic and social conditions of the nineteenth century, was now applied to a war and a society for which it was not conceived. The birthmarks from the political conditions of the nineteenth century proved to be particularly enduring in the dualism of the Reich and the cities or districts, which lasted until the end of the war. This dualism, in turn, gained a momentum at this time that was to be particularly disastrous for those women and families who received Family Aid. The economic and social conditions of wartime society differed most decisively from those of the nineteenth century in the high degree of urbanization and thus in the greater number of individuals who were chiefly dependent on money income and who now, consequently, required financial support. In Berlin, for example, the number of applications for assistance during the war of 1870–1871 was 16,760, 15,671 of which were approved. By the end of 1914, in comparison, the number of approved aid applications had already risen to 81,264.[147]

The codification of Family Aid dated back to a Prussian law of 1850, which, in turn, was a side-effect of the events of 1848–1849.[148] Before then, the responsibility to provide for needy dependants of conscripted soldiers in Prussia lay solely with the communities; they determined the form, scope and execution of such assistance. The inadequacy of this arrangement was revealed in the partial mobilization of the territorial army (*Landwehr*) in 1839–1840. In order to remedy this, private aid organizations were founded with some financial support from the Prussian War Ministry in the individual districts of the territorial army battalions (*Landwehrbataillonsbezirke*). These organizations were assigned, as required, to look after the families of soldiers. By 1848, approximately two-thirds of the army-battalion districts had such organizations. Their activity, however, which was organized on a voluntary basis and neither standardized nor coordinated by a higher organization, also proved to be insufficient. Because the communities could not or did not want to pay such war support, and were not legally bound to provide certain minimum benefits, and because private welfare efforts were insufficient in scope to offer an actual remedy, countless families of conscripted soldiers remained inadequately provided for or completely without financial help. A Prussian law of 27 February 1850 ruled that administrative districts and free cities – as opposed to the more solvent communities – pay a minimum in financial aid to families of conscripts. A refund by the state was not planned; the districts and cities were supposed to raise the necessary means according to the proportion of their other contributions. Based upon proven need, the wives and children under 14 of conscripted reserve or territorial army troops were eligible to receive assistance. Siblings, relatives in ascending line and children over 14 could be included if they had already been supported by the draftee. In 1867, the law was applied to the North German Confederation (*Norddeutscher Bund*) and, in the following years, introduced in a series of southern German states. In 1868, it was altered to include the dependants of other categories of troops. In the wars of 1864 and 1866, the raising of the funds for Family Aid had been left up to the districts and the cities. After their financial assistance proved to be inadequate during the war of 1870–1871 and consequently had to be supplemented by private funds and state aid to the poor, the Reich, through a law of 4 December 1871, approved that those districts that lay within the states of the North German Confederation be reimbursed out of French war contributions for the minimum aid allowances they had paid. As a result of this law, the Reich transferred approximately 25 million marks to the individual states. It refused, however, to grant the districts' and states' demand that they also be reimbursed for those expenditures for Family Aid that went beyond the minimum allowance, which, in itself, had proved to be inadequate in the majority of cities and districts. The Reich justified its refusal by saying that it could not control whether the districts and cities had actually increased Family Aid only to the level of need, which was a condition of their activity. Here, one of the configurative problems that would be exacerbated in the First World War became obvious. The dualism between the responsibility of the Reich and that of the districts and cities made (against the letter of the law, which stipulated that the districts alleviate need) the minimum allowance the chosen target of the districts, because only this would possibly be reimbursed by the Reich.

The urging of the Prussian War Ministry to increase the assistance minimum and the necessity to bring the legislation into line with Article 58 of the imperial constitution, which stipulated that the Reich bear the costs of waging war, led, in the second half of the 1880s, to a new draft of the Family Aid law of 1850. This draft recognized the Reich's obligation, in principle, to reimburse this aid. The emphasis here, however, lay on the words "in principle." The Reich insisted that the extent and the amount of the remuneration, as well as the method of establishing these, be regulated through a special law after the end of the next war. This provisional arrangement was justified by the Reich's necessity to give priority to the direct costs of war and by its renewed refusal to issue the delivering agencies – the administrative bodies now responsible for this aid, which in Prussia were identical with the districts and the free cities – with *carte blanche*. The government wanted to reserve for itself the right to examine after the end of a war whether the administration of Family Aid through the delivering agencies – the Reich itself lacked the necessary administrative bodies to achieve this objective – was appropriate and not, because of the expectation of an automatic refund, too generous. After the imperial government also made it known that, in the event of an unfortunate end to a war, it would not even be able to guarantee its reimbursement of the minimum allowance, the Reichstag refused, in 1887, to accept this version of the law.

In the final form of the law, passed on 28 February 1888 and officially entitled "Law concerning the support of families of conscripted men," the Reich was obligated to reimburse minimum benefits, which was the job of the delivering agencies to provide; when this refund should occur, however, was to be arranged through a special law. The delivering agencies were also obligated to support dependants of conscripts beyond the minimum allowance, until the alleviation of their need. The most important changes to legal family assistance, as it was defined in 1888, were the increase in the minimum allowance and the further expansion of the circle of recipients. The dependants of men in the reserves (*Reserven*), militia, the replacement reserves (*Ersatzreserven*), the Home Guard and the navy, as well as those of men on leave and volunteers, were now entitled to receive financial aid. The definition of "eligible dependents" was extended to include a conscript's legitimate children under 15, his legally recognized illegitimate children and his relatives in ascending line and siblings, as well as his wife's relatives in ascending line and her children from a previous marriage – all these only if they had heretofore been supported by the conscripted man. Distant relatives, divorced wives and illegitimate children remained expressly exempt from this definition.

During the First World War, no fundamental changes were made to this legal and organizational basis of Family Aid. Through modifications in the level of support and the circle of those entitled to receive it, the imperial government attempted, however, to adapt the law to the changed conditions. First of all, the war-economy legislation of 4 August 1914 increased the minimum allowance from 6 to 9 marks in summer and from 9 to 12 in winter, as well as extending aid entitlement to include the dependents of nursing personnel and the illegitimate children of conscripts.[149] By the end of the war, the minimum allowance had been raised to 25 marks for wives and 15 marks for supported children, among others; the differentiation in the minimum for the summer and winter months was dropped. Successively, the dependants of cooks employed by the army, of men in the volunteer Motorized Corps (*freiwillige Motorkorps*), of soldiers who completed their period of service during the war, of conscripts who were interned in foreign countries or otherwise prevented from returning home, and those of wartime volunteers were taken up into the circle of individuals entitled to assistance. Former wives of conscripted soldiers who had been innocent with regard to the divorce and whom, consequently, these men had been required to support now had a legitimate claim to such aid, as did the conscript's parentless grandchildren, stepsiblings and stepchildren, foster parents and children, if they had previously been supported by him, as well as any illegitimate children, even those not fathered by the conscript, his wife had brought into the marriage.

During the war, Family Aid thus developed an unstoppable tendency toward universalization. Consequently, what was originally planned as special assistance for a clearly demarcated group of persons became an obligation on behalf of the state to support large sections of the wage-earning population, as well as those, such as individuals in trade, retail and agriculture, who were self-employed. Thus, after soldiers – particularly those who were competent only for garrison duty and therefore not deployed on the front – detailed to war production had refused on numerous occasions to be transferred to a factory because, as they argued, their dependants would thereby lose their Family Aid, these men received the difference between their wages and their Family Aid from war-welfare funds.[150] And those skilled workers who were called back from the front frequently also received Family Aid for a period of time as "money to tide them over."[151] The high number of longer-term conscripts and the reliance of the vast majority of their dependants on money income rendered more than one-sixth of the population in this way state pensioners during the course of the war. Already by the end of 1915, the number of families receiving government assistance was estimated at roughly 4 million, that of supported individuals at 11 million.[152] Proceeding from the results of the wartime population census of 5 December 1917, which put the German population at the end of 1917 at 62,615,275 persons and 14,850,186 households (including institutional households),[153] then the percentage of households receiving such financial assistance was almost one-third of the total number, and the percentage of such individuals a good one-sixth. This percentage was, towards the end of the war and particularly in the larger cities, considerably higher. At the beginning of 1918, 26.4% of the population in Düsseldorf and 28.5% of the population in Barmen received Family Aid,[154] over one-third of the households in Charlottenburg and half of those in Neukölln got assistance,[155] as did one-fourth to one-third of the population in Frankfurt-on-Main.[156]

The financial expenditure was correspondingly high. For the entire German Empire, the minimum allowances advanced by the delivering agencies amounted to 93.4 million marks in August 1915; in August 1916, the sum was 128.3 million marks,[157] which had increased to 130 million marks a month by November 1916.[158] In Prussia, over 4 billion marks were spent on Family-Aid minimums – exclusive of the additional expenditures of the delivering agencies – between August 1914 and October 1918 (see Table 15).

In comparison to these figures, the total state revenues of Prussia, collected from taxes and the running of the railways (pure proceeds), came to 6.2 billion marks for the period January 1914–December 1918.[159] Of Prussia's expenditure for minimum assistance, 331.3 million marks were apportioned to the administrative region of Düsseldorf and 307.6 million marks to the administrative region of Potsdam, which were the two regions in Prussia that had given out the greatest sums for minimum aid allowances.[160]

The additional benefits, beyond the minimum allowance, that the delivering agencies awarded to "war families" diverged greatly in amount. In mid-1915, the delivering agencies made a 35% contribution to imperial allowances; in Bavaria, this figure was 18%.[161] From place to place, the difference ranged from 0 to 100: Some, above all rural, districts did not pay anything; some large

Table 15. Monthly Expenditures for Family Aid (Minimum Allowances) in Prussia, 1914–1918

| | In Millions of Marks | | | | |
	1914	1915	1916	1917	1918
January		39.8	79.3	114.7	108.8
February		41.2	79.6	110.7	104.0
March		45.6	80.5	111.3	104.8
April		47.9	79.5	108.0	104.4
May		50.7	80.3	108.9	103.6
June		51.7	79.2	108.7	101.6
July		53.8	79.4	107.3	102.0
August	16.3	56.5	78.8	107.0	100.8
September	28.1	58.5	79.6	105.2	100.1
October	31.9	60.2	82.0	105.7	100.3
November	35.3	74.5	81.7	108.5	
December	38.6	80.2	131.5	117.7	
Total for 1914–1918: 4,166.3 million marks					

Source: ZStA Merseburg, Rep. 77, Tit. 332g, Nr. 27, Beiheft 3, Bd. 1-7 (rounded numbers; the total sum is my own calculation).

cities, at least at the beginning of the war, contributed 100% to the minimum allowance, contributions which do not necessarily seem to have increased in relation to the progressive increase in the minimum allowance during the course of the war. The rest of the cities and districts fell somewhere in between, predominantly on the lower half of the scale. By the end of February 1915, the city of Berlin, for example, with approximately 90,000 "war wives" receiving assistance, had paid an additional 8.5 million marks in city supplements (excluding rent subsidies) to the 8.6 million marks for minimum allowances. By comparison, in the Grand Duchy of Baden, where 10.25 million marks had been expended on Family Aid by the end of December 1914, only 2.26 million marks of this had gone to supplementary financial assistance.[162]

In many cases, the wartime financial support given by the state and communities was supplemented by larger companies and trade unions, which provided the dependants of their conscripted workers or members with additional benefits. These benefits decreased, however, with the duration of the war.

For many cities and districts, raising the means necessary to finance Family Aid, which represented the largest share of municipal welfare expenditures during the war,[163] developed into a financial and political high-wire act. The total, direct burden of the war, up to its conclusion, on the communities of the German Empire was, roughly estimated, 4 billion to 4.5 billion marks. The Reich contributed only a small part of this sum. At the end of 1914, and again at the end of 1915, the Reichstag approved a fund of 200 million marks to assist the communities in their wartime welfare work, an amount which was later increased. The German states received a monthly installment of 10 million marks at the beginning of the war – by the end, this sum was almost 48 million marks – which they could then divide among themselves and redirect to their respective communities. The communities used an estimated 80% of these means on Family Aid.

In view of the great expenditure made by communities to support "war families," this was anything but sufficient. The Reich's reimbursement of minimum allowances proceeded at a very sluggish pace and consequently could not provide a solution to the cities' financial problems. The first refund installment, paid out in 1916, covered only one-quarter of the delivering agencies' expenditures for minimum allowances made from the beginning of the war until 1 June 1916, and by the war's end, even financially weak cities, such as Barmen, could only credit a good half of the money the Empire owed them as "received." The numerous initiatives from cities and municipal associations as well as the Prussian government, which were intended to induce the Reich to repay the minimum allowances more quickly and completely during the war itself, failed because of the decisive opposition of the Imperial Office of the Treasury (*Reichsschatzamt*) and the imperial chancellor. They justified their rejection of these repayment requests with the absolute financial and political priority of military expenditure.[164] Even the promised reimbursement of the interest that the communities had to pay for the money they now had to acquire on the money market only occurred after the end of the war, as did the refund of the remaining minimum allowances. Thus, as the Prussian minister of the interior explained to the chairmen of the regional councils in the end of September, this state of affairs would unfortunately endure and the reimbursement of minimum allowances before the end of the war: "[is] not possible, in view of the obligation of the Reich's financial administration to have all available means ready to preserve the strike capability of the army. On the other hand, however, an interruption in Family Aid, upon whose regular progress rests the willingness to fight of those fathers facing the enemy, must not occur."[165]

The minister referred the communities to the money market in order to meet their financial need. There, however, the cities and districts did not have an easy time. Part of the reason for their difficulties lay in the fact that, before the war, they were already in relatively high debt.[166] In addition, the communities, in borrowing money on the money market, came into increasing competition with the Reich, which likewise covered part of its financial needs there. In this situation, the delivering agencies resorted to the most varied improvisations. Some succeeded in obtaining credit from regional insurance institutions; others used the opportunity, created for this purpose, to draw a three-month bill on the Prussian state, which they repeatedly prolonged, and still other delivering agencies transferred their claim to be reimbursed for minimum allowances from the Reich to banking institutions, which then granted them the corresponding credit.

Additionally, numerous delivering agencies endeavored to reduce the financial burden of Family Aid by other methods, namely by taking every opportunity to cut their expenditures for this assistance. One such possibility, and the one with the greatest impact, existed in counting every other considerable income of "war wives" and "war families" toward their Family Aid. This possibility was then exploited by the cities and districts to the greatest degree, in manifest opposition to the interests of state economic and social policy. The intention of the state's entire wartime labor-market policy, which was intimately connected with Family Aid, was that aid recipients would not be kept from taking up employment in the war industry by such accounting practices. This intention was in part subverted by the conflict of financial and political interests between the Reich and the delivering agencies and, consequently, the central objective of the state here, namely to foster the soldiers' readiness for action through the financial support of "war families,"[167] could only partially come to fruition.

After this brief description of the financial and political aspects of Family Aid, two questions remain to be answered in relation to this essential socio-political institution of the war period. Firstly, we need to examine the mental correlate – and particularly that of the female population – of this state maintenance, which was completely new in scope. We need to explore, in other words, how governmental support structured reality in the perception of the women concerned, as well as in the attributions that this social group, set off from wartime society through decisions of social policy, experienced from outside. Here, the question is one of the concrete construction of the societal paradigm "war wife." The second pertinent question concerns the consequences of Family Aid on the material situation of wage-earning women and families.

In the preceding analysis, we have already seen that certain generalized ideas existed about the "war wife," i.e. that the social group delimited by this expression in contemporary discourse bore expectations, fears, etc. that went beyond the pure definition of "Family Aid recipient." These preconceptions were revealed, for example, in the discussions about the role of "war wives" in the mobilization of labor for the war economy, their approach to sexuality, their function of socialization with regard to male adolescents and the form of their written communication with family members, and above all husbands, on the front, namely the much-lambasted "letters of lament." The characteristic feature of these generalized views about the "war wife" was that they, in their respective context of use, were simultaneously the cause for and the consequence of the increased attention that the authorities and the general public (media, churches, associations, political parties, etc.) devoted to the group of female aid recipients. In all of these contexts of use, the term "war wife" was not least a term of control, which prescribed conduct that was considered "correct" for "war wives" and rendered their "false" conduct an object of scandal. This was also true of the other contexts in which this term was used, in particular those that concerned these women's behavior as consumers and the much-reproached demands they raised as such.

The description of "war wives" as extravagant was already a topos in the first months of the war, and remained one for its duration. Thus, the Berlin chief of police, like many authorities, complained about the fact: "that [it is], above all, the wives of combatants [who] use the money they are provided with improperly. It is significant that the refreshment rooms of the department stores are almost always full."[168] In the first months of the war, it was women's consumption of tortes and other expensive baked goods that was criticized; later, when these goods were no longer available, it was their cinema-going that often came under fire. There were municipalities that deemed it necessary to officially intervene and issued announcements, such as the following: "It has been repeatedly observed that war wives who receive municipal assistance regularly go to the cinema. As this is not compatible with the objectives of the assistance, we want to draw attention to the fact that, in the future, these women will lose this municipal assistence."[169]

Although there was a real basis in fact for the complaints about "war wives'" conspicuous consumption, especially in the second half of the war, when luxury consumption was often the only kind that was realizable with money, it is unmistakable that the authorities and public opinion derived the right to control the assisted from Family Aid. The magazine *Vorwärts* mocked this claim to moral consumption control – a claim with which the labor movement had also been plagued – through the publication of the following "letter:"

> Earlier, it was the champagne-drinking and the auto-driving of the journeyman bricklayer that did not permit some good souls to sleep. Today, it is the war wife, frittering away her war assistance in cafés on cake and whipped cream, that robs many of their more or less well-earned night's rest . . .. As certain as it now is that journeyman bricklayers have already drunk champagne, even without dying from it, it is also certain today that there are war wives whom, when they eat cake and whipped cream, even the whip won't stir. And it's good for those who still can get it.[170]

Closely related to the reproach that "war wives" wasted the money they received from state support was the complaint, raised with equal frequency, of their "covetousness." And if this "covetousness" was expressed in concrete demands on the authorities, then it was considered particularly reprehensible. Thus, the Landrat in Itzehoe explained that the food riots that broke out on 24 January 1917 in that and other neighboring cities and lasted for a longer period of time were instigated

> by a number of undisciplined war wives who are catered for by the local soup kitchen and who came together for this occasion and apparently planned this excess. It is precisely these women who have

been catered for, free of charge, by the city of Itzehoe since the beginning of the war who laze away the day and spend their Family Aid on unnecessary trinkets. For weeks, this group had already discussed among itself that the food in the soup kitchen was bad . . .

and had ultimately rioted with the soldiers because of a shortage of potatoes.[171] The demanding behavior of women whose economic position had improved through their receipt of Family Aid was especially emphatically denounced. As the Deputy General Command of the 1st Bavarian Army Corps Munich wrote in its monthly report of May 1917: "By the way, we should note the phenomenon . . . that some war wives, in particular those from the lower classes, who, thanks to the statutory assistance of the Reich etc., are better off than in peacetime, become very demanding and then are discontented that they, despite the money, cannot buy more food than is permitted by ration cards."[172]

It needs to be emphasized that the different ways of looking at "war wives" "from above" in all the contexts of use mentioned (wage labor, family, sexuality and consumer behavior) were of a completely negative shade: The term "war wives" delimited a social group for which one was very often inclined to ascribe a tendential or acute violation of the rules as its typical characteristic.

The next important question is how the content of this term "war wives" was constituted "from below." In answering this question, we need to explore whether the group of Family Aid recipients was not only delimited and invested with specific attributes from the outside, but also by the respective women and families themselves, and, if this were the case, what content these individuals gave the term.

An unambiguous answer exists to the first part of the question: The recipients of Family Aid developed a definite "we-feeling," which was clearly due, in large part, to the fact that they were completely aware of the negative and controlling aspects of their description by the authorities and in the press. A Saxon "war wife," in a letter to her husband, who was a prisoner of war, analyzed the situation as follows:

what is sometimes rumored by people is indescribable. Recently it was even reported, it was even said to a war wife's face, that the war wives take no notice of the war, since they can sleep long, go for walks, and the husband even sends a heap of money home, naturally it can't be made bad enough this couple of marks pay is not such a big heap. Oh how gladly would I trade with them [those women who were not war wives] especially I and your children we have to bear it the longest. We have to pay for it twice and have to buy everything from our assistance at exactly the same price as those whose husbands are at home and earn a lot of wonderful money. They make more progress than us, where you poor men have had to slave away for them from the beginning one might also say in the far distance and perhaps you will return sick and broken what do we have from that and now they want to envy us too much attention is paid to us war wives I don't need anyone to do that.[173]

The relatives of "war wives," in particular their conscripted husbands, reacted sensitively to the negative implications of the term "war wife" and confronted it with the opposite valuation. So reasoned a sergeant during a train ride in August 1917:

one would like to participate in everything, if only it would happen justly; one man lost his entire living through the war and his family was allocated the low Family Aid . . . additionally, there was an article in the newspaper recently, in which the war wives were described as lazy. The writer of the article does not seem to know that women have to stand in line and run around half the day in order to obtain food for their families. If one does not come at the right time, then one gets absolutely nothing.[174]

This "we-feeling" expressed itself in collective action aimed at increasing Family Aid. "War wives storm the city halls and demand help,"[175] and "A movement, with the goal of attaining an increase in the assistance of the Reich, has seized hold of the local war wives"[176] reported the distressed city administrations to the imperial government.

The second part of the question, namely that of the meaning women themselves gave to their existence as "war wives," is much more difficult to answer. Of particular interest here is whether or not female Family-Aid recipients' feelings of self-worth increased as a result of the state's new respect for women's role as housewives and mothers.

There are certain clues that speak for such a development. It was fostered, in part, by the repeatedly emphasized opinion, expressed by the state, as well, that Family Aid was something completely different from poor aid: It was not state or municipal charity, but rather the fulfillment of a moral claim.[177] This led to the fact that these women and their relatives regarded state financial assistance, in the sense of a "moral economy," as an entitlement because of their status as "war wives" – an expectation that hardly any of the se women could have held before the war. In 1917, however, a woman could write to her boyfriend, a prisoner of war: "Soon we are going to have to glue our mouths shut [because there is nothing to eat.] Come back . . . and marry me, so that the state also has to provide for me and I won't have to hang around with strangers in other cities."[178]

Accordingly, these women also developed a self-conscious and demanding attitude with respect to the authorities. Confident in the legitimacy of their claim to all state and municipal assistance, they were willing to achieve their objective, if necessary, by providing false financial details to the authorities, who had to verify financial need as a condition of granting Family Aid. To "war wives," the voluntary assistants at the aid offices – mostly women from the lower and middle bourgeoisie – who were responsible for Family Aid allocations were

> in general, not up to the task. Their clumsiness did not escape their notice. The women by no means behaved only in a passive manner with respect to their judges; rather, the relationship showed a certain reciprocity. Resourceful women quickly found out, as well, that the truth, i.e. the actual financial circumstances, did not need to coincide completely with the answers to the questions [the assistants] posed and turned their experiences into educational work in the waiting room, with appropriate descriptions of the assistants in charge: the witch, the angel, the good . . . The female assistants were occasionally backed into a corner by the women's replies and in order to get rid of them, gave them a small amount of (supplementary) assistance. [The resulting] differences in the assessment of need, manifest in the granting of special subsidies, became known from the opinions war wives exchanged among themselves and were even amplified in the transfer from one person to the next, without the women recognizing the reasons for this phenomenon . . . The result was that each of the women, in the course of a conversation, complained about the injustice that prevailed in the distribution of war aid and always felt herself to be the most disadvantaged . . . Judgments on respective need were generally alien to the imagination of those supported because, to them, only their identity as war wife mattered. And what one of them received from the delivering agencies, the others demanded without question, in so far as it pertained to the satisfaction of basic needs.[179]

Conscripted husbands were equally convinced of the justice of that "moral economy." The municipal authorities of Lauban already explained this in late 1914:

> Even proceeding from the mildest interpretation of the term "need," one encounters great difficulties because it is impossible to measure precisely the conditions of the individual. And when, after having diligently examined and subsequently turned down an application, one has to hear from a warrior in the field that, while he is sacrificing life and health for the Fatherland, the home authorities have pettily denied a "few pennies' worth" of support to his family, then recourse to the letter of the law is of no help. For the feeling of the people proceeds from the assumption that the state has a general obligation to support them, which has nothing to do with examining an individual's specific need.[180]

This and other initiatives to abrogate the examination of need, however, did not succeed.[181]

Family Aid also led to rising expectations among another group: Poor-aid recipients compared their "legal aid for emergency need" to the support according to need that the recipients of Family Aid received. These individuals perceived the financial differential that resulted when poor aid was transferred to Family Aid and consequently "approached the Poor Relief Office and demanded a raise."[182] This change in expectations can be interpreted as one of the developments of the war that had consequences lasting beyond it; it therefore indicates the important impetus the First World War gave to the development of the welfare state.

We can perceive definite elements in both the perception and behavior of women and families receiving Family Aid that support the conclusion that women could have gained greater self-confidence from their existence as "war wives." The extent of this consequence of Family Aid was limited by clear countertendencies, however. The generally poor "image" of "war wives" must have prevented women from giving this term an unambiguously positive connotation. Additionally, in spite of all the differences between Family Aid and poor aid, many women found it humiliating that, for the first time in their lives, they had to apply for financial assistance, especially since the inspection of their entire financial, health and work circumstances was not always performed by public servants who were very obliging in dealing with "war wives."[183]

The effect Family Aid had on the familial arena seems to have been more important, however, than its aforementioned impact on women's self-definition in their "public" role. As recipients of Family Aid and in the absence of their husbands, many women had control over the family's entire cash income for the first time. This enabled them to see the previous mode of allocation within the family, by which the husband had frequently received the largest share of the money or goods, from another perspective. Countless reports, such as that of the Augsburg District Office (*Bezirksamt*), contained the observation

> that many war wives, especially those with a large number of children, have never had so much cash for their household at their disposal as now. With rather strong words about their husbands, many have admitted this to me personally, with the observation that they do not have to worry as much now as before the war, when their husbands had spent almost all of their earnings on drink and had hardly anything left for their wives and children.[184]

An examination of the effects such wartime experiences of women had on familial structures and forms of allocation in the post-war period, after their husbands had returned home, is beyond the scope of this study. The assumption, however, that, after such experiences, these women were generally prepared to re-establish the status quo with regard to family income after their husbands' return is perhaps the most implausible of all possible developments.

In terms of the material consequences of Family Aid on the lifestyle of aid recipients, we need to differentiate these according to both time and region. First of all, there was the clear country–city difference: In rural areas, where the cost of living was lower and access to natural goods easier, Family Aid proved to be adequate in the majority of cases. Rural women receiving assistance could afford either to deposit part of the money in the bank or to keep children at home, who otherwise would have been sent to work for farmers.[185] In urban areas, on the contrary, Family Aid was only sufficient in the very first months of the war. Before cost-of-living increases spiraled out of control, Family Aid had given some working-class families the opportunity to retrieve valuables, pawned years before, from the pawnshop, to outfit their children in new clothing, and to set aside savings.[186] In the majority of cases, however, this phenomenon must have been limited to large families of unskilled workers, whose income before the war was extremely low.[187] From 1916, at the latest, the increased prices alone, which were not compensated for by the sporadic increases in Family Aid, had already made it practically impossible for urban "war wives" and their families to live solely from this assistance.[188] Additionally, in the second half of the war, another factor limited the effectiveness of the material assistance provided by Family Aid. As a result of the scarcity and governmental regulation of consumer goods, money completely lost its function as a general means of exchange. With the transition from the consumer-goods market to a governmentally regulated shortage of consumer goods, money alone did not grant access to scarce goods anymore – if we disregard the few, atypical top earners who could afford exorbitant black-market prices. In the following section, we will analyze the changes this development caused in the provision of wage-earning women with consumer goods.

The Provision with Consumer Goods: Housework, Family "Squirrels" and Public Morale

The lack of foodstuffs, the price increases and the problems of state rationing bestowed housework with an even greater significance for the livelihood of individual families than before the war. Already before 1914, it was the performance, household practice and experience of housewives in dealing with the consumer-goods market that had first made it possible for working-class, white-collar and civil-servant households to cover the most essential everyday needs with their tight family budget. Under the aggravated living conditions of wartime, housewives increasingly compensated for the shortage in the family's income with prolonged and intensified housework. In addition to this, housewives had yet another task to perform: After the consumer-goods market had conclusively collapsed in 1916,[189] and government rationing only insufficiently replaced it in its function of providing food, it remained up to individual women and families how to obtain the food they needed. Under these conditions, housework took on a perceptibly different character. Since the changes that shaped wartime housework worked in different directions, this character manifested, so to speak, schizophrenic traits. On the one hand, tasks that, in the pre-war period, had increasingly been removed from urban households and allocated to the consumer-goods market once again became part of the work of the individual household. During the course of the war, the household economy essentially returned to being a quasi-subsistence economy. On the other hand, the logic of state management and rationing extended itself into individual households and caused the connection between their economic and societal functions to become stronger than ever before. Soon government rationing controlled not only the allocation of food – ration cards served not as a guarantee of certain amounts of food, but rather as a ban against obtaining more than these limited amounts – but also its use in individual families. And decision-makers sought to gain entry into every kitchen not only through rationing itself, but also through the accompanying opportunities for influencing women politically. Through propaganda measures and the wartime cooking courses that the authorities and women's organizations arranged, housewives were supposed to gain the knowledge of home economics and consciousness necessary to perform their housework, now at last honored as a patriotic task, in a manner that would support the state.

Contemporary observers already perceived that the wartime household economy bore the characteristics of a quasi-subsistence or individualized economy.[190] The most conspicuous aspect of this development was the increase in the home-production of foodstuffs in and by urban households. Apartments, basements and balconies became populated with rabbits, chickens, goats and pigs. Garden plots and leasehold property, which were made available by city administrations and businesses for this purpose, allowed urban families to grow their own potatoes, fruit and vegetables. The military and civil authorities welcomed and supported families' efforts to provide for themselves, since they had an equally positive influence on the food situation and on the population's morale. As the Deputy General Commands reported in March 1917:

> Whoever could somehow make it possible, even those from the poorer population, has cultivated a piece of land with vegetables and potatoes. To this end, available and suitable sites were put at [their] disposal. These people use their breaks at work and the time after work to tend their gardens, and thus no time remains for brooding and talking politics.[191]

Industries were requested to grant their workers the necessary time to garden their property.[192] From time to time, allotment leaseholders gave up tilling their parcels of land; with increasing famine, thieves harvested the crops in their stead. Buying and dealing with purchased goods, also, increasingly required an expenditure of work and time that rendered the term "consumption" a euphemism. The "time-consuming nature of food-shopping and the involved management"[193] of food even won housewives sympathetic remarks from the authorities, who otherwise assessed them rather critically. The head of the War Food Office, despite his aversion to the "senseless beverage" coffee, even set 370,000 tons of barley aside a year in order not to deprive the "sorely afflicted housewives" of their "brown beverage."[194] The food, kerosene or shoe "polonaises" in front of stores became the characteristic feature of housework during the war: "Whoever, on these chilly spring nights," read one such article, published in the *Berliner Tageblatt*, devoted to this wartime phenomenon of waiting in line,

does not shy away from a walk through the streets of the city, will, already before midnight, see figures, loaded down with household utensils, stealing back and forth in front of the covered markets. At first, there are only a few, but with the approach of midnight, the groups become real crowds. These are predominantly composed of women. In the beginning, they crouch down on the steps of the surrounding shops and on the iron park fences. Soon, however, one [woman] comes and lays a palliasse down near the entrance, on which she makes herself comfortable. That is the signal for general movement. Behind the happy owner of the palliasse, a second woman sets up a deck chair. Close to her, another, less demanding [woman] sits down on a simple wicker chair she transported from her apartment, which is God only knows how far away. A fourth only has a "stick" . . . The others stand there apathetically, some are sleeping as they stand, and the moonlight makes their pale faces appear even paler. Policemen appear and walk morosely up and down. Morning dawns. New throngs draw near. Women with strollers . . . Now the coffeepots and sandwiches are going to be brought out. Some of the women reach for their knitting in order to shorten the leaden hours. Finally, the selling begins. And the result: a paltry half a pound or, when one is especially lucky, a whole pound of meat, lard or butter for half of the shoppers, whereas the others have to go away empty-handed.[195]

Having to stand in line for food or for clothing, shoes, soap and ration cards was not the only factor that made running a household more difficult during the war. The more the quality of food deteriorated, for example, the more time and energy were necessary to prepare it. Or, the more infrequently clothing or food was allocated, the more intensively women had to stretch what was available through economizing or mending. Garbage was processed for reuse; in individual households, food was canned or made into preserves. The dictates of supply, which government rationing brought with it, meant that housewives were confronted with unfamiliar goods[196] and that their efforts to run an organized household were often made impossible by the unpredictability of allocations. As the Deputy General Commands wrote in their monthly report for April 1917:

> The population finds it – and rightly so – particularly annoying that one does not know, even in the middle of the month, which goods are available that month and in what amounts the individual foodstuffs will be distributed . . . Obviously, it is impossible to think of managing one's household in a well-ordered fashion, if one does not know how to conserve the provisions one has. This especially applies to the household of the worker who is not well-off, in which no stores have been saved from the previous month. Thus, one often hears animated complaints from these circles about the deplorable state of affairs. The trade unions even fear that the peace in the factories, which has been maintained up to now, might be disturbed because of this.[197]

Many local associations eventually decided to control not only the allocation of food rations, but also their use. This was applied, in particular, to the consumption of potatoes. Government supervisors and random spot checks were supposed to guarantee that potatoes were stored properly and that, in those cases where potatoes were transferred to households to be stored in the cellar for a certain period of time, their consumption did not exceed the per-head allowance. If these potato checks revealed that the consumption of potatoes did in fact exceed the ration level, the municipalities then resorted to punitive measures. If inspectors came across stores of potatoes that exceeded the allocated amount, these households were then convicted of black-marketeering. If they discovered empty cellars, this was an unwelcome side effect of consumption checks: Some families, out of fear that their provisions would be confiscated, had, as a precaution, already eaten them.[198] This fear was not unfounded.

Sometimes potato rations were retroactively cut, which meant that, from the potatoes they already had in storage, consumers were required to return the specific amount that, according to the new ration allowances, they would no longer receive. This measure hit precisely those families which had used their provisions the most economically especially hard.[199]

Because of their plight, housewives became the most vociferous critics of government rationing. Conversely, housewives were cast as accomplices in the failure of rationing. Already in the pre-war debates about the "normal" problems low-income families had in keeping house and feeding their members, scolding housewives had played an important role.[200] During the war, these complaints gained in resonance, in particular those about "women of the poorer classes who, because of their lack of experience in home economics, do not know how to help themselves with regard to the shortage of potatoes and fat."[201] Women's organizations and civil authorities developed initiatives to give housewives the necessary domestic knowledge and the requisite psychological tools that would then enable them to weather the food shortage through rational and "patriotic" housekeeping. If the "scapegoat" character which public attention conferred upon housework had been less pointed, then we could almost speak of a revaluation of such work in and through the war. The bourgeois women's movement and the Association of German Housewives (*Verband Deutscher Hausfrauen*), which it had founded, developed the liveliest activities.[202] With state support, the BDF carried out training in public speaking for men and women, food exhibits and traveling cooking classes; the publication of the *Hauswirtschaftliche Korrespondenz* and cooking demonstrations were intended to teach women "how to economize out of love of the Fatherland."[203] The nation had suddenly discovered that the trenches ran through the kitchens of German housewives,[204] and these housewives were to come through their battles in "this holy war" victoriously, so that, one day, it could be said: "The German housewife had won it."[205] The propaganda campaign initiated in 1915 for proper wartime nutrition was supposed to "connect the gentleness of the dove with the cleverness of the snake,"[206] particularly in the effort to familiarize housewives with previously unknown foods, such as porridge, and get them to use them. As Anna Lindemann recommended in her lecture "The Adaptation of the Individual

Household to the Current Situation," given at the 1915 seminar to train the National Women's Service,

> Move women to return to the customs of their forefathers and to make a soup for breakfast . . . Very many of these soups can be made sweet; porridge can be enjoyed with milk and sugar. We can learn a lot here from the Scottish population. It inhabits a country whose landscape is poor and mountainous; in terms of its nature, the population is more like the Germans than the remaining inhabitants of Great Britain. In most districts, this population feeds itself with oatmeal, milk and herring. It is simultaneously a highly intelligent population, whose descendants can be found in high positions in British business and in the British administration. In lonely mountain regions, you can find men there who read the Bible in the original while shepherding . . . The Scot eats oats for breakfast, lunch and dinner; and if we do not have excessively large stores of oats even by the new harvest, we still want to make use of all that is still there.[207]

Women were not only reproached for providing poorly for their family members, however, but also for providing for them too well. A lack of awareness of the broader perspective of the war economy was frequently denoted as the true "failure" of German housewives during the war, whereby women, with their "selfless individualism,"[208] only took the provision of their dependants into consideration, not the functioning of the provision for the whole. The housewife has

> been preached to, from early adolescence on, that the main duty of the good, competent housewife is, without consideration for someone else or something else, to care for her personal household and the circle of people who belong to it. Here lie the roots of today's inclination to violate the laws of rationing. This does not occur out of personal self-interest, but rather, in most cases, out of familial self-interest and seems to the housewives, therefore, as something not only allowed, but imperative, which they innocently pride themselves on, without understanding that this feeling, this philosophy of life has become a degenerate concept today.[209]

At the beginning of the war, reproaches about women's lacking an appropriate perspective of "the whole" had concerned the panic-buying with which many housewives – as well as many communities – had reacted to mobilization and through which they had driven up prices. In the second half of the war, this reproach signified something completely different, namely that few housewives, in the interest of providing for themselves and their families, shyed away from violating the legal regulations of the war economy and of society in general. Since even the most frugal housekeeping could not stretch the short supply of food enough to be sufficient, women turned to self-help, and providing for one's existence became a crime. The lack of interest women showed for the big picture, in that they violated laws and ignored the moral code the authorities and others had formulated for the war economy, was probably less a result of an overarching housewives' ideology than women's reaction against the slow starvation facing them and their dependants. They knew "that it is scientifically proven and generally – indeed, one can even say officially – recognized that individuals subsisting on the amount of food stipulated by the regulations will surely fall prey to malnutrition, which will endanger their lives."[210]

This fact was aptly demonstrated by the conditions in institutions, such as old-age homes, whose occupants literally did not receive anything to eat beyond their allotted rations,[211] as well as by the deaths that resulted from too many scruples in obeying the dietary regulations.[212] Above all, however, this was confirmed by the deterioration in health that women and men who had remained at home could observe in themselves, their children and in other family members. As commentary on a photograph that a prisoner of war had sent home, one individual wrote back in March 1917:

> gotten a little thin, but, dear Hans, don't think that we at home look better. Sometimes I can barely stand up, I'm so weak and worn out, and I have already been faced several times with the decision to go back to the front voluntarily. I experienced really hard days out there, but lived considerably better. So, dear Hans, patiently wait for the end of this genocide, because, here at home, we also aren't spared anything.[213]

The increased mortality rate among the civilian population starkly illustrates a general loss of strength on the part of those left at home. This increase in the mortality rate can be deduced from the development of the female mortality rate, which was not influenced by military deaths,[214] from 1914 to 1918 as compared with that of 1913. We can already observe a notable increase in mortality among female infants and adolescents up to 15 years of age in 1915. One year later, this increase especially affected the age groups from 5 to 20 and above 85 years, a trend that intensified in 1917 and then also extended to include the age group from 20 to 85 years of age. In 1918, when the great influenza epidemic struck, the mortality rate among the female population from 5 to 35 years of age increased by 100% as compared to 1913, whereas it rose by almost 200% in the age group from 15 to 25 years. These numbers suggest a particularly severe exhaustion among young women who had suffered four years of war work and war rations. Due to the better food provisions in rural areas, the wartime mortality rate exhibits a clear difference between the city and the country starting at the end of 1916 and the beginning of 1917. The number of deaths in the Mark Brandenburg, to which the Berlin suburbs belonged, increased almost by half compared to 1913. The number of deaths also rose faster in Anhalt, the Rhine province, Saxonia, Berlin, the three Hanseatic cities and in Westphalia than the average for the entire Reich or Prussia. In Württemberg, Baden and Bavaria, on the other hand, the mortality rate increased less dramatically.[215] Infant deaths, which, from 1915 to 1917, had been lower than in 1913, rose above the latter year's figure in 1918; they did not, however, reach the infant mortality rate of 1910–1911.[216]

Compared to the increase in mortality among the female population between 1914 and 1918, the infants' state of health during the war seems rather favorable. If we consider, however, that the number of children per family was lower than before the war, which actually should have improved the diet and care of infants, the fact that their mortality rate did not permanently decline also points to inadequate dietary and health conditions. Under wartime conditions, furthermore, a relatively well-nourished infant lived on the "substance" of its mother: The women economized on their own diet in order to provide for their children, so that a well-fed infant was often accompanied by a malnourished mother.[217] The total number of Germans who died because of malnutrition during the First World War is estimated at 700,000.[218]

Not even the most intensive and economical housekeeping could guarantee the survival of urban populations after – at the latest – 1916, when rationing became ubiquitous and the rations constantly smaller. In this situation, women and families, no longer in single instances, but as the whole, broadened the methods by which they provided for their livelihood. As the Deputy General Commands reported in April 1917:

In the realm of nutrition, the situation has deteriorated so far that even otherwise trustworthy parts of the population, who have long sought to obey the conspicuous rationing regulations, are now providing for themselves best as they can without regard to the laws. They call it self-help and even consider it legally justifiable because, in their minds, the authorities are negligent in their duty to equally and adequately care for the population.[219]

The "family squirrel"[220] became the symbol of illegal self-provision and represented the most conspicuous and widespread variant of this practice: the foraging or "squirreling" trips to the country, through which urban populations, by circumventing the rationing and maximum-price regulations, procured food directly from its rural producers. Soon the trains of "squirrels" were carrying hundreds of people, who, either in "screaming, sweating and schlepping hordes"[221] or in small groups, worked their way through the rural catchment areas of the cities, from farm to farm, in order to find something edible that they could then buy or barter. Contrary to the widely held opinion that foraging was a privilege of the rich, it was very frequently working-class families who used their connections to relatives and acquaintances in the country to obtain additional food through these means.[222] In the summer of 1917, the Munich police headquarters, "which had let its people fan out as 'test squirrels,'" ascertained that, apart from through violence, food was only obtainable in the country through connections.[223] In some cities, there was "such a crowd of working-class women, who, equipped with baskets, travel to the neighboring districts," at weekends, "that the entrance to the train station is completely obstructed."[224]

As a result of the increase in passengers, the railway administration, to the annoyance of the military authorities, instituted special "squirrel trains" in some areas.[225] Soon foraging was no longer only a weekend activity: Many male and female workers did not enter employment or took leave from their job in order to acquire food in this more promising, direct way instead.[226] Eventually, the state included the population's illegal self-provision in its calculations for food rationing: In some cases, for example, small and medium-size cities, because of their better connections to the surrounding agricultural countryside, received fewer allocations of meat. The populations of these cities thus had the implicit task of procuring the rest for themselves.

In addition to foraging in a narrower sense, i.e. to consumers' on-site buying or exchanging of agricultural products, other illegal practices of obtaining food also existed. The commercial black market, to which an estimated half a million people devoted themselves in the second half of the war,[227] supplied financially solvent individuals with additional rations. In some locations, tourism blossomed during the war, since it offered materially more affluent city dwellers the possibility of buying into the better nutritional situation of the rural population for several weeks. This industry lived almost exclusively from the black market. As the District Office of Berchtesgaden reported in June 1918: "The tourist industry lives like lilies of the valley, the municipal association cannot give them anything and the heavenly Father feeds them anyway."[228]

Falsified and stolen ration cards were put into circulation,[229] and a comprehensive, illegal barter economy developed on the black market. As was reported in Deputy General Commands' monthly reports for August 1918:

> Bartering has become the predominant factor in the entire turnover of goods . . . The shoemaker promises to make a pair of boots if two pounds of butter are delivered; the innkeeper allows the farmer to stay the night despite overcrowding, if he leaves a loaf of cheese behind; the bottled-beer dealer delivers bottled beer in exchange for a carton of eggs; the individual who brings the coach builder a chicken gets his wheel repaired first, and that's how it proceeds in every business.[230]

"Squirrels" *en route* to the country often encountered sections of the rural population traveling in the opposite direction, toward the city, where they could trade food for services and products that they required for their household and farm. Even flying "squirrels" were observed: Soldiers in the air force landed their planes in the flat countryside and sold off their supplies of gasoline for food.[231] Even the small trader gradually forgot "completely that it is his duty to sell for money and is only going to barter the sales goods provided to him by state authorities, if indeed he does not prefer to keep these goods for himself."[232]

Theft also increased during the war, in particular the robbing of fields, which, "through . . . [its] expansion, is becoming a danger to the public" and against which the few unconscripted policemen were powerless.[233] Contemporary observers estimated that "approximately 50% of all rationed foodstuffs was distributed to the population through government rationing; the other half, on the contrary, followed 'twisted paths' to come into its possession."[234]

With several foodstuffs, it was suspected that larger amounts of them were illegally sold than the government rationing program was provided with.[235] The authorities also got a sense of the enormous scope of illegal food supplies through the spot checks they carried out. One investigation, conducted among approximately 8,000 shipyard workers in October 1917, revealed that 7,000 of them, through foraging trips, had stocked up on enough potatoes to last until the next harvest.[236] In a small village in the area governed by the Deputy General Command Hannover, 13,400 eggs and 3,700 pounds of meat, which stemmed from the black market, were confiscated in the course of two months,[237] and a one-day inspection of railway traffic in the Prüm District in June 1917 brought in approximately 36 pounds of butter, 421 eggs, 500 kilograms of flour, almost 30 pounds of peas, 80 pounds of potatoes, 42 pounds of veal, 12 pounds of ham and one pound of bacon in contraband.[238]

Despite the decline in recording and prosecution during the war due to the personnel shortage in the police and the judiciary, wartime criminal statistics also reflect the extent to which crime had become a normal form of providing for oneself (see Tables 16 and 17).

In comparison to the average of the years 1911 to 1913, the female crime rate in 1917 had clearly risen.[239] The increase concerned, above all, the younger age groups, up until age 30, and crimes against property. Among convicted women, it was the number of women with no previous record that rose during the war. This increase refers to the fact that violations of the law had also become common in those classes of the population that otherwise were not "criminal."

The decline in offenses against the state and public order – in which only adolescents had no part[240] – was based on the fact that very heterogeneous criminal offenses were summarized under this category and that some of these lost their meaning in the war economy. The decrease in the number of convicted violations of the health and safety regulations for female workers, for example, can be explained by the *de facto* abolition of these regulations. The ordinances governing shop-closing times, working on Sunday and license obligations were more

Table 16. The Female Crime Rate in 1917 in Comparison to
the Average Rate of the Years 1911–1913

Age	Increases and decreases in percent			
	Total	Crimes against the state and public order	Crimes against persons	Crimes against property
under 15	+90.9	+17.2	−21.2	+94.3
15–18	+54.9			+69.1
18–21	+63.3	−6.3	−22.3	+95.1
21–25	+54.7	−42.5	−25.2	+112.2
25–30	+13.4	−53.4	−27.6	+75.9
30–40	−8.1	−59.7	−34.6	+54.8
40–50	−8.5	−58.5	−32.5	+58.1
50–60	−6.1	−62.0	−31.4	+64.1
over 60	−20.7	−95.9	−36.6	+38.2
All age groups	+14.5	−55.3	−31.0	+75.6

Source: Koppenfels, S. von. *Die Kriminalität der Frau im Kriege.* Kriminalistische Abhandlungen 11. Franz Exner, ed. (Leipzig, 1926), 14.

seldom violated because business in shops, restaurants and inns
greatly slackened during the war.[241] The increase in those offenses
that fell under "violence and threats against public officials," in
which, above all, married women between 30 and 60 years of
age were involved, reflect the collisions of women and civil
servants over government rationing. The most marked rise was
that in the number of crimes against property (see Table 18). As
the Deputy General Commands reported in July 1918:

> The very worst consequence of state control, which has grown like
> a weed, is the immeasurable dishonesty and unscrupulousness that
> have implanted themselves in the soul of the people. The compulsion
> to circumvent the law, the compulsion to illicitly deal on the black
> market or to obtain, through forbidden manipulations inclusive of
> theft, basic necessities for oneself has given rise to a general indiffer-
> ence about obeying the law and completely silences the voice of
> conscience. People steal and take wherever they can. The plundering
> of complete trains by the employees, including the civil servants, is
> the order of the day. The selling of entrusted state property for
> personal profit is growing at a frightening rate. It is impossible to

The Family in the First World War

Table 17. Women's Offenses against the State and Public
Order, 1911–1917

	Women were convicted because of:			
Year	Offenses against female-employment regulations, etc.	against ordinances governing shop-closing times and working on Sunday	regarding licence obligations, etc.	violence and threats against public officials
1911	1,517	4,300	4,096	984
1912	1,547	4,714	4,005	1,021
1913	1,418	5,222	4,032	1,073
1914	1,236	4,495	3,497	943
1915	461	2,584	2,346	986
1916	335	1,891	1,438	1,224
1917	174	675	754	1,256
Year	trespassing	freeing of prisoners	other crimes and offenses against the state	
1911	2,163	126	136	
1912	2,022	146	137	
1913	1,933	145	187	
1914	1,633	110	181	
1915	1,555	92	171	
1916	1,690	156	268	
1917	1,634	220	1,028	

Source: Same as Table 16, page 17.

have enough guardposts and sentries, because one always has to experience again that the guards also steal.[242]

The women convicted of petty larceny in 1917, whose number was twice as high as that in 1913, had usually stolen food from stores or potatoes or other crops from fields. Those women convicted of receiving stolen goods had been caught doing business on the black market. The majority of document falsification

Table 18. Female Crimes against Property, 1911–1917

Women were convicted because of:

Year	Larceny		Embezzlement		Receiving Stolen Goods	Fraud	Falsification of Documents
	petty	grand	repeated offence				
1911	19,803	1,026	2,447	5,027	2,269	3,720	1,102
1912	19,951	1,025	2,282	5,144	2,393	3,874	1,095
1913	18,199	963	2,152	4,985	2,446	3,774	1,228
1914	19,572	902	2,017	4,748	2,159	3,461	1,241
1915	21,176	1,433	2,174	3,847	3,054	3,563	1,257
1916	25,453	1,918	2,766	4,650	4,862	4,371	2,022
1917	37,735	2,942	3,223	5,941	7,734	4,774	3,337

Source: Same as Table 16, page 33.

cases involved women who had manipulated their food-ration cards and ration coupons.

The rationing authorities considered the black market the "most dangerous scourge . . . from which our Fatherland is currently suffering,"[243] since it deprived them of a large part of the food they could have used for state allocations. They were, consequently, in a tight spot. If they wanted to prevent at least a part of this food from vanishing into "squirrel pockets," they would have to take up the fight against the "family squirrels," because, of all the ways of obtaining food illegally, it was the population's efforts to provide for itself that caused the greatest and most continuous loss. On successful foraging weekends, entire areas of the countryside were "picked over," leaving the resident farmers unable to fulfill their food-delivery obligations and reducing the food allocations of the cities affected even more. In Württemberg, foragers in the summer of 1917 set out:

> on Saturday and Sunday ever more frequently with large milk cans. How detrimental the effect of such carryings-on is to the milk provision of a large city can be seen in the case of Stuttgart, which, on Sundays and Mondays, receives 15,000 liters of milk, or approximately one-sixth of what it receives on the remaining days of the week. And the report of a milkman is indicative: "The town of E. can deliver 500 more liters of milk again because, with the new schedule, the squirrels can no longer reach Stuttgart with the evening trains."[244]

It was a vicious circle: The more meager the rations allocated by the state became, the greater the proportions assumed by the black market; the more food the "squirrels" carried away from the black market, the less remained for government allocation. The state had to wage a victorious fight against illicit trading in order to maintain its system of rationing. Ending or even only obstructing illegal self-provision would have condemned a large part of the population to a state-prescribed death of starvation, however. Not even the authorities declared themselves in favor of an unconditional battle against the black market under these circumstances. It was clear to them, as it was to the population that received its rations from them, that the black market was necessary for survival. Aside from the fact that, for this reason, the authorities considered the fight against illicit trading only partially desirable, this fight was almost impossible to wage. In essence, one would have had to station a police officer behind every customer. Out of consideration for public morale, which had been the driving force at the beginning of the war to inaugurate rationing and the highest-price policy, the authorities now deemed it imperative to stop at the decisive point. The population had reacted bitterly to the authorities' efforts, which had been half-hearted at best, to restrict its illegal self-provision through hand-luggage and mail inspections, claiming that the state was morally unjustified in so doing. Governments and authorities elevated this widespread view to a *de facto* law of their behavior, in that they no longer judged their own policy according to the criterion of efficiency, but according to whether or not it would be supported by "the healthy judgment of the population." As the minister of the interior of Bavaria wrote to the district police authorities in 1917:

> During wartime, in which the population's judgment about the authorities, in particular, is rasher and more agitated than usual, any action [against the "family squirrels"] would only result in general bitterness and, what has already been observed on more than one occasion, unruliness. Simultaneously it would also immensely damage the reputation of the authorities themselves and of the present state as a whole, without ultimately achieving anything more than an empty performance according to the letter of the law. Our time is really too difficult and the morale of the population, which is already put to a severe test of endurance, too valuable a good for such action, because it is of decisive importance for the general will to survive . . . Today more than ever before, the police's entire performance has to be reasonable and decent in terms of its content and the form of enforcement; it has to be supported by the healthy judgment of the population.[245]

In spite of this restraint from governments and public officials, the population always assumed the worst if authority was concerned. The people suspected that the authorities in charge had pursued the "squirrels" on behalf of the more well-to-do part of the population, which, instead of having to forage for itself, could continue to provide for itself on the less conspicuous commercial black market. And they believed that the goods confiscated from "squirrels" did not find their way back into the state's ration provisions, but into the pots of the auditors.[246] Because of the population's general mistrust of the organs of the state, Bavaria's Ministry of the Interior rejected the proposal at the beginning of 1918 to allow policemen to receive a percentage share of the "squirrel booty" they had seized. In explanation of its refusal, the ministry said that this would possibly increase the effectiveness of state control, but not necessarily its popularity: "This would clearly invite references to the times of the robber barons, which are already mentioned today in complaints from squirrels."[247]

Women, in particular, when their arduously won products of foraging were confiscated by surveillance officials and they were reported to the police for violating the rationing laws, showed "little sense of the abstractness of the punishment."[248] As one woman from Silesia wrote to a prisoner of war in February 1917:

> And then I travel for two days together with two or three women and one goes from house to house and one still has to properly plead for money before one gets anything to buy that's how it looks like beggars the women go around. Then you know that with [food] coupons there's too little to live on and too much to die . . . But that's not all. Us poor women what shall we say we come from the [train] station with the goods then sometimes one or two gendarmes come and take the goods from the women don't pay for it they only write a ticket then comes wailing and complaining looks like the first day of the war is that justice in the world.[249]

These measures not only incurred the population's bitterness, but also increased its willingness to resist. Without any sense of wrongdoing, individuals circumvented state controls wherever possible. A favorite trick to evade inspections at train stations was to exploit the "halo" of soldiers in combat dress and have them bring food through the barriers.[250] Hardly any public official dared to inspect soldiers in this instance, and if they did, they then had to fear for their lives. In Altötting, for example, a tumult broke out in September 1918 when the mill inspector of the State Grain Authority (*Landesgetreidestelle*) confiscated bread cereals that had been brought there by local working-class families to be illegally ground. Approximately 400 people immediately assembled in front of the mill. "With the most terrible threats, the masses, some of whom were equipped with iron bars, logs, cudgels, stones and firearms, demanded the repeal of the mill blockade and waited for [the inspector] to arrive at the mill." After an official at the District Office had, as a precaution, hidden the inspector inside his building, a part of the crowd moved there and aggressively demanded his surrender. Another group collected at the train station in order to be able to intercept him as he departed. In the end, the official from the District Office had to drive the representative of the State Grain Authority to the train station in a neighboring town.[251]

As we have seen, in the course of the war the population learned to disregard the state in its capacity as the authority responsible for setting norms and for control. Additionally, it also learned a completely new form of providing for its livelihood, which consisted in blackmailing government officials in their capacity as the authority responsible for allocating food rations. The population's displeasure over the food situation increasingly erupted in spontaneous demonstrations, rock-throwing at the windows of official buildings and walkouts. Besieged city governments now saw no other way of defusing this particularly critical situation than to permit, preventatively or after its emergence, additional food to be allocated. The military authorities sharply criticized this practice because they feared that the entire population would learn the wrong lesson. As was written in the Deputy General Commands' monthly reports of March 1917: "If the riots result in city governments' handing over food or giving out bread without ration cards, then the people will conclude that there must be enough provisions available and will thus see causing trouble as an effective means of getting their wishes fulfilled."[252]

The civil authorities were also completely aware of the problematic nature of this action; they did not dare, however, to refrain from using the one social palliative at their disposal. Urban populations exploited this opportunity to increase their rations. The workers in factories and companies threatened walkouts and then carried out their threats; housewives and adolescents demonstrated after they had read in the newspaper or heard rumors that riots and strikes had resulted in an improvement in food provisions in this city or in that town.[253] To the chagrin of local governments, the network of informal communication also functioned in the opposite direction: One of the factors that triggered the food riots that broke out in Barmen in February 1917 was the rumor that Barmen potatoes had been transported to Essen in order to settle the strike there.[254]

The significance that families' individual strategies to provide for themselves, as well as the disregard these expressed for the state's regulatory mechanisms and its authority in general, had for wartime society ultimately went well beyond the scope of rationing. The behavior and perceptions tied to this self-provision not only undermined the principle and the efficiency of the government's rationing policy, they also proved to have exceedingly serious consequences for the relationship between the state and the population in general. The subversive strategies that, above all, working-class women developed during the war to fulfill their responsibility of providing for their families turned into strategies of subversion that, in the end, irrevocably destroyed the consensus of wartime society between the rulers and the ruled.

Notes to Chapter 4

1. O. M. Graf, *Wir sind Gefangene. Ein Bekenntnis* (München, 1978), 205.
2. K. Hausen, "Familie als Gegenstand historischer Sozialwissenschaft. Bemerkungen zu einer Forschungsstrategie," *GG* 1 (1975): 182.
3. Hausen, "Familie," 208. The concept, recommended by Karin Hausen, represents the clarification of Heller's concept of reproduction, which underlies this work. See my introduction.
4. O. Riebicke, *Was brauchte der Weltkrieg? Tatsachen und Zahlen aus dem deutschen Ringen 1914/18* (Leipzig, 1936), 36.
5. F.-W. Henning, *Das industrialisierte Deutschland 1914 bis 1972* (Paderborn, 1975), 34.
6. *Die Kriegsvolkszählungen vom Jahre 1916 und 1917 in Bayern.* Beiträge zur Statistik Bayerns 89. Bayerisches Statistisches Amt, ed. (München, 1919), 29. These are estimates too. The results are proved on the local level. Thus, the report of the Neukölln War Administration report states that 34.6% of all male inhabitants were conscripted. *Kriegsverwaltungsbericht der Stadt Neukölln 1914–1918*, Statistisches Amt, ed. (Neukölln, 1921), 13.
7. *Bulletin der Studiengesellschaft für soziale Folgen des Krieges*, vol.: *Deutschland*, 2nd expanded ed. (Kopenhagen, 1919), 16.
8. E. v. Wrisberg, *Heer und Heimate 1914–1918* (Leipzig, 1921), 89ff.
9. F. Burgdörfer, *Krieg und Bevölkerungsentwicklung* (München and Berlin, 1940), 11.
10. *Bewegung der Bevölkerung in den Jahren 1914 bis 1919.* Statistik des Deutschen Reiches 276 (Berlin, 1922), XXX.
11. *Bulletin*, 16; *Kriegsvolkszählungen in Bayern*, 82. The report of the Neukölln War Administration even proceeds from the statistic that 75% of the men conscripted in Neukölln were married. *Kriegsverwaltungsbericht der Stadt Neukölln*, 13. Of the 1.9 to 2.4 million Germans who were killed during the First World War, 69% were single and 31% were married. This means that between

589,000 and 744,000 marriages ended because of the death of the husband. *Bewegung der Bevölkerung*, LVIII.

12. Letter excerpt, March 1917: HStA/Kr, I. Bayerisches AK München 1979.

13. O. A. Wolff, *Zur wirtschaftlichen Lage der Handlungsgehilfinnen während des Krieges*, diss. (Stuttgart, 1918), 40.

14. P. Marschalck, *Bevölkerungsgeschichte Deutschlands im 19. und 20. Jahrhundert* (Frankfurt/M., 1984), 148.

15. The following examination of the migration of the population during the First World War concerns only the immediate period of the war. For a description of the longer-term demographic consequences of the First World War, see E. Heinel, "Die Bevölkerungsbewegung im Deutschen Reich in der Kriegs- und Nachkriegszeit," diss. (Berlin, 1927); Burgdörfer, *Krieg und Bevölkerungsentwicklung*; id., *Volk ohne Jugend* (Berlin, 1934); id., *Geburtenschwund. Die Kulturkrankheit Europas und ihre Überwindung in Deutschland* (Heidelberg et al., 1942); A. zu Castell, "Die demographischen Konsequenzen des Ersten und Zweiten Weltkriegs für das Deutsche Reich, die Deutsche Demokratische Republik und die Bundesrepublik Deutschland," in W. Dlugoborski, ed., *Zweiter Weltkrieg und sozialer Wandel* (Göttingen, 1981), 117ff.; Marschalck, *Bevölkerungsgeschichte*, 53-71.

16. Here and in what follows, unless otherwise noted: *Bewegung der Bevölkerung*, I-LXVII.

17. R. Meerwarth, "Die Entwicklung der Bevölkerung in Deutschland während der Kriegs- und Nachkriegszeit," in R. Meerwarth et al., *Die Einwirkung des Krieges auf Bevölkerungsbewegung, Einkommen und Lebenshaltung in Deutschland* (Stuttgart et al., 1932), 32.

18. Letter excerpt, March 1917: HStA/Kr, I. Bayerisches AK München 1979.

19. Ibid.

20. The *Statistik des Deutschen Reiches* calculated an absence of 3.3 million births for the years 1915 to 1919. S. I. Marschalck not only extrapolates from the figures in 1913, but also takes the declining trend in the birthrate between 1913 and 1924 into account. He thereby arrives at a figure of 2.2 million births, cited here in the text, that did not occur as a result of the First World War. Marschalck, *Bevölkerungsgeschichte*, 148.

21. Heinel, "Bevölkerungsbewegung," 67. For the question of abortion, see also the section of this chapter entitled "Child-Rearing and Adolescent Socialization."

22. *Bewegung der Bevölkerung*, III.

23. *Kriegsvolkszählungen Bayerns*, 105-112, 116ff; unless otherwise noted, also valid for the following data. The statistics about the change in the size of households are cited from U. Daniel, *Arbeiterfrauen in der Kriegsgesellschaft. Beruf, Familie und Politik im Ersten Weltkrieg* (Göttingen, 1989), 136-137.

24. *Die Frau in der bayerischen Kriegsindustrie nach einer amtlichen Erhebung aus dem Jahre 1917*. Beiträge zur Statistik Bayerns 92. Bayerisches Statistisches Landesamt, ed. (München, 1920), 20. The results of the wartime apartment censuses unfortunately do not provide any information about the increase in the number of single households. The development of the stock of small apartments is listed separately; those apartments that included up to two rooms and a kitchen or up to three rooms without a kitchen were considered "small apartments." *Reichswohnungszählung im Mai 1918*.

Statistik des Deutschen Reiches 287, Statistisches Reichsamt, ed. (Berlin, 1919), 7, 20-24.

25. For an example of the frequent complaints about women's sexual depravity during the war, see M. Bauer, *Der große Krieg in Feld und Heimat* (Tübingen, 1921), 153-157.

26. Result of a survey by the Chairman of the Düsseldorf Regional Council in his district, second half of 1915; Polizeidirektion Dresden to Regierungspräsident Düsseldorf, 8 October 1915; and *passim*: HStA Düsseldorf, Regierung Düsseldorf 30457. Gesundheitsbericht 1914-1918 für den Regierungsbezirk Aachen, 29: HStA Düsseldorf, Regierung Aachen 6935.

27. Testimony by members of the Reichstag Committee to Combat Venereal Disease, upon returning from the front: ZStA Potsdam, Reichsministerium des Innern 9344, Bl. 237ff., p. 3 of the minutes.

28. M. Liepmann, *Krieg und Kriminalität in Deutschland*, Wirtschafts- und Sozialgeschichte des Weltkrieges, German series (Stuttgart et al., 1930), 152.

29. A. Salomon, *Charakter ist Schicksal. Lebenserinnerungen*, R. Baron and R. Landwehr, eds. (Weinheim and Basel, 1983), 164.

30. M.-E. Lüders, *Fürchte dich nicht. Persönliches und Politisches aus mehr als 80 Jahren* (Köln, 1963), 62-63. In the early days of the war, Lüders was engaged by the German military administration in Belgium to care for prostitutes. M. Hirschfeld and A. Gaspar, eds., *Sittengeschichte des Ersten Weltkriegs* (Hanau, n.d. [1929]), 231-280; H. Dolsenhain, ed., *Das Liebesleben im Weltkriege* (Nürnberg, 1919), 9-12, 22. For information about the surveillance of prostitutes, see K. Meyer, "Krieg und Frauenkrankheiten", diss. (Halle, 1916), 11.

31. For the years 1903-1913, the average number of individuals in the German army infected with venereal disease a year was 20.4 per thousand. With the start of positional warfare, the number of cases of venereal disease among front soldiers rose. In the first three years of the war, the number of individuals with venereal disease, at 15.4 per thousand, was indeed below the pre-war level, which, increasing to 20.2 per thousand, it almost reached in the fourth year of the war. Under the conditions of war, these statistics took on quite a different significance, however. Among soldiers who were not deployed on the front, the infection rate increased to 27.5 individuals per thousand. General Staff Doctor Merkel, "Die Gesundheitsverhältnisse im Heer," in F. Bumm, ed., *Deutschlands Gesundheitsverhältnisse unter dem Einfluß des Weltkrieges*. Wirtschafts- und Sozialgeschichte des Weltkrieges 1, German series (Stuttgart et al., 1928), 182-183. See here, as well, Hirschfeld and Gaspar, eds., *Sittengeschichte*, 171-194; Jungblut, "Die Geschlechtskrankheiten im deutschen Heere während des Weltkrieges 1914-1918," in *Mitteilungen der Deutschen Gesellschaft zur Bekämpfung der Geschlechtskrankheiten* 21.1/2 (1923/24), 2-5; P. Lissmann, *Die Wirkungen des Krieges auf das männliche Geschlechtsleben* (München, 1919), 23-24 and *passim*; Preußisches Kriegsministerium to Reichsamt des Innern, 7 April 1915: ZStA Potsdam, Reichsministerium des Innern 12868, Bl. 68ff.; Notes about a meeting, re. the spread of venereal disease in the army and measures to prevent its transfer to the home front, 29 March 1915: ibid., Bl. 117; Minutes of the commissary consultation in the Imperial Office of the Interior, 29 May 1915: ZStA Potsdam, Reichsministerium des Innern 11869, Bl. 284; HStA Düsseldorf, Regierung Düsseldorf 30457 and 30458, *passim*.

32. Präsident des Reichsversicherungsamts to Staatssekretär des Innern, 22

The War from Within

April 1915: ZStA Potsdam, Reichsministerium des Innern 12868, Bl. 191ff.; Generalgouvernement Brüssel to Reichsamt des Innern, 21 September 1915 an: ibid., Bl. 264.

33. Letter from Otto H., dated 11 February 1917, rpt. in: V. Ullrich, *Kriegsalltag. Hamburg im Ersten Weltkrieg* (Köln, 1982), 102.

34. Minutes of a meeting, re. venereal disease, 26 November 1915: ZStA Potsdam, Reichsministerium des Innern 11869, Bl. 119. The social doctor A. Blaschko deemed that the distribution of prophylactics to soldiers would, "to many, equal a provocation to extra-marital sexual intercourse." A. Blaschko, "Die Prostitution in Kriegszeiten," *Deutsche Strafrechts-Zeitung* 1 (1914): 494.

35. Notes about a meeting, re. the spread of venereal disease in the army and measures to prevent its transfer to the home front, 29 March 1915: ZStA Potsdam, Reichsministerium des Innern 12868, Bl. 119. Statement from Dr. Schultzen of the Prussian War Ministry.

36. The suspicion that the army was propagating contraceptive techniques was expressed by Professor K. Oldenberg at the conference "Preservation and Increase of the Strength of the German People" in Berlin. See *Die Erhaltung und Mehrung der deutschen Volkskraft. Verhandlungen der 8. Konferenz der Zentralstelle für Volkswohlfahrt in Berlin vom 26.–28. Oktober 1915* (Berlin, 1916), 29.

In the negotiations about the law against the prevention of births, a draft of which was laid before the Reichstag in February 1918, representatives of the government argued for a ban on condoms, irrespective of the fact these existed as the only effective means against the transmission of syphilis. M. Flesch, "Der Entwurf eines Gesetzes zur Bekämpfung der Geschlechtskrankheiten und eines Gesetzes gegen die Verhinderung von Geburten im Deutschen Reich," *Annalen für Sozialpolitik und Gesetzgebung* 6 (1919): 147. Before the war, contraception with condoms was particularly widespread in the middle classes, whereas *coitus interruptus* was the most important means of birth control in the working classes. Here, see M. Marcuse, "Zur Frage der Verbreitung und Methodik der willkürlichen Geburtenbeschränkung in Berliner Proletarierkreisen," *Sexual Probleme* 9 (1913): 779.

37. Ludendorff to Stellv. Gen.kdo.s, 17 May 1918: HStA/Kr, Stellv. Gen.kdo. I. Bayerisches AK München 967. The comparison between the "house of shame" and the "field of honor" is taken from a letter by Pastor K. from Mönchengladbach, in which he condemns the authorities for this fact. See his correspondence with the authorities in HStA Düsseldorf, Regierung Düsseldorf 30457.

38. Ludendorff to Stellv. Gen.kdo.s, 17 May 1918: HStA/Kr, Stellv. Gen.kdo. I. Bayerisches AK München 967; Preußisches Kriegsministerium to Stellv. Gen.kdo.s, 15 May 1916: HStA Düsseldorf, Regierung Düsseldorf 30457.

39. Chef des Feldeisenbahnwesens, 20 May 1918: HStA/Kr, Stellv. Gen.kdo. I. Bayerisches AK München.

40. J. Jadassohn, "Geschlechtskrankheiten," in Bumm, ed., *Deutschlands Gesundheitsverhältnisse*, 1: 257-258; Camp Bürgermeister (District Düsseldorf) to Moers Landrat, 28 April 1918: HStA Düsseldorf, Regierung Düsseldorf 8057; Vorstand der Landesversicherungsanstalt Rheinprovinz to Regierungspräsident Aachen, 20 June 1916: HStA Düsseldorf, Regierung Aachen 6913; R. Stern, *Die Bedeutung des Kampfes gegen die Geschlechtskrankheiten, Referat vom 20.7.1916*. Special supplement 10 to *Amtliche Mitteilungen der Landes-*

versicherungsanstalt Rheinprovinz 9.

41. Lissmann, *Wirkungen*, 23-24; Stern, see previous endnote; "Denkschrift der Obersten Heeresleitung über die deutsche Volks- und Wehrkraft," draft presented by the head of the Front Health Authority, von Schjerning, to the Supreme Command, 30 August 1917: ZStA Potsdam, Vetreter des Reichskanzlers bei der OHL 31, 12-13; Schultzen of the Prussian War Ministry (see endnote 35), Bl. 117.

42. "Vorschläge betr. vorbeugende Maßnahmen zur Verhinderung eines weitgehenden sittlichen Verfalls und einer Verseuchung der durch die Rück-wanderung des Heeres in Mitleidenschaft gezogenen Bevölkerung," anonymous in Kriesersatz- und Arbeitsdepartement, to Demobilmachungsamt, 14 November 1918: ZStA Potsdam, Reichsministerium für wirtschaftliche Demobilmachung 21, Bl. 8ff.

43. See, for example, Bayerischer Innenminister to Regierung Oberbayerns, 28 June 1918: HStA/Kr, Stellv. Gen.kdo. I. Bayerisches AK München 1372.

44. Kriegsgesundheitsbericht für den Regierungsbezirk Düsseldorf 1.8.1914-31.12.1918: HStA Düsseldorf, Regierung Düsseldorf 8148, 21-22; Polizeidirektion Dresden to Regierungspräsident Düsseldorf, 8 October 1915: HStA Düsseldorf, Regierung Düsseldorf 30457; Gesundheitsbericht des Regierungbezirks Aachen 1914-1918, 29: HStA Düsseldorf, Regierung Aachen 6935.

45. Kriegsgesundheitsbericht für den Regierungsbezirk Düsseldorf 1.8.1914-31.12.1918, 22: HStA Düsseldorf, Regierung Düsseldorf 8148. These findings are not valid for all larger cities; in Leipzig, for example, the number of "secret prostitutes" who were apprehended as well as that of those individuals infected by them seems to have sunk during the war. E. Voigtländer, "Die Entwicklung der Verwahrlosung in den Jahren 1914-1920," *Zentralblatt für Vormundschaftswesen, Jugendgerichte und Fürsorgeerziehung* 13 (1921/22): 196.

46. Gesundheitsbericht des Regierungsbezirks Aachen 1914-1918, 29: HStA Düsseldorf, Regierung Aachen 6935; Jahresbericht der Münchener Polizei-direktion, re. wartime prostitution, 1914: HStA/Kr, Stellv. Gen.kdo. I. Bayerisches AK München 2278.

47. Gesundheitsbericht des Regierungsbezirks Aachen (see previous endnote), 29.

48. Polizeiverwaltung/Oberbürgermeister Krefeld to Regierungspräsident Düsseldorf, 13 August 1915: HStA Düsseldorf, Regierung Düsseldorf 30457.

49. Oberbürgermeister Mülheim a.d.R. to Regierungspräsident Düsseldorf, 18 August 1915: ibid. For further information about the increase in extramarital relationships during the war, also see Hirschfeld and Gaspar, eds., *Sittenge-schichte*, 97ff., 102-103. As examples of the countless publications about women's "immorality" during the First World War see Bauer, *Der große Krieg, passim*, and B. Grabinski, ed., *Weltkrieg und Sittlichkeit. Beiträge zur Kulturgeschichte der Weltkriegsjahre* (Hildesheim, 1917), 137-166.

50. Polizeidirektion Essen to Regierungspräsident Düsseldorf, 20 August 1915: HStA Düsseldorf, Regierung Düsseldorf 30457.

51. Bayerisches Kriegsministerium to Stellv. Gen.kdo.s, 19 August 1915: HStA/Kr, Stellv. Gen.kdo. I. Bayerisches AK München 2278.

52. The wife of a conscripted roofer, for example, who was placed under surveillance by the chairman of the regional council in Münster, "even though

her surrendering for money was not proven," was only successful in obtaining
after first consulting an attorney and furnishing a character reference. Quote
from Regierungspräsident Münster to Oberpräsident, 22 January 1915; Oberpräsident Münster to attorney, 19 February 1915: StA Münster, Oberpräsidium
6020. In contrast to the practice before the war, women and girls under
21 were also placed under increased vice-squad supervision; Klingelhöffer's
statements at the conference "Preservation and Increase of the Strength of the
German People," (see endnote 36 above), 227–228; Polizeidirektion Dresden
to Regierungspräsident Düsseldorf, 8 October 1915: HStA Düsseldorf, Regierung
Düsseldorf 30457.

53. Polizeidirektion Dresden to Regierungspräsident Düsseldorf, 8 October
1915: HStA Düsseldorf, Regierung Düsseldorf 30457.

54. Stellv. Gen.kdo. XX. AK Allenstein, Verordnung zur Verhinderung der
Verbreitung von Geschlechtskrankheiten, 12 May 1916: HStA/Kr, Stellv. Gen.kdo.
I. Bayerisches AK München 967. There had to be at least three months between
the two warnings.

55. See the answers to the poll conducted by the Chairman of the Düsseldorf
Regional Council in August 1915 in HStA Düsseldorf, Regierung Düsseldorf
30457. Also see Oberpräsident Magdeburg to Regierungspräsident, 1 March 1915,
and Oberpräsident Magdeburg to Innenminister, 29 April 1915: ZStA Potsdam,
Reichsministerium des Innern 12093, Bl. 220–221.

56. The police administration of Düsseldorf reported the prostitution of
suspicious "war wives" to the city's War Aid Commission. Several communities
attempted to cut the aid of unfaithful "war wives" but did not receive the approval
of the supervisory authorities for this action. Polizeiverwaltung/Ober-
bürgermeister Düsseldorf to Regierungspräsident Düsseldorf, 28 August 1915:
HStA Düsseldorf, Regierung Düsseldorf 30457; Newspaper excerpt: ZStA
Potsdam, 61 Re1/7971, Bl. 62.

57. Pastor H. Priebe: "Kriegerfrauen! Helft euren Männern den Sieg
gewinnen!", Berlin, 1916, 7: StA Münster, Oberpräsidium 4126; Preußisches
Kriegsministerium to Stellv. Gen.kdo.s, 15 February 1917: HStA/Kr, MKr 2331.

58. War-industry meeting of the Chairman of the Düsseldorf Regional Council,
14 December 1914: ZStA Merseburg, Rep. 77, Tit. 332r, Nr. 123, Bl. 35.

59. The most original analysis of this "love of prisoners," i.e. of women's
positive emotional attitude toward prisoners of war that had been generally
observed, was made by a Viennese neurologist. In addition to compassion and
romanticism, he made the following diagnosis: The "battle between the sexes,"
which rages as an "eternal war" between men and women, had only seemingly
abated during the war. In reality,

women are using the war in order to conquer men's position and to perhaps
occupy it permanently... This battle between the sexes turns the man
into the woman's natural enemy. In this roundabout way, the man's enemy
becomes the woman's ally. The love of prisoners stems from these sources.
Women love the enemy because (not in spite of the fact!) the men hate them.
They follow a dark yearning to take revenge on men and to insult them in a
particularly painful manner. The men of this nation are being devalued. They
aren't men at all and the men of foreign blood are only being used as a means
to express this contempt for the man close [to the women] more strongly.
The formula is thus: I love you because our men hate you.

The Family in the First World War

W. Stekel, *Unser Seelenleben im Kriege. Psychologische Betrachtungen eines Nervenarztes* (Berlin, 1916), 62-69.

Concerning the problemic nature of the relationships between German women and prisoners of war during the First World War, also see Ch. Beck, ed., *Die Frau und die Kriegsgefangenen*, vol. 1, pt. 2: *Die deutsche Frau und die fremden Kriegsgefangenen* (Nürnberg, 1919), *passim*, and Hirschfeld and Gaspar, eds., *Sittengeschichte*, 114-120.

60. The German word is *Franzmänner* and is a derogatory term for French men. [Translator]

61. Stellv. Gen.kdo. I. Bayerisches AK München to Bezirksamt Lauf, 18 August 1918; Gendarmeriestation Röthenbach b. Lauf, 23 August 1918: HStA/Kr, Stellv. Gen.kdo. I Bayerisches AK München 1578. Working-class women's relationships with prisoners of war are also mentioned in the reports of the Factory Inspectorate. See, for example, *Jahresberichte der Gewerbeaufsicht*, Regierungsbezirk Potsdam, 1: 95.

62. Bezirksamt Aichach to Regierungspräsidium München, 22 February 1918: HStA/Kr, Stellv. Gen.kdo. I Bayerisches AK München 1962. Also see: Memorandum of a meeting, re. the establishment of War-Industry Offices, 18 January 1917, 25-26: BA/MA, RM 3/1003.

63. Zusammenstellung der Monatsberichte der stellvertretenden Generalkommandos über Volksstimmung und Ernährung, 3 May 1917, 28: Stellv. Gen.kdo. XIV. AK Karlsruhe: BA/MA, RM3/4670. Cited in the following as "Monatesberichte."

64. Bezirksamt Traunstein to Regierung Oberbayern, 2 December 1917: HStA/Kr, Stellv. Gen.kdo. I. Bayerisches AK München 1960.

65. Bezirksamt Eggenfelden 2. November 1917 to Regierung Niederbayern: HStA/Kr, Stellv. Gen.kdo. I. Bayerisches Ak München 1960.

66. ZStA Potsdam, 61Re1/1966, 1967, 1969.

67. *Berliner Volkszeitung*, 13 December 1916: "Doppelselbstmord zweier Kriegerfrauen aus Scham": ZStA Potsdam, 61 Re1/7969, Bl. 168.

68. *Deutsche Tageszeitung*, re. the decree of the High Command in the Marches, 21 December 1916: ZStA Potsdam, 61 Re1/7969, Bl. 174. The decree provided for up to one year in prison for offenders.

69. Collection of petitions, anonymous letters, etc.: HStA/Kr, Stellv. Gen.kdo. I. Bayerisches AK München 949.

70. Anna T. to Stellv. Gen.kdo. I. Bayerisches AK München, 4 November 1916: HStA/Kr, Stellv. Gen.kdo. I. Bayerisches AK München 54.

71. *Berliner Tageblatt*, 19 October 1918: "Amnestie für Kriegerfrauen."

72. Of the almost 1.7 million military persons who died during the First World War, close to one third were married. Consequently, approximately 500,000 women and families were already affected by this. Heinel, "Bevölkerungsbewegung," 21, and *Bewegung der Bevölkerung*, XLIX. Robert, "the father" in Leonhard Frank's 1916/17 story of the same name, was one of the literary personifications of those who remained at home to cope with the experience of death. "Fallen on the field of honor" was how it was formulated in the message that Robert received in the summer of 1916 communicating the death of his only son:

> Honor (*Ehre*). That was one word and consisted of four letters. Four letters that, together, formed a lie of such infernal power that an entire people could

have been bound by these four letters and, by virtue of its own free will, pulled into the most atrocious suffering. The field of honor was not visible, not imaginable, was not comprehensible to Robert. It was not a field, not soil, not land, was not fog and not air. It was absolute nothingness. And that is what he should hold on to. His entire life long.

The story appeared in *Die weißen Blätter* 3: 11 (1916) under the title "The Waiter." Rpt. in M. Reich-Ranicki, ed., *Anbruch der Gegenwart. Deutsche Geschichten 1900–1918* (München, 1983), 521

For more concerning literary efforts to process the experience of death and the loss of friends, spouses and family members, see B. Hüppauf, "'Der Tod ist verschlungen in den Sieg.' Todesbilder aus dem Ersten Weltkrieg und der Nachkriegszeit," in B. Hüppauf, ed., *Ansichten vom Krieg. Vergleichende Studien zum Ersten Weltkrieg in Literatur und Gesellschaft* (Königstein/Ts., 1984), 55–91, especially 62–68, and K. Latzel, *Vom Sterben im Krieg. Wandlungen in der Einstellung zum Soldaten-tod vom Siebenjährigen Krieg bis zum II Weltkrieg* (Warendorf, 1988).

73. Bericht des Berliner Polizeipräsidenten, 30 November 1914: ZStA Potsdam, Reichskanzlei 2398/1, Bl. 53. With regard to the stance of the churches during the war, see W. Pressel, *Die Kriegspredigt 1914–1918 in der evangelischen Kirche Deutschlands* (Göttingen, 1967); H. Missalla, *"Gott mit uns." Die deutsche katholische Kriegspredigt 1914–1918* (München, 1968); K. Hammer, *Deutsche Kriegstheologie 1870–1918* (München, 1974); R. van Dülmen, "Der deutsche Katholizismus und der Erste Weltkrieg," *Francia* 2 (1974): 347–376.

74. On several occasions, unsuspecting individuals had had their letters to conscripted relatives returned with the stamp "Recipient killed in action." The authorities, consequently, instructed the regional post office to ask first the local authorities in such cases if the relatives had already been notified. War-industry meeting of the Chairman of the Düsseldorf Regional Council, 14 September 1914: ZStA Merseburg, Rep. 77, Tit. 332r, Nr. 123, Bl. 16 and War-industry meeting of the Chairman of the Düsseldorf Regional Council, 19 October 1914: ibid., Bl. 2.

75. E. Glaeser, *Jahrgang 1902* (Berlin, 1931), 270–271.

76. Bezirkskommandos Landau, monthly report to Stellv. Gen.kdo. II. Bayerisches AK Würzburg, 28 September 1916: HStA/Kr, MKr 12842; Bezirksamts Neu-Ulm, monthly report to Stellv. Gen.kdo. I. Bayerisches AK München, 26 October 1916: HStA/Kr, Stellv. Gen.kdo. I. Bayerisches AK München 1946; Magistrat Rosenheim, monthly report to Stellv. Gen.kdo. I. Bayerisches AK München, 2 November 1916: ibid., and Bezirkamts Friedberg, monthly report to Stellv. Gen.kdo. I. Bayerisches AK München, 27 October 1916: ibid.

77. Bezirksamt Friedberg, Bezirkskommando Landau and Magistrat Rosenheim (see previous endnote).

78. Garnisonsältester Kaufbeuren, 16 November 1916: HStA/Kr, Stellv. Gen.kdo. I. Bayerisches AK München 1947. See, as well, Glaeser's vivid description of men's increasing unwillingness to get a medical; Glaeser, *Jahrgang 1902*, 289–290.

79. P. L. Berger and H. Kellner, "Die Ehe und die Konstruktion der Wirklichkeit. Eine Abhandlung zur Mikrosoziologie des Wissens," *Soziale Welt* 16 (1965): 228.

80. 11. Bayerisches Infantrie-Division to Bayerisches Kriegsministerium, 15 December 1915: HStA/Kr, MKr 2330. Official complaints about the damaging

consequences of marital correspondence resulting from women's negative accounts of the home front lasted the entire war. For a few further examples, see: Monatsberichte, 3 August 1917, 8: BA/MA, RM3/4670; Report of the Office for Social Policy, 1 December 1915, 4-5: HStA/Kr, MKr 14029. The most prominent mention of these "letters of lament" was made by Adolf Hitler in *Mein Kampf*: Just like enemy propaganda, "the letters of lament direct from the home front had long exercised their effect" on the front. "It was no longer even necessary that the opponent forwarded them to the German front via pamphlets, etc. . . . The front was still flooded by this poison, which thoughtless women fabricated at home." Adolf Hitler, *Mein Kampf* (Berlin, n.d.), 208.

81. Approximately 3,000 letters to and approximately 9,000 letters from prisoners of war passed through Railroad Post Office I in Munich everyday. This correspondence was between German prisoners in France and Italy and their friends and relatives in Bavaria, Saxony and Silesia; Militärische Überwachungs- stelle at Bahnpostamt 1 München to Chef des Stellvertretenden Generalstabs der Armee Abt. IIIb, 12 May 1917: HStA/Kr, Stellv. Gen.kdo. I. Bayerisches AK München 1539. At this post office, over 70,000 letters were examined daily; Undated compilation of the Deputy General Command of the 1st Bavarian Army Corps Munich: HStA/Kr, Stellv. Gen.kdo. I. Bayerisches AK München 1943. The collection of letter excerpts from March 1917 can be found in: HStA/Kr, Stellv. Gen.kdo. I. Bayerisches AK München 1979. On the criteria of selection and the underlying social-scientific question, see the undated compilation of the Deputy General Command of the 1st Bavarian Army Corps Munich cited above, *passim*.

82. HStA/Kr, Stellv. Gen.kdo. I. Bayerisches AK München 1979.

83. Wirtschaftsstelle München-Süd to Stellv. Gen.kdo., 21 January 1918: HStA/ Kr, Stellv. Gen.kdo. I. Bayerisches AK München 1961.

84. Letter, 2 March 1917: HStA/Kr, Stellv. Gen.kdo. I. Bayerisches AK München 1979.

85. B. von Brentano, *Theodor Chindler. Roman einer deutschen Familie*. (Frankfurt/M., 1979), 307.

86. Johanna B. to Julius B., 8. October 1914, rpt. in Ullrich, *Kriegsalltag*, 23. Concerning the alienation of conscripted men and their relatives in general, see: A. Schütz, "Der Heimkehrer," in A. Schütz, *Gesammelte Aufsätze* (Den Haag, 1972), 2: 70-84; W. Waller, *Veteran Comes Back* (New York, 1944); D. Wecter, *When Johnny Comes Marching Home* (Cambridge, 1944); R. J. Lifton, *Home from the War* (New York, 1973); R. W. Whalen, *Bitter Wounds. German Victims of the Great War, 1914-1939* (Ithaca, NY, and London, 1984).

87. Marcuse, "Zur Frage," *passim*. Also see U. Linse, "Arbeiterschaft und Geburtenentwicklung im Deutschen Kaiserreich von 1871," *AfS* XII (1972): 205- 271, especially 224-229.

88. Marcuse, "Zur Frage," 775, 777.

89. Regierungspräsident Düsseldorf to Oberbürgermeister and Landräte, 9 June 1917: HStA Düsseldorf, Regierung Düsseldorf 43053 I, Bl. 13f.

90. S. Koppenfels, *Die Kriminalität der Frau im Kriege*, Kriminalistische Abhandlungen 11 Franz Exner, ed. (Leipzig, 1926), 31-32. The welfare doctor Bumm estimated the number of abortions at up to 40% of all pregnancies; E. Bumm, "Not und Fruchtabtreibung," *Münchener medizinische Wochenschrift* 70.50 (1923): 1471.

91. Koppenfels, *Kriminalität*, 32.

92. Heinel, *Bevölkerungsbewegung*, 67.
93. Ibid., 56-57.
94. Letter excerpt, 14 March 1917: HStA/Kr, Stellv. Gen.kdo. I. Bayerisches AK München 1979.
95. Karl Alexander von Müller to Bayerisches Kriegsministerium, 31 August 1916: HStA/Kr, MKr 2335. One intermediary agent of the Bavarian War Ministry, who was from the country himself, asserted that the women's movement was responsible for the spread of contraceptives among the rural population of Bavaria:

> Apparently, female emissaries would be sent from women's associations with emancipatory leanings to the country in order - often through the mediation of female teachers - to effect the destruction of the family structure, the basis of which was the subordination of the woman to the man, to attempt to cast doubt upon the respect of male authority, and furthermore, to support a special female lifestyle with special interests. Although it cannot be proven, one probable result of these endeavors is the rampant use of contraceptives and the consequent decline in the birthrate, which, in light of the regular granting of leave, can by no means be explained by the men's absence.

Memorandum about the report of an intermediary agent of the Bavarian War Ministry, September 1916, 2-3: HStA/Kr, MKr 17146

The bourgeois women's movement did not reject wartime population policy out of hand, but its stance was reserved. Above all, the movement criticized the fact that women themselves, as those principally affected by such considerations, were merely objects of a policy designed and directed by male politicians and specialists. As Adelheid Steinmann commented, somewhat smugly, in *Jahrbuch des BDF* in 1918: With regards to "some efforts to combat the decline in the birthrate," women are reproached

> for only thinking about themselves, not about the Fatherland, and for endangering the future of the nation. One can hear, in all seriousness, that one has to make women understand that they have a state function to perform with child-bearing . . . One hears this the most often from those circles that are otherwise the least inclined to grant women state functions.

A. Steinmann, "Die Frau in der Familie," *Jahrbuch des BDF 1918: Frauenaufgaben im künftigen Deutschland* (Berlin, 1918), 44

Also see G. Bäumer, *Lebensweg durch eine Zeitenwende* (Tübingen, 1933), 302-305.

96. Saalmann, "Ein Beitrag zur Frage der Bevölkerungspolitik nach dem Kriege," *Zeitschrift für Bevölkerungspolitik und Säuglingsfürsorge* 10 (1918): 233.
97. This observation, which was made by contemporaries about Vienna, can be applied without hesitation to conditions throughout the German Reich; A. Haberda, "Gerichtsärztliche Erfahrungen über die Fruchtabtreibung in Wien," *Vierteljahresschrift für gerichtliche Medizin und öffentliches Sanitätswesen* 56, 3rd ed. (1918): 59. In many cases, the birth of children in working-class families could be traced back to these families' lack of efficiency in using contraceptives rather than to their desire or planning for children; for this, see

Marcuse, "Zur Frage," *passim*. In looking back on the life of her parents, one daughter of a north German working-class family reported that her parents' knowledge about contraception came from a book in which the days on which a woman could not conceive were mixed up with those on which she could; D. Kachulle, ed., *Die Pöhlands im Krieg. Briefe einer Arbeiterfamilie aus dem Ersten Weltkrieg* (Köln, 1982), 19-20. The family had five children.

98. Memorandum about the commissary meeting in the Prussian Ministry of the Interior, re. combating the decline in the birthrate, 13 October 1915: ZStA Potsdam, Reichsministerium des Innern 9343, Bl. 8-9, *passim*.

99. For this, see the respective Memorandums about the commissary meetings in the Prussian Ministry of the Interior, re. combatting the decline in the birthrate on 13 October 1915, 17 March 1916, 8 April 1916, 9 May 1916, 6 June 1916, 9 September 1916, 27 September 1916, 2 November 1916, 6 December 1916, 21 December 1916, all in: ZStA Potsdam, Reichsministerium des Innern 9343, Bl. 8-9, 15ff., 25-30, 31ff., 36-40, 164-185, 225-240, 251-256, as well as Preußischer Innenminister to Vizepräsident des Staatsministeriums, re. draft of a report to the Emperor about the consultations of the Ministerial Commission on the decline in the birthrate, 8 March 1917: ZStA Potsdam, Reichsministerium des Innern 9344, Bl. 3-6; Memorandum about the causes of the decline in the birthrate and proposed measures to combat it, edited in the Ministry of the Interior, Berlin 1915: ZStA Potsdam, Reichsministerium des Innern 9342, Bl. 6ff.; "Denkschrift der Obersten Heeresleitung über die deutsche Volks- und Wehrkraft": ZStA Potsdam, Vertreter des Reichskanzlers bei der OHL 31. This draft, created by the head of the Front Health Authority, von Schjerning, was sent to the Supreme Command on 30 August 1917.

100. See, for example, Preußischer Innenminister to Staatssekretär des Reichsschatzamts, 28 September 1916: ZStA Potsdam, Reichsministerium des Innern 9343, Bl. 188; as well as the Memorandums from the commissary meetings (see previous endnote). For additional information on this subject, see P. Weindling, "The Medical Professions, Social Hygiene and the Birth-Rate in Germany, 1914-1918," in R. Wall and J. Winter, eds., *The Upheaval of War. Family, Work and Welfare in Europe, 1914-1918* (Cambridge, 1988), 417-437.

101. See the statement of the President of the Imperial Health Office on the Bundesrat's petition of the Berlin Society for Racial Hygiene, re. suitability for marriage, a comment which also contains a detailed description of German and international policy on this matter; Präsident des Kaiserlichen Gesundheitsamts to Staatssekretär des Innern, 11 December 1917: ZStA Potsdam, Reichsministerium des Innern 9379, Bl. 5-15.

102. The petition originated from the Berlin Society for Racial Hygiene; ZStA Potsdam, Reichsministerium des Innern 9379, Bl. 70-71. Also see C. Usborne, "Pregnancy is the Woman's Active Service: Pronatalism in Germany during the First World War," in Wall and Winter, eds., *Upheaval*, 389-416.

103. Preußischer Innenminister, 18 May 1918: HStA Düsseldorf, Regierung Düsseldorf 53851.71. 18. Bericht des Berliner Polizeipräsidenten, 30 November 1914: ZStA Potsdam, Reichskanzlei 2398/1, Bl. 53. With regards to the stance of the churches during the war, see W. Pressel, *Die Kriegspredigt 1914-1918 in der evangelischen Kirche Deutschlands* (Göttingen, 1967); H. Missalla, *"Gott mit uns." Die deutsche katholische Kriegspredigt 1914-1918* (München, 1968); K. Hammer, *Deutsche Kriegstheologie 1870-1918* (München, 1974); R. van

Dülmen, "Der deutsche Katholizismus und der Erste Weltkrieg," *Francia* 2 (1974): 347-376.

104. E. Wex, *Die Entwicklung der sozialen Fürsorge in Deutschland 1914-1927* (Berlin, 1929), 17-18, 26ff.

105. Regarding the role of health insurance in wartime social work, see A. Lauter, "Die deutsche Sozialversicherung vom Kriegsausbruch bis zum Frieden von Versailles," diss. (München, 1920/21), 139-160. For information about wartime social security in general, see F. Kleeis, *Die Geschichte der sozialen Versicherung in Deutschland* (Berlin, 1928, rpt. Berlin, 1981), 210 to the end. On infant welfare during the war, see H. Künkel, "Die Wohlfahrtspflege, ihr Begriff und ihre Bedeutung, unter besonderer Berücksichtigung der Familienfürsorge in der Provinz Brandenburg," diss. (Würzburg, n.d. [1920]), *passim*.

106. What follows is based on A. Fischer, *Staatliche Mütterfürsorge und der Krieg* (Berlin, 1915), 10-18.

107. Ibid., 4. For information about Alfons Fischer, see K.-D. Thomann, *Alfons Fischer (1873-1936) und die Badische Gesellschaft für soziale Hygiene* (Köln, 1980).

108. For this, see BA Koblenz, R 36/1143, *passim*.

109. Lauter, "Sozialversicherung," 33.

110. Regarding the corresponding efforts before 1914, see U. Frevert, "'Fürsorgliche Belagerung:' Hygienebewegung und Arbeiterfrauen im 19. und frühen 20. Jahrhundert," *GG* 11 (1985): 420-446.

111. Professor Hecker at the conference "Preservation and Increase of the Strength of the German People" (see note 36), 87-88; Kriegsgesundheitsbericht für den Regierungsbezirk Düsseldorf, 1.8.1914-31.12.1918: HStA Düsseldorf, Regierung Düsseldorf 8148. The Gesundheitsbericht für den Regierungsbezirk Aachen, 1914-1918, 60: HStA Düsseldorf, Regierung Aachen 6935, and the abovementioned Kriegsgesundheitsbericht für den Regierungsbezirk Düsseldorf refer to the shortage of milk as the reason.

112. Dr Bornstein at the conference "Preservation and Increase of the Strength of the German People" (see note 36), 124.

113. A survey conducted by a Berlin factory insurance company in 1915 of 367 mothers revealed that the shortage of milk as well as mothers' weakness and malnutrition were named as the most frequent reasons for stopping nursing; A. Bluhm, "Zur Kenntnis der Gattungsleistungen der Industriearbeiterinnen im Kriege," *Archiv für Rassen- und Gesellschafts-Biologie* 1 (1918/19): 77. The Maternity Benefit also did not bring about any far-reaching change in those regions where nursing one's own children was traditionally frowned upon; 17. Jahres- und Kassenbericht des Kinderfürsorgevereins für das Land Bayern, München 1917: Jahresbericht für 1916, 15: HStA/Kr, MKR 14383.

114. On adolescents and the youth-policy social reformers and the state in imperial Germany, see K. Saul, "Der Kampf um die Jugend zwischen Volksschule und Kaserne. Ein Beitrag zur 'Jugendpflege' im Wilhelminischen Reich 1890-1914," *MGM* 9 (1971), vol. 1, 97-143; K. Saul, "Jugend im Schatten des Krieges. Vormilitärische Ausbildung - Kriegswirtschaftlicher Einsatz - Schulalltag in Deutschland 1914-1918," *MGM* 34 (1983), vol. 2, 91-184; Th. Nipperdey, "Jugend und Politik um 1900," in Th. Nipperdey, *Gesellschaft, Kultur, Theorie* (Göttingen, 1976), 338-359; J. Reulecke, "Bürgerliche Sozialreformer und Arbeiterjugend im Kaiserreich," *AfS* 22 (1982): 299-329; K. Tenfelde, "Groß-

stadtjugend in Deutschland vor 1914," *VSWG* 69 (1982): 182–218; E. Domansky, "Politische Dimensionen von Jugendprotest und Generationenkonflikt in der Zwischenkriegszeit in Deutschland," in D. Dowe, ed., *Jugendprotest und Generationenkonflikt in Deutschland, England, Frankreich und Italien im 20. Jahrhundert* (Bonn-Bad Godesberg, 1986), 113–137; D. Peukert, *Grenzen der Sozialdisziplinierung. Aufstieg und Krise der deutschen Jugendfürsorge von 1878 bis 1932* (Köln, 1986). In terms of the history of youth policy in the twentieth century, see C. Hasenclever, *Jugendhilfe und Jugendgesetzgebung seit 1900* (Göttingen, 1978).

115. As before, female adolescents continued to be treated almost primarily as prospective wives and mothers by this age-specific social policy. Schools, communities and socio-political organizations were supposed to give them the necessary qualifications in housekeeping and infant welfare. See, for example, Reports from the Düsseldorf administrative district, re. youth welfare and occupational choice of school-leavers, 1915 and 1916: HStA Düsseldorf, Regierung Düsseldorf 33120. The number of official complaints about, in particular, male adolescents was immense; for some examples, see Civil Servant Bracht at a demobilization meeting in the Reichstag, 15 January 1918: BA Koblenz, NL 151/159, 2ff.; Monatsberichte, 3 July 1918, 22: BA/MA, RM3/7795.

116. Contemporary literature about the "waywardness" of male adolescents is quite comprehensive. See, for example, Minde, "Die zunehmende Verwahrlosung der Jugend," *Deutsche Strafrechts-Zeitung* 2 (1915): 501–506; Köhne, "Die Jugendlichen und der Krieg," *Deutsche Strafrechts-Zeitung* 3 (1916): 13–18; Rupprecht, "Die Jugendstraffälligkeit in Bayern im Frieden und im Kriege," *Deutsche Strafrechts-Zeitung* 3 (1916): 128–134; "Ungeeignete Maßnahmen gegen Minderjährige," *Korrespondenzblatt der Generalkommission der Gewerkschaften Deutschlands* 26 (11.3.1916): 116–117; Kronecker, "Strafvorschriften gegen die Verwahrlosung Jugendlicher," *Leipziger Zeitschrift für deutsches Recht* 10.8 (1916): 576–584; B. Fränkel, *Maßnahmen zur Bekämpfung der Verwahrlosung der Jugend* (Breslau, 1916); Prölß, "Kriegsjugendschutz," *Deutsche Juristenzeitung* 22 (1917): 185–190; E. Voigtländer, "Veränderungen der Verwahrlosung während des Krieges," *Mitteilungen der Deutschen Zentrale für Jugendfürsorge* 13 (1918): 24–26; E. Voigtländer, "Die Entwicklung der Verwahrlosung in den Jahren 1914–1920," *Zentralblatt für Vormundschaftswesen, Jugendgerichte und Fürsorgeerziehung* 13 (1921/22): 193–197; G. Moses, *Zum Problem der sozialen Familienverwahrlosung unter besonderer Berücksichtigung der Verhältnisse im Krieg*. Beiträge zur Kinderforschung und Heilerziehung 175 (Langensalza, 1920).

117. "Jahresbericht der Gewerbeaufsicht des Regierungsbezirks Breslau 1914–1918," in *Jahresberichte der Gewerbeaufsicht 1914–1918*, 1: 389.

118. "Gewerbeaufsichtsbericht Schwarzburg-Sondershausen 1914–1918," ibid., 3: 10. Almost every report of the Factory Inspectorate during the First World War included such complaints; they were raised, in particular, in urban-industrial regions.

119. As evidence of the numerous complaints about the moral waywardness of male adolescents, see, in addition to the *Jahresberichte der Gewerbeaufsicht 1914–1918, passim*, Ullrich, *Kriegsalltag*, 33; Stellv. Gen.kdo. I. Bayerisches AK München, Monatsbericht, April 1918, 5: HStA/Kr, MKr 12848; Memorandum of the High Command in the Marches, re. the 18 March 1916 announcement of

forced savings for adolescents, 19 August 1916: HStA Düsseldorf, Regierung Düsseldorf 33555.

In the somewhat obscure 1919 publication *Das Liebesleben im Weltkriege*, which nevertheless contains interesting individual observations, E. Iros reported about the "cock of the walk" syndrome exhibited by men who had not been drafted and, above all, by male adolescents who earned good wages. According to Iros, the sight of "very young lovers" had caused a sensation, both in industrial areas and in the country. Sixteen- and seventeen-year-old boys had supposedly already had permanent relationships as, earlier, the pupils at the secondary modern schools (*höhere Mittelschule or Realschule*) or the Berlin apprentices in the clothing industry, and the sexual style of these lower classes seemed to have become the common property of all male adolescents during the war. E. Iros, in H. Dolsenhain, ed., *Das Liebesleben im Weltkriege* (Nürnberg, 1919), vol. 1, part 2, 3rd and 4th half-vol.: 21-22.

[In this period, primarily members of the upper and upper-middle classes attended the gymnasium, which was – and is – prerequisite for a university education. Mittelschule or Realschule was more for members of the lower-middle class. Translator]

120. The number of unexcused absences for both boys and girls continued to increase in the post-war period. Liepmann, *Krieg*, 88.

121. In 1882, 30,697 juveniles between the ages of 12 and 17 were convicted. In 1896, this number was 43,962, which signified an increase of 43%. For every 10,000 juveniles in 1882, there were 568 convictions, as compared to 1896, where there were 697 (+22%). Fränkel, *Maßnahmen*, 3. Between 1909 and 1913, the number of juveniles convicted by local and district courts rose from 1,419 to 2,058 (+45.7%) in Munich, from 1,866 to 3,102 (+66%) in Nuremberg and from 447 to 645 (+44.3%) in Augsburg. For the same period of time, the number of persons convicted overall only rose 12.4%. Rupprecht, "Jugendstraffälligkeit," 129.

122. Voigtländer, "Veränderungen," 25.

123. On the history and critique of the term "waywardness," see A. Gregor and E. Voigtländer, *Die Verwahrlosung männlicher Jugendlicher*, pt. 1 of *Die Verwahrlosung, ihre klinisch-psychologische Bewertung und ihre Bekämpfung* (Berlin, 1918), 3; M. Kieper, *Lebenswelten 'verwahrloster' Mädchen* (München, 1980), 17-24; M. Kieper, "'Verwahrlosung'," in H.-J. Petzold and H. Speichert, eds., *Handbuch pädagogischer und sozialpädagogischer Praxisbegriffe*, (Reinbek, 1981), 482ff.; W. Reichel, "'Verwahrlosung'," in G. Rexilius and S. Grubitzsch, eds., *Handbuch psychologischer Grundbegriffe* (Reinbek, 1981), 1194-1198; K. Horn, "Gewalt versöhnt nicht mit Normen," in *Erziehung in geschlossenen Heimen*, Bundesjugendkuratorium, ed. (München, 1982), 13-14; Peukert, *Grenzen*, 54-67, 107-115, 151-162.

124. Landrat Dinslaken to Regierungspräsident Düsseldorf, 24 December 1915: HStA Düsseldorf, Regierung Düsseldorf 33120.

125. Landrat Krefeld to Regierungspräsident Düsseldorf, 28 December 1915: ibid. Where women were awarded any active function in socialization, it was predominantly a negative one. Thus, for example, female workers in factories were held to be jointly responsible for juveniles' indiscipline. *Jahresberichte der Gewerbeaufsicht 1914-1918, passim.* Normally, however, women were found to be too "weak" or "soft" in their capacity as mothers to be able to have

any influence on their children's lifestyle. This topos endured beyond the war; as late as 1927, Friedrich Zahn attributed the "waywardness" of youth during the war to women's great softness. F. Zahn, "Die deutsche Familie und der Wiederaufbau unseres Volkes," *Allgemeines Statistisches Archiv* 16 (1927): 8.

126. Preußischer Kriegsminister to Vizepräsident des preußischen Staatsministeriums, 2 February 1915: ZStA Potsdam, Reichskanzlei 2398/1.

127. Ibid. and Saul, "Jugend," 97, 103. In the labor movement, a clear mistrust of this institution prevailed. In Hamburg, party and union leaders had agreed in 1914 that the working-class youth should be included in the "Youth Army." This decision had to be withdrawn following the protests of youth organizations and party meetings. Ullrich, *Kriegsalltag*, 33ff. For this, also see Saul, "Jugend," 97–100 and G. Fiedler, *Jugend in Krieg. Bürgerliche Jugendbewegung, Erster Weltkrieg und Sozialer Wandel (1914–1923)* (Köln, 1989), 76–80.

128. Landrat Solingen to Regierungspräsident Düsseldorf, 15 January 1916: HStA Düsseldorf, Regierung Düsseldorf 33120.

129. Thus, in May 1916, the rumour circulated in the 1st Bavarian Army Corps Munich that the Youth Army had shot hundreds of people during the revolts over price increases in Berlin, among them the members' own mothers. At least one set of parents withdrew its son from the Munich army association because of this. Stellv. Gen.kdo. I. Bayerisches AK München, 22 May 1916: HStA/Kr, Stellv. Gen.kdo. I. Bayerisches AK München 1723.

130. For this and the following, see the Memorandum of the High Command in the Marches, re. the 18 March 1916 announcement of forced savings for adolescents: HStA Düsseldorf, Regierung Düsseldorf 33555.

131. Ibid., 9.

132. *Kriegsverwaltungsbericht Neukölln*, 328. In April 1916, the Chairman of the Arnsberg Regional Council reported to the Prussian Minister for Trade and Industry about the migration of male adolescent workers out of Berlin. See his letter of 27 April 1916: StA Münster, Oberpräsidium 6801.

133. "Jahresbericht des Landespolizeibezirks Berlin 1914–1918," in *Jahresberichte der Gewerbeaufsicht 1914–1918*, 1: 238.

134. See, for example, Monatesberichte, 3 July 1918, 23: BA/MA, RM3/7795, about the introduction of forced savings for adolescents in Alsace-Lorraine.

135. For a detailed version of this episode, see F. Boll, *Massenbewegungen in Niedersachsen 1906–1920. Eine sozialgeschichtliche Untersuchung zu den unterschiedlichen Entwicklungstypen Braunschweig und Hannover* (Bonn, 1981), 217–234. Several Deputy General Commands only introduced forced savings for adolescents who were conspicuously "extravagant;" such was the case with the Army Corps Kassel, for example.

136. "Jahresberichte der Gewerbeaufsicht Hamburgs und Bremens 1914–1918," in *Jahresberichte der Gewerbeaufsicht 1914–1918*, 3: Hamburg: 29, Bremen: 54.

137. "Jahresbericht des Regierungsbezirks Koblenz 1914–1918," ibid., 1: 932.

138. Oberpräsident Münster to Stellv. Gen.kdo. VII Münster, 19 May 1916: StA Münster, Oberpräsidium 6801; Regierungspräsident Münster to Stellv. Gen.kdo. VII Münster, 17 August 1916: ibid.: Regierungspräsident Arnsberg to Stellv. Gen.kdo. VII Münster, 30 September 1916: ibid. See also the additional documents pertaining to these discussions in the Army Corps Münster's sector.

139. Minutes of a meeting, 20 October 1916, 1–6: HStA Düsseldorf, Regierung Düsseldorf 33555.

140. Ibid., 9. Regarding the stance of the trade unions and employers, see also the enclosure to the letter the Chairman of the Arnsberg Regional Council wrote to the Chief Chairman in Münster, 3 November 1916: StA Münster, Oberpräsidium 6801. The civil administrations also remained firm in their rejection of forced savings, and this time their ranks included the chairman of the Arnsberg Regional Council: StA Münster, Oberpräsidium 6801, *passim*.

141. Stellv. Gen.kdo. VII. AK Münster to Preußische Kriegsminister, 16 January 1917: ibid. In terms of the compulsory-savings discussion in other German states, see HStA/Kr, MKr 12649, 12650 and 12848, which concerns Bavaria and Baden.

142. A *Malter* was a measurement used in Prussia. It was equivalent to 695.5 liters. [Translator]

143. Glaeser, *Jahrgang 1902*, 292ff.

144. For rationing and prices policy during the First World War, see Daniel, *Arbeiterfrauen*, 183–215.

145. "The history of the collapse of the power that was legitimate until 1918 (in Germany) shows how the dissolution of the bond to tradition through the war, on the one hand, and the loss in prestige through defeat, on the other, in connection with the systematic habituation to illegal behaviour in equal measure shattered the obedience to army and work discipline and thus prepared the coup against established authority." M. Weber, *Wirtschaft und Gesellschaft*, 5th rev. ed. (Tübingen, 1972), 155.

146. G. Albrecht, "Die Unterstützung der Familien Einberufener. Entwicklung und gesetzliche Grundlagen," *Jahrbücher für Nationalökonomie und Statistik* 151 (1940): 66.

147. M. Hoffmann, "Das Gesetz betreffend die Unterstützung von Familien in den Dienst eingetretener Mannschaften vom 28.2.1888/4.8.1914 und seine Anwendung," diss. (Berlin, 1918), 8, 15.

148. The information in the following section is found in Hoffmann, "Gesetz," 1–37, and Albrecht, "Unterstützung," 67–71.

149. This and what follows is according to Albrecht, "Unterstützung," 71–74, and Hoffmann, "Gesetz," 38–67. The entire package of the War Economy Law of 4 August 1914 is printed, with detailed commentary, in I. Jastrow, *Im Kriegszustand* (Berlin, 1914), 139ff., 145–158; see also B. Kundrus, *Kriegerfrauen. Familienpolitik und Geschlechter verhältnisse im Ersten und Zweiten Weltkrieg* (Hamburg, 1995).

150. Reichsamt des Innern to Bundesregierungen, 9 January 1917: GLA Karlsruhe, 456 EV8/111, and J. Fichtel, "Der Familienlohn," diss. (München, 1926), 27.

151. Stellv. Gen.kdo. VII. AK Münster to Preußisches Kriegsministerium, 6 June 1915: ZStA Potsdam, Reichsministerium des Innern 12092, Bl. 95–96.

152. Memorandum of a meeting about Family Aid between the Imperial Office of the Interior, the state governments, trade unions, representatives of industry, and congresses of municipal authorities, etc., 11 November 1915: ZStA Potsdam, Reichsministerium des Innern 12094, Bl. 212ff. With these estimates, the figures for Bavaria were projected onto the Reich; the delivering agencies' reports for the entire area of the Reich were not available.

153. *Hauptergebnisse der Volkszählung im Deutschen Reich am 5.12.*

The Family in the First World War

1917, Volkswirtschaftliche Abteilung des Kriegsernährungsamts, ed. (Berlin, 1918), 2.

154. J. Reulecke, "Städtische Finanzprobleme und Kriegswohlfahrtspflege im Ersten Weltkrieg unter besonderer Berücksichtigung der Stadt Barmen," *Zeitschrift für Stadtgeschichte, Stadtsoziologie und Denkmalpflege* 1 (1975): 70.

155. Wex, *Entwicklung*, 15.

156. Ch. Klumker and B. Schmittmann, eds., *Wohlfahrtsämter* (Stuttgart, 1920), 12.

157. In August 1916, the amount for the city-state Lubeck of 225,000 marks was added up by the authorities as an estimate. Nachweisung über die gezahlte Familienunterstützung: ZStA Potsdam, Reichsministerium des Innern 12129, Bl. 68-69.

158. Hoffmann, "Gesetz," 59.

159. Calculated according to *Statistisches Jahrbuch für den preußischen Staat* 16 (1920): 320.

160. Calculated according to Nachweisungen über die gezahlte Familienunterstützung: ZStA Merseburg, Rep. 77, Tit. 332g, Nr. 27, Beiheft 3, Bd. 1-7. These are the minimum allowances in Prussia for 1914 to 1918.

161. Excerpts from communications of the Royal Bavarian State Ministry of the Royal House, Royal Bavarian State Foreign Ministry and Royal Bavarian State Ministry of the Interior, re. the wartime activities of the state's domestic administration: ZStA Potsdam, Reichsministerium des Innern 12094, Bl. 184-185.

162. P. Hirsch, "Die Kriegsfürsorge der deutschen Gemeinden," *Annalen für soziale Politik und Gesetzgebung* 4 (1916): 263-264.

163. For this and the following information, see Reulecke, "Städtische Finanzprobleme," 68-77.

164. Staatssekretär des Reichsschatzamts to Preußischer Innenminister, 15 August 1914: ZStA Potsdam, Reichsministerium des Innern 12089, Bl. 254-257; Reichsschatzamt/Reichskanzler to Preuâischer Innen- und Finanzminister, 30 September 1915: ZStA Merseburg, Rep. 120BB VII 1, Nr. 3i, Bd. 2, Bl. 337-346; Commissary meeting in the Imperial Office of the Interior between the Imperial Treasury, Imperial Naval Office, Imperial Office of the Interior, Ministry of the Interior, Ministry for Trade and Industry and the War Ministry, 7 July 1916: ibid.

165. Preußischer Innenminister to Regierungspräsidenten, 30 September 1914: ZStA Potsdam, Reichsministerium des Innern 12089, Bl. 203-204.

166. At the beginning of the war, the indebtedness of the communities lay at 7.5 billion marks, to which still another 60 to 70 million marks of short-term debt were added. By the same point in time, the Reich had taken out approximately 5 billion marks in loans. J. Reulecke, "Wirtschaft und Bevölkerung ausgewählter Städte im Ersten Weltkrieg (Barmen, Düsseldorf, Essen, Krefeld)," in J. Reulecke, ed., *Die deutsche Stadt im Industriezeitalter. Beiträge zur modernen deutschen Stadtgeschichte* (Wuppertal, 1980), 115.

167. See, for example, Reichsamt des Innern, 25 January 1915, 2: BA/MA, RM31/958.

168. 26. Stimmungsbericht des Berliner Polizeipräsidenten, 23 January 1915: ZStA Potsdam, Reichskanzlei 2398/1, Bl. 183; report no. 37, 17 April 1915 is identical. The increasing opinions of contemporaries about "war wives'" behaviour as consumers was not limited to urban areas. Rural "war wives" were also reproached for squandering their war aid in the city. See, for example,

Memorandum about a meeting, re. the establishment of War Industry Offices, 18 January 1917, 17-22: BA/MA, RM31/1003.

169. Weida Board of Aldermen (Saxony-Weimar), as quoted in *Vossische Zeitung*, 22 August 1916. The emphasis of this announcement lay on the municipal Family Aid and not on the statutory minimum aid provided by the Reich, since the latter was not allowed to be cut.

170. *Vorwärts*, 7 June 1915.

171. Landrat Itzehoe about the riots in Itzehoe, Glückstadt and Lägerdorf, 29 January 1917: ZStA Merseberg, Rep. 197A, Io, Nr. 1, Bd. 2, Bl. 31-35.

172. Monatsbericht des Stellv. Gen.kdo.s I. Bayerisches AK München für Mai 1917, 5 June 1917, 2: HStA/Kr, MKr 12844; identical are the Monatsberichte, 3 July 1917: BA/MA, RM3, 5 (XX. AK Allenstein).

173. Letter from a Saxony "war wife" to her husband, a prisoner of war, March 1917: HStA/Kr, Stellv. Gen.kdo. I. Bayerisches AK München 1979.

174. Bericht der Eisenbahnüberwachung, Kriminalwachtmeister H., re. the surveillance of the railway route Munich-Ulm-Kempten-Munich on 7 August 1917, 8 August 1917: HStA/Kr, MKr 11484.

175. Reichsverband Deutscher Städte to Reichsamt des Innern, 27 September 1915: ZStA Potsdam, Reichsministerium des Innern 12093, Bl. 117.

176. Magistrat Kattowitz to Reichsamt des Innern per telegraph, 6 October 1915: ibid., Bl. 164.

177. Staatssekretär des Reichsmarineamts to Marinestation Ostsee, 18 May 1915: Zusammenstellung der Grundsätze über die Anwendung des Gesetzes vom 28. Febr. 1888 in der Fassung des Gesetzes vom 4. August 1914: BA/MA, RM31/958. See also Hirsch, "Kriegsfürsorge," 264-265. The idea of a "moral economy" that developed during the war through the example of families with conscripted members did not only concern Family War Aid. Already at the beginning of the war, "the opinion, which was difficult to combat, had spread that war participants, along with their families, were relieved of paying any rent." *Kriegsverwaltungsbericht der Stadt Neukölln*, 344. The term "moral economy" is used here as a prescientific collective name for widespread public perceptions of a "just" social and economic policy. The term is not, however, used in exactly the same sense in which Edward P. Thompson introduced it. If one remains true to its original meaning, then the term can only partially be applied to the First World War. As with Thompson's examples from eighteenth-century England, the question during the years 1914 to 1918 was also one of the population's generalized ideas about what was economically "fair" or "unfair," ideas that the authorities shared to a certain extent. During the First World War, however, these ideas were not based on legitimations through tradition and were also not concerned with a generalization of the money economy, in which Thompson embedded the term "moral economy." E. P. Thompson, "The Moral Economy of the English Crowd in the 18th Century," *Past and Present* 50 (1971), 76-136.

178. Letter to a prisoner of war from Planitz, 4 March 1917: HStA/Kr, Stellv. Gen.kdo. I. Bayerisches AK München 1979.

179. Hoffmann, "Gesetz," 283-284, 301-302.

180. Magistrat Lauban, Petition to abolish the need clause, 18 November 1914: ZStA Potsdam, Reichsministerium des Innern 12091, Bl. 27-28.

181. See, for example, Preußischer Kriegsminister to Reichsamt des Innern,

26 October 1914; Preußischer Innenminister to Reichsamt des Innern, 4 November 1914: ZStA Potsdam, Reichsministerium des Innern 12089. The War Minister was for, the Minister of the Interior against abolishing the need clause. Even the Commission for the Imperial Budget (*Kommission für den Reichshaushaltsetat*) in the Reichstag had proposed a motion to abolish the need clause; ibid. 12091, Bl. 152.

182. Wex, *Entwicklung*, 16.

183. A. Blos, *Kommunale Frauenarbeit im Kriege* (Berlin, 1917), 7-8. Complaints about the authorities' poor treatment of "war wives" were on the agenda all throughout the war; see, for example, Reichsamt des Innern 26 July 1918: HStA/Kr, Stellv. Gen.kdo. I. Bayerisches AK München 882.

184. Bezirksamt Augsburg to Stellv. Gen.kdo. I. Bayerisches AK München, 19 December 1916: HStA/Kr, Stellv. Gen.kdo. I. Bayerisches AK München 980. Also there see Bericht der Polizeidirektion München to Stellv. Gen.kdo. I. Bayerisches AK München, 28 December 1916, and Bezirksamt Vilsbiburg to Stellv. Gen.kdo. I. Bayerisches AK München, 23 December 1916.

185. See, for example, Vorstand des Gesamtverbandes der christlichen Gewerkschaften to Stellvetreter des Reichskanzlers, 5 October 1914: ZStA Potsdam, Reichsministerium des Innern 12089; *Jahresbericht der Gewerbeaufsicht 1914- 1918*, 1: 411-412; Monatsberichte, 3 February 1917: BA/MA, RM3/4670.

186. 18. Bericht des Berliner Polizeipräsidenten, 30 November 1914: ZStA Potsdam, Reichskanzlei 2398/1, Bl. 53.

187. Compare with the chapter 2. Trade-union representatives estimated that, in November 1915, the number of families who were better-off financially than before the war because of Family War Aid was 1,000, at the highest, 10,000. Memorandum on the meeting between the Imperial Office of the Interior, federal governments, congresses of municipal authorities, industry- and trade union representatives, re. Family Aid, 11 November 1915: ZStA Potsdam, Reichsministerium des Innern 12094, Bl. 212ff.

188. See, for example, Regierungspräsident Magdeburg, September 1917: ZStA Merseburg, Rep. 77, Tit. 1059, Nr. 3, Beiheft 2, Bd. 1, Bl. 183.

189. Additionally, see E. Lederer's analysis of the collapse of the money economy; E. Lederer, "Die ökonomische Umschichtung im Kriege," *Archiv für Sozialwissenschaft und Sozialpolitik* 45 (1918/19): 1-39, 430-463, esp. 9-13. The expression "collapse of the money economy" does not imply that a complete relapse to barter-economic forms of intercourse had occurred during the First World War; a money economy, albeit in limited form, continued to exist. For this, see A. Dopsch, *Naturalwirtschaft und Geldwirtschaft in der Weltgeschichte* (Wien, 1930; rpt. Aalen, 1968), 251-252. What had collapsed, however, was the function of a "normal" money economy to maintain the exchange of goods for money as the rule of circulation. Regarding wartime food rationing and prices policy, see Daniel, *Arbeiterfrauen*, 183-215.

190. G. Briefs, "Entwicklung und Verfassung der Hauswirtschaft innerhalb der Volkswirtschaft," in G. Briefs et al., eds., *Hauswirtschaft im Kriege*. Beiträge zur Kriegswirtschaft 25 (Berlin, 1917), 30; M Voß-Zietz, "Praktische Hauswirtschaft im Kriege," in ibid., 61.

191. Monatsberichte, 3 July 1917, 3: BA/MA, RM3/4670.

192. Stellv. Gen.kdo. VIII. AK Koblenz to Handelskammern und industrielle Vereinigungen, 7 February 1917: HStA Düsseldorf, Regierung Aachen 8067.

193. Monatsberichte, 3 May 1917, 28: BA/MA, RM3/4670.

194. Memorandum of the official meeting of the Chairmen of the Regional Councils, Berlin, 11 October 1916: HStA Düsseldorf, Regierung Düsseldorf 14920, Bl. 283–284. The only other population group that received an allocation of a group-specific consumer good out of consideration for morale was the population of Bavaria: It received a greater allotment of beer. A. Skalweit, *Deutsche Kriegsernährungswirtschaft*. Wirtschafts- und Sozialgeschichte des Weltkriegs, German series (Stuttgart et al., 1927), 80.

195. *Berliner Tageblatt* 256, 19 May 1916; as quoted in Skalweit, *Deutsche Kriegsernährungswirtschaft*, 200ff.

196. I. von Blanquet, "Die Kriegsernährungswirtschaft der Stadt Cassel und ihre Lehren für die öffentliche Lebensmittelversorgung," diss. (Köln, 1923), 63–64. There was a lot of mistrust of, among other things, frozen meat, which was seldom sold to consumers before the war.

197. Monatsberichte, 3 April 1917, 44: BA/MA, RM3/4670.

198. Monatsberichte für August, 12: ibid.

199. Monatsbericht des bayerischen Kriegsministerium/Pressereferat für Dezember 1916, 23: HStA/Kr, MKR 12843, and Monatsbericht des bayerischen Kriegsministerium/Pressereferat für Februar 1917, 18: ibid.; von Blanquet, "Kriegsernährungswirtschaft," 45. Such confiscation campaigns were carried out in Munich and Nuremberg, among other cities.

200. See, for example, F. Kalle and O. Kamp, *Die hauswirtschaftliche Unterweisung armer Mädchen* (Wiesbaden, 1889), III. Compare this with G. Tornieporth, *Studien zur Frauenbildung* (Weinheim and Basel, 1979), 85–174.

201. See, for example, Monatsberichte, 3 August 1917, 7, 63: BA/MA, RM3/4670; Regierungspräsident Düsseldorf to (Ober)Bürgermeister and Landräte, 17 May 1916: HStA Düsseldorf, Regierung Düsseldorf 33094; A. von Harnack, *Der Krieg und die Frauen* (Berlin, 1915), 15–16. To representatives of the bourgeois women's movement, communicating knowledge of home economics and national economics to working-class women had already been an important matter of concern before 1914. Their commentary on the complaints about housewives' lack of home-economic skills thus contained a certain amount of smugness:

> [Before the war,] the communication of technical ability and rational sense in the breadth and depth of a woman's tasks in the house, the family and the national community was, despite all the warnings, generally left to coincidence and to the personal decision of each individual woman. The use of the cheap cliché: "To whom God gives a task, he also gives reason" regarding the education and training of women will probably be bitterly avenged now. What every social worker had experienced a thousand times in the life of widows, the requirement that they, suddenly unprepared, unschooled, simultaneously have to be father and mother, breadwinner and child-rearer, today counted for millions of German women of all classes and stations: Know everything, be capable of everything, do everything!

> M.-E. Lüders, *Das unbekannte Heer. Frauen kämpfen für Deutschland 1914–1918* (Berlin, 1937), 24

202. The Association of German Housewives held its first general assembly in Hamburg in June 1916 and its second in Munich in June 1917. In 1913, it had

114 affiliated associations with over 100,000 members. ZStA Potsdam, 70Re2/ 18, Bl. 291. One of the association's wartime activities with the most lasting effect was its propagation of red beets, which the Imperial Office for Fruit and Vegetables had requested since the population did not know what to do with the vegetable. Ibid., Bl. 399. For the development of the housewives' organization during the Weimar Republic, see R. Bridenthal, "'Professional' Housewives: Stepsisters of the Women's Movement," in R. Bridenthal et al., eds., *When Biology Became Destiny: Women in Weimar and Nazi Germany* (New York, 1984), 153-173.

203. A. Lindemann, "Anpassung des Einzelhaushalts an die jetzige Lage," in A. Lindemann, ed., *Unsere Ernährung in der Kriegszeit. Neun Vorträge, gehalten bei dem Lehrkursus des Nationalen Frauendienstes im Stuttgarter Landesgewerbemuseum, 22.–24. Februar 1915* (Berlin, 1915), 57. Also see E. Schumacher, *Die Kriegspflichten der Hausfrau* (Bonn, 1915), *passim*.

204. A. von Zahn-Harnach, *Die arbeitende Frau* (Breslau, 1924), 93.

205. F. Wohltmann, *Unsere Volksernährung und die deutsche Hausfrau* (Berlin, 1915), 32.

206. Lindemann, "Anpassung," 55.

207. Ibid., 51.

208. G. Bäumer, *Lebensweg durch eine Zeitenwende* (Tübingen, 1933), 278.

209. Voß-Zietz, "Praktische Hauswirtschaft im Kriege," 43. Additionally, see Lindemann, "Anpassung," 64-65; Steinmann, "Die Frau in der Familie," 38-39.

210. Monatsbericht des Stellv. Gen.kdo.s II. Bayerisches AK Würzburg für August 1918: HStA/Kr, MKr 12849, D., Bl. 1.

211. Bericht der Wissenschaftlichen Deputation für das Medizinalwesen to Preußischer Innenminister, 18 July 1917: HStA Düsseldorf, Regierung Düsseldorf 38865, 63-64, 70. For this, also see H. Rubner, "Der Gesundheitszustand im allgemeinen," in Bumm, ed., *Deutschlands Gesundheitsverhältnisse*, 72-75, 82.

212. See, for example, the obituary the Munich historian Hermann von Grauert wrote for his colleague Albert Hauck in 1919: "He supposedly pursued conscientiousness to such lengths during the war that, in his own diet, he did not permit himself to exceed the ration quantities that were alloted to him. As a result of this, he presumably died of enfeeblement." As cited in K. L. Ay, *Die Entstehung einer Revolution. Die Volksstimmung in Bayern während des Ersten Weltkriegs* (Berlin, 1968), 122. Marie-Elisabeth Lüders' mother also died in this way, of a state-decreed malnutrition. Lüders, *Fürchte dich nicht*, 74.

213. Letter, 24 March 1917: HStA/Kr, Stellv. Gen.kdo. I. Bayerisches AK München 1979.

214. During the air raids of the First World War, "only" 273 civilians died in Prussia and 220 in Baden. Heinel, *Bevölkerungsbewegung*, 10. Regarding the development of the mortality rates of the male and female German populations between 1914 and 1918, see ibid., Table 50, and Marschalck, *Bevölkerungsgeschichte*, 169.

215. Heinel, *Bevölkerungsbewegung*, 139-140.

216. In terms of an exact calculation of infant mortality rates between 1914 and 1918 that takes the high yearly drop in the number of births into account, see *Bewegung der Bevölkerung*, LVIII–LXVI.

217. Dr Czerny, director of the children's hospital at the Berlin hospital Charité, before the Investigating Committee on the German collapse, in *Die*

Ursachen des deutschen Zusammenbruchs im Jahre 1918, Zweite Abteilung: Der innere Zusammenbruch, A. Philipp, ed. (Berlin, 1928), ser. 4, 4:196. For this, also see Medizinalrat Dr Ritter at the Herford meeting on the war economy in the Minden administrative district, 27 October 1917: HStA Düsseldorf, Regierung Düsseldorf 14916, p. 7 of the minutes.

218. Heinel, *Bevölkerungsbewegung*, 12. The military losses in the First World War amounted to between 1.9 and 2.4 million soldiers. Marschalck, *Bevölkerungsgeschichte*, 148.

219. Monatsberichte, 3 April 1917, 8: BA/MA, RM3/4670. See also, among others, Memorandum on the sixth consultation with representatives of the state, province and district price offices, Dresden, 15 December 1917: ZStA Potsdam, Reichsministerium des Innern 10144, Bl. 156ff., 9.

220. The terms "hamster" (*Hamster*) and "squirrel" (*Hamsterer*) were used synonymously during the First World War.

221. Regierungspräsident Mittelfranken to Bayerischer Innenminister, 17 June 1917; as cited in Ay, *Entstehung*, 116.

222. Monatsberichte, 3 November 1916, 32: BA/MA, RM3/4670; Monatsberichte, 3 May 1917, 15: ibid.; Monatsberichte, 3 July 5: ibid.; Monatsberichte, 3 August 1917, 18: ibid.

223. Ay, *Entstehung*, 116.

224. Monatsberichte, 3 March 1917, 16: BA/MA, RM3/4670.

225. Monatsberichte, 3 August 1918, 11: BA/MA, RM3/7796; File note of the State Secretary of the War Food Office, re. a meeting in War Food Office, 11 November 1918: ZStA Potsdam, Reichsministerium des Innern 10146, Bl. 438-441.

226. Magistrat Wandsbek, 24 September 1917: ZStA Merseburg, Rep. 77, Tit. 1059, Nr. 3, Beiheft 2, Bd. 1, Bl. 214. The trainstation Winsen/Luhe, for example, was positioned in the middle of a main delivery route for new potatoes. From 10 to 19 July 1918 - i.e. at the height of the harvest - the station sold between 1,600 and 4,400 tickets to Hamburg each day, whereas, toward the end of the month, that number was only between 300 and 490. From time to time, the "squirrels" gathered the potatoes from the fields themselves and disappeared without paying. Monatsberichte, 3 August 1918, 11: BA/MA, RM3/7796.

227. Memorandum on the sixth consultation with representatives of the state, province and district price offices, Dresden, 15 December 1917, 15: ZStA Potsdam, Reichsministerium des Innern, 10144, Bl. 156ff.

228. Bezirksamt Berchtesgaden to Regierung Oberbayern, 14 June 1918: HStA/Kr, Stellv. Gen.kdo. I. Bayerisches AK München 1966.

229. Monatsberichte, 3 March 1917, 9: BA/MA, RM3/4670. In terms of this, see also HStA Düsseldorf, Regierung Düsseldorf 14196 and 14917, *passim*.

230. Monatsberichte, 3 August 1918, 12: BA/MA, RM3/7796.

231. Bayerisches Kriegsministerium to Stellv. Gen.kdo.s etc., 5 May 1918: HStA/Kr, Stellv. Gen.kdo. I. Bayerisches AK München 557.

232. Monatsberichte für November 1917, 22: HStA/Kr, MKr 12852.

233. War-economy meetings of the governments of the Rhine province and of Westphalia, 4 May 1917: HStA Düsseldorf, Regierung Düsseldorf 14916. In addition, see Monatsberichte, 3 February 1917, 16: BA/MA, RM3/4670; Monatsberichte, 3 August 1917, 5: ibid.; Monatsberichte, 3 August 1918, 12: BA/MA, RM3/7796. In June 1917, the mayor of Orsoy demanded that the draft

board of Moers transfer individuals required to do emergency labor service to his city to watch over the fields. The mayor wrote:

The city of Hamborn lies across from us. Every day, countless dubious elements, who have their eye on our produce or get up to all sorts of mischief in the fields and meadows, come from there. On Sundays, the number of visitors increases into the thousands. The local police administration, with only one single policeman, is powerless in the face of these masses.

Orsoy Bürgermeister to Einberufungsausschuß Moers, 2 June 1917: HStA Düsseldorf, Regierung Düsseldorf 15274

234. Monatsberichte, 3 April 1918, 14: BA/MA, RM3/7794. Also see Monatesberichte für Dezember 1917, 17: HStA/Kr, MKr 12852.
235. Obmann of Stellv. Gen.kdo.s III. Bayerisches AK Nürnberg, 6 February 1918: HStA/Kr, Stellv. Gen.kdo. I. Bayerisches AK München 2399. Zimmermann assumes that approximately one-eighth to one-seventh of grain, flour and potato sales and one quarter to one-third of milk, butter and cheese sales were made on the black market, as was one-third to one half of egg, meat and fruit circulation. Zimmermann, "Veränderungen," in Meerwarth et al., *Einwirkung*, 441.
236. Monatsberichte für Oktober 1917, 21: HStA/Kr, MKr 12852.
237. Monatsberichte, 3 August 1917, 18: BA/MA, RM3/4670.
238. Monatsberichte, 3 July 1917, 79: ibid.
239. The development of female criminality was depicted here not only because the majority of "family squirrels" were women, but also to facilitate a comparison with the relevant pre-war statistics. A similiar comparison cannot be made for the male population because of conscription. For more information on this, see Koppenfels, *Kriminalität, passim*.
240. One of the reasons why the crime rate increased so dramatically among female adolescents under 15 and those between 15 and 18 during the war was the participation of these two groups in crimes against property. The other was that, in view of the numerous ordinances directed at adolescents – the restriction of visits to restaurants, cafés and cinemas, the ban on loitering in public squares and streets, on smoking in public, etc. – it was almost impossible for such individuals not to violate some regulation. See von Koppenfels, *Kriminalität*, 15-16.
241. Before the war, it was married women, above all, who were convicted of violating their license obligations. Consequently, their share of those women convicted during the war could drop, without necessarily corresponding to the general trend. For this, see ibid., 14, 19 and *passim*.
242. Monatsberichte, 3 July 1918, 22: BA/MA, RM3/7795.
243. Memorandum on the sixth consultation with representatives of the state, province and district price offices, Dresden, 15 December 1917: ZStA Potsdam, Reichsministerium des Innern, 10144, Bl. 156ff.
244. Monatsberichte, 3 July 1918: BA/MA, RM3/7795, 65.
245. Bayerischer Innenminister to Distriktspolizeibehörden, 11 September 1917: HStA München, MInn 66329.
246. Monatsberichte, 3 July 1918, 21-22: BA/MA, RM3/7795; Monatsberichte, 3 May 1918, 15-16: ibid.; Monatsberichte, 3 June 1918, 20-21: ibid.; Monatsberichte, 3 February 1918, 15: BA/MA, RM3/7794; Monatsberichte, 3 April 1918,

16: ibid. In addition to this, also see W. Albrecht, *Landtag und Regierung in Bayern am Vorabend der Revolution von 1918* (Berlin, 1968), 224-232. The population's mistrust of authority was also fueled by those instances where it became public that certain individuals had received preferential "food" treatment. It thus caused a considerable stir when, after the private export of food from Bavaria had been banned, the Bavarian Minister-President Hertling, who had been named chancellor of the Reich, could still receive food sent from Bavaria without a problem in August 1917. Ay, *Entstehung*, 161-162.

247. This position of the responsible consultant in the Bavarian Ministry of the Interior is quoted in ibid., 168.

248. Memorandum on the sixth consultation with representatives of the state, province and district price offices, Dresden, 15 December 1917, 17: ZStA Potsdam, Reichsministerium des Innern, 10144, Bl. 156ff. Even the prosecuting attorneys seemed to have little understanding of the abstractness of the punishment. Toward the end of the war, a witty, but loyal prosecuting attorney published his war experiences on the "home front," a large section of which was devoted to the "squirrel" problem. The task of the prosecuting attorney's office, wrote Karl Giesecke, was to "honor" every forager reported to the police "with a ticket, according to their earnings and fortune. This is anything but pleasant for us, but there has to be a punishment, and whoever wants to forage should not allow himself to be searched." K. Giesecke, *Im Kampf an der inneren Front. Meine Kriegserlebnisse als Staatsanwalt* (Leipzig, 1918), 41 and *passim* - includes an impressive panorama of the illegal war economy.

249. Letter of a Silesian to a prisoner of war, 20 February 1917: HStA/Kr, Stellv. Gen.kdo. I. Bayerisches AK München 1979.

250. Memorandum on the sixth consultation with representatives of the state, province and district price offices, Dresden, 15 December 1917, 12, 20: ZStA Potsdam, Reichsministerium des Innern, 10144, Bl. 156ff. In addition, see Monatsbericht des Stellv. Gen.kdo. I. Bayerisches AK München für Juni 1917: HStA/Kr, MKr 12844, as well as Bayerisches Kriesgministerium to Stellv. Gen.kdo.s, 15 September 1917: HStA/Kr, Stellv. Gen.kdo. I. Bayerisches AK München 808.

251. Bezirksamt Altötting to Stellv. Gen.kdo. München, 16 September 1918: HStA/Kr Stellv. Gen.kdo. I. Bayerisches AK München 1372.

252. Monatsberichte, 3 March 1917, 12: BA/MA, RM3/4670. In addition to this, see also Monatsbericht des Stellv. Gen.kdo.s München für Juni 1918: HStA/ Kr, MKr 12849 and Stellv. Gen.kdo. VII AK Münster to Regierungspräsident Düsseldorf, 7 September 1918: HStA Düsseldorf, Regierung Düsseldorf 9081.

253. Here see, for example, Monatsberichte, 3 April 1917, 12: BA/MA, RM3/ 4670; Stadtmagistrat Bayreuth to Stellv. Gen.kdo. III. Bayerisches AK Nürnberg, 6 August 1917: HStA/Kr, MKr 2497.

254. Between 8,000 and 10,000 people participated in these riots in Barmen. They first besieged and then seriously damaged the city hall, cut the hoses of the fire department, which had been called in against them, and plundered and demonstrated for days, until, finally, the military moved in. ZStA Merseburg, Rep. 197A, Io, Nr. 2, Bl. 226ff. See here, as well, L. Stern, ed., *Die Auswirkungen der Großen sozialistischen Oktoberrevolution auf Deutschland*. Archivalische Forschungen zur Geschichte der Arbeiterbewegung (Berlin, 1959), 4:377-378.

5

The Fight over the Meaning-Endowment of the War

Demobilization began with the feelings . . . Popular mood precedes events.[1]

For more than four years, the First World War shaped life and death in Europe. In Germany, the months in which it began and in which it ended became fixed terms. "August 1914" stood – and stands – for an unprecedented mass enthusiasm that, with only few exceptions, infected the entire society. November 1918 lent its name to a revolution, in which the war and imperial Germany found their end. The socio-psychological basis of the November Revolution was not a revolutionary mass movement, nor was it a counterpart to the "August experience" under the opposite circumstances. Rather, this radical political change of 1918 and 1919 was prepared and facilitated by a development that had lasted the entire war and increasingly gained in effectiveness. In the course of this development, a large section of the population revoked its loyalty to the belligerent German state. At the end of 1917, military observers held that current popular opinion "no longer approves of the state, which wants to continue the war indefinitely, until it has triumphed to the death and will perhaps only stop when the entire world and everyone in it are destroyed."[2]

In the end, the vast majority of the German population found its own state, rather than that the military opponent, to be a threat, and there only needed to be more political groups willing and able to act in order to convert this attitude of the population – which was competent to act on the local level, but not on that of the entire state – into organized political action. "As I stood last week and read a telegram about the Revolution in Petersburg," reported one Munich woman to Styria in March 1917:

I heard someone behind me say, too bad that it's not in Berlin. I looked around and it was German soldiers in battle dress . . . They need another war bond now . . . Mrs H., I and Mrs J. had the money, but they tell us that we would do better to bury it than to give it for a war bond. For letting us and our children live in want and go hungry. Let those sign the bonds who have enough butter and meat, as it's commonly called without ration coupons, they can pay 6 marks a pound. That's why I don't believe in God anymore, because one sees how things are and the purse is considered God. My brother has money, too, but he also doesn't give it away, even though he's so Christian. He says he also doesn't want to hear anything about love of one's country, and love of one's homeland, because the Fatherland doesn't give us anything, if we don't work, then we don't have anything. The [Fatherland] is for those who can afford it.[3]

The "August Experience" lost its society-shaping force and became one of the "ideas of 1914," which were preserved primarily by intellectuals, artists and full-time propagandists and whose area of influence was almost exclusively limited to printed and published material. This occurred when the population began to realize that the war would last longer and claim more human lives and material sacrifices than had been expected. The first consequences of the war's transition from event to permanent state[4] were already apparent by the end of 1914. In December of that year, the public opinion reports from Berlin's chief of police, which kept the government informed at regular intervals throughout the entire war about the morale and conduct of the capital's inhabitants, registered the first complaints of the "faint-hearted." "The number of women dressed in black is multiplying rapidly, and gives a gloomy cast to the Christmas mood," wrote the police chief. Although working-class circles had also condemned Liebknecht's special vote in the Reichstag against war credit at the outset, by the end of 1914, their judgment was already "more benign."[5] By March 1915, the price increases and the more difficult conditions of life had already led to a "certain longing for peace"[6] and "war-weariness."[7] In July 1915, the government had to hear from the chief of police's reports that "particularly among working-class women, . . . a sometimes very deep desire for peace has asserted" itself.[8] It only lasted three months until the mood among the Berlin women waiting in line for food became "as unpleasant as possible, at times even bitter," and "often enough expressed itself in abuse of the government."[9] By 1916 and 1917, already the majority of the population no longer wanted to hear anything about the war.

> The number of housewives who express their displeasure openly is growing steadily, and an exceedingly disturbing irritation at times prevails among the lower classes of the people . . .[10]

> The question of war aims preoccupies only a proportionally small fraction of the population. To by far the largest majority, only one question seems important: When will the war come to an end.[11]

"The people said that 'enthusiasm is not a herring that one can salt.'"[12] The Bavarian War Minister saw things similarly. In September 1918, the Prussian War Ministry circulated the proposal of a Reichstag representative to inaugurate "a fountain of youth of new enthusiasm for the Fatherland," whereby soldiers departing for the front would be honored at public rallies as defenders of the Fatherland. To this, the Bavarian War Ministry laconically commented that the last incidents as transports of reinforcements departed for the "battlefield" showed "that the participation of the people in this is unwelcome."[13]

To the people, their participation in the war no longer seemed desirable anyway. If, at the beginning of the war, the authorities could barely ward off the hordes of "war mischief makers"[14] – as the volunteers for the war were called by their less voluntary comrades[15] – by 1915, applications for deferment had already begun to pile up on their desks.[16] The situation throughout Germany was similar to that in Berlin, namely that it was women, and above all working-class women, who first publicly expressed their displeasure about wartime conditions. Since 1916/1917, the vast majority of the population had been classified as war-weary,[17] and it was working-class women, be they housewives or industrial workers, who voiced this opinion most radically. In the autumn of 1918, the military authorities on the home front finally warned that the general "apathy of the masses" could possibly constitute "the precursor of a mood . . . that will eventually demand peace at any price. It should be mentioned in this connection that in the lower levels of society, particularly from the mouths of women, one can hear comments to the effect that it is, in the end, immaterial whether the Rhineland is German or French."[18]

Civil authorities across Germany, who had subjected the morale of the people to meticulous observation since 1916, concurred with the conclusion of the Altötting District Office[19] that the "general dissatisfaction" had become "especially sharp, in particular through the conduct of trouble-loving women, who incite their husbands."[20] Their almost identical analyses of the dividing line that separated the war-weary part of the population from the part that was willing to hold out can be summarized in several pairs of opposites: The potential for protest was,[21] reported the civil authorities, more marked among women than men, stronger in the cities than in the country, influenced the working class more than the bourgeoisie and, within the working class, unorganized workers more profoundly than organized labor, and was deepest among the "uneducated" classes, whereas, according to military reports about morale, the "educated" classes' willingness to "hold out" only began to slacken shortly before the war's conclusion.[22]

Theoretical models of class or stratum alone cannot depict the mixed nature of this protest potential in terms of where it was posited in society. Such approaches wield explanatory power only for those dividing lines that run between the usual social classes, such as that between the working and the middle classes.[23] Other social groups and the attitudes that are assigned to them elude class and stratum analyses. This is partly because they contradict such an analysis (as the critical stance of unorganized in comparison to that of organized labor or the city–country opposition) partly because they are too diffuse (as the fairly indefinite categories of "the educated" and "the uneducated") and partly because these are not provided for in such a class or stratum analysis (as the gender-specific structure of the protest potential). If we seek to provide an explanation that is compatible with contemporary descriptions of this potential for protest, then we cannot use impoverishment theories as a basis for argument. The contrast between urban and rural areas could indeed be explained as a direct consequence of the deterioration of living conditions during the war, as perhaps could that between organized and unorganized labor. This reasoning cannot be applied to the difference between the working and middle classes in terms of their willingness to persevere with the war, however. The economic position in particular of "salaried workers," i.e. of white-collar employees in business and administration, whose salary could not even remotely keep pace with the price increases, was often no less desperate than that of workers.[24] No matter how we define the category of "the educated," it, too,

cannot simply be equated with the materially advantaged of wartime. Likewise, gender-specific differences cannot be deduced
solely from the economic situation. A hypothesis that takes the
social heterogeneity of the protest potential into account must
necessarily, therefore, be a syncretic one.

The explanatory approach I use here proceeds from the
premise that a critical stance toward the war and toward the
society that was waging it was developed above all by those
sections of the civilian population to which the following three
conditions applied:

1 Those levels of the population that were affected most
strongly by the material deprivations of wartime and the resulting
regulatory measures of the state and in whose life and work
situation these two elements intervened most sustainedly were
especially critical of the war and its consequences. This stratum
included urban families who were dependent upon a money
income and, in particular, the women who were responsible for
feeding them.

2 A critical attitude developed more freely in those individuals
and groups that were less directly threatened by the application
of state sanctions. This was valid for the majority of women.
Financial sanctions against them, such as the revocation of their
Family Aid, were ruled out because of the detrimental effect the
authorities feared these sanctions would have on morale at
the front. The use of violence against demonstrating women,
who possibly even had small children with them, would have
meant breaking a societal taboo, an action from which state
organs recoiled.[25] Lastly, the notorious threat of being sent to
the trenches was one that could not be applied to women.[26]

3 Criticism of the war circumstances predominated in those
strata of the population that were less easily influenced by the
state-national meaning-endowment, which was important for
the population's perseverance during the First World War. This
applied to those whose access to and consequent ability to be
influenced by existing institutions and procedures of societal
meaning-endowment, such as schools, newspaper-reading, vocational training, cultural consumption, and organizations and
associations of various natures, was limited.[27] This hypothesis
is based on the theory that participation in the arenas that
are summarized in the sociology of knowledge under the term
"secondary sozialization" decisively determines the degree of

identification with which individuals and collectives fit the structures of their everyday lives into meaning-endowments. These meaning-endowments are not themselves rooted in this everyday world and are, by virtue of their own material and emotional structures of relevance, possibly contradictory. The internalization of supra-individual structures of relevance of a religious, political or social nature should therefore be understood as a learning process, which, in societies based upon the division of labor, is predominantly mediated in an institutionalized form. Schools and universities, newspapers and the arts, vocational training programs and professional organizations, sports associations and political parties practice contents, rituals and areas of knowledge that, for all their differences, have something in common: They bind individual meaning-endowments into supra-individual contexts of meaning. Where this bond has developed biographically and historically, it is also socio-psychologically effective and thereby potentially employable. Associations, sects and trade unions can mobilize their members for specific objectives, just as a state can mobilize its population – provided that the union of individual structures of relevance with supra-individual structures withstands the demands made upon it. In terms of the First World War, this means that, under the heavy physical and psychological burdens of wartime, the identification with the belligerent state collapsed first among those individuals and in those social strata whose participation in the symbol production of society was less pronounced. This characteristic distinguishes the unorganized workforce from trade-union members and from large parts of the middle classes, the "uneducated" from the "educated," and, not least, women in large part from men. In the nineteenth century, for example, girls attended elementary school more irregularly than boys and, beyond reading lessons, were seldom given the opportunity to learn writing and arithmetic.[28] In imperial Germany, with the exception of home-economics classes at school, which were oriented toward work in the family, girls were excluded from vocational training programs,[29] and, before 1914, a higher-school or university education was a rarity for women. Moreover, secondary education was based upon an image of women that defined women's life-world not as an integral part of society as a whole, but as a space supposedly outside the realm of society.[30] In addition, women were organized much less frequently in political parties, associations or organizations and were consequently much less intensively integrated into the network of magazines and events that these supported.[31]

During the First World War, the military authorities continually stressed that the population's will to "hold out" extended just as far as the participation in the fate of the entire society made possible through "education." As the Deputy General Command of the 1st Bavarian Army Corps Munich wrote in October 1917:

> A colossal rift [divides] our people: On the one side, the masses who, often unfortunately without a wider perspective, are opposed to the war, resigned and bowing to the unavoidable, and who more or less allow themselves to be depressed by the side-effects of the war. On the other side, the educated, who are more in a position to take their focus off the pettinesses of everyday life, to experience global events more consciously and to express their opinion about them.[32]

Even Social-Democrat functionaries adopted this point of view. As the Social Democrat Eduard David said in a meeting in 1916 between the leaders of the Reichstag and the chancellor, "The uneducated have no political goals, from which to draw their powers of resistance."[33] Women, it was believed, particularly lacked satisfactory comprehension of the big picture. After a detailed reading of letters that women had written to their family members on the front or in prison camps, the military authorities reached the conclusion that it seemed "most difficult of all to teach the people the meaning of the war. One usually encounters a hopeless, shallow utilitarian point of view in these letters, a lack of any horizon and breadth of perspective."[34]

In 1918, Sebastian Schlittenbauer, the general secretary of the Bavarian Christian Farmers' Association (*Bayerischer christlicher Bauernverein*) as well as the Center Party's representative in the Bavarian Landtag, impressed his view on the Bavarian government that only the introduction of women's right to vote would lead to women's greater identification with the interests of the state. Said Schlittenbauer:

> The low morale stems mainly from the fact that, although the German woman does not fail in her work, she does fail in her conception of things. Compared to the French woman and the English woman, the German woman is lacking in political consciousness, which puts the Fatherland above individual interests. Anyone who takes the train, anyone who has the opportunity in the waiting room to listen to the

talk of women, must . . . often be astonished at the short-sightedness of the remarks of German women. Their constant complaints, their eternal accusations, their wishes and demands, which are not influenced by any consideration of the Fatherland, their letters of lament to their husbands and sons at the front are the main cause of the poor morale in the army . . . In the long run, it will no longer do that our German girls receive absolutely no political-civic instruction in school, and in the long run, it will no longer do that we exclude women so totally from political life. How shall the woman have an understanding of state emergencies in the hour of danger if, in the hours of peace, she is never trusted with the spirit and essence of the state. I emphatically support the right of women to vote . . . It is too deeply rooted in the welfare of the state itself.[35]

The social composition of the protest potential proves that the population's growing dissatisfaction with the war and the state was a question of the "intensification of class difference, which, in comparison to earlier decades, had shifted,"[36] and which was equally determined by mental and economic factors. The main emphases of wartime social protest also show that the social tensions of the war years cannot *only* be interpreted as class difference. The population's criticism was directed primarily at the inequality it saw in consumer-good and food provision. One component of this bitterness about the unequal access to food, which the population regarded as a serious violation of its right to social justice, was a critique of the better-off upper strata of society:

if the big people had to live on the starvation diet of the ration cards the war would already be long done unfortunately one sometimes sees such fat dumplings running around who surely say that they are not like the beggars, thank God, that we have it, you can see how you get along . . . but the ordinary people are robbed of the little they have, and the big ones are hauling away the goods by the truckload.[37]

In addition, however, the principle of an equal and thereby just distribution of goods, as defined by popular opinion, was to have universal validity. Not only was the inequality between rich and poor seen as a violation of this principle of social justice, but also that between the city and the country, between two local associations with different provisions regulations, and between workers who did heavy labor and were thereby entitled to additional pay and workers who did – and were – not. Even the traditional lines of socio-psychological tension became more marked under the influence of this wartime postulate of justice. In southern Germany, for example, and especially in Bavaria, criticism of the insufficient rations crystallized into a more sharply accentuated hatred of Prussia.[38] Complaints about colleagues who were entitled to additional pay, the neighboring community with bigger butter rations, and the farmers who withheld their products or only sold them for black-market prices were just as vehement as the bitterness about the better-off circles of the population. And at the center of all the criticism concerning the various forms of injustice stood the state, which seemed either to cause them, or at least to permit their existence. Consequently, exactly that situation arose which the government had feared since the beginning of the war and which it had wanted to prevent through state rationing: The food problem became, in the truest sense of the word, a political issue. The "pulse of public opinion is by and large located in the human stomach:" so wrote the Deputy General Command of the 3rd Bavarian Army Corps Nuremberg in September 1917.[39] The protest, however, was directed much less against the shortage as such, as against the governments and civil authorities, by whose measures a large part of the population felt betrayed and cheated. Criticism and indignation was triggered, on the one hand, by what was seen as the unfair inequality in food allocation between social groups and classes and, on the other, by the inequality in food allocation between different regions and categories of labor, which was considered equally egregious. This inequality cannot be analyzed within the framework of a class model: It was not the food situation *per se* that was the political issue, but the population's perception that the inequality inherent in this situation was caused by state measures and was thereby subject to moral criteria.

> In the poorer elements of the population, an ever-increasing irritation and bitterness is gaining ground. This can be put down to the inequality in lifestyles and the not always just manner of food distribution rather than to the prevailing food shortage itself. "The manner of food distribution, which has been tolerated all too long, could easily be avoided, is laborious and even unjust," said a report of the Royal Police Headquarters of Munich, "is a far more dangerous enemy for public order and security than the lack of food, with which everyone has to come to terms and does come to terms, as soon as a

guarantee exists that preferential treatment and other injustices are excluded from food allocations."[40]

It is a strange phenomenon that the people can reconcile itself to any deprivation, but that nobody can tolerate it if someone else has a little bit more than himself. If one could succeed in spreading the certainty that the unpleasantnesses with the food situation would be evenly distributed, then the dissatisfaction would disappear immediately.[41]

If government authorities could have given the population the certainty that wartime society was organized according to the principle of social justice, then they would have pursued this route, completely new for imperial Germany, of legitimizing state power – despite the fact that, before August 1914, these same government authorities would have emphatically rejected such a principle as "Social-Democratic."[42] They saw that they were incapable of doing this, however. Optimizing food allocations until they even approximately satisfied the demand for social justice was not, in view of the desperate food situation and existing political conditions, which did not permit a decisive infringement upon agrarian and entrepreneurial interests,[43] in the realm of the possible. Consequently, only one possibility remained for decision-makers, that of trying to change the opinion of the population about food allocations and thereby about wartime society in general through deliberate propaganda.

This path was also followed. Through the establishment of propaganda institutions, "enlightenment" campaigns of various kinds, the use of theatre, photographs and cinema, and through the employment of countless intermediary agents, governments and the military, civil authorities and political parties, trade unions, churches, associations and women's movements strove to gain opinion-forming influence over the critical elements of the population. All of these endeavors soon came up against the same problem, however: The majority of the population had reached the point of forming its own opinion about the war; it did this not only independently of official announcements and censored media, but in enlightened contradiction to these. And the majority thereby came to the conclusion that enough was enough, as is witnessed in this letter a Hamburg woman wrote to her conscripted husband, a carpenter, in October 1917: "If there are no more vacations, then you all have to take a vacation and say: Now, we are ending it all. For this fighting has been going on long enough. We want to be human beings once again and live among human beings. For this is no life anymore."[44]

Informal Communication and Collective Action

Initially, public opinion was the one good that was successfully nationalized during the First World War. Printed materials were censored, army reports were the "muse of the General Staff,"[45] and public performances and events required official authorization and were subject to police surveillance.[46] Every medium of public communication was controlled by the government. This state monopoly had no competition as long as the majority of the population believed in the continuation of the identity between their own interests and those of the state. This belief faded in direct proportion to the increase in the length of the war, the sacrifice of human life and the material deprivation, and then became its opposite. In the second half of the war, the majority of the population tended to be critical of, if not hostile toward, the state, and nothing was better suited to make something implausible than its official announcement. In August 1918, Deutelmoser, head of the News Department of the Foreign Office (*Nachrichtenabteilung des Auswärtigen Amts*), could only ascertain that, "Almost nobody here believes the authorities anymore, least of all when they try to speak officially encouragingly."[47]

Since it was common knowledge that the media stood under state and military censorship, this mistrust also applied to newspaper reports. Army reports increasingly lost credibility as well, while accounts from soldiers on leave about the situation at the front and in the army gained in persuasive power. In this situation of sharp social tensions, coupled with the uncertainty about the "real" state of the war that had developed since the controlled media were no longer considered credible sources of information, a network of informal communication arose spontaneously, awkwardly and uncontrollably.[48] This network spanned the entire territory of the Reich, including the front. In it, a "counter-public" (*Gegenöffentlichkeit*) was established, which, in the form of rumors, slogans, jokes and tall tales, commented on, analyzed, caricatured and, above all, criticized the war and its concomitants. In addition to the greatly increased correspondence between

241

family members and acquaintances during the war, the most important trading centers of informal communication were those places where, owing to wartime conditions, people gathered. These included the queues in front of stores and government offices, the notice boards where army reports were publicly posted, and train compartments, in which women on foraging trips and soldiers on vacation leave met and used the opportunity to exchange opinions and experiences. To the authorities, women and soldiers on leave from the front counted as the most important sources and informers in this informal system of communication.[49] The civil and military bureaucracies could not agree, however, whether it was the civilians who thereby demoralized the front soldiers in this way or whether the inciting influence of the soldiers was greater on those who had stayed behind. One general probably came the closest to the truth, when he complained, in the spring of 1918, that soldiers on leave brought the ill-feeling to the home front and returned to the front wearier of the war than before. As he said, "It has thus come to a cycle, to an ever-rising antipathy to the war."[50]

The authorities had no effective means at their disposal with which to combat this flood of rumors and other sensationalist forms of popular knowledge about the war. Official denials in the daily newspapers would only have encouraged the wider circulation of such information. Legal measures were useless, since the authorities could scarcely ever get hold of the individuals responsible for spreading the rumors and defeatist comments. Beyond this, the juridical formulation of the offense proved to be problematic. Several Deputy General Commands did indeed make the telling of rumors a punishable offense, at least as far as the respective rumors dealt with the military situation. The valid regulations were either so broadly interpreted, however – as by the 14th Prussian Army Corps Karlsruhe – that they rendered the spreading of all false information about the war a punishable offense, whereby, as the Bavarian War Ministry complained, "only *alarming*, untrue news about the war was to be prohibited."[51] Or they threatened only the "thoughtless" spreading of rumors and thereby allowed their "unintentional" telling to go unpunished, as in the 3rd Bavarian Army Corps. Or, instead of concentrating only on false accounts about the war, these regulations made the telling of any false rumor a punishable offense, and were therefore scarcely applicable.

The authorities did want, at the least, to keep communication among the people under surveillance, however. Since 1916/1917, there had been a *de facto* obligation to notify the authorities of all rumors, an obligation which was otherwise only customary for the outbreak of contagious diseases.[52] As a result of this, the Deputy General Commands and municipal administrations began to keep detailed records of the rumors that appeared in their area of surveillance. Their notes give a good overview, in terms of contents, of the opinions about the war and wartime conditions that circulated through the population in the form of rumors, jokes, sayings or even in the "artistic" form of rhymes.[53] As official reports verify, this network of informal communication conveyed much more than mere news; it also carried vivid and meaningful descriptions of individual phenomena that, independent of the truthfulness of their contents, reflected and reinforced the perception of wartime society as a whole.

Rumors that had anything good to report were rare. When such rumors did occur, they usually referred to an allegedly imminent improvement in the supply situation,[54] or they announced the end of the war or a partial peace with one of Germany's military opponents sometime in the immediate or foreseeable future.[55] The authorities considered the effects of these positive reports on the population's morale to be as dangerous as negative ones, since the hoped-for events generally did not occur and the hope, as a result, turned into disappointment.

The conditions within the army and the course of military events were intensely analyzed within this network of informal communication. Apart from the success or failure of certain military campaigns and the consequent number of casualties, it was the conditions behind the lines that received particular attention. Unofficial reports recounted the excessive high-life that rear-echelon officers led, which was supposedly organized with the food to which the front officers were actually entitled.[56] In the autumn of 1918, these two strains of unofficial reporting about military matters merged with the rumor, spread throughout the Empire, that the last German offensive had failed because "the men, as a result of their starvation, only advanced to the first supply office, which they raided, and could then not be induced to move forward."[57]

Assertions that many of the soldiers reported as "having fallen on the field of honor" were actually terribly maimed or mentally ill and had been put into institutions, where they were to be hidden from their relatives, were also widely disseminated.[58]

Denser still was the informal reporting about the food situation of the civil population, which was especially feared by the authorities as a source of unrest. This reporting also functioned according to the principle of adding a hint of the absurd to the reality of wartime society, thereby rendering the reported events a caricature. The reports asserted that, in large cities such as Munich, Vienna or Berlin, hundreds of people starved to death daily and that the corpses had to be removed with moving vans or streetcars,[59] while farmers and municipal associations hoarded food or allowed it to go to waste. Thus, 30,000 rotten eggs were supposedly buried in the Field of Mars in Munich,[60] and, as an economic and political variation of the legend of the flying Dutchman, an entire train full of rotten eggs was said to have been seen on a secret trip through Germany.[61] Even the Bavarian Minister of the Interior, Brettrich, personally asked the Wolfratshausen District Office in March 1917 if the town were actually hoarding 800,000 eggs, as rumors alleged, because the municipal association wanted to wait until there was a complete million.[62] The increasingly frequent claims made by individuals that, as prisoners of war in England, they had had to unload sacks of flour (or of other natural products of high nutritional value) from their own farms or that, after the sinking of an English ship, they had seen crates of eggs, sacks of flour, etc. with the label "Municipal Association (*Kommunalverband*) Schwabmünich" (here, one inserted the name of the city or community in which the rumor was currently circulating) in the water aroused particular bitterness.[63] Popular opinion concluded from this – when it did not already assume it from the outset – that business-minded German traders or government authorities were conducting a flourishing food trade with perfidious Albion.

In addition to military matters and the food situation, this unofficial formation of opinion focused on political conditions in a narrower sense. Such reports contained the popular explanation of why the war was still going on. In Bavaria in the summer of 1917, it was said that the war, in reality, had long been lost, but that "the big leaders still want to do in masses of people so that they won't get any revolution afterwards."[64] A sharper version of the rumor asserted that "according to published surveys, only 45% of the people were destroyed by the war and that there will be no peace until 75% are done in. It is inevitable."[65] Other reports claimed that Germany could have already had peace in 1916, if the industrialists of the war industry had not objected to it "because they had not yet earned enough to cover their rising costs."[66]

Additionally, countless other rumors circulated about the most varied subjects. Some of them confirm that the network of informal communication often came closer to the truth than published opinion. In September 1918, for example, the population of Munich, including upper-middle classes, was suddenly seized by the "very disturbing delusion" that the Empire would become a republic and that war bonds would thereby be rendered worthless.[67] In the summer of 1917, news that the emperor had been the victim of an assassination attempt in Austria and was seriously wounded circulated through the population of Bavaria. This, the people thought, served him right since "Austria's wanted to conclude peace for a long time, but the Prussian swine keeps holding it up." At the end of June, there had actually been an assassination attempt, which the media was not allowed to report. According to internal statements of the War Press Office [*Kriegspresseamt*], an intoxicated mentally disturbed man had flung a package against the emperor's car and consequently damaged a headlight.[68]

Another variety of rumors distinguished itself in that it pushed to the limit the level of absurdity that people, under the conditions of war, were likely to consider possible. Thus, civilians and soldiers reported in the middle of 1916 that "The war against the English is a phoney one, because, in his heart, the emperor sticks with the English. He's got his money in the Bank of England, that's why he doesn't want to ruin it with the English."[69] Simultaneously, the rumor circulated among dog owners that the Deputy General Command Munich wanted to have all the dogs slaughtered.[70] In Bavaria, the growing resentment against Prussia ensured the wide dissemination of reports that the United States had offered the Bavarian government 4 billion marks to break with Prussia, or that Hindenburg had fought a duel with the crown prince of Bavaria.[71]

The reality content of these rumors varied as greatly as the state's true share of responsibility for the outrages against which they inveighed. It ranged from completely erroneous claims, such as the last one, to virtually prophetic insights into the actual

situation, such as the report concerning the imminent transformation of the German Empire into a republic. In general, this
informal communication constituted, so to speak, a half-authentic
medium: In it, the deplorable wartime conditions and certain
political and economic interests were hypostatized to a degree
that confirmed the growing perception of the totality of wartime
society as negative and ridiculous.

Informal communication was the medium through which the
population incited itself far more lastingly and more effectively
than would have been possible through the agitation of the
organized war opposition constituted by the Independent Social
Democratic Party of Germany and Spartakus.[72] It radicalized the
population, suffering from the deprivations of wartime, to the
point where the dissatisfaction changed into collective action
and led to spontaneous disturbances. The counterpublic of the
people not only produced and intensified the prevailing mood
but often even supplied the trigger for food riots and strikes,
which, beginning at the end of 1915 and increasingly from 1916
on, turned communities into secondary theatres of war. These
episodes of collective action often began with the rumor that, at
a certain baker's, one could get bread without ration coupons. A
large crowd then quickly assembled at the indicated place; if its
hopes were disappointed, it plundered the shops or marched to
the city hall, thereby setting off a chain reaction of further
episodes of spontaneous collective action. Such disturbances, in
turn, led to countless new rumors that, through their accounts
of the numerous dead that supposedly lay in the streets after the
suppression of such and such a demonstration or such and such
a strike, heated the people's anger to boiling point.[73] Housewives
and female workers demonstrated the greatest inclination to
become violent and composed the vast majority of strikers and –
together with adolescents and schoolchildren – demonstrators.
"There is no doubt," explained Colonel von Wrisberg of the
Prussian War Ministry in August 1917: "that the previous strikes
and, above all, the disturbances of the peace that grew out of
them were caused by women and adolescents. Our old workers
are probably disciplined and usually have no connection with
these agitations."[74]

It was this form of social protest – everyday, shaped by women
and adolescents and erupting spontaneously in the streets or at
the factory – that was typical for the First World War, not the

strikes and demonstrations, political in the more narrow sense of the word, that ensued in 1917 and, above all, in 1918. In the second half of the war, these spontaneous disturbances, which were motivated almost without exception by the difficulties of everyday life and with whose complaints large segments of the population concurred, became a ubiquitous and permanent dis-ruptive factor, which terrified the authorities and brought the governability of the cities into question. In order to illustrate the progression of such protest and to serve as one example of many, the following report, completely typical of its kind, about the disturbances in Tangermünde on 17 August 1916 shall be recounted in detail.

After the distribution of butter had been delayed for a few days, approximately 100 women collected on 17 August at 11 a.m. in front of the Tangermünde city hall. The majority of these women worked in the local canning factory. A group of women entered the building, wanting to speak to the second mayor, who was responsible for allocations. They were told that the butter would be distributed on 19 August.

> Those women who stood directly next to the second mayor and spoke to him were satisfied with the information they had received; whereas those who were standing further away heckled him. He asked the former to communicate the facts to these women and to calm them down, which they promised to do. The crowd then dispersed, some supposedly said "We'll be back in the afternoon!" The crowd knew that, at 5 o'clock, a meeting of the municipal council was to take place and they apparently wanted to pester the arriving council members. Since the meeting, due to special circumstances, had, as an exception, already begun at 4 o'clock, this was not successful. Large crowds of people did indeed gather between 4 and 5 o'clock, their ranks increasingly reinforced by adolescent boys and girls, as well as schoolchildren, and which, by moderate estimations, reached 1,000 persons by 7 o'clock. There was incessant screaming and howling; insulting and mocking remarks were also shouted at the authorities and it seemed as if, not the provision of butter, but rather the desire for scandal and mischief played the main role. At around 7 o'clock, the second mayor stepped in front of the city hall and once again told those women who were standing nearest that the distribution of butter, for reasons that he had already communicated, could only take place on Saturday. These women, too, were satisfied with the information they had received; since, however, the crowd that was standing behind them constantly screamed and howled, he

asked these women to communicate this information to the others and to calm them down, which they promised to do, and then went back inside the city hall. Between 7 and 8 o'clock, the crowd diminished slightly – presumably people were eating their supper – only to reappear around 8.30 in considerably larger numbers and then attack the house of a member of the board of the Tangermünde dairy, in whose cellar 800 kilograms of butter were supposedly stored. Large stones were taken out of the gutter, other stones retrieved from other streets where they lay, and were thrown against the house; by 11 o'clock, all of the windows in the house were broken, [and] one had already attempted to break in the door with large stones, as well. The police officers were powerless against this; many were slightly injured from the stone-throwing. When the second mayor left city hall at 7.30, he was insulted by being pelted with honey.

Ultimately, the military was called in. Because of the rumors concerning its arrival,

the agitation of the crowd increased and the attacks on the house became more violent, so that the troops who intervened were only successful in suppressing the throngs after a half an hour. As soon as it was driven into one street and the soldiers turned around, the crowd followed them, and the intervention of the Home Guard company was required to disperse the crowd. A number of persons were arrested for creating a public nuisance as well as for breaching the peace. When the troops were present, the mob shouted that they would gather again on the same day and later if there were still no butter. In the evening, the crowd, which at first had consisted only of working women, was composed primarily of women, as well as young girls and adolescent boys, and unfortunately also a large number of schoolchildren. In addition, there were a number of shady elements, who used the opportunity for scandal. Even if, in the beginning, the formation of the mob was caused by the butter shortage, in the course of time, it took on the character of a demonstration.[75]

Because of their spontaneous and unorganized character, which sometimes lent such collective action an "element of carnival,"[76] these riots offered the authorities no means with which to prevent them. The trade unions, whose integration into the warring society[77] helped to pacify organized workers, perceived themselves as incapable of influencing non-union workers, in particular women. As was reported in the Deputy General Commands reports for June 1916:

Labor leaders have . . . indicated that they would do everything possible to prevent such disturbances and strikes over food provisions,
but that they no longer have their people in hand. Besides that, very
many unorganized workers would be involved, over whom they have
no influence. In particular, it is the countless female workers who
constantly agitate and stir things up.[78]

If representatives of the trade unions or of the Social Democratic Party dared to approach a throng of demonstrating women
with the intention of pacifying them, they then had to hear jeers,
such as "You yourselves belong to the big people. You only take
care of yourselves and have no heart for the ordinary people!"
Or, as official reporters commented, they displayed "clear signs
of great agitation, yes, almost fear."[79]

The effective combating of this agitation also failed because
of a lack of personnel. In Nuremberg, for example, which had
experienced the first big street riots in June 1916, only 54 of the
original 380 police officers were still in service after two years
of war. Of these, only 12 men were available for deployment
against disturbances, the remaining being either too old or unfit
for such activity. The 260 auxiliary policemen hired as replacements – the majority of whom were unemployed workers – had
proved too willing to take sides with the demonstrators during
the course of such interventions.[80] Even the deployability of
the military as the last reserve for fighting riots was called
into question by the fact that the soldiers' sympathies lay with
the demonstrators – largely due to the relationships that had
developed between women and soldiers stationed on the home
front. In such cases, the soldiers made sure, at the outbreak of a
riot, that the barracks were empty, or simply took the side of
the demonstrating women.[81] Toward the end of the war, women
could almost count on soldiers' assistance, as is evidenced by
the following conversation that twenty to thirty Straubing
women held in a train compartment in September 1918 about
the upcoming celebration of their hometown's 700th anniversary:

Now the king's coming to us – As if we really needed him! – He
should stay at home with his fools – Our mayor, that idiot, went to
Munich just to invite the king – And then, they're crying about the
debts – The decorations'll also cost money – They're even going to
have festival grub – We don't need this shit – Let him come – We've
gotten everything ready – and we'll receive him with rotten potatoes.
They're thinking that putting the military there will help them –

The soldiers are going to be with us – They've had enough of this whole damn business, too.[82]

The number of women who were convicted of disturbing the peace and other violations against public order did indeed clearly increase in comparison to pre-war figures. In 1913, 273 individuals were convicted of disturbances of the peace, rioting, etc., 187 of whom were women and 9 of whom were adolescents. In 1917, of the 1,198 individuals convicted of such offenses, 1,028 were women and 553 were juveniles.[83] In light of the enormous scope of these riots during the war, however, the number of women on whom the state could execute the normative power of law was actually very small. Because of the explosive political force implicit in any action against female food rioters, it was more helpful for maintaining the "*Burgfrieden*" if only a relatively small number of women were apprehended and convicted. In view of the "disturbing political consequences of punishments," the authorities preferred, in some cases, to dismiss all legal proceedings, as was done when, following the first food riots of the war in Berlin in October 1915, approximately seventy individuals, predominantly women, were facing conviction.[84] In 1918, the authorities resorted to one last means of combating riots: They used tear-gas grenades to disperse the crowds. The planned outfitting of police stations in big cities with such grenades did not make much progress, however, since these weapons were in short supply and had actually been intended for enemy soldiers.[85] After the First World War, tear gas became standard equipment in the fighting of internal riots. At least in this area, there is no doubt about the modernizing effects of the war.

Public-Opinion Polling and Propaganda

The alarming development of the population's morale, which made the "endurance of the scaffolding of public opinion"[86] seem increasingly questionable, led the authorities to adopt extraordinary measures. In order to be able to "continuously put a finger on the pulse of the people,"[87] they covered the Empire with a network of observation stations. From the last garrison down to the smallest community, military and civil authorities in the second half of the war had to report all important developments and events that could provide information about public opinion. In order to monitor communication in train compartments, which were considered breeding grounds of "belly-aching," an organization of railway surveillance was established, which was to report on conversations overheard and graffiti on the toilet walls.[88] "A vast number of paid and unpaid informers from all circles of society"[89] was employed by the Counter-Intelligence Department (*Abwehrabteilung*) of the Deputy General Staff (*stellvertretender Generalstab*).

One of the most comprehensive public-opinion polling campaigns was arranged, on orders from the military government in Munich, by a professor of the art who was working at the Railway Post Office as a non-commissioned officer involved in censoring letters. In order to be able to better inform government officials about morale and, simultaneously, to preserve the material for posterity for socio-political and folkloristic studies, this professor introduced a letter-copying service at the Post Office Board of Censors. Of the letters that daily passed through the Railway Post Office I in Munich, over 70,000 were inspected and then excerpted according to their representativity. Out of the correspondence that was affected by these measures, which included mail within the states of Bavaria, Baden, Saxony and Silesia, as well as that sent from these areas to German prisoners of war, officials created a representative cross-section of the patterns of perception that letter-writers developed in and about the war. Opinions that were only "poor imitations of newspaper articles" were, "because of the similar style," eliminated. What remained, it was hoped, was the authentic opinion of the people, but as the Deputy General Command of Munich noted: "one must unfortunately say that the overall impression of our people's mental state, which one gains from reading these letters over a longer period of time, . . . cannot exactly be called uplifting."[90]

The excerpts from the letters give a very vivid insight into the perceptions of classes that, for the historian, remain speechless in "normal times" because of the lack of written records. The plentitude of such records in this instance was due to the separation of spouses and relatives during the war, which transformed letters into a means of mass communication.[91]

The knowledge that the authorities thus acquired about public opinion led to the urgent demand for countermeasures. If, during the war, the population had decision-makers to consider its morale "as a military means of war as such,"[92] then these had also thereby learned the historical force that the state's direction of patterns of perception could have. "The war had taught the value of propaganda if nothing else."[93] The German people were still lacking, diagnosed the War Press Office in September 1917, "in a strong national self-consciousness, one that completely governs the inner life of the individual . . . [They are like] good and well-behaved children, who must actually be told, however, what they have to do."[94]

Governments, the military and civil servants discovered the creation of meaning for the entire society as a new area of state responsibility.[95] The defeatist stance that the population took up with regard to the war and the state that was waging it could not be suppressed. Decision-makers realized, consequently, that this attitude had to be confronted with a positive meaning, one that was able to establish the validity of affirmative patterns of perception. Above all, the "enlightenment," as the authorities termed their new area of responsibility,[96] was supposed to counter the most dangerous components of the people's perception of the war: the view that conditions would be better if the war were over, the lack of individual identification with wartime society as a whole and the belief that the misery of the war was absolutely meaningless.[97]

I want to outline two of the most rigorously conceived developments of such conceptions of meaning-endowment here. Even though they found no practical application during the war, they impressively document contemporary experimentation with the medium of state self-representation and propaganda, which was entirely new in scope. The idea of establishing the person of the emperor as the identification symbol for the people was suggested by the head of the War Food Office, von Batocki, in March 1917. To this end, von Batocki believed that an "especially clever and tactful" journalist should be assigned to the emperor; his sole function would then be to provide ideas for campaigns that would demonstrate the emperor's closeness to the people. Von Batocki proposed two possible such campaigns. One was that the emperor come to Berlin and then receive individuals from all classes of society; the second was that he exploit, with "systematic skill," such opportunities as the "hero's death" of Prince Friedrich Karl.[98] The exposé "Freedom in Germany" that Friedrich Naumann sent to the imperial chancellor in October 1917[99] provides a second example of these conceptions of meaning-endowment. In it, he demanded "the conscious establishment of the German legend at home," which should counter the "legend of German unfreedom," which Germany's opponents used for war propaganda. As in the enemy states, where the battle against the German Reich as tyranny incarnate had been turned into a mission, Naumann argued, that the German state also had to give its people a sense of what they were fighting and suffering for. The enemy states of the West each possessed a "sort of national music" – the French the idea of freedom and the English the ideal of inviolability – which they had, together with American ingredients, now melted together into a "sort of political world religion," from which, said Naumann, "central Europeans and especially we Germans are to be excluded. The material war has thereby become an affair of fundamental convictions in the style of the old wars of religion." Above all, the Germans needed to follow the suit of the French and construct their own idea of freedom. According to Naumann, "The times demand a representation of history from the standpoint of the liberal development of the people." This portrayal, he said, needed to be based on the age of the Wars of Liberation, the Paulskirche in 1848–1849 and the announcement of universal suffrage in the Reich in 1871, and now (in the war) in Prussia. Thereby, Naumann thought, the enemy "slander, as if we were wild animals in the Garden of Eden," could be opposed with a specifically German message, one with which the people could identify. This message was that Germany was the only nation in which the inhabitants had gained liberal and social rights through the state and not in opposition to it.[100]

In general, however, the authorities saw their task of wartime "enlightenment" more practically: to "work on the people"[101] with all possible means. Therein, one of the most important objectives was to "gain access to working-class women."[102] The Deputy General Staff was in charge of organizing the "enlightenment" in the army; the Deputy General Commands were responsible for agitation within the civil population of Prussia. Since 1916, Bavaria had built up an organization independent of the Reich; this organization came under the jurisdiction of the Bavarian Ministry of the Interior and thus, in contrast to Prussia, under that of the civil authorities.[103] The manner of proceeding, however, was similar throughout the Empire. The military and civil authorities recruited individuals from all sectors of the population, who were then supposed to act as "multipliers of opinion." Both sets of authorities placed particular value on the cooperation of non-government organizations of every persuasion, since each "– be it political or unpolitical, scientific, religious, social or economic – . . . [constitutes] a body through whose circulation system one can pump a stream of trust and confidence into all of its limbs, if only the leaders want to."[104]

In the end, consequently, trade unions and entrepreneurs' associations, chambers of commerce and the Fatherland Party (*Vaterlandspartei*), women's societies and socio-political organizations, the German National Association of Commercial Clerks (*Deutschnationaler Handlungsgehilfenverband*), churches,[105] teachers, professors, artists and many others became involved in lifting the general morale, a task which they performed both in their respective hometowns and on lecture or business trips.[106] The collaboration of women and women's organizations was especially encouraged, since, through it, the authorities hoped to attain better access to the female population.[107] Finally, those individuals who enjoyed the trust of the people were also supposed to be made useful to these ends. Since soldiers on leave from the front were considered "unconditional authorities on everything that concerned the war," the "truly tremendous power . . . that the accounts of front soldiers wielded on the home front" was to be deployed to increase the population's will to "hold out" instead of undermining it. With this aim in mind, "more educated" and "reliable" soldiers were granted special leave, on the provision that they then strove to build up the population's morale.[108]

The authorities preferred such methods of indirect opinion manipulation to centrally controlled mass campaigns and a single propaganda organization, not least because, in view of the population's vast mistrust of authority and its intentions, the state's power to shape public opinion no longer reached very far. As Lieutenant Colonel von Kreß, representative of the Bavarian War Ministry, said at an October 1917 "enlightenment" meeting at the War Press Office in Berlin:

> [It is important] to make nothing emanating from the government public, because what we intend with the entire enlightenment program on the homefront is nothing other than to counter certain opinions that are part of the mass psychosis resulting from the war. How shall one oppose this through any other means but those of

mass suggestion? One can never practice this, however, on someone who is equipped with a certain aversion to this enlightenment,
and that is every individual as soon as he becomes aware that the
instruction comes from official channels.[109]

The work of this multitude of government intermediaries
was supported by the use of leaflets and posters – the specific
model here was the agitation methods of the Left[110] – slide
shows, orchestral and theatrical performances, traveling cinemas,
rhetorical schooling and the distribution of argumentation
aids.[111] One Deputy General Command even maintained an acting
company, which traveled around the country, and many others
organized trips, during which farmers could view factories and
urban poverty, or civilians inspect models of frontline trenches.
In 1918, the imperial government established the Central Office
for Domestic Propaganda (*Zentralstelle für Heimataufklärung*),
which, together with employers' associations, the Office of
Social Policy (*Büro für Sozialpolitik*) and the Cultural League
of German Scholars and Artists (*Kulturbund deutscher Gelehrter
und Künstler*),[112] was to coordinate and intensify official and
other propaganda activities.[113] The focus of these efforts became
advertising campaigns, in which the population was to be moved
to subscribe to war bonds.

As, despite all of this propagandist activity, the people's morale
increasingly deteriorated, the government did eventually try to
bring a certain degree of centralization to its "enlightenment"
efforts. The War Press Office, established in 1915, was anything
but the "spiritual War Food Office" that Reichstag representative
Matthias Erzberger had demanded. Its endeavors in the realm of
propaganda were so unsuccessful that, toward the end of the
war, it was judged to be "one of the saddest phenomena of the
entire war period."[114] The Supreme Command, too, urged that
the "fruitless appearances on the home front," which undermined the morale of the army, be put to an end.[115]

The most far-reaching of the imperial government's propaganda efforts were in the realm of state film policy. The years
1917 and 1918 mark the transition from a prohibitive state film
policy, which had been pursued heretofore, to a manipulative
one.[116] If, before the war and during its first two years, the
authorities had primarily considered cinemas and the new medium of film as threats to the adolescents' moral condition, they
now recognized "the extraordinary power of film to influence

the masses."[117] Already in 1916, the Prussian War Ministry had hired the private German Bioscope Company (*Deutsche Bioscop-Gesellschaft*") to produce entertaining, anti-French films, under the stipulation that its involvement in this project did not become known. The German Picture Company (*Deutsche Lichtspiel-gesellschaft*), which was backed by the major industrialist Alfred Hugenberg, also produced patriotic films with government participation.[118] In 1917, the Photograph and Film Office (*Bild-und Filmamt*, hereafter referred to as Bufa) was established. It was developed out of the Counter-Intelligence Agency (*Abwehr-stelle*) of the Foreign Office with the objective of "using film in the national interest in such a way that it, on the one hand, has an enlightening effect and, on the other, influences the feelings of the people in appropriate ways."[119] The foundation of the *Universum-Film-AG* (Ufa, after 1918 becoming the biggest German film company) followed at the end of 1917. Ufa's purpose was to conceal the official nature of film support; the Reich, however, had substantial influence over the management of the company.[120]

In terms of quality, the government's initial efforts in propaganda-film production left much to be desired. The impression the enlightenment officers had about the first Bufa films "was not necessarily satisfying." They found the scenes of the front senti-mental and artificial and recommended that the films on no account be shown to soldiers.[121] And despairing cinema owners complained that it was "asking too much [of the audience] if it had to watch the same three-quarters of an hour or even longer of falling grenades, trenches, desolate terrain, prisoners, etc."[122] A start had been made, however, and, in the inter-war period, Ufa was to develop into the dominant company of the German film industry.

In the end, the German advertising industry, sensing the com-pletely new opportunities for professionalization, also introduced diverse initiatives into the realm of opinion manipulation.[123] The time was too short, however, and the terrain of state propaganda still too unfamiliar for the efforts of this and other industries to have a marked effect on popular morale. The population's negative attitude to the war proved to be resistant to all attempts to influence it. As the Deputy General Commands saw it, this was particularly so "because women and adolescents are, for the most part, impervious to any sort of enlightenment and reject every attempt in this direction with the catchword 'cheap propaganda.'"[124] And, as one District Office in Bavaria complained, with especially seditious women and adolescents, "enlightenment" was perhaps more damaging that useful since it "would probably only provoke counter agitation, which would then find a receptive audience."[125]

The individuals within the military and civilian bureaucracy responsible for propaganda were conscious of the fact that the development of state opinion-manipulation would only come to fruition in terms of effectiveness after the war. Considerations of how the governments and authorities should gain access to the construction of reality "from below" and of what organizational measures they should then pursue were, consequently, already conceived with an eye towards that time. For then, as was repeatedly stressed, the societal and political conflicts, which had heretofore been subdued, would erupt, and the Prussian House of Representatives (*Abgeordnetenhaus*) – independent of any eventual changes in suffrage – would also no longer serve as a counterbalance to the Reichstag and the Social Democrats represented there. In order to surmount these difficulties, decision-makers believed it would be necessary that "as much of our population as possible take conscious part in social life . . . To clarify knowledge about the state in this regard remains the most important task of civil enlightenment."[126]

The technique of "clarifying the knowledge of the state" or, in the language of the philosopher Ernst Cassirer, consciously to create the myth of the state, originated in the First World War. Its practical application flourished especially in the preparation and execution of the Second World War. As Cassirer wrote in 1944/1945 with regard to Nazi Germany:

The new political myths do not freely flourish on their own . . . Instead, they are artificially created objects, cultivated by very dextrous and clever craftsmen . . . In the future, it will be possible to produce myths in the same sense and with the same methods as any other modern weapon, as machine guns or airplanes . . . This has changed the entire form of our social life . . . Even the most horrible despotic systems contented themselves with only forcing certain rules of behavior on human beings. They did not occupy themselves with people's feelings, judgments or thoughts . . . The modern political myths, however, proceeded in a different way. They did not begin by demanding or outlawing certain actions. They set out to change human beings in order to regulate and govern their actions. The political myths acted like a snake trying to paralyze its victims before attacking them. Human beings surrendered to them without any substantial resistance. They were conquered and subjugated before they realized what had happened.[127]

Notes to Chapter 5

1. J. Hofmiller, *Revolutionstagebuch 1918/19. Aus den Tagen der Münchener Revolution* (Leipzig, 1938), 21. Entry from 17 September 1918.

2. Monatsbericht des Stellv. Gen.kdo.s München für November 1917: HStA/Kr, Stellv. Gen.kdo. I. Bayerisches AK München 2398. Conclusions such as Michael Stürmer's that the social system of First World War Germany was "a military government supported by a consensus of the masses" implicitly absolve the society of the German Empire – to the detriment of the "masses" – of responsibility for the side-effects and resulting costs of the war. In this instance, Stürmer's implicit meaning becomes clearer when considered with the sentence immediately preceding that quoted here: "The German Empire ended in the first days of the world war." These conclusions clearly do not correspond to the source findings. M. Stürmer, *Das ruhelose Reich. Deutschland 1866–1918* (Berlin, 1983), 380.

3. Letter, 19. March 1917: HStA/Kr, Stellv. Gen.kdo. I. Bayerisches AK München 1979.

4. This concept, which also serves as the title of chapter 2, about the first months of the war, is adopted from E. Stransky. E. Stransky, *Krieg und Geistesstörung* (Wiesbaden, 1918), 32.

5. 19. Bericht des Berliner Polizeipräsidenten, 5 December 1914: ZStA Potsdam, Reichskanzlei 2398/1, Bl. 76, and 20. Bericht des Berliner Polizeipräsidenten, 12 December 1914: ibid., Bl. 106.

6. 32. Bericht des Berliner Polizeipräsidenten, 6 March 1915: ibid. 2398/2, Bl. 83

7. 34. Bericht des Berliner Polizeipräsidenten, 20 March 1915: ibid., Bl. 148.

8. 43. Bericht des Berliner Polizeipräsidenten, 10 July 1915: ibid. 2398/3, Bl. 187–188.

9. 50. Bericht des Berliner Polizeipräsidenten, 18 October 1915: ibid 2398/4, Bl. 153.

10. 58. Bericht des Berliner Polizeipräsidenten, 5 February 1916: ibid. 2398/5, Bl. 181.

11. 85. Bericht des Berliner Polizeipräsidenten, 18 June 1917: ibid. 2398/10, Bl. 292.

12. G. Grosz, *Ein kleines Ja und ein großes Nein. Sein Leben vom ihm selbst erzählt* (Reinbek, 1974), 101.

The Fight over the Meaning-Endowment of the War

13. Circular memorandum of the Prussian War Minister, 2 September 1918: HStA/Kr, MKr 2345.

There had been several riots in Bavaria, for example, when, at the time of transport, soldiers, unwilling to do active service, united with bystanders and together attacked the escorting officers. See, for example, K. L. Ay, *Die Entstehung einer Revolution. Die Volksstimmung in Bayern während des Ersten Weltkriegs* (Berlin, 1968), 186–187.

14. The sense of this cannot be fully translated into English. The German word used, *Kriegsmutwilliger*, does not actually exist and involves a play on the words *Kriegsfreiwilliger*, or war volunteer, and *mutwillig*, or mischievous. [Translator]

15. R. Meier, *Feldpostbriefe aus dem Ersten Weltkrieg 1914–1918* (Stuttgart, 1966), 48.

16. Kriegsbericht des Regierungspräsidenten Düsseldorf, 15 April 1915: ZStA Merseberg, Rep. 77, Tit. 332r, Nr. 123, Bl. 48. Military doctors became judges of life and death; for more on this, see E. Glaeser, *Jahrgang 1902* (Berlin, 1931), 289–290, and A. Adler, *Die andere Seite. Eine massenpsychologische Studie über die Schuld des Volkes* (Wien, 1919), 5–6.

17. See, for example, Zusammenstellung aus den Monatsberichten der stellvertretenden Generalkommandos, 3 October 1916, 3: BA/MA, RM3/4670: "Without being a pessimist, one can say that the vast majority of the people are war-weary." In this chapter, these monthly reports will be abbreviated as "Monatsberichte." The identical sentiment is expressed in, among others, Bezirksamt Memmingen to Stellv. Gen.kdo. München, 28 October 1916: HStA/Kr, Stellv. Gen.kdo. I. Bayerisches AK München 1946. The eldest at the garrison of Kaufbeuren introduced his November 1918 report about morale with the following remarks: "A joke was told me recently: What is the difference between the morale in Germany and in Austria? The answer: With us, it's optimistic, but serious; there, it's pessimistic, but merry. By and large, I would like to endorse that." Garnisonsältester Kaufbeuren, 16 November 1916: HStA/Kr, Stellv. Gen.kdo. I. Bayerisches AK München 1947.

18. Monatsberichte, September 1918, 9: HStA/Kr, MKr 12853.

19. Bezirksamt Altötting to Regierung Oberbayern, 21 September 1918: HStA/Kr, Stellv. Gen.kdo. I Bayerisches AK München 1969.

20. See, for example, Bayerisches Kriegsministerium to Kommandeure der mobilen Formationen, 11 August 1917: HStA/Kr, Stellv. Gen.kdo. I. Bayerisches AK München 1373; Meeting in the War Press Office, re. propaganda, 18 May 1917, item 3: ZStA Potsdam, Reichsministerium des Innern 12475, Bl. 112; Sächsischer Innenminister to Kreishauptmannschaften, 8 April 1917, rpt. in *Ursachen und Folgen. Vom deutschen Zusammenbruch 1918 und 1945 bis zur staatlichen Neuordnung in der Gegenwart. Eine Urkunden- und Dokumentensammlung zur Zeitgeschichte* (Berlin, n.d.), vol. 1:200.

21. When the term "social protest" or its compounds, such as "protest potential," are used here, they are to be understood, following the suggestion of H. Volkmann and J. Bergmann, "as prescientific collective terms of an archetype of social behavior, which takes shape in varying forms of expression. This archetype has roots in the social structure, violates social and/or legal norms and is – innovatively or restoratively – goal-oriented." H. Volkmann and J. Bergmann, eds., *Sozialer Protest. Studien zu traditioneller Resistenz und kollektiver Gewalt in Deutschland vom Vormärz bis zur Reichsgründung* (Opladen, 1984),

14. Regarding the discussion of "social protest" as a historical concept, see Ch. Tilly et al., *The Rebellious Century, 1830-1930* (New York, 1975), *passim*: R. Tilly, ed., "Sozialer Protest," *GG* 3.2 (1977); D. Puls, ed., *Wahrnehmungsformen und Protestverhalten. Studien zur Lage der Unterschichten im 18. und 19. Jahrhundert* (Frankfurt/M., 1979); R. Wirtz, *"Widersetzlichkeiten, Excesse, Crawalle, Tumulte und Skandale." Soziale Bewegung und gewalthafter sozialer Protest in Baden 1815-1848* (Frankfurt/M., 1981). In terms of the role of women in social protest, see M. I. Thomis and J. Grimmett, *Women in Protest, 1800–1850* (London and Canberra, 1982); L. A. Tilly, "Women's Collective Action and Feminism in France, 1870-1914," in L.A. Tilly and Ch. Tilly, eds., *Class Conflict and Collective Action* (Beverly Hills and London, 1981), 207-231; C. Honegger and B. Heintz, eds., *Listen der Ohnmacht. Zur Sozialgeschichte weiblicher Widerstandsformen* (Frankfurt/M., 1981).

22. On the higher morale among organized workers, see, for example, Bayerisches Kriegsministerium to Kommandeure der mobilen Formationen, 11 August 1917: HStA/Kr, Stellv. Gen.kdo. I Bayerisches AK München 1373; Monatsbericht des Presserefats des bayerischen Kriegsministeriums für Oktober 1917: HStA/Kr, MKr 12845; Monatsbericht des Stellv. Gen.kdo.s III. Bayerisches AK Nürnberg für August 1917, 2-3: ibid.

In terms of the morale of the middle classes, see Monatsberichte, 3 May 1918, 20: BA/MA, RM3/7795; Monatsbericht des Stellv. Gen.kdo.s II. Bayerisches AK Würzburg für Oktober 1917, Bl. A, 1., 2: HStA/Kr, MKr 12845. The middle classes' willingness to persevere with the war seems to have begun to falter sooner than that of the "intellectuals," however. See, for example, Monatsbericht des Pres-sereferats des bayerischen Kriegsministerium für August 1917: HStA/Kr, MKr 12845, 2-3.

Regarding the city-country opposition, see, for example, Monatsbericht des Stellv. Gen.kdo.s I. Bayerisches AK München für Oktober 1916: HStA/Kr, MKr 12842 and Preußischer Innenminister to Kriegsministerium, 5 May 1916: ZStA Potsdam, Reichsministerium des Innern 12475, Bl. 26-29.

In terms of the "intellectuals'" morale, see Monatsberichte des Stellv. Gen.kdo.s I. Bayerisches AK München für Oktober 1917: HStA/Kr, MKr 12845; Minutes of the meeting of the intermediary agents, 22 June 1918: HStA/Kr, Stellv. Gen.kdo. I. Bayerisches AK München 2396, Bl. 2; Monatsbericht des Stellv. Gen.kdo.s VII. AK Münster, end of 1917: ZStA Potsdam, Reichskanzlei 2398/11, Bl. 55ff.; Regierungspräsident Düsseldorf 23 August 1918: ZStA Merseburg, Rep. 77, Tit. 1059, Nr. 3, Beiheft 2, Bd. 3, Bl. 561. The majority of those who supported the war-objectives discussion also came from "intellectual" circles, whereas, in the rest of the population, the wish for a negotiated peace prevailed.

For more on women's morale, see those sources cited in endnote 18.

23. For such an analysis, see J. Kocka, *Klassengesellschaft im Krieg. Deutsche Sozialgeschichte 1914-1918* (Göttingen, 2nd expanded ed. 1978), *passim*.

24. Ibid., 71-76.

25. See, for example, Polizeidirektion München to Stellv. Gen.kdo. München, 15 August 1918, rpt. in Ay, *Entstehung*, 187-188: At the demonstration in Munich on 14 August, the police, "despite repeated efforts, were unfortunately unsuccessful in arresting a woman, who was holding a small child and who, as the main ringleader, was behaving in a particularly unruly manner, since she immediately threatened to scream and thereby would have gained the

unconditional support of the entire crowd."

26. With regard to the morale of the Berlin workforce, the Berlin Police Commissioner reported in May 1918, for instance:

The workers, intimidated by the course of the last strike and its consequences [several strikers were sent to the front], are, in general, particularly concerned with not giving their employers and the authorities any reason to complain, in order to avoid being sent from their current, well-paid jobs to the front. The women do indeed grumble, and also get carried away and abuse the government. Their influence on the working men is, however, extremely slight.

97. Bericht des Berliner Polizeipräsidenten, 22 May 1918: ZStA Potsdam, Reichskanzlei 2398/11, Bl. 291

27. This thesis is based on the sociology of knowledge developed following the tenets of Max Weber and Alfred Schütz. For this, see chapter 1 and the literature cited there.

28. J. Zinnecker, *Sozialgeschichte der Mädchenbildung. Zur Kritik der Schulerziehung von Mädchen im bürgerlichen Patriarchalismus* (Weinheim and Basel, 1973), 80–84.

29. A. Puhlmann, *Mädchenerziehung in der bürgerlichen Gesellschaft* (Köln, 1979), 48–49; G. Tornieporth, *Studien zur Frauenbildung* (Weinheim and Basel, 1979), 7.

30. Zinnecker, *Sozialgeschichte*, 135–141 and *passim*. Also see I. Brehmer et al., eds., *"Wissen heißt leben . . ." Beiträge zur Bildungsgeschichte von Frauen im 18. und 19. Jahrhundert*. Frauen in der Geschichte IV (Düsseldorf, 1983): M. Simmel, *Erziehung zum Weibe. Mädchenbildung im 19. Jahrhundert* (Frankfurt/M., 1980).

31. Until 1908, women were forbidden to join a political party. A statistical inquiry into the behavior of male and female readers, conducted between 1922 to 1926 at the Leipzig Municipal Library, also illuminates the gender-specific participation in the societal production of symbols. The lending figures for individual titles and specific subjects for this period of time were then used to analyze reading behavior according to gender and class. The following figures are percentages.

Subject	Working-Class		Bourgeois		Total	
	Women	Men	Women	Men	Women	Men
Narrative Literature	73.1	45.3	62.4	45.0	66.8	45.2
Poetry and Drama	5.7	4.4	8.0	7.4	7.0	6.0
Didactic Literature about technology, science, politics, etc.	21.3	50.3	29.6	47.5	26.2	48.8

The study concluded that the commonality in women's reading behavior, which even cut across class lines, was just as distinctive as the gender-specific differences in general and those within each class. When compared with those of the working class, however, the gender-specific difference in the bourgeoisie became increasingly less significant. The author of the study summarized the main focus of women's "typical" reading matter as follows:

> Absence of any interest in what is not connected to their own life, rejection of the dissolution of the material, concrete world in favor of abstract concepts. Complete lack of interest in everything that appears like "jurisprudence," but even in every cognitive system connected to it . . . Life in the imagination, life in the sensual perception . . . The vivid yet simultaneously human world filled with the senses is what is absolutely attractive.

> W. Hofmann, *Die Lektüre der Frau. Ein Beitrag zur Leserkunde und zur Leserführung* (Leipzig, 1931), 30, 39–40 and *passim*. Quote appears on p. 193

32. Monatsbericht des Stellv. Gen.kdo.s I. Bayerisches AK München für Oktober 1917: HStA/Kr, MKr 12845. The same sentiments are expressed in, among others, Monatsbericht des Stellv. Gen.kdo.s II AK Würzburg für Oktober 1917: ibid., and Monatsbericht des Stellv. Gen.kdo.s I. Bayerisches AK München für September 1917: ibid.

33. Eduard David, SPD, at the meeting of the Reichstag party leaders with the chancellor, 5 September 1916: ZStA Potsdam, Reichskanzlei 2398/7, Bl. 209ff.

34. Monatsbericht des Stellv. Gen.kdos. I. Bayerisches AK München für April 1917, 17: HStA/Kr, MKr 12844.

35. Dr Sebastian Schlittenbauer, Regensburg, 30 September 1918: HStA München, MInn 66332. This deals with the copy of a letter that Schlittenbauer had sent to the district secretary of the Bavarian Farmers' Association on the same day.

36. Monatsbericht des Stellv. Gen.kdo.s II. Bayerisches AK Würzburg für August 1918, Bl. 1: HStA/Kr, MKr 12849.

37. Letter from Upper Bavaria, 11 March 1917: HStA/Kr, Stellv. Gen.kdo. I. Bayerisches AK München 1979. For this, see also Kocka, *Klassengesellschaft*, 33–51 and the identical references cited there.

38. With regard to the complaints of injustice, see, along with the previous endnote: Monatsberichte, April 1916, 6: BA/MA, RM3/4670; Monatsberichte, 3 October 1916, 22–23: ibid.; Monatsberichte, 3 November 1916, 25: ibid.; Monatsberichte, 3 January 1917, 30: ibid.; Monatsberichte, 3 June 1918, 56, 65: ibid., 7795; Monatsbericht des Kriegsversorgungsamts Hamburg, 24 June 1918, 1: StA Hamburg, Kriegsversorgungsamt Ia 19b, Bd. 2.

The following is quoted as an example of the legends and rumors that Bavarian soldiers and civilians spread from 1915 at the latest about the Prussian–Bavarian conflict:

> Outside of Verdun, Bavarian troops had to recapture a position five times that Prussian troops had lost. At the end, the Bavarians were so incensed that one Bavarian regiment turned against the Prussians, so that there were dead and wounded among them. As punishment, the Bavarian regiment was supposed to be decimated. King Ludwig . . . broke off his friendship with the emperor because of this and, when the emperor said that the king should stay at home, the king declared that, if he went home, he would also take his troops with him. Filled with consternation about this, the emperor, incognito, secretly went to Munich to sort out the affair.

The Fight over the Meaning-Endowment of the War

Report of a Senior Front Police Officer to the Prussian War Ministry, which then sent it to the Bavarian War Ministry on 31 August 1916: HStA/Kr, MKr 2335

In 1916, an anonymous individual circulated the following verse version of Bavaria's hatred of Prussia: "You wickedly deceived German people, now you don't have any butter, / And believe - already in a few weeks, completely without fodder. / For all this, are the Prussians guilty, the arrogant, fresh - / Instead of France, it'd be better to slit the Prussians' throats." [In the original German, this poem was also intended to rhyme: *"Du arg betrogenes Deutsches Volk, jetzt bist Du ohne Butter, / Und glaub' in wenig Wochen schon so gänzlich ohne Futter. / An all dem sind die Preußen schuld, die arroganten, frechen - / Statt Frankreich, wär es besser wohl - die Preußen abzustechen."* Translator] Professor Gottinger, München, to Referent of the Bayerisches Kriegsministerium, 30 August 1917: HStA/Kr, MKr 2334. Toward the end of the war, the increasing aversion to Prussia led, in Bavaria, to the Hindenburg myth being turned on its head; the general chief of staff was now called a "mass murderer" and "mass butcher" by the population. Vertrauensmann Augsburg, 29 August 1918: HStA/Kr, Stellv. Gen.kdo. I. Bayerisches AK München 1980. It was popularly reported about the "iron soldier" - a wooden figure into which one could hammer a nail after having made a contribution to the war-chest - that "When he is completely nailed up, he can go to the General Staff." [In German, this colloquial saying involves a play on words. The past tense of the verb "to nail up" is *vernagelt*, which is the same word as that for the adjective "small-minded." Translator] Hofmiller, *Revolutionstagebuch*, 24.

39. Monatsbericht des Stellv. Gen.kdo.s III. Bayerisches AK Nürnberg für September 1917, 2: HStA/Kr, MKr 12845.

40. Monatsbericht des Stellv. Gen.kdo.s I. Bayerisches AK München für März 1917, 4 July 1917, 1: HStA/Kr, MKr 12844.

41. Monatsberichte, 3 January 1917, 7-8: BA/MA, RM3/4670. For more about inequality as a motive for social protest during the First World War, see also Kocka, *Klassengesellschaft*, 44ff.

42. This is emphasized in, among others: Lecture of the War Minster at the Council of State meeting, 9 October 1916: HStA/Kr, MKr 14363, 8; Excerpt from the letter von Batocki, head of the War Food Office, wrote to Ludendorff, 3 February 1917: ZStA Merseburg, Rep. 90a Y.IX.5b, Nr. 4, Bl. 36ff., 4.

43. Cf. R. G. Moeller, "Peasants, Politics and Pressure Groups in War and Inflation: A Study of the Rhineland and Westphalia, 1914-1924," diss. (University of California, Berkeley, 1980), 165-275; J. Flemming, *Landwirtschaftliche Interessen und Demokratie. Ländliche Gesellschaft, Agrarverbände und Staat 1890-1925* (Bonn, 1978), 76-143; M. Schumacher, *Land und Politik. Eine Untersuchung über politische Parteien und agrarische Interessen 1914-1923*, Beiträge zur Geschichte des Parlamentarismus und der politischen Parteien 65 (Düsseldorf, 1978), 33-84. Regarding the general domestic constellation of power and interests in the German Empire during the war, see H.-U. Wehler, *Das deutsche Kaiserreich 1871-1918* (Göttingen, 1988), ch. 8, and Kocka, *Klassengesellschaft*, 96-137.

44. V. Ullrich, *Kriegsalltag. Hamburg im Ersten Weltkrieg* (Köln, 1982), 98.

45. Adler, *Die andere Seite*, 4.

46. On press policy during the First World War, see K. Mühsam, *Wie wir belogen wurden. Die amtliche Irreführung des deutschen Volkes* (München, 1918); W. Nicolai, *Nachrichtendienst, Presse und Volksstimmung im Weltkrieg* (Berlin, 1920); W. Vogel, *Die Organisation der amtlichen Presse- und Propagandapolitik des Deutschen Reiches von den Anfängen unter Bismarck bis zum Beginn des Jahres 1933.* Special issue of *Zeitungswissenschaft* 16. 8/9 (1941): 8–9. (Berlin, 1941); K. Koszyk, *Deutsche Pressepolitik im Ersten Weltkrieg* (Düsseldorf, 1968); K. Koszyk, "Pressepolitik und Propaganda im Ersten Weltkrieg," *Francia* 3 (1975): 465–475; W. Deist, ed., *Militär und Innenpolitik im Weltkrieg 1914–1918* (Düsseldorf, 1970), 1: doc. nos. 31–75 (concerning censorship); H. D. Fischer, "Die Münchner Zensurstelle während des Ersten Weltkriegs. Alfons Falkner von Sonnenburg als Pressereferent im Bayerischen Kriegsministerium in den Jahren 1914 bis 1918/19," diss. (München, 1973); H. D. Fischer, ed., *Pressekonzentration und Zensurpraxis im Ersten Weltkrieg* (Berlin, 1973); A. G. Marquis, "Words as Weapons: Propaganda in Britain and Germany during the First World War," *JCH* 13 (1978): 467–498; S. Quandt and H. Schichtel, eds., *Der Erste Weltkrieg als Kommunikationsereignis* (Gießen, 1993); M. Creutz, *Die Pressepolitik der Kaiserlichen Regierung während der Ersten Weltkriegs* (Frankfurt/ M., 1996).

47. Head of the News Department of the Foreign Office, re. the propaganda question, 19 August 1918, quoted in *Ursachen und Folgen*, 2:287.

48. "Informal communication" is defined here as interpersonal lines or networks of communication that are independent of the dominant communication system and through which rumors, jokes, watchwords, etc. are circulated. F. Dröge, *Der zerredete Widerstand. Soziologie und Publizistik des Gerüchts im Zweiten Weltkrieg* (Düsseldorf, 1970), 12 and *passim*. Additionally, see W. B. Lerg, *Das Gespräch. Theorie und Praxis der unvermittelten Kommunikation* (Düsseldorf, 1970), 88–171 and *passim*.

In terms of the role of informal communication within the framework of a theory of collective action, see N. J. Smelser, *Theorie des kollektiven Verhaltens*, W. R. Heinz et al., eds. (Köln, 1972), 37ff., 94–97 and *passim*. In Smelser's approach, rumors, ideologies and superstition represent "generalized ideas through which individuals become activated to participate in episodes of collective action." Ibid., 94. "Collective action" is defined as "goal-oriented action through which individuals attempt to rearrange their social environment . . . Furthermore, during collective episodes, individuals attempt to redefine this environment on the basis of a particular type of idea, which I call a generalized idea." N. J. Smelser, "Fragen über Reichweite und Problembereiche einer Theorie kollektiven Verhaltens," in W. R. Heinz and P. Schöber, eds., *Theorien kollektiven Verhaltens. Beiträge zur Analyse sozialer Protestaktionen und Bewegungen*, 2 vols (Darmstadt and Neuwied, 1973), 80.

49. See, for example, HStA/Kr, MKr 2330–2348, *passim*; Preußischer Kriegsminister to Stellv. Gen.kdo.s, 2 September 1915: HStA/Kr, MKr 11484; Chef des Generalstabs der Armee IIIb to Kriegsministerien, 5 June 1917: ibid.

Even several years later, Georg Michaelis, previous head of the Imperial Grain Office and later imperial chancellor, still commented about women's queuing during the war with noticeable bitterness. Wrote Michaelis, "This was where housewives and mothers got the poison and the bile, with which, together with low-quality food substitutes, they cooked meals for their husbands and children." G. Michaelis, *Für Staat und Volk. Eine Lebensgeschichte* (Berlin, 1922), 288.

50. W. Scheller, *Als die Seele starb. 1914–1918. Das Kriegserlebnis eines Unkriegerischen* (Berlin, 1931), 48. On the morale of soldiers at the front, see, in addition to the literature cited in the introduction, L. Scholz, *Seelenleben des Soldaten an der Front. Hinterlassene Aufzeichnungen des im Kriege gefallenen Nervenarztes* (Tübingen, 1920).

51. File note of Department R in the Bavarian War Ministry, 26 February 1917: HStA/Kr, MKr 2331. Emphasis in the original.

52. Kriegspresseamt Berlin to Militärstellen des Heimatgebiets, 13 January 1917: ibid. One doctor who served as an honorary intermediary agent for the government despaired of the vast number of rumors circulating. His idea for countering this, that "the intermediary agents who are absolutely reliable create an information office for rumors," was never put into action, however. Ay, *Entstehung*, 181.

53. The mood of the people was often communicated poetically. In a March 1917 letter, for example, it was reported that children in Munich sang the following song: "Dawn, O dawn, without coupons, there is no bread, and when the sirens blow, into the cellar I must race, I and a few friends." [In the original German, this song rhymes: *Morgenrot, Morgenrot, ohne Marken gibts kein Brot, und wenn die Sirenen blassen muß ich in den Keller rasen, ich und mancher Kamerad.* Translator] Letter from Munich, March 1917: HStA/Kr Stellv. Gen.kdo. I. Bayerisches AK München 1979. In Jülich, the following version of this song circulated: "Dawn, O dawn, England knows no hunger yet, France still bakes fresh rolls, Russia still has pig's feet, Germany only has jam and kohlrabi." [Again, this song rhymes in German: *Morgenrot, Morgenrot, England hat noch keine Not, Frankreich backt noch frische Brötchen, Rußland hat noch Schweinepfötchen, Deutschland nichts als Marmelade und dazu noch Erdkolrabien.* Translator] Monatsberichte, 3 January 1917, 5: BA/MA, RM3/4670. For other versions of this song, as well as examples of other critical folk-songs, see W. Steinitz, *Deutsche Volkslieder demokratischen Charakters aus sechs Jahrhunderten* (Berlin, 1979), 2: 339–420, and R. Busch, "Imperialismus und Arbeiterliteratur im Ersten Weltkrieg," *AfS* 14 (1974): 293–350, esp. 320–327.

54. See, for example, Monatsberichte, 3 November 1916, 34: BA/MA, RM3/4670. In some cases, such positive rumors created the positive event they announced through their circulation. In April 1917, for example, the Bavarian police came upon a group of approximately 400 individuals, above all women and children, in the woods, illegally collecting firewood. The thirteen individuals who were reported for violating the forest laws declared that they had "heard a rumor . . . that the Krupp company in Essen had purchased this section of the woods from the state and had no objection to people chopping down the wood." Monatsbericht des Stellv. Gen.kdo. III. Bayerisches AK Nürnberg für April 1917, 2 May 1917: HStA/Kr, MKr 12844.

55. See, for example, Monatsberichte, 3 December 1916, 11: BA/MA, RM3/4670, and HStA/Kr, MKr 2330-2348, *passim.*

56. See, for example, Monatsbericht des Stellv. Gen.kdo.s I. Bayerisches AK München für Oktober 1916, 2: HStA/Kr, MKr 1282; Bezirksamt Miesbach to Regierung Oberbayern, 7 October 1917: HStA/Kr, Stellv. Gen.kdo. I. Bayerisches AK München 1958.

57. Vertrauensmann Augsburg, 29 August 1918: HStA/Kr, Stellv. Gen.kdo. I. Bayerisches AK München 1980. For this, also see Monatsbericht des Stellv. Gen.kdo.s München, 10 September 1918: HStA/Kr, Stellv. Gen.kdo. I. Bayerisches AK München 2398.

58. See, for example, HStA/Kr, Stellv. Gen.kdo. I. Bayerisches AK München 1723, *passim.*

59. See, for example, Monatsbericht des Stellv. Gen.kdo.s München für November 1917: HStA/Kr, Stellv. Gen.kdo. I. Bayerisches AK München 2398, and Monatsbericht des Stellv. Gen.kdo.s München für Mai 1918: ibid.

60. Report about the railway rumors, 5 July 1917: HStA/Kr, Stellv. Gen.kdo. I. Bayerisches AK München 1723.

61. *Münchener Post,* 20 June 1916.

62. Bezirksamt Wolfratshausen to Regierung Oberbayern, 24 March 1917: HStA/Kr, Stellv. Gen.kdo. I. Bayerisches AK München 1951.

63. The Bavarian Minister of the Interior Brettreich felt obliged to counter these rumors and argued that "flour sacks, be they empty or full, do not swim." Innenminister Brettreich to Vaterländische Volkshilfe, 24 August 1917: HStA/Kr, MKr 2335.

64. Report about the railway rumors, 5 July 1917: HStA/Kr, Stellv. Gen.kdo. I. Bayerisches Ak München 1723.

65. Police Officer's report to his office, 12 June 1917: HStA/Kr, MKr 2333.

66. Bezirksamt Rosenheim to Stellv. Gen.kdo. München, 19 October 1918: HStA/Kr, Stellv. Gen.kdo. I. Bayerisches AK München 1970.

67. Report from an intermediary agent, 27 September 1918: HStA/Kr, Stellv. Gen.kdo. I. Bayerisches AK München, 1981, Bl. 113.

68. Report about the railway rumors, 5 July 1917: HStA/Kr, Stellv. Gen.kdo. I. Bayerisches Ak München 1723; Kriegspresseamt, 14 July 1917: ibid.

69. Historian Karl Alexander von Müller's report to the Bavarian War Ministry about morale in Bavaria, 31 August 1916, 3: HStA/Kr, MKr 2335.

70. Kartell der Stammbuch führenden Spezialklubs Frankfurt/Main to Stellv. Gen.kdo. München, 21 August 1916: HStA/Kr, Stellv. Gen.kdo. I. Bayerisches AK München 949. The military authorities denied this immediately.

71. Monatsbericht des Stellv. Gen.kdo.s München für August 1918: HStA/Kr, Stellv. Gen.kdo. I. Bayerisches AK München 2398; Monatsbericht des Stellv. Gen.kdo.s München für September 1918: ibid.; Vertrauensmann Oberstaufen, 23 August 1918: HStA/Kr, Stellv. Gen.kdo. I. Bayerisches AK München 1980.

72. By comparison, Friedhelm Boll asserts the hypothesis that the Social-Democratic opposition, above all, and the MSPD, to a certain extent, could be considered bearers of the counterpublic during the First World War. F. Boll, "Spontaneität der Basis und politische Funktion des Streiks 1914-1918. Das Beispiel Braunschweig," *AfS* 17 (1977): 340 and *passim*; F. Boll, *Massenbewegungen in Niedersachsen 1906-1920. Eine sozialgeschichtliche Untersuchung zu den unterschiedlichen Entwicklungstypen Braunschweig und Hannover* (Bonn, 1981), 147-150 and *passim.* In view of the fact that the network of informal communication, as well as the vast majority of food riots, was not under the influence of the Social Democrats, Boll's hypothesis, in this form, is not particularly convincing.

73. See, for example, ZStA Merseberg, Rep. 197A, Io, Nr. 1, Bd. 2, *passim*; War Office /Technical Staff about the strike, 26 April 1917: HStA/Kr, MKr 17306;

Note about Senator Sander's speech to the Hamburg Senate on 8 September 1916, re. the riots that had just ended in Hamburg: StA Hamburg, Kriegsakten des Senats AIIP 233; Monatsberichte, 3 February 1917, 29: BA/MA, RM3/4670.

74. Minutes of a meeting in the Prussian War Ministry, re. the strike movement, 13 August 1917, 3: HStA/Kr, MKr 17306; Beauftragter des Bayerischen Kriegs-ministeriums in Preußisches Kriegsamt to Bayerisches Kriegsministerium, 14 August 1917: ibid. See also the minutes of this same meeting in: BA/MA, RM3l/ 2383, Bl. 100–106, and HStA/Kr, MKr 12842–12853. The report about the militarization of factories, which the Prussian War Office sent on 16 March 1918, contained, among "several special tips," the piece of advice that "Women [are] particularly difficult." Preußisches Kriegsamt to Stellv. Gen. kdo.s, etc., 16 March 1916: HStA/Kr, MKr 17306.

75. Regierungspräsident Magdeburg to Preußischer Innenminister, 9 September 1916: ZStA Merseburg, Rep. 197A, Io, Nr. 1, Bd. 2, Bl. 14ff.

76. Monatsberichte, 3 March 1917, 9: BA/MA, RM3/4670.

77. For this, see H.-J. Bieber, *Gewerkschaften in Krieg und Revolution. Arbeiterbewegung, Industrie, Staat und Militär in Deutschland 1914–1920*, 2 vols. (Hamburg, 1981), 220–253, 487–504, as well as Berichte des Büros für Sozialpolitik: HStA/Kr, MKr 14029, *passim*, and Kocka, *Klassengesellschaft*, 51–57.

78. Monatsberichte, June 1916, 13: BA/MA, RM3/4670. The Office for Social Policy made the following comment:

> As little as one would question the loyalty of Prussian civil servants, because a lot of luggage is now being lost by the railway, as little as one can make the post office morally responsible for the theft of packages by its temporary employees, it is equally impossible to reproach the trade unions for a lack of discipline, which is displayed by a workforce that is fundamentally different from that earlier organized in them.

> Report of the Office for Social Policy, 15 September 1917, 4–5: HStA/Kr, MKr 14029

79. Vorstand des Stadtmagistrats Bayreuth to Regierung Oberfranken, 17 September 1917: HStA/Kr, MKr 17161.

80. K.-D. Schwarz, *Weltkrieg und Revolution in Nürnberg. Ein Beitrag zur Geschichte der deutschen Arbeiterbewegung* (Stuttgart, 1971), 148–151.

81. See, for example, Garnisonskommando Augsburg to Stellv. Gen.kdo. München, 26 December 1917: HStA/Kr, Stellv. Gen.kdo. I. Bayerisches AK München 557; Bayerisches Innenministerium to Regierung Oberbayern, 28 June 1918: HStA/Kr, Stellv. Gen.kdo. I. Bayerisches AK München 1372. The soldiers also sided with the "squirrels" when their foraged goods were confiscated at the train station; see, for example, Bayerisches Kriegsministerium to Stellv. Gen.kdo.s, 15 September 1917: HStA/Kr, Stellv. Gen.kdo. I. Bayerisches AK München 808.

82. "In view of the times," the celebration was ultimately cancelled. Ay, *Entstehung*, 122.

83. See S. von Koppenfels, *Die Kriminalität der Frau im Kriege* (Leipzig, 1926), 17, 23; M. Liepmann, *Krieg und Kriminalität in Deutschland*. Wirt-schafts- und Sozialgeschichte des Weltkriegs, German series (Stuttgart et al., 1930), 24.

84. Meeting of the Prussian State Ministry, 25 October 1915: ZStA Merseburg, Rep. 90a Y.IX.5a, Nr. 2, Bl. 148ff., 16–17; Erster Staatsanwalt des Landgerichts I Berlin to Polizeipräsident Berlin, 4 December 1915: ZStA Merseburg, Rep. 197A, lo, Nr. 1, Bd. 1, Bl. 36. For evidence that it was primarily women who were concerned, see Ay, *Entstehung*, 184, note 2.

85. HStA/Kr, MKr 2497, *passim*; Stellv. Gen.kdo. I München to Standortälteste, 29 August 1918: HStA/Kr, Stellv. Gen.kdo. I. Bayerisches AK München 557; Bayerisches Kriegsministerium to Bayerisches Staatsministerium des Innern, 23 July 1918: HStA/Kr, Stellv. Gen.kdo. I. Bayerisches AK München 1373.

In Bavaria, tear-gas bombs were used in Ingolstadt, for example, where there were riots in May 1918 after police had arrested and beaten up a war invalid. The outraged crowd first tried to obtain the invalid's release through negotiation and then, when this proved unsuccessful, set fire to the city hall. In a letter, dated 22 June 1918, to the Upper Bavarian government, Bavarian Minister of the Interior Brettreich wrote of the event: "Only after hours of raging and after several insufficient interventions by the armed authorities could the rioting be suppressed through the use of tear-gas bombs." As cited in Ay, *Entstehung*, 187.

86. Monatsbericht des Stellv. Gen.kdo. III. Bayerisches AK Nürnberg für Juni 1918: HStA/Kr, MKr 12849, Bl. 2

87. Kriegspresseamt Berlin to Leiter des Vaterländischen Unterrichts, 26 October 1917: Copy of the War Press Office's report for the Supreme Command about enlightenment at the Deputy General Commands: HStA/Kr, MKr 2336.

88. The surveillance of train stations originated at the level of the individual Deputy General Commands in 1915 and 1916; by 1917, this practice had spread across the entire Reich. HStA/Kr, MKr 11484, *passim*. It was originally conceived as a measure that would lead to the apprehension of deserters and foreign spies. Nicolai, *Nachrichtendienst*, 41–42.

89. Memorandum of the Bavarian War Ministry, March 1918: HStA/Kr, MKr 2339.

90. Compilation of the Deputy General Command Munich, undated: HStA/Kr, Stellv. Gen.kdo. I. Bayerisches AK München 1943; "Leitsätze für die Briefab-schriften" by Adolf Shinnerer: ibid. The quotes in the text also come from these two sources. Only the excerpts for March 1917 (found in HStA/Kr, Stellv. Gen.kdo. I. Bayerisches AK München 1979) seem to have been supplied.

91. According to O. Riebicke, roughly 8 million letters and packages were, on average, sent to members of the military each day during the war. In 1918, the number was over 4 million. Conversely, at the beginning of the war, members of the military sent close to 6 million letters each day to the home front. During the course of the war, this number increased to almost 8 million. Thus, the average number of daily military letters was approximately 14 million at the beginning, and 19 million towards the end of the war. In addition to this mail between the military front and the home front, there were also those letters and cards exchanged within the military, which amounted to more than one million each day. O. Riebicke, *Was brauchte der Weltkrieg? Tatsachen und Zahlen aus dem deutschen Ringen 1914/18* (Leipzig, 1936), 111.

92. Bayerisches Kriegsministerium to Kommandeure der mobilen Form-ationen, 11 August 1917: HStA/Kr, Stellv. Gen.kdo. I. Bayerisches AK München 1373.

The Fight over the Meaning-Endowment of the War

93. A. Mendelssohn-Bartholdy, *The War and German Society. The Testament of a Liberal* (New York, 1971), 76. In its own way, the Berlin Dada movement of the immediate post-war period took up the forward-looking aspects the war had revealed in this area. In addition to the "head Dadaist" and other functionaries, the movement named George Grosz "propaganda Dadaist," "what," as Grosz said,

> is between the name and the sentence, in small print, "what am I thinking today?" on my calling card. I had to find a motto that would benefit the good thing of Dadaism. Something like "Dada is here" or "Dada will vanquish" or "Dada, Dada above all!" We printed these slogans on small leaflets and soon the shop windows, coffee-house tables, house doors and the like all over Berlin were plastered with them. It was really alarming.
>
> The *B.Z. am Mittag* printed an entire article about the the Dadaist danger.
>
> Grosz, *Ein kleines Ja*, 131

The genesis and organization of Germany's "enlightenment" policy in the First World War have already been well researched and need not be recapitulated here. For literature pertaining to this subject, see, in addition to that cited in endnote 46, H. Thimme, *Weltkrieg ohne Waffen. Die Propaganda der Westmächte gegen Deutschland, ihre Wirkung und ihre Abwehr* (Stuttgart and Berlin, 1932); Vogel, *Organisation, passim*; Deist, ed., *Militär*, vol. 1, doc. nos. 124-183, vol. 2, doc. nos. 321-370 (concerning "enlightenment"); K. W. Wippermann, *Politische Propaganda und staatsbürgerliche Bildung. Die Reichszentrale für Heimatdienst in der Weimarer Republik* (Köln, 1976), 21-48; D. Stegmann, *Die Erben Bismarcks. Parteien und Verbände in der Spätphase des Wilhelminischen Deutschlands. Sammlungspolitik 1897-1918* (Köln and Berlin, 1970); D. Stegmann, "Die deutsche Inlandspropaganda 1917/ 18. Zum innenpolitischen Machtkampf zwischen OHL und ziviler Reichsleitung in der Endphase des Kaiserreichs," *MGM* 12 (1972): 75-116; M. Shorer, "Roles and Images of Women in World War I Propaganda," *Politics and Society* 5 (1975): 469-486; G. Mai, "'Aufklärung der Bevölkerung' und 'vaterländischer Unterricht' in Württemberg 1914-1918," *Zeitschrift für Württembergische Landesgeschichte* 36 (1977): 199-235; G. D. Stark, "Cinema, Society, and the State: Policing the Film Industry in Imperial Germany," in G. D. Stark and B. K. Lockner, eds., *Essays on Culture and Society in Modern Germany* (Arlington, Tex., 1982), 122-166; H. Barkhausen, *Filmpropaganda für Deutschland im Ersten und Zweiten Weltkrieg* (Hildesheim et al., 1982), 21-181; K.-P. Müller, "Organisation, Themen und Probleme der Volksaufklärung in Baden 1914 bis 1918," *ZGO* 134 (1986): 329-358. In terms of the historical development of propaganda in the nineteenth and twentieth centuries, see U. Daniel and W. Siemann, eds., *Propaganda. Meinungskampf, Verführung und politische Sinnstiftung (1789-1989)* (Frankfurt/M., 1994).

94. Kriegspresseamt Berlin to Bayerisches Kriegsministerium, 19 September 1917: HStA/Kr, MKr 2335.

95. Mai, "'Aufklärung,'" 230.

96. This was later rechristened "patriotic instruction" in the jargon of the military authorities. For this, see Hindenburg's decree of 15 September 1917, rpt. in Deist, ed., *Militär*, vol. 2, doc. no. 337, 860-864.

97. See, for example, Preußisches Kriegsministerium to Preußischer Innenminister and Preußischer Unterrichtsminister, March 1916: ZStA Potsdam, Reichsministerium des Innern 12475: Stellv. Gen.kdo. VII. AK Münster, 12 July 1917: HStA/Kr, MKr 2333; Monatsbericht des Stellv. Gen.kdo.s München für Oktober 1918, 4: HStA/Kr, MKr 12850.

98. Note from von Batocki to the chancellor, 18 May 1917: ZStA Potsdam, Reichskanzlei 2398/10, Bl. 224-225.

99. ZStA Potsdam, Reichskanzlei 2398/11, Bl. 61-78. According to a handwritten additional remark, this piece was written "by a German officer." H. Thimme asserts that Friedrich Naumann was its author. Thimme, *Weltkrieg*, 241-242.

100. In terms of the English, French and above all the German meaning-endowment of the war, see R. Rürup, "Der 'Geist von 1914' in Deutschland. Kriegsbegeisterung und Ideologisierung des Kriegs im Ersten Weltkrieg," in B. Hüppauf, ed., *Ansichten vom Krieg. Vergleichende Studien zum Ersten Weltkrieg in Literatur und Gesellschaft* (Königstein/Ts., 1984), 1-30, here 14-15 and *passim*, as well as Thimme, *Weltkrieg*, 208-247.

101. Dr. A. Messmer from Vaterländische Volkshilfe München to Pressereferat des Bayerisches Kriegsministeriums, 28 July 1917: "Aufklärung zur Hebung der Volksstimmung," 1: HStA/Kr, MKr 2334.

102. Meeting about enlightenment in the War Press Office, 18 May 1917: ZStA Potsdam, Reichsministerium des Innern 12475, Bl. 112. Also see Kriegspresseamt, 19 May 1917: "Richtlinien für die Aufklärung des Kriegspresseamts über einzelne z. Zt. wichtige Fragen": ibid.

103. For this, see Wippermann, *Politische Propaganda*, 21-48; Nicolai, *Nachrichtendienst*, 35-43, 113-136; Ay, *Entstehung*, 62ff.; W. Albrecht, *Landtag und Regierung in Bayern am Vorabend der Revolution von 1918* (Berlin, 1968), 124-134, 198-208, 232-252; Bavarian Ministry of the Interior to Bavarian Foreign Ministry, re. building up the propaganda organization in Bavaria, 14 June 1918: HStA/Kr, MKr 2342. The Bavarian government preferred this arrangement because it kept the military out of politics and strengthened the federalist principle. See Plans from the Bavarian War Ministry re. enlightenment activity, 5 December 1917: HStA/Kr, MKr 2337; Memorandum of the Bavarian War Ministry, re. Prussia's efforts to centralize power in the area of enlightenment *vis-à-vis* Bavaria, March 1919: HStA/Kr, MKr 2339. With regard to how propaganda was organized in Württemberg, see Mai, "'Aufklärung,'" *passim*.

104. Richtlinien für den Aufklärungsdienst in der Heimat, 10 March 1918, 6-7: ZStA Potsdam, Reichsministerium des Innern 12298, Bl. 185ff.

105. Together, the People's Association for Catholic Germany and the Protestant Church founded "Patriotic Help for the People" in Bavaria, which employed numerous government intermediary agents and initiated propaganda campaigns. For this, see Albrecht, *Landtag*, 201ff.; Tätigkeitsbericht der Vaterländischen Volkshilfe pro 1917 vom 1.1.1918: HStA/Kr, MKr 2338.

106. On the role of the trade unions and employer organizations in domestic propaganda, see Bieber, *Gewerkschaften*, 471-486. In 1918, the Nuremberg War Office bureau established that

The attempt to go over the heads of the trade unions in order to influence the workers "enlightenedly" would not only bring practically no success, but rather, would also have very alarming side-effects, since the impression would be given that one had intentionally worked against the trade unions. The previous cooperation of the trade-union leaders with this branch of the War Office would thereby be endangered. This cooperation is directed toward making the influence of the trade unions on the working masses utilizable for the maintenance of economic peace and to transfer the responsibility for the workers' behavior to the trade-union leaders.

Kriegsamtsstelle Nürnberg to Bayerisches Kriegsamt, 13 September 1918: HStA/Kr, MKr 2353

Regarding the All-German Association, see A. Kruck, *Geschichte des Alldeutschen Verbandes 1890–1939*. Veröffentlichungen des Instituts für Europäische Geschichte Mainz 3 (Wiesbaden, 1954); L. Werner, *Der Alldeutsche Verband 1890–1918. Ein Beitrag zur Geschichte der öffentlichen Meinung in Deutschland in den Jahren vor und während des Weltkriegs* (1935; rpt. Vaduz, 1965); G. Eley, *Reshaping the German Right. Radical Nationalism and Political Change after Bismarck* (New Haven, 1980); K. Schilling, "Beiträge zu einer Geschichte des radikalen Nationalismus in der Wilhelminischen Ära 1890-1909," diss. (Leipzig, 1968).

107. See, for example, Kriegspresseamt Berlin to Frauenorganisationen, 18 September 1917: HStA/Kr, MKr 2335; Kriegspresseamt Berlin to Frauenorganisationen, 1 March 1917: ibid., 2331.

108. Stellv. Gen.kdo. XIII. AK Stuttgart, 19 July 1917: HStA/Kr, Stellv. Gen.kdo. I. Bayerisches AK München 1722; Mai, "'Aufklärung,'" 215.

109. Minutes of the enlightenment meeting in the Berlin War Press Office, 10 December 1917: HStA München, MInn 66330, 3: Lieutenant Colonel von Kreß, representative from the Bavarian War Ministry, about Bavarian propaganda.

110. See, for example, Preußisches Kriegsministerium to Reichskanzler, 10 September 1916: ZStA Potsdam, Reichskanzlei 2398/7, Bl. 248; Oberbürgermeister/Polizeiverwaltung Düsseldorf to Regierungspräsident Düsseldorf, 11 February 1918: HStA Düsseldorf, Regierung Düsseldorf 14966.

111. In the training sessions on discussion, answers to the most important complaints of the population were formulated. See, for example, circular memorandum of the Berlin War Press Office, 21 September 1917: HStA/Kr, Stellv. Gen.kdo. I. Bayerisches AK München 2399. This document offers possible replies to the question of why those individuals who are safe at the home front, in particular, sing about a "hero's death."

112. Hermann Sudermann, Walter Rathenau, Heinrich von Gleichen and the Africa researcher Leo Frobenius sat on the executive board of the "Cultural League." Wippermann, *Politische Propaganda*, 26-27.

113. On this, see Wippermann, *Politische Propaganda*, 21-48. The Central Office for Domestic Enlightenment developed its real effectiveness during the Weimar Republic as the Imperial Headquarters for Domestic Service and was temporarily closed during the Third Reich. In 1952, it was converted into the Federal Headquarters for Political Education. Ibid., 15. For more information about the Central Office, also see Stegmann, "Deutsche Inlandspropaganda," 90-93, as well as J. K. Richter, *Die Reichszentrale für Heimatdienst. Geschichte der ersten politischen Bildungsstelle in Deutschland und Untersuchung ihrer Rolle in der Weimarer Republik* (Berlin, 1963).

114. Representative Müller-Meiningen at the enlightenment meeting in the Bavarian Ministry of the Interior, 5 November 1918, p. 8 of the minutes HStA/Kr, MKr 2347. Matthias Erzberger had originally wanted to establish the "intellectual War Food Office" in the Ministry of Culture as an information office for patriotic inquiries. M. Erzberger to Staatssekretär von Jagow im Auswärtigen Amt, 28 August 1916: ZStA Potsdam, Reichskanzlei 2398/7, Bl. 124ff.

115. Generalstabschef to Preußisches Kriegsministerium, 9 March 1917: ZStA Potsdam, Reichskanzlei 2398/10, Bl. 100ff; Generalstabschef to Reichskanzler, 17 August 1917: ibid., Bl. 382ff.; Generalstabschef to Preußischer Kriegsminister and other Kriegsministerien, Reichskanzler, etc., 15 November 1917: ZStA Potsdam, Reichskanzlei 2398/11, Bl. 91ff. Regarding the differences between the Supreme Command and civilian leadership of the Reich in questions of domestic propaganda, see Stegmann, "Deutsche Inlandspropaganda," *passim*.

116. For this, see Stark, "Cinema," *passim*, and Barkhausen, *Filmpropaganda*, 21–181.

117. "Bericht über die Tagung vom 7.–10.8.1917 in Berlin." Kriegspresseamt Berlin, ed. (1917), 9.

118. Stark, "Cinema," 161.

119. Lecture "Das Bild- und Film-Amt und seine Aufgaben," given by Dr. Wagner of Bufa on 7 August 1917 for the participants at the enlightenment conference in Berlin, 7–10 August 1917. Rpt. in "Bericht über die Tagung vom 7.–10.8.1917 in Berlin." Kriegspresseamt Berlin, ed. (1917), 17.

120. Reichsamt des Innern to Bundesregierungen, etc., 12 March 1918: HStA/Kr, MKr 2341. For the history of the Ufa see: K. Kreimeier, *The Ufa Story. A History of Germany's Greatest Film Company 1918–1945* (New York, 1996).

121. Report of the Bavarian participant, re. the meeting of the War Press Office with the Enlightenment Officers, 6–9 August 1917: HStA/Kr, MKr 2334.

122. Petition of a Munich cinema owner, Autumn 1917, as cited in Ay, *Entstehung*, 65.

123. "As long as German advertising work is not consciously united [and] uniformly directed by a far-sighted, industrious expert, then the individual, divided pieces are just pieces and not an entire work . . . Advertising people are to be brought into the leading posts of our news offices." "Mitteilungen des Vereins Deutscher Reklamefachleute," September 1918. As cited in R. Lebeck and M. Schütte, *Propagandapostkarten I* (Dortmund, 1980), 7ff.

124. Monatsberichte, 3 August 1917, 5: BA/MA, RM3/4670. For this, also see Monatsbericht des Kriegsversorgungsamts Hamburg, 24 May 1917, 1–2: StA Hamburg, Kriegsversorgungsamt Ia 19b, Bd. 2.

125. Monatsbericht des Stellv. Gen.kdo.s I. Bayerisches AK München für Juli 1918, 2: HStA/Kr, MKr 12849.

126. Conference of the Heads of Patriotic Instruction at the Deputy General Commands, 15–16 May 1918, p. 10 of the minutes: HStA/Kr, MKr 2342.

127. E. Cassirer, *Vom Mythus des Staates* (Zürich, 1949), 367–368, 374. See also the simultaneously devastating and forward-looking criticism Adolf Hitler made of propaganda during the First World War in *Mein Kampf*, in the chapter entitled "War Propaganda."

6

Summary and Conclusion

Emancipation from the system is progress.[1]

Karl Gutzkow

We have a recommendation for the honorable Senate of the City of Hamburg: We want to have our men and sons back and we don't want to go hungry any longer – Peace has to be made. The honorable Senate must stand by us in this, otherwise we are going to do something else.

Quoted from a letter from "several war wives of Hamburg" to the
Hamburg Senate, dated 11 August 1916[2]

Where women's history is concerned, the question of the longer-term meaning of events, structures and historical problems sooner or later runs aground on the shallows inherent in past and contemporary definitions of the term "emancipation." The problematic nature of this concept, its expressly enigmatic character, is a result of its career as a weapon in political discourse. This had already begun in the first decade of the nineteenth century, when "emancipation" was used as a term of agitation in the debates concerning the political, legal and social equality of Catholics and Jews, workers and women.[3] With regard to women, "emancipation" meant – and still means today – a progressive movement: Women's liberation from traditional legal, political and social bonds with the goal of greater equality in the respective present and with the expectation of a freer society in the future. Consequently, as soon as the term "emancipation" enters into historical analysis without reflection, its originally critical content quickly becomes an affirmative, backward-looking meaning-endowment of the respective present. In this retrospective reflection, the time axis imperceptibly changes from framing its respective political context to being its measuring rod. Corresponding to the temporal dynamic of progress, which always resonates in the concept of "emancipation," whoever speaks today about women's "emancipation" in the past is, by definition, more emancipated, i.e. he or she is a contemporary of the past's future. From such a perspective, it is a short step to the reverse conclusion, that we can establish "emancipatory" features in the past where the past resembles the present. Then, no longer is "emancipation from the system . . . progress," as Karl Gutzkow proclaimed in 1835, but rather "emancipation" is equivalent to the progress of the system itself (in the direction of the present).[4]

Out of well-founded mistrust of this mirror on the wall, which always reflects "how we, in the end, brought things so marvelously far,"[5] current research in women's history seldom engages the concept of "emancipation." Rather, as is the case with the history of everyday life and out of similar motives of criticizing the present, such research is increasingly directed toward examining women's resistance, refusal and protest in history.[6] Where this manner of approaching the past present is pursued without reflection, however, it too is afflicted with an anachronistic "bias," which is likewise fed by present-oriented wishful-thinking. Against the background of actual political and ecological grassroots movements and forms of protest that are not incorporated into the traditional party system, a backward-looking analysis of non-conformist behavior that was negatively sanctioned by the respective authorities often runs the risk of turning into retrospective idealization. It is, consequently, often assumed that "criticism of the system" was the driving force behind protest movements and actions in the past – especially if, in terms of their contents, opponents or forms, these exhibit certain similarities with contemporary sources of protest – even when these movements objectively expressed "criticism within the system" and possibly did not even perceive themselves as "critical of the system." The subjectively intended meaning of such actions and movements, therefore, might actually have been something completely different than it, because of this idealization, is interpreted to be.[7]

Just as with "emancipation," the perception and intention of the respective actors have to be our criteria for deciding whether the use of the concept "resistance" is meaningful or not. And, when examining "emancipatory" tendencies or the "resistant" actions of social groups, we always need to determine whether their material and mental consequences extended beyond the given context. With all efforts to endow a movement or a period or a social group with meaning after the fact – independent of whether these emphasize "emancipation" or the alternatives that were submerged in the historical process – we must proceed with particular caution when examining conditions of life that, as in the First World War, were shaped by extreme deprivation and misery. This is not the case because we are unable to discover links for this or that reading of the past here – such links exist and are accessible. Nor is caution required exclusively for reasons of professional ethics, as Theodor Lessing maintained.[8]

The reason, rather, is of another nature. Looking back on the four years of perpetual crisis that the First World War represented on both the individual and the collective level, we can only speculate about the extent to which individuals, in the midst of their desolate and chaotic life situation, perceived the wartime changes that we might label "emancipatory" or "resistant" tendencies as such. It is hardly possible, in other words, to measure how far contemporaries could filter these changes out of the individual and general chaos as single tones, instead of simply seeing them as one exception among many that the catastrophe of war had brought with it, to be forgotten as soon as possible after its conclusion. Both "emancipation" and "resistance" are ultimately terms belonging to the history of everyday experience because they depict phenomena that only take on concrete form in the perception of the individuals in question. This does not mean that intersubjectively verifiable criteria cannot be established for both interpretative approaches. Such criteria, however, can describe nothing more than a question-driven heuristics: If these criteria can be applied to a specific fact, then the question remains whether we can find clues in the handed-down or reconstructed perception of the concerned individuals that this fact could have had the same meaning for them as we assume.

In applying this approach to working-class women in the First World War, we confront a problem, a problem which plagues the concept of "emancipation" itself: No discussed catalog of criteria exists for what is to be understood by "emancipation." It also does not make sense here to create such a catalog *ad hoc*, according to the question of which economic, social or mental changes under which concrete circumstances could be described as "emancipatory." For the purposes of this concluding summary and evaluation, I shall instead pursue a more pragmatic path and summarize the most important results of the three main sections of this work in light of the following questions:

- What changes did the First World War entail for the life and working conditions of urban working-class women?
- How far did the effects of these changes extend beyond the conclusion of the war?
- Which of these changes improved the life and working conditions of working-class women in the longer term?

I will then summarize women's "resistance" in the First World War in a similar manner as that used for bpowomen's "emancipation." Here, the pertinent framing questions are:

- To what extent was criticism within viz. of the system, for example, articulated in working-class women's social protest?
- In other words, which ways of perception shaped this criticism?
- To what degree did this criticism exert longer-term, decisive influence on the development of society as a whole and on the role of working-class women in said development?

Emancipation on Loan: Female Wage Labor, 1914–1918

Contrary to the prevailing opinion, the quantitative development of female employment in the First World War predominately followed the pre-war pattern. The female labor potential that can be ascertained from statistics did not increase more than the average between 1914 and 1918. Consequently, we cannot assume that the number of those women who took up employment for the first time because of the war was very significant. Correspondingly, the number of employed women did not increase exceptionally between the occupational census of 1907 and that of 1925. In 1907, 30.5%, or 8.5 million, of the total female population of 27.9 million was employed. In 1925, by comparison, 35.6%, or 11.5 million, of the total female population of 32.2 million was working. In the same period of time, the number of employed men rose from 61.4%, or 16.7 million, of the total male population of 27.1 million to 68.0%, or 20.5 million, of the total male population of 30.2 million. The percentage increase in male employment between 1907 and 1925 was thus slightly more marked than that in female employment, namely 6.6% in comparison to 5.1%.[9] The military and civil authorities did indeed strive to mobilize women for the war industry, where an increasingly urgent labor shortage prevailed. Their efforts, however, which became more centralized and intense during the second half of the war, did not succeed in rectifying this labor shortage by employing more women.

The reason why this official mobilization of women failed lay on several levels. On the political and administrative level, it was the inefficiency and internal contradictions of the general organization and its concrete measures that prevented the authorities from substantially influencing the wartime labor market. On the structural level, it was the incongruence between the supply and demand of labor that obstructed their efforts to employ more women in war-industry concerns. For armaments production it was not simply more workers that were sought, but skilled workers. Instead of hiring women, who, as a rule, were not qualified for skilled labor, armaments-factory owners endeavored to obtain military deferments for their own skilled workers or, when this proved unsuccessful, employed foreign workers or prisoners of war. They preferred this option to employing women in part because skilled workers could be found within these two groups and in part because foreigners and, above all, prisoners of war could be paid less and treated worse than German women.

And finally, on the level of the life circumstances and experiences of women themselves, there were several factors that robbed women of their interest in working in the war industry. Women knew that their employment in the armaments industry – i.e. in branches of industry that had principally hired male labor before the war – would only be temporary and that, at the end of the war, they would have to give up their new positions to the returning soldiers. They consequently could not foster any hopes that their move into these usually better-paid, "male" branches would be permanent. Women who had dependants to provide for were the least likely to consider industrial work. Women who did not earn wages were by no means unemployed, but rather, in the majority of cases, were indispensable labor for their families – and this was not only true of wives and mothers. This fact of women's existence proved to be an important obstacle in mobilizing women for the war industry. Even if these women could have found other accommodation for their children and other dependants during their work shifts, so little remained of their wages – after transportation costs, the wear and tear on clothes and shoes, and child-care costs were deducted – that working did not seem to be worthwhile. Either these women succeeded in supporting themselves and their dependants from the money they received either as unemployment benefit or as Family Aid – something which became "easier" during the war since essential consumer goods were longer available to buy and thus had to be produced by one's own labor – or they took on piecework commissions. Even independent of whether they had children or dependants to support, women inexperienced in factory work frequently preferred to do homework, presumably because this work represented a less decisive break from the previous conditions of their lives. Although wartime home-workers also primarily produced items for the army, labor-market authorities found the increase in their numbers undesirable for labor-market policy since the productivity of this workforce was considerably lower than that of its industrial counterpart.

Despite these obstacles to women's mobilization there was still a very clear rise in the number of women employed in war-industry concerns. As we have seen, this new female workforce of the war industry was recruited predominantly from women who had heretofore worked in other industrial sectors or in non-industrial jobs. Especially for maids, agricultural workers and workers in industries, such as the textile industry, whose production either stagnated or decreased during the war, the war boom represented a chance to move out of occupations that either paid less or involved a greater degree of personal dependence. Here, as with the surge of women into office jobs with the military and war societies, the great number of women who changed employment out of their own initiative supports the premise that these women subjectively perceived the open-ing of new fields of work as a chance to improve their situation. This premise is also verified by contemporary surveys, where, for example, women employed during the war in "male positions" in the metal industry asserted that they wanted to keep their new jobs beyond the end of the war. Thus, by broadening the spectrum of jobs open to women, the war did bring, objectively as well as subjectively, a change for the better and, thereby, an opportunity for emancipation (in the sense outlined above).

Moreover, the trends observed during the war – namely the migration of female labor out of domestic service and agriculture as well as the increased employment of women in heretofore predominantly "male" positions in the metal, electric or chemical industries, or in offices – were not confined to those four years. They had already begun before 1914 and became increasingly pronounced after 1918.[10] It is difficult to determine the extent to which the war accelerated this shift in women's areas of work – and for the same reason that we must, in the end, put a question mark against the chance for emancipation offered by these new fields. The changes that the war had brought with it here were, for the most part, undone during the course of demobilization in 1918 and 1919, beginning with the positions that women found more attractive. White-collar employees' employment with the military authorities and war societies ended when these organizations were closed down. And women had to leave industrial positions previously occupied by men when the soldiers returned home. Thus, whether the shift in women's professions portrayed by the occupational census of 1925, in comparison with that of 1910, was actually intensified by wartime experiences or by the ensuing inflationary period must remain open until female employment during this latter period has been more thoroughly examined. Another question, to answer which likewise requires further study of the post-war period, is whether women who experienced that they were indeed capable of performing jobs previously declared as "male" during the war at least carried this recognition – if not the actual position – into the post-war period, as something they could build upon. After the decisive intrusion of demobilization, however, the impact of the First World War could only prove, in both cases, to be of an indirect nature.

By contrast, another development linked to wartime female wage labor did have direct consequences that extended beyond the period of the war itself: the intensification of socio-political activity aimed at wage-working women. There was an upswing of such activity in the second half of the war and, although its effectiveness was certainly limited by the difficult material and personal conditions of wartime and by the lack of receptiveness the majority of relevant military superiors displayed for such socio-political endeavors, it did indeed bear innovative traits. In so far as working-class women got to experience this expanded socio-political activity at all – because of these limitations, most wage-working women were not reached by such efforts – they clearly perceived it as positive.[11] Here as well, however, the end of the war entailed a step backwards, since, as a rule, this social policy, "by women for women," driven was generally not incorporated into the post-war social policy of either the individual German states or the central government.[12] Only at the lowest administrative levels did the Women's Departments of the War Office bureaus have any sort of future. In Prussia, 18 Women's Departments were annexed to the chief regional councils or administrative regions in June 1919.[13] This transfer of the regional Women's Departments to the civil authorities had been arranged for by the Demobilization Office (*Demobilmachungsamt*).[14] After overcoming the internal bureaucratic conflict that had arisen regarding the financing of and responsibility for the Women's Departments, the Prussian government, as of 1 October 1919, took over the costs for these entities, which were, by that time, actually under the jurisdiction of the chairmen or chief chairmen of the regional councils.[15] At least some of the institutions and individuals that had been in charge of social policy for female wage labor during the war also remained active after it. In this, we see the impact of the First World War, which intensified the institutionalization of female social work, which had already begun before August 1914.[16] In so far as this development contained aspects emancipatory for women, these applied more to the – predominantly bourgeois – women, to whom, as a result of this professionalization, new fields of work and new positions were permanently opened up, than specifically to working-class women. As a result of the First World War, the social net was thus strengthened to a certain extent in its aftermath, but these benefits still did not necessarily extend to urban female workers. The further-reaching consequences of wartime social policy can consequently be seen less in the realm of women's emancipation – as far as this concerned working-class women – and more in connection with the general development that led to the modern welfare state.[17]

Beyond this, the financial assistance of male and female textile workers during the war also represented an essential step in the shaping of the welfare state. In providing it, the Reich and the individual German states recognized, for the first time to this extent, their responsibility for the material support of unemployed

workers. These "embryonic" unemployment benefits, which
were later extended to workers in other branches of industry,
such as those of clothing and tobacco-processing, and which, in
the case of the textile industry, primarily served to support
unemployed female workers, existed as a precursor to state
unemployment insurance, which was begun in 1927.

Finally, the wages, working conditions and qualifications
structure of industrial labor, as well as the way in which this
work was perceived, both by the women performing it and by
other social groups, still need to be addressed. In this instance,
as well, the issue is whether we can ascertain improvements that
possibly promoted the emancipation of working-class women in
the sense discussed above.

With regard to women's working conditions and qualifications
structure, the effects of the First World War proved to be primarily negative. The opportunities that women, as well as
adolescents, had for receiving job qualifications declined relatively during this period because efforts initiated before the
war to improve these two groups' level of qualification were
interrupted and replaced by short-term, specialized training
programs. In absolute terms, the working conditions for both
female and adolescent workers deteriorated as a result of the *de
facto* repeal of industrial health and safety regulations.

The other two parameters of female wage labor, namely the
wage scale and patterns of perception, need to be considered in
more detail. The difference between female and male wages
declined by a few percentage points between 1914 and 1918,
to which the greater demand for female labor and the fact that a
greater number of women moved into "male industries," where
the wages were higher, contributed equally. The most important
reason for this convergence in male and female wages, however,
was that, in spite of the rise in nominal wages – which was
somewhat more marked for women than for men – the war years
were characterized by a clear drop in real wages. Apart from
those instances where the wages for skilled workers had risen
sharply, the more the level of general wages approached subsistence level, the more wages themselves levelled off. This was
because the lowest wage-earners, in particular female employees,
were the first to reach the point where wages stopped being a
meaningful way in which to secure one's livelihood. Under these
conditions and in light of the fact that the loss in real wages was

intensified during the second half of the war by the impossibility of obtaining essential consumer goods with money, the slight improvement in female workers' nominal wages did not translate into any actual improvement in their material situation. Thus, if considered structurally, the First World War did represent an important stage along the way towards bringing women's wages into alignment with men's.[18] From the perspective of the history of everyday life, however, the slight percentage gain women experienced in their wages did not, when considered against the background of the more concrete and pressing circumstances of life during the war, represent a factor that could have furthered women's emancipation.

The most important change in the way in which female war-time wage labor was perceived – both by women themselves and by others – was its promotion to a subject of positive national interest. If, before the war, the discussion of female employment was dominated by considerations of the possible and actual consequences it would have on the family, on men and male wages, as well as on working women's health and "moral" condition, these were now eclipsed by the revaluation of this work as a patriotic service to the war economy. To working women, who had heretofore received little public support for their occupational activities, this development offered a chance for increased professional and personal self-confidence and thereby a gain in emancipation. One essential qualification needs to be made here, however. The high public regard that female wage labor enjoyed during the war should not conceal the fact that such labor was only a stopgap, the continuation of which after the war was by no means desired. Women's employment in "male positions" was not welcomed as such, but rather as a necessity of the war economy. The consequent public esteem for working women referred exclusively and unanimously to their function as "place-holders," so long as the emergency of war and the shortage of labor endured. It by no means led to a greater societal acceptance of women's wage labor in general. The official consensus was that, after demobilization, female workers, who had first occupied their jobs for the first time during the war, should again concede them to men. This expectation, which the actual course of demobilization was then supposed to meet, was also common knowledge among working women themselves. Since their retention of these positions had at no point in time been considered seriously in public discourse, they could likewise only view their wartime employment as temporary. The two changes in female wartime wage labor that could be considered the most emancipatory – the ideological revaluation of such labor and the partial nullification of the gender-specific labor market – consequently only achieved a temporary improvement in working-class women's situation: an emancipation on loan.

Emancipation from the System: Women in Urban Working-Class Families, 1914–1918

The drastic changes that the war wrought in the everyday life of the urban population shaped the family, as the social institution responsible for managing everyday life, in equally decisive ways. Generally speaking, the First World War's central impact on the family was to shift the relationship between its two primary functions. The family's reproductive functions, namely the bearing and raising of children, as well as the care and emotional stabilization of adults, receded markedly during the war. The primary reasons for this were the drop in the number of marriages and the separation of countless spouses and families, both of which were due to conscription. By contrast, the tasks that families and especially women had to perform with regard to the production and consumption of goods grew rapidly. This was not only caused by the fact that urban families, out of necessity, had to produce their own foodstuffs during the war. Buying consumer goods also became more difficult and required more time, especially in the second half of the war, because of the general food shortage and rationing. Moreover, since the collapse of the money and consumer-goods market in 1916, women and families had increasingly turned to illegal means to provide for their existence, which were particularly labor-intensive and time-consuming. Economic performance thus became the defining feature of family life during the war.

As we have seen, the decline in the family's reproductive performance as well as the drastic rise in its economic tasks resulted in structural problems for wartime society as a whole. Governments and bureaucracies, on the one hand, and families and women, on the other, developed conflicting perceptions of these problems and conflicting strategies for dealing with them. And, where neither side proved strong enough to assert itself over the other – as was, with far-reaching consequences, the case with food rationing – these perceptions and strategies mutually cancelled each other out. Consequently, a highly complex structural and mental relationship developed in the First World War between families, or the women who were responsible for them, and the authorities. In comparison to the pre-war period, relations between "the" family and "the" state became more acute; state intervention in family life and its consequences expanded, both in scope and intensity. Simultaneously, the family's significance as a factor the state had to reckon with in its actions rose, as did that of women and families' willingness to perceive themselves as independent actors with regard to the state. This structural and mental intensification in family–state relations led, at the same time, to an increase in both the opportunities for various conflicts to emerge and the willingness to wage them.

The most glaring and immediate change that the war produced in the realm of family reproduction was the decline in the number of marriages and births. The actual meaning of this development, however, lay neither in its statistical significance, nor in the fact that a drop in the birthrate was an automatic consequence of the military conscription of marriageable and fertile men. Rather, both governments and bureaucracies and women and their husbands, under the influence of wartime conditions, gained a heightened awareness that the questions of whether women had children, and if so, how many, could or had to be consciously decided. The number of children in pre-war families was by no means always a result dictated by nature, but rather, was one that one or both marital partners had also tried, increasingly with more rather than less success, to control. The war, however, gave these efforts new impetus, as the population considerably improved its knowledge concerning contraceptives and its determination to put this knowledge to use. At the same time, on the political level, governments and bureaucracies included the control of – or the attempt at controlling – the population's reproductive behavior as one of their responsibilities.

The state and the military, in effect, provided the initial impetus for this development. On the one hand, conscription reduced the number of actual and potential fathers. On the other, since so much value was placed on their physical and psychological stability – at least until their deployment at the front – conscripted men were referred, with the tolerance and even support of the military leadership, to extramarital sexual services and schooled in prophylactic methods to protect them from contracting venereal disease. Preventative measures against venereal disease were in part identical with those against conception. The military, therefore – together with the population's network of informal communication, in which women shared pertinent information with one another – was largely responsible for raising the level of such sexual knowledge. At the same time, both the state and the population developed an increased need to plan pregnancies, but for opposing reasons. Through an intensified pro-natal social policy as well as corresponding legal and propaganda measures, governments and bureaucracies attempted to slow down any further decline in the birthrate. In contrast to this, the population, in light of the war, understood pregnancy-planning to mean the planned prevention of pregnancy. To it, wartime society did not seem to be a suitable environment for children. The extremely desperate conditions of life during the war rendered child-rearing an almost insoluble task. Moreover, the experience of a present, in which it was normal that thousands of men were killed on the front daily, left the population pessimistic about the future, in which female children seemed destined to starve and male children destined for the mass grave.

The people's growing inner rejection of the conditions of war lent a political cast to their desire to restrict the number of children they had. In executing their pro-natal policies, the Empire, German states and communities overlooked the population's conscious will to control its fertility, and, to all appearances, did not even seem to recognize this as an essential factor. Their catalog of measures and regulations were designed for a population that did not develop and implement strategies itself, but rather was externally oriented and could be controlled in its behavior through bans, such as that on abortion, and positive incentives, in particular the improved socio-political care for mothers and small children. As a result of this, the fundamental impact of wartime pro-natal policy did not lay in its immediate effectiveness, which, in view of the population's attitude, was slight, but in its precursory role. Population policy, understood as the state's specific exertion of influence on the reproductive behavior of the population, was established as a task of government. The elaboration of pro-natal social policy by the Reich, the states and the communities simultaneously marked a further stage in the development of the modern welfare state.

The drop in the birthrate was perhaps the most conspicuous consequence of the decreased reproductive performance of the wartime family, but it certainly was not the only one. As we have seen, other problems also resulted from the manifold, often long-term and sometimes final separation of marital spouses and families that followed the conscription of the men. During the war, the emotional relationships of family members and, above all, of husbands and wives, were confined to the few days of leave that soldiers had and to written correspondence, which, for the first time, became a mass phenomenon. Consequently, on the individual level, these relationships manifested signs of estrangement. On the societal level, these emotional relationships, exactly because of their reduced form, served to intensify the weariness with the war, both at home and on the front. After it had become the residue of the central socio-psychological function of marriage and family – i.e. the meaning-endowing unity and site of the construction of a common reality – the correspondence between front and homeland, in particular that from "war wives" to their enlisted husbands, fulfilled this task of intensifying war weariness. This was only done partially, but in its limitedness, very emphatically. Since women had to restrict themselves to the essential when communicating with their husbands, fathers and sons, they persistently described the difficulties and deprivations of their and their children's everyday lives in very drastic terms. The authorities, consequently, came to fear this interfamilial communication as a source of subversive opinions.

A further problem resulted from the fact that the physical separation of countless married couples effectively removed sexual intercourse from the context of marriage. This development led to a rise in prostitution – both behind the lines and in Germany itself – and consequently to the spread of venereal disease, particularly to classes and regions previously untouched by the disease. Furthermore, nonmarital and extramarital sexual relationships became more widespread, which was more difficult for the authorities to combat than prostitution and venereal disease because they could not rely on the vice squad and the epidemic police. Reality and public norm by no means ran parallel here, however. Already before the war, extramarital relationships had entailed, particularly for women, moral and sometimes legal sanctions. During it, two categories of women's nonmarital and extramarital relationships came to be viewed as virtually unpatriotic. The first category consisted of the suspected or actual extramarital relationships of "war wives," whose sexual conduct the authorities observed particularly closely because of its possible effects on front morale. The second concerned all women who, whether married or not, had formed relationships with prisoners of war. If the civil and military authorities learned of these increasingly common liaisons, they punished the parties concerned with court convictions and time in the public stocks. The connection the authorities made between sexuality and patriotism was applied exclusively to women; soldiers and officers behind the lines were not held to the same moral standard. This fact did not go unnoticed or uncriticized by contemporary observers, especially by women.

The last problem to be analyzed within the parameters of the decline of the wartime family's reproductive performance is adolescent socialization. According to the perception of the civil and, in particular, the military authorities on the home front, the conscription of fathers, teachers and policemen had robbed society of its central disciplinary authorities; this had proved to be especially detrimental for working-class youths. Mothers, it was believed, lacked the necessary singlemindedness and authority to control their sons. This, combined with the increased financial independence, personal freedom and self-esteem that working-class male adolescents had gained as a result of their increased importance as family providers and as labor in the war industry, had led to their alarming rebelliousness, criminality and waywardness. It was the military authorities, in particular, who tried to replace the missing male authority figures by decree; the most spectacular of these legislative measures was the forced-savings program for adolescents. They were confronted with the problem, however, that these incomplete working-class families had a completely different way of perceiving the same facts. The military authorities had concluded that the working-class family's socialization of male adolescents was deficient from this group's increased theft, frequent absence from school and its general rebelliousness, which was manifested not least in the fact that, next to women, adolescents constituted the majority of the participants in demonstrations and riots. These damning statistics by no means reflected a fundamental "waywardness" in family relations, as the authorities assumed, however, but often its opposite, namely the functioning of familial socialization under the special conditions of wartime. In that they stole, foraged and demonstrated together with women, adolescents contributed to the family's income, often as direct "accomplices" of their mothers. The generation gap, at least as it was characterized in the years 1914 to 1918 by public officials and social-policy experts, occurred, if at all, in the factory, in the streets and between working-class youths and the authorities. It did not occur in the family.

Of the war-induced changes in the realm of familial repro-ductive performance, the general trend toward conscious family planning bore clear emancipatory traits. It was a factor that, both in the short term as well as beyond the war's conclusion, could improve women's and families' material situation and give them new chances to plan the course of their lives. Of a more ambivalent nature, however, were the consequences of those wartime developments that can be classified as trends toward a relativization of marriage and family as the normal state of human and especially female existence. These trends included the fact that more women, in particular "war wives" and laborers in the war industry, lived alone, either temporarily or indefinitely; that, as a result of the massive death toll of eligible men, fewer women could count on getting married; and finally, that individuals entered into nonmarital or extramarital relationships more fre-quently. For women who knew how to fill this leitmotif of female biography, which such doubts about the possibility of marrying and starting a family represented, with individual meaning, in that they embraced new forms of life and work, these developments held emancipatory content, objectively as well as subjectively. Most women, however, seem to have considered these developments not as an enhancement of their options, but as an impediment to traditional life plans, namely as their inability to make the choice they preferred, that of marrying and having children. This is reflected in the expression "surplus of women," a manner of speaking adopted by women themselves, which betrayed an underlying feeling of low self-esteem as a surplus and thereby superfluous part of the population. The consequences that the increase in nonmarital and extramarital relationships entailed for individual women were, presumably, of an equally double-edged nature. If, for some women, the liberating and enhancing aspects of such experiences predominated, most women probably considered these experiences an emergency solution not chosen for its own sake. Moreover, it was an emergency solution severely sanctioned by the authorities and published opinion, as far as it concerned women, whereby the double moral standard that had also been valid before the war received a patriotic slant.

With regard to the family's functions of production and consumption, the first important wartime change we examined was in the family's income. The introduction of Family Aid at the beginning of the war, which was to compensate "war families" for money income they lost through the conscription of their male wage-earners, turned the state and communities into a central source of familial income. Never before had so many women and families been supported by the state for such a long period of time – up until the end of the war, if the men concerned survived the war; in some cases, after the war, as well – to such an extent.

The next essential factors that influenced the wartime family's budget were the increase in the cost of living and the partial collapse of the money economy in the second half of the war. Most consumer goods continuously became more expensive and increasing numbers of them ultimately disappeared from the market altogether, and thus could not be purchased with money. In the first months of the war, Family Aid had raised the standard of living of some families, particularly those with the lowest incomes and the greatest number of children. For the rest of the war, however, this support became less important for the population's livelihood, as did money income in general.

For urban families, nonmonetary strategies of existential provision took on an importance in the First World War that they had not had since the beginning of urbanization and the general rise of a capitalistic market economy in the nineteenth century. In connection with this, the character of the urban household economy changed decisively and in diverging ways. On the one hand, the household economy was bound more directly to its societal context, more strongly supervised and more clearly perceived in terms of its relevance for society as a whole. Officials responsible for food rationing set limits on how much food each household could consume, and then conducted inspections to ensure that these limits were being adhered to. Parallel to these measures, the authorities and associations, in particular women's associations, engaged in public-relations work, which was supposed to make women aware of the importance of their behavior in terms of home economics and to induce their conformity to food-rationing policies.

On the other hand, the partial collapse of the money economy led to a certain economic independence on the part of single families. Through the family's taking on or extending its own production of foodstuffs, its economy developed characteristics of a quasi-subsistence economy. Furthermore, in that women and families turned with increasing frequency to illegal methods to provide for themselves and "squirreled," plundered and stole, or, through their participation in demonstrations and strikes, collectively tried to force the state to improve care, they not only circumvented state-rationing policy, but also undermined its already low effectiveness and reputation to a lasting and irrevocable degree. The population perceived the authorities to be culpable in their inability to provide it with enough consumer goods to meet the minimum existential need. This perception became the driving force behind the negative attitude that gradually asserted itself in almost all classes of society and among working-class women in particular. It was first directed against the poor food provisions, and then, ultimately, against the war and the state that was waging it.

In the final analysis, the effects of the war on familial production and consumption were extremely ambivalent. In some cases, the payment of Family Aid temporarily improved "war wives and families'" financial situation in comparison to the prewar period. In all cases, even though its importance greatly decreased during the second half of the war, this state support became an essential factor for safeguarding the existence of the family. The fact that women, to a larger degree, now had control over this income, as their husbands or other male family members had had over their own earnings before the war, objectively and subjectively gave them more independence and, correspondingly, more self-confidence. This was clearly reflected in "war wives'" attitude and behavior towards the authorities. Although we unfortunately cannot explore here whether this development found longer-term expression in the reconfiguration of intrafamilial power relations in women's favor, it seems reasonable to suppose that a social history of the family in the Weimar Republic would elicit an affirmative answer. The aforementioned emancipatory aspects of Family Aid were not completely annulled, but they were relativized by the fact that they were inseparably bound up with the negative image of "war wives." When "war wives" were mentioned in public discourse, the intention was frequently one of admonition and they were the targets of official criticism. They were, it was maintained throughout the war, too extravagant, shirked work essential to the war effort, neglected their children, were unfaithful to their husbands, were too demanding and, above all, too critical. Those "war wives" who were aware of the negative tone of published opinion certainly knew how to counter this with self-confident remarks and behavior. The possibility, however, of their developing an unbroken feeling of self-worth from the receipt of state aid – which, in essence, had laid the very groundwork for the negative connotations of the "war wife" image, since women derived extensive control over their livelihood through this money – was thereby greatly reduced.

The changed role of housework during the war was of a similarly contradictory nature. On the one hand, in the context of the war industry, housework – and thereby women's housework as a societally relevant activity – experienced a clear revaluation. We should also not forget, however, that this increased official attention and recognition was coupled with an intensification of actual and moral control and a visible tendency to assume that women's deficiency in running a household was one of the causes for the poor food situation. Working-class women, in particular, asserted the reports of the authorities, women's associations and others, lacked the home-economics knowledge needed to cope with the difficult food situation during the war and the ability to keep, not only the welfare of their own family, but that of the entire society in mind. The reproach that women were unqualified to run a household was not only inseparable from public attention to the societal relevance of housework, it was also one of its driving motives. Through lectures, cooking courses and other measures, housewives were supposed to become competent to fulfill their important societal function in the first place. In this respect, the revaluation of housework during the First World War by no means signified a corresponding revaluation of the women running these households, but rather their characterization as chronically underqualified.

The belief that housewives in general, and working-class women in particular, lacked an understanding of the big picture was the second essential educational motive behind the increased public interest in housework between 1914 and 1918. Women were supposed to be taught that they acted against the common good if they placed feeding their own family above adhering to rationing regulations, i.e. if they foraged, bartered and stole, if they complained about conditions, and if they expressed their displeasure in food riots and thereby attempted to blackmail – in part successfully – the state and the communities. Instead of trying to help themselves, women were to learn to persevere without complaining and to trust in the authorities. Instead of complying with this catalogue of virtues for subjects, working-class women acted independently and autonomously and sought, in their own way, to ensure the existence of their dependants. In so doing, these women not only proved their ability to cope with crises of survival; they also exhibited a remarkable degree of independence with regard to the norms, ideologies and regulatory mechanisms of wartime society. This independent attitude of the majority of working-class women ultimately manifested itself in their general rejection of the war, and of the government and military leadership responsible for it – a rejection in which women, as a result of their responsibility to feed their families, felt themselves completely justified. In this attitude, the emancipatory potential created by the changes in the family's productive and consumptive performance expressed itself in the most unambiguous way. Against this background, women emancipated themselves – to fall back on the words of Karl Gutzkow – from the system. The spontaneous and unorganized manner in which they did this allowed women to become a fundamental force in disrupting the war-societal system. It did not, however, offer them the means to change it.

The Fight over the Meaning-Endowment of the War

Working-class women's emancipation from the system of wartime society also expressed itself in the active role that they played in the fight over endowing the war with societal meaning. Working-class women were the first to express criticism of the war, and they did so most emphatically. They were also the ones who, together with soldiers on leave from the front, maintained the network of informal communication, through which anti-war sentiment spread ever further at home and on the front, until, in the end, it took hold of the vast majority of the population. Not least, it was at them that governments, military and associations directed their propaganda to "hold out" and their "enlightenment" activity, in the context of which the people's attitudes were monitored ever more intensely and ever more instruments were deployed to influence them.

In their negative perception of the war and of war society, women proved to be resistant to all efforts to reinstate the *Burgfrieden* mentality of the first months of the war. The belligerent state, conversely, could be partially influenced by women's perceptions, but, ultimately, not restructured by them. The end of the war was caused by Germany's military collapse, and the end of the Reich executed through organized political activities of a parliamentary or extraparliamentary nature.[19] Women, in undermining support for the belligerent state in the population with such sustained effort, had laid the groundwork for the course these developments would take, the rapid pace of which cannot be understood without this prehistory. Their influence, however, came to an end with the end of the war. One last time, the form of social protest that had distinguished itself by its spontaneous and unorganized rule-breaking and episodes of collective action and which had already been a female domain in preindustrial societies, became a mass phenomenon. After the war, social protest was not carried out with the same intensity. In and during the November Revolution, the process of resolving conflicts of interest was once again mediated and institutionalized. The parties, in particular the Social Democrats, returned, after more than four years of existing in the shadows, as organized political actors. And with the workers' and soldiers' councils, new ones were temporarily established. Women were not involved in the first or in the second development to any great extent.

Organized, mediated and institutionalized political action remained, in essence, a male domain, a fact that was only slightly moderated, in comparison to the pre-war period, by female suffrage,[20] and one that by and large still holds true today. The question of why women continue to be underrepresented in the realm of organized political action cannot be pursued here. The results of this study, however, suggest an answer to the question of why specific, female forms of spontaneous and unorganized collective action seem to be so tied to their respective historical context, in this instance the First World War, that they find no continuation beyond it and why, despite their not insignificant influence within the given situation, these forms do not have any observable, longer-term consequences for the form of social relations and women's role in them. Such forms of collective resistance are sparked by concrete aspects of the present that the individuals, primarily women, involved want to end. They do not, however, carry a concrete blueprint for an alternative reality with long-term perspective, toward whose realization life and action are to be directed and against whose background the respective present appears in need of improvement. Consequently, the conditions that call such resistance into being simultaneously mark its boundaries. The protest against this or that social ill ultimately ends with it. Spontaneous and unorganized collective action neither shapes ideas of inequality and oppression, from which one can then abstract, nor is it shaped by them. The subversive foundation that endows such action with meaning is intrinsic to the concrete situation. The vehemence of such action is grounded in this, as is, however, its longer-term ineffectiveness. To return once again to the distinction made above, wartime social protest objectively as well as subjectively articulated criticism *of* the system, not only *in* the system. The system that was meant, however, was the war and the ruling circles who, in the population's perception, had to accept responsibility for the war and its consequences. For a society that was no longer waging war, however, this perception offered the means neither for explanation nor for action. If women and others had, from 1914 to 1918, emancipated themselves from the system, then, in the years following, the system emancipated itself from them once again.

Notes to Chapter 6

1. K. Gutzkow, *Philosophie der Tat und des Ereignisses* (1835), as cited in K. M. Grass and R. Koselleck, "Emanzipation," in O. Brunner et al., eds.,

Summary and Conclusion

Geschichtliche Grundbegriffe. Historisches Lexikon zur politisch-sozialen Sprache in Deutschland (Stuttgart, 1975), 2: 168.

2. As cited in V. Ullrich, *Kriegsalltag. Hamburg im Ersten Weltkrieg* (Köln, 1982), 56.

3. For this, see Grass and Koselleck, "Emanzipation," 153–197.

4. The term "emancipation" shares this aspect of explicitly or implicitly idealizing the present – which is not to be confused with the close relation, be it intentional or unintentional, every historical analysis has to the conditions and ways of thinking of its own present – with a considerable number of theoretical approaches of "modernization." For this, see H.-U. Wehler, *Modernisierungstheorie und Geschichte* (Göttingen, 1975), 11–30, 44 and *passim*.

5. J. W. v. Goethe, *Urfaust*, Berlin ed. (Berlin and Weimar, 1973), 8: 13.

6. See, for example, C. Honegger and B. Heintz, eds., *Listen der Ohnmacht. Zur Sozialgeschichte weiblicher Widerstandsformen* (Frankfurt/M., 1981); M. I. Thomis and J. Grimmett, *Women in Protest, 1800–1850* (London and Canberra, 1982); L. A. Tilly, "Women's Collective Action and Feminism in France, 1870–1914," in L. A. Tilly and Ch. Tilly, eds., *Class Conflict and Collective Action* (Beverly Hills and London, 1981), 207–231.

On working-class men and women's collective protest and resistance, see the literature cited in note 10 of chapter 1, and W. Albrecht et al., "Frauenfrage und deutsche Sozialdemokratie vom Ende des 19. Jahrhunderts bis zum Beginn der 20er Jahre," *AfS* 19 (1979): 459–510, esp. 502–503. On such protest during the Second World War, see T. W. Mason, *Arbeiterklasse und Volksgemeinschaft. Dokumente und Materialien zur deutschen Arbeiterpolitik 1936–1939* (Opladen, 1975); H. Elling, *Frauen im deutschen Widerstand 1933–1945* (Frankfurt/M., 1978); L. Eiber, "Frauen in der Kriegsindustrie," in M. Broszat et al., eds., *Bayern in der NS-Zeit* (München, 1981), 3: 569–644; G. Schefer, "Wo Unterdrückung ist, da ist auch Widerstand – Frauen gegen Faschismus und Krieg," in *Frauengruppe Faschismusforschung, Mutterkreuz und Arbeitsbuch. Zur Geschichte der Frauen in der Weimarer Republik und im Nationalsozialismus* (Frankfurt/M., 1981); A. Kuhn and V. Rothe, *Frauen im deutschen Faschismus*, 2 vols. (Düsseldorf, 1982); G. Szepansky, *Frauen leisten Widerstand: 1933–1945* (Frankfurt/M., 1983); R. Wiggershaus, *Frauen unterm Nationalsozialismus* (Wuppertal, 1984); C. Sachse, "Fabrik, Familie und kein Feierabend. Frauenarbeit im Nationalsozialismus," *Gewerkschaftliche Monatshefte* 9 (1984): 566–579.

On the problematization of the term "resistance," see M. Broszat, "Resistenz und Widerstand. Eine Zwischenbilanz des Forschungsprojekts," in M. Broszat et al., eds., *Bayern in der NS-Zeit*, 4: 691–709. In terms of the problematization of women's resistance in the Third Reich, also see U. Frevert, *Frauen-Geschichte: Zwischen bürgerlicher Verbesserung und neuer Weiblichkeit* (Frankfurt/M., 1986), 232–243.

7. This is especially, if not exclusively, valid for examinations of National Socialism. It will suffice to mention one example. In her study *Frauen unterm Nationalsozialismus* (see previous endnote), Renate Wiggershaus cites boycotting a Nazi meeting, not hanging a Nazi flag outside one's house, refusing to accept the Mother's Cross, reporting sick, and working slowly and poorly at one's job as manifestations of female resistance, and weights them equally with working in the underground, hiding an individual sought by the Gestapo and

sabotaging weapons in an armaments factory (119, 130). Of one woman who, under very arduous circumstances, visited her husband in a concentration camp, Wiggershaus asserts that she thereby "opposed the National-Socialist system" (126). The fact that this man was in a concentration camp does indeed say something about the system, and the fact that his wife visited him there does indeed say something about this woman's strength and perhaps also something about her relationship to her husband. Her visit says very little, however, about her relationship to the system. With this distinction between "critique in the system" and "critique of the system," under no circumstances mean that individual or collective resistance that does not reveal a corresponding consciousness of the individuals or groups involved should be considered less valuable in comparison to conscious opposition. Such a stance has to be ruled out not least because the intensity and amount of the physical and psychological suffering that the respective individuals had to bear on account of their actions was primarily the same – whether the resistance was subjectively intentional or not. The difference lies not in the valuation, but in the facts.

8. See above, introduction.

9. R. Bridenthal and C. Koonz, "Beyond *Kinder, Küche, Kirche*: Weimar Women in Politics and Work," in R. Bridenthal et al., eds., *When Biology Became Destiny: Women in Weimar and Nazi Germany* (New York, 1984), 44, 60.

10. For this, see W. Müller et al., *Strukturwandel der Frauenarbeit 1880– 1980* (Frankfurt and New York, 1983); G. Wellner, "Industriearbeiterinnen in der Weimarer Republik: Arbeitsmarkt, Arbeit und Privatleben 1919-1933," *GG* 7 (1981): 534-554; R. Stockmann, "Gewerbliche Frauenarbeit in Deutschland 1875-1980. Zur Entwicklung der Beschäftigtenstruktur," *GG* 11 (1985): 447-475.

11. Cf. U. Daniel, *Arbeiterfrauen in der Kriegsgesellschaft. Beruf, Familie und Politik im Ersten Weltkrieg* (Göttingen, 1989), 100-106.

12. Marie-Elisabeth Lüders was one of several individuals who worked to achieve the incorporation of the Women's Departments. For this, see BA Koblenz, NL 155/160, *passim*. Whereas, in Württemberg and Baden, the central Women's Departments were successfully transferred to the civil government, the Women's Department in Bavaria was dissolved on 1 April 1919. In Prussia, the FAZ was replaced in the Ministry of the Interior with a Women's Department Headquarters. This does not seem to have been more than a purely administrative and technical link for those Women's Departments that continued to exist in the chief regional councils or the administrative regions. In terms of the imperial government, by the middle of 1919, only one woman was employed in the Labor Ministry – as a consultant for individuals who had lost a husband or father in the war, whereas there were no women working in the Imperial Ministry of the Interior or for the Imperial Commissioner for Housing. Parliamentary questions of all women in the National Assembly re. demobilization, 20 August 1918, printed in *Archiv für Frauenarbeit* (1919): 109. On the transition of the Women's Departments in Prussia, see BA Koblenz, NL 151/160, *passim*.

13. Preußischer Innenminister to Finanzminister, 4 June 1919: ibid. At the beginning of 1919, in answer to a petition, a considerable number of the chairmen and chief chairmen of regional councils had pronounced themselves in favor of keeping the Women's Departments. See the copy of their positions in ibid.

Summary and Conclusion

14. Preußischer Innenminister to Reichsamt für wirtschaftliche Demobilmachung, 22 January 1919: ZStA Potsdam, Reichsarbeitsministerium 33073, Bl. 36.

15. Preußischer Innenminister für Volkswohlfahrt to Oberpräsidenten, 7 October 1919: HStA Düsseldorf, Regierung Düsseldorf 33138; Preußischer Innenminister für Volkswohlfahrt to Oberpräsidenten, 11 November 1919: ibid.

16. For this, see Ch. Sachße, *Mütterlichkeit als Beruf. Sozialarbeit, Sozialreform und Frauenbewegung 1871-1929* (Frankfurt/M., 1986), 151-173, as well as Frevert, *Frauen-Geschichte*, 155ff.

17. L. Preller, H.-J. Puhle and Christoph Sachße, among others, stress the important role the First World War in general played in this development. See L. Preller, *Sozialpolitik in der Weimarer Republik* (Kronberg/Ts. and Düsseldorf, 1978), 5; H.-J. Puhle, "Vom Wohlfahrtsausschuß zum Wohlfahrtsstaat," in G. Ritter, ed., *Vom Wohlfahrtsausschuß zum Wohlfahrtsstaat. Der Staat in der modernen Industriegesellschaft* (Köln, 1973), 49; Sachße, *Mütterlichkeit*, 151.

18. In the initial post-war period, the difference in male and female wages partially further decreased, and partially increased. Up until 1924, the period of inflation brought a strong alignment of wages with it. In this period, however, as during the war, it was real wages that were brought into line with the subsistence level, not women's wages with men's. Once the inflation was over, this tendency toward wage alignment logically stopped again. The difference in male and female wages stabilized for the rest of the Weimar Republic at the level reached at the end of the inflation years. This level was slightly higher than that of the pre-war period. For this, see Wellner, "Industriearbeiterinnen," 547-548: A. Karbe, *Die Frauenlohnfrage und ihre Entwicklung in der Kriegs- und Nachkriegszeit* (Rostock, 1928), 100-101 and *passim*; S. Bajohr, *Die Hälfte der Fabrik. Geschichte der Frauenarbeit in Deutschland 1914 bis 1945* (Marburg/L., 1979), 41-56; G. Bry, *Wages in Germany, 1871-1945* (Princeton, NJ, 1960), 95-96.

19. On the November Revolution, see G. P. Meyer, *Bibliographie zur deutschen Revolution 1918/19* (Göttingen, 1977); V. Ullrich, *Die Hamburger Arbeiterbewegung am Vorabend des Ersten Weltkriegs bis zur Revolution 1918/19*, 2 vols. (Hamburg, 1976); W. J. Mommsen, "Die deutsche Revolution 1918-1920. Politische Revolution und sozialer Protest," *GG* 4 (1978): 362-391; H.-J. Bieber, *Gewerkschaften in Krieg und Revolution. Arbeiterbewegung, Industrie, Staat und Militär in Deutschland 1914-1920*, 2 vols. (Hamburg, 1981); M. Scheck, *Zwischen Weltkrieg und Revolution. Zur Geschichte der Arbeiterbewegung in Württemberg 1914-1920* (Köln and Wien, 1981); E.-H. Schmidt, *Heimatheer und Revolution 1918. Die militärischen Gewalten im Heimatgebiet zwischen Oktoberreform und Novemberrevolution* (Stuttgart, 1981); D. Lehner, *Sozialdemokratie und Novemberrevolution* (Frankfurt and New York, 1983); W. Bramke, "Zum Verhalten der Mittelschichten in der Novemberrevolution," *ZfG* 31 (1983): 691-700; H. A. Winkler, *Von der Revolution zur Stabilisierung. Arbeiter und Arbeiterbewegung in der Weimarer Republik 1918 bis 1924* (Berlin and Bonn, 1984); U. Kluge, *Die deutsche Revolution 1918/19. Staat, Politik und Gesellschaft zwischen Weltkrieg und Kapp-Putsch* (Frankfurt/M., 1985); K. Schönhoven, ed., *Die Gewerkschaften in Weltkrieg und Revolution 1914-1919*. Quellen zur Geschichte der deutschen Gewerkschaftsbewegung im 20. Jahrhundert 1 (Köln, 1985); W. Wette, "Die militärische

Demobilmachung in Deutschland 1918/19 unter besonderer Berücksichtigung der revolutionären Ostseestadt Keil," *GG* 12 (1986), 63-80; W. Deist, "Der militärische Zusammenbruch des Kaiserreichs. Zur Realität der 'Dolchstoßlegende,'" in U. Büttner, ed., *Das Unrechtsregime. Internationale Forschungen über den Nationalsozialismus. Fs. W. Jochmann zum 65. Geburtstag* (Hamburg, 1986), 1: 101-129; H. Beyer, *Die Revolution in Bayern 1918-1919* (Berlin, 2nd, expanded ed. 1988); Ch. Sternsdorf-Hauck, *Brotmarken und rote Fahnen. Frauen in der bayerischen Revolution und Räterepublik 1918/19* (Frankfurt/M., 1989); H. Konrad and K. M. Schmidlechner, eds., *Revolutionäres Potential in Europa am Ende des Ersten Weltkriegs. Die Rolle von Strukturen, Konjunkturen und Massenbewegungen* (Wien and Köln, 1990).

20. The catchy, but incorrect assertion that the introduction of women's suffrage in Germany can be understood as a reward for female participation in the war (see, for example, A. Marwick, *War and Social Change in the Twentieth Century. A Comparative Study of Britain, France, Germany, Russia and the United States* (London, 1974), 49) has already been rejected by Barbara Greven-Aschoff: B. Greven-Aschoff, *Die bürgerliche Frauenbewegung in Deutschland 1894-1933* (Göttingen, 1981), 159. The wartime debate on suffrage - in which women's right to vote was not discussed - proves the accuracy of this rejection, as does the hesitant manner in which women's suffrage was introduced in the last days of the German Empire. On this issue, see L. Bergsträßer, *Die preußische Wahlrechtsfrage im Kriege und die Entstehung der Osterbotschaft 1917* (Tübingen, 1929); R. Patemann, *Der Kampf um die preußische Wahlreform im Ersten Weltkrieg*. Beiträge zur Geschichte des Parlamentarismus und der politischen Parteien 26 (Düsseldorf, 1964); R. J. Evans, *Sozialdemokratie und Frauenemanzipation im deutschen Kaiserreich* (Berlin and Bonn, 1979), 302-311; R. J. Evans, "German Social Democracy and Women's Suffrage, 1891-1918," *JCH* 15 (1980): 533-557.

Select Bibliography

I. Unpublished Sources

(General sources. The actual records used are listed individually in the German edition of this book, Arbeiterfrauen in der Kriegsgesellschaft. Beruf, Familie und Politik im Ersten Weltkrieg, *beginning on page 369.)*

Staatsarchiv Detmold: M1IE; L 103
Hauptstaatsarchiv Düsseldorf: Regierung Düsseldorf; Regierung Aachen
Bundesarchiv/Militärarchiv Freiburg i. Br.: RM3; RM20; RM23; RM31; RM43; PH2; N38; N46; MSG 767, 768, 779/780.
Staatsarchiv Hamburg: Politische Polizei; Kriegsakten des Senats; Kriegsversorgungsamt.
Generallandesarchiv Karlsruhe: Stellvertretendes Generalkommando XIV. AK.
Bundesarchiv Koblenz: R36; R43I; R86; NL 151.
Zentrales Staatsarchiv Merseburg: Rep. 77; Rep. 90A Y.IX; Rep. 120C VIII 1; Rep 197A; Rep 120BB VIII.
Hauptstaatsarchiv/Kriegsarchiv München: MKr; Stellvertretendes Generalkommando I. Bayerisches AK München; Postprüfstelle Ludwigshafen; Militärische Überwachungsstelle des I. Bayerischen AK München.
Hauptstaatsarchiv München/Abt. 2: MInn; MH.
Staatsarchiv Münster: Oberpräsidium; Regierung Arnsberg.
Zentrales Staatsarchiv Postdam: (old) Reichskanzlei; Reichsamt/Reichsministerium des Innern; Reichsjustizamt/Reichsjustizministerium; Reichsschatzamt/ Reichsfinanzministerium; Reichsarbeitsministerium; Reichswirtschaftsministerium; Reichsministerium für Ernährung und Landwirtschaft; Reichsamt/ Reichsministerium für wirtschaftliche Demobilmachung; Vertreter des Reichskanzlers bei der OHL; Auswärtiges Amt/ Presseabteilung; Reichstag; 62 DAF 3; 61Re 1; Reichsgetreidestelle; Zentralstelle für Beschaffung der

Select Bibliography

Heeresverpflegung; Reichsbekleidungsstelle; Reichsgemein-
schaft Deutscher Hausfrauen.
Staatsarchiv Potsdam: Pr. Br. Rep. 30 Berlin C Polizeipräsidium.

II. Published Sources and Literature

Adam, B. *Arbeitsbeziehungen in der bayerischen Großstadt-
metallindustrie von 1914 bis 1932.* München, 1983.
Adams, M. C. C. *The Great Adventure. Male Desire and the
Coming of World War I.* Bloomington and Indianapolis, 1990.
Adler, A. *Die andere Seite. Eine massenpsychologische Studie
über die Schuld des Volkes.* Wien, 1919.
Albrecht, G. *Übergangswirtschaft und Arbeiterfrage.* Berlin,
1917.
——. "Soziale Probleme und Sozialpolitik in Deutschland während
des Weltkrieges." *Jahrbücher für Nationalökonomie und
Statistik* 144 (1936), 96–107, 214–232.
——. "Deutschlands soziale Kriegsvorbereitung vor dem Weltkriege." *Jahrbücher für Nationalökonomie und Statistik* 143
(1936), 484–495.
——. "Die Unterstützung der Familien Einberufener. Entwicklung
und gesetzliche Grundlagen." *Jahrbücher für Nationalökonomie und Statistik* 151 (1940), 66–84.
Albrecht, W. *Landtag und Regierung in Bayern am Vorabend
der Revolution von 1918.* Berlin, 1968.
—— et al. "Frauenfrage und deutsche Sozialdemokratie vom Ende
des 19. Jahrhunderts bis zum Beginn der 20er Jahre." *AfS* 19
(1979), 459–510.
Altmann, S. P. *Soziale Mobilmachung.* Mannheim, 1916.
Amberger, W. *Männer, Krieger, Abenteurer. Der Entwurf des
"soldatischen Mannes" in Kriegsromanen über den Ersten
und Zweiten Weltkrieg.* Frankfurt/M., 1984.
Anz, Th. and Vogl, J., eds. *Die Dichter und der Krieg. Deutsche
Lyrik 1914–1918.* München, 1982.
*Arbeitsverhältnisse und Organisation der häuslichen Dienst-
boten in Bayern.* Beiträge zur Statistik Bayerns 94. Bayerisches
Statistisches Landesamt, ed. München, 1921.
Arnstadt, A. *Der Weltkrieg und die deutsche Volkswirtschaft.*
Langensalza, 1916.
Ashworth T. *Trench Warfare 1914–1918. The Live and Let Live
System.* London, 1980.

Audoin-Rouzeau, S. *Men at War 1914–1918. National Sentiment and Trench Journalism in France during the First World War. Reports from the French Trenches.* Oxford, 1992.

Augeneder, S. *Arbeiterinnen im Ersten Weltkrieg. Lebens- und Arbeitsbedingungen proletarischer Frauen im Österreich.* Wien, 1987.

August 1914: Ein Volk zieht in den Krieg. Berliner Geschichtswerkstatt, ed. Berlin, 1989.

Ay, K. L. *Die Entstehung einer Revolution. Die Volksstimmung in Bayern während des Ersten Weltkriegs.* Berlin, 1968.

Bach, F. W. *Untersuchungen über die Lebensmittelrationierung im Kriege.* München, n.d. [1919].

Bäumer, G. "Der weibliche Arbeitsmarkt im Kriege," in G. Bäumer, *Weit hinter den Schützgräben. Aufsätze aus dem Weltkrieg.* Jena, 1916, 142–151.

—. *Lebensweg durch eine Zeitenwende.* Tübingen, 1933.

—. *Heimatchronik während des Weltkriegs.* Berlin, 1930.

Bailey, S. "The Berlin Strike of January 1918." *CEH* 13 (1980), 158–174.

Bajohr, S. *Die Hälfte der Fabrik. Geschichte der Frauenarbeit in Deutschland 1914 bis 1945.* Marburg/L., 1979.

Barbusse, H. *Das Feuer. Tagebuch einer Korporalschaft.* Zürich, 1979.

Barkhausen, H. *Filmpropaganda für Deutschland im Ersten und Zweiten Weltkrieg.* Hildesheim et al., 1982.

Baudis, D. "Deutschland und Großbritannien in der Zeit des Ersten Weltkriegs. Versuch einer vergleichenden Betrachtung einiger Aspekte der wirtschaftlichen und sozialen Entwicklung." *JbWG* (1981), pt. 3, 49–78; pt. 4, 205–216.

—. "Auswirkung des Krieges auf die Lage der Volksmassen in Berlin 1917/18." *JbWG* 2 (1987), 9–27.

— and Nussbaum, H. *Wirtschaft und Staat in Deutschland vom Ende des 19. Jahrhunderts bis 1918/1919.* Vol. 1 of *Wirtschaft und Staat in Deutschland. Eine Wirtschaftsgeschichte des staatsmonopolistischen Kapitalismus in Deutschland vom Ende des 19. Jahrhunderts bis 1945*, 3 vols. H. Nussbaum and L. Zumpe, eds. Vaduz, 1978.

Baur, M. "Der Beschäftigungsgrad der Industriearbeiterinnen in Zeiten sinkender Konjunktur . . ." Diss., München, 1923–1926.

Beaufort, J. M. de. *Behind the German Veil: A Record of a Journalistic War Pilgrimage.* New York, 1918.

Beck, Chr., ed. *Die Frau und die Kriegsgefangenen*, vol. 1, pt. 2: *Die deutsche Frau und die fremden Kriegsgefangenen*. Nürnberg, 1919.

Becker, J.-J. *The Great War and the French People*. Oxford et al., 1986.

— and Audoin-Rouzeau, S., eds. *Les Sociétés européennes et la guerre de 1914–1918*. Paris, 1990.

Becker, U. *Die Entwicklung des Frauenerwerbs seit der Jahrhundertwende*. Bleicherode, 1937.

Beckmann, M. *Briefe im Kriege 1914/1915*. München and Zürich, 1984.

Beloff, M. *War and Welfare. Britain 1914–1945*. London, 1984.

Bendit, L. "Der Krieg und der deutsche Arbeitsmarkt." Diss., Erlangen, 1920.

Benjamin, D. "Die soziale Lage der Berliner Konfektionsheimarbeiterinnen mit besonderer Berücksichtigung der Kinderaufzucht." Diss., Greifswald, 1925.

Berger, P. L. and Kellner, H. "Die Ehe und die Konstruktion der Wirklichkeit. Eine Abhandlung zur Mikrosoziologie des Wissens." *Soziale Welt* 16 (1965), 220–235.

Berger, P. L. and Luckmann, Th. *Die gesellschaftliche Konstruktion der Wirklichkeit. Eine Theorie der Wissenssoziologie*. Frankfurt/M., 1982.

Berger, P. L. and Pullberg, S. "Verdinglichung und die soziologische Kritik des Bewußtseins." *Soziale Welt* 16 (1965), 97–112.

Berger, R. *Die häuslichen Dienstboten*. M.-Gladbach, 1916.

—. *Die häuslichen Dienstboten nach dem Kriege*. M.-Gladbach, n.d.

Bergsträßer, L. *Die preußische Wahlrechtsfrage im Kriege und die Entstehung der Osterbotschaft 1917*. Tübingen, 1929.

Bericht über die Verwaltung der Stadt Gelsenkirchen in der Zeit vom 1. April 1903 bis 31. März 1920. Gelsenkirchen, 1921.

Berichte des Berliner Polizeipräsidenten zur Stimmung und Lage der Bevölkerung in Berlin 1914–1918. Publication of the Staatsarchiv Potsdam, vol. 22. I. Materna and H.-J. Schreckenbach, eds. Weimar, 1987.

Bessel, R. "'Eine nicht allzu große Beunruhigung des Arbeitsmarktes.' Frauenarbeit und Demobilmachung in Deutschland nach dem Ersten Weltkrieg." *GG* 9 (1983), 211–229.

—. "The Great War in German Memory: The Soldiers of the First

World War, Demobilization, and Weimar Political Culture." *German History* 6 (1988), 20-34.

— and Feuchtwanger, E. J., eds. *Social Change and Political Development in Weimar Germany*. London, 1981.

Bevölkerung und Wirtschaft 1872-1972. Statistisches Bundesamt Wiesbaden, ed. Stuttgart et al., 1972.

Bewegung der Bevölkerung in den Jahren 1914 bis 1919. Statistik des Deutschen Reichs 276. Berlin, 1922.

Beyer, F. *Der Arbeitseinsatz in der Wehrwirtschaft*. Berlin, 1936.

Beyer, H. *Die Revolution in Bayern 1918-1919*, 2nd expanded ed. Berlin, 1988.

Bieber, H.-J. *Gewerkschaften in Krieg und Revolution. Arbeiterbewegung, Industrie, Staat und Militär in Deutschland 1914-1920*, 2 vols. Hamburg, 1981.

Bierbrauer, W. "Die Einwirkungen des Krieges und der Nachkriegszeit auf die Wohnbautätigkeit unter besonderer Berücksichtigung von Rheinland und Westfalen." Diss., Münster, 1921.

Binding, R. G. *Wir fordern Reims zur Übergabe auf.* n.p., 1935.

Blei, F. *Erzählung eines Lebens*. Leipzig, 1930.

Blos, A. *Kommunale Frauenarbeit im Kriege*. Berlin, 1917.

—. *Die Frauenfrage im Lichte des Sozialismus*. Dresden, 1930.

Blücher von Wahlstadt, E. Fürstin. *Tagebuch*. München, 1924.

Boak, H. L. "Women in Weimar Germany: The 'Frauenfrage' and the Female Vote." In Bessel and Feuchtwanger, eds., *Social Change*, 155-173.

Bock, G. "Historische Frauenforschung: Fragestellungen und Perspektiven," in K. Hausen, ed., *Frauen suchen ihre Geschichte. Historische Studien zum 19. und 20. Jahrhundert*. München, 1983, 22-60.

Boll, F. "Spontaneität der Basis und politische Funktion des Streiks 1914-1918. Das Beispiel Braunschweig." *AfS* 17 (1977), 337-366.

—. *Massenbewegungen in Niedersachsen 1906-1920. Eine sozialgeschichtliche Untersuchung zu den unterschiedlichen Entwicklungstypen Braunschweig und Hannover*. Bonn, 1981.

Bott, J. P. "The German Food Crisis of World War I. The Cases of Coblenz and Cologne." Diss., University of Missouri-Columbia, 1981.

Boyd, C. E. *Nationaler Frauendienst: German Middle Class Women in Service to the Fatherland, 1914-1918*. Athens, Ga., 1979.

Brandt, O. *Die deutsche Industrie im Krieg 1914/15*. Berlin, 1915.

Braun, G. *Der Soziallohn und seine wirtschaftliche Bedeutung*. Berlin and Leipzig, 1922.

Braybon, G. *Women Workers in the First World War. The British Experience*. London and Totowa, N.J., 1981.

Brentano, B. von. *Theodore Chindler. Roman einer deutschen Familie*. Frankfurt/M., 1979.

Brezina, E. *Internationale Übersicht über Gewerbekrankheiten nach den Berichten der Gewerbeinspektion der Kulturländer über die Jahre 1914–1918*. Berlin, 1921.

Bridenthal, R. et al., ed. *When Biology Became Destiny: Women in Weimar and Nazi Germany*. New York, 1984.

Briefs, G. "Kriegswirtschaftslehren und Kriegswirtschaftpolitik." *Handwörterbuch der Staatswissenschaften* 5 (Jena, 1923), 984–1022.

— and Stadthagen, H. *Die Preisprüfungstellen*. Beiträge zur Kriegswirtschaft 22/23. Berlin, 1917.

— et al. *Die Hauswirtschaft im Kriege*. Beiträge zur Kriegswirtschaft 25. Berlin, 1917.

Brüggemeier, F. J. and Kocka, J., eds. *Geschichte von unten – Geschichte von innen. Kontroversen um Alltagsgeschichte*. Hagen, 1985.

Bry, G. *Wages in Germany, 1871–1945*. Princeton, 1960.

Buchner, E. (= Eduard Mayer). *1914–1918. Wie es damals daheim war. Das Kriegstagebuch eines Knaben*. Nürnberg, 1930.

Bulletin der Studiengesellschaft für soziale Folgen des Krieges, vol.: *Deutschland*, 2nd expanded ed. Kopenhagen, 1919.

Bumm, E. "Not und Fruchtabtreibung." *Münchener medizinische Wochenschrift* 70.50 (1923), 1471–1472.

Bumm, F., ed. *Deutschlands Gesundheitsverhältnisse unter dem Einfluß des Weltkriegs*. Wirtschafts- und Sozialgeschichte des Weltkriegs 1, German series. Stuttgart et al., 1928.

Bundschuh, H. "Lohn- und Lebensverhältnisse der Arbeiter in der Industrie des Neckartales mit Beschränkung auf die standortlich gebundene Industrie." Diss., Heidelberg, 1923.

Bur, L. *Die Umwälzung der deutschen Volkswirtschaft im Kriege*. Abhandlungen aus dem Staatswissenschaftlichen Seminar zu Straßburg 34. Straßburg, 1918.

Burchardt, L. "Die Auswirkungen der Kriegswirtschaft auf die deutsche Zivilbevölkerung im Ersten und Zweiten Weltkrieg." *MGM* 15 (1974), 65-97.

—. "The Impact of the War Economy on the Civilian Population of Germany during the First and Second World War," in W. Deist, ed., *The German Military in the Age of Total War*. Leamington, 1985, 40-70.

Burgdörfer, F. *Volk ohne Jugend*. Berlin, 1934.

—. *Krieg und Bevölkerungsentwicklung*. München and Berlin, 1940.

—. *Die Kulturkrankheit Europas und ihre Überwindung in Deutschland*. Heidelberg et al., 1942.

Busch, R. "Imperialismus und Arbeiterliteratur im Ersten Weltkrieg." *AfS* 14 (1974), 293-350.

Buß, E. "Die Frauenarbeit im Dienst der preußisch-hessischen Staatseisenbahnen und ihre Entwicklung während des Krieges." Diss., Göttingen, 1919.

Cadogan, M. and Craig, P. *Women and Children First. The Fiction of Two World Wars*. London, 1978.

Carsten, F. L. *War Against War. British and German Radical Movements in the First World War*. London, 1982.

Cartarius, U. *Deutschland im Ersten Weltkrieg*. München, 1982.

Cassirer, E. *Der Mythus des Staates*. Zürich, 1949.

Castell, A. zu. "Die demographischen Konsequenzen des Ersten und Zweiten Weltkriegs für das Deutsche Reich, die Deutsche Demokratische Republik und die Bundesrepublik Deutschland," in W. Dlugoborski, ed., *Zweiter Weltkrieg und sozialer Wandel*. Göttingen, 1981, 117-137.

Cecil, H. and Liddle, P. eds. *Facing Armageddon: The First World War Experienced*. London, 1996.

Chemnitz, W. *Frauenarbeit im Kriege (1914-1918)*. Berlin, 1926.

Condell, D. J. L. *Working for Victory? Images of Women in the First World War, 1914-1918*. London, 1987.

Conze, W. *Der Strukturwandel der Familie in industriellen Modernisierungsprozeß. Historische Begründung einer aktuellen Frage*. Vortragsreihe der Gesellschaft für westfälische Wirtschaftsgeschichte 23. Dortmund, 1979.

Craig, D. and Egan, M. *Extreme Situations. Literature and Crisis from the Great War to the Atom Bomb*. London, 1979.

Creutz, M. *Die Pressepolitik der kaiserlichen Regierung während des Ersten Weltkriegs*. Frankfurt/M., 1996.

Select Bibliography

Curtin, D. Th. *The Land of Deepening Shadow: Germany at War*. New York, 1917.

Dammer, S. *Mütterlichkeit und Frauendienstpflicht. Versuch der Vergesellschaftung "weiblicher Fähigkeiten" durch eine Dienstverpflichtung. Deutschland 1890–1918*. Weinheim, 1988.

Daniel, U. "Fiktionen, Friktionen und Fakten – Frauenlohnarbeit im Ersten Weltkrieg," in G. Mai, ed., *Arbeiterschaft 1914–1918 in Deutschland. Studien zur Arbeitskampf und Arbeitsmarkt im Ersten Weltkrieg*. Düsseldorf, 1985, 277–323.

—. "The Politics of Rationing, Versus the Politics of Subsistence: Working-Class Women in Germany, 1914–1918," in R. Fletcher, ed., *Berstein to Brandt: A Short History of German Social Democracy*. London, 1987, 89–95.

—. "Women's Work in Industry and Family, 1914–1918," in R. Wall and J. Winter, eds., *The Upheaval of War: Family, Work and Welfare in Europe, 1914–1918*. Cambridge, 1988, 267–296.

—. *Arbeiterfrauen in der Kriegsgesellschaft. Beruf, Familie und Politik im Ersten Weltkrieg*. Göttingen, 1989.

—. "Gender and Work: The Impact of War (1914–1918 and 1939–1945) in Germany," in E. Aerts, ed., *Women in the Labour Force. Comparative Studies on Labour Market and Organization of Work since the 18th Century*. Leuven, 1990, 90–98.

—. "Der Krieg der Frauen 1914–1918: Zur Innenansicht des Ersten Weltkriegs in Deutschland," in G. Hirschfeld and G. Krumeich, eds., *"Keiner fühlt sich hier mehr als Mensch . . .".* Essen, 1993, 131–149.

—. "Kultur und Gesellschaft. Überlegungen zum Gegenstandbereich der Sozialgeschichte." *GG* 19 (1993), 69–99.

— and Siemann, W. *Propaganda, Meinungskampf, Verführung und politische Sinnstiftung (1789–1989)*. Frankfurt/M., 1994.

—. "Clio unter Kulturschock. Zu den aktuellen Debatten der Geschichtswissenschaft," *GWU* 48 (1997), 195–218, 259–278.

Davis, B. "Food Scarcity and the Empowerment of the Female Consumer in World War I Berlin," in V. de Grazia et al., eds., *The Sex of Things. Gender and Consumption in Historical Perspective*. Berkeley et al., 1996, 287–310.

Dazur, D. "Der deutsche Arbeitsmarkt seit Kriegsbeginn und die Bekämpfung der Arbeitslosigkeit durch das Reich." Diss., Würzburg, 1920.

Decken, A. E. von der. "Ein Vergleich des Gesundheitszustandes der deutschen Frau im jetzigen Krieg zum Weltkrieg auf Grund von Untersuchungen des Krankengeschichtenmaterials des Marienkrankenhauses Freiburg i. Br." Diss., Tübingen, 1945.

Deist, W., ed. *Militär und Innenpolitik im Weltkrieg 1914–1918*, 2 vols. Düsseldorf, 1970.

—. "Armee und Arbeiterschaft 1905-1918." *Francia* 2 (1974), 458-481.

—. "Der militärische Zusammenbruch des Kaiserreichs. Zur Realität der 'Dolchstoßlegende'," in U. Büttner, ed., *Das Unrechtsregime. Internationale Forschungen über den Nationalsozialismus. Fs. W. Jochmann zum 65. Geburtstag*, vol. 1. Hamburg, 1986, 101-129.

Delatour, Yvonne. "Le Travail des femmes pendant la première guerre mondiale et ses conséquences sur l'évolution de leur rôle dans la société." *Francia* 2 (1974), 482-501.

Delbrück, G. von. *Die wirtschaftliche Mobilmachung in Deutschland 1914*. Published posthumously by J. von Delbrück. München, 1924.

Deutelmoser, E. "Die amtliche Einwirkung auf die deutsche Öffentlichkeit im Kriege." *Die deutsche Nation* 10 (1919), 18-22.

Deutscher Textilarbeiterverband. *Jahrbuch 1918*. Berlin, 1919.

Deutschland im Ersten Weltkrieg, 3 vols. Berlin, vol. 1, 1971, vols. 2 and 3, 1970.

Dolsenhain, H., ed. *Das Liebesleben im Weltkriege*. Nürnberg, 1919.

Domansky, E. "Politische Dimensionen von Jugendprotest und Generationenkonflikt in der Zwischenkriegszeit in Deutschland," in D. Dowe, ed., *Jugendprotest und Generationkonflikt in Deutschland, England, Frankreich und Italien im 20. Jahrhundert*. Bonn-Bad Godesberg, 1986: 113-137.

Dopsch, A. *Naturalwirtschaft und Geldwirtschaft in der Weltgeschichte*. Wien, 1930; new ed. rpt. Aalen, 1968.

Dornberger, P. and Fromm, E. *Frauen führen Krieg. Aufzeichnungen*. Berlin, 1977.

Doty, M. Z. *Short Rations: An American Woman in Germany, 1915–1916*. London, 1917.

Dröge, F. *Der zerredete Widerstand. Soziologie und Publizistik des Gerüchts im Zweiten Weltkrieg*. Düsseldorf, 1970.

Duby, G. and Lardreau, G. *Geschichte und Geschichtswissenschaft. Dialoge.* Frankfurt/M., 1982.

Dülmen, R. van. "Der deutsche Katholizismus und der Erste Weltkrieg." *Francia* 2 (1974), 347–376.

Dünner, J. *Der deutsche Arbeitsnachweis im Kriege bis zum Erlaß des Hilfdienstgesetzes.* Regensburg, n.d. [1918].

Duisberg, C. "Die soziale Lage der Arbeiterschaft in der chemischen Großindustrie vor dem Weltkriege und ihre weitere Entwicklung." Diss., Würzburg, 1920.

Eckardt, G. *Industrie und Politik in Bayern 1900–1919. Der Bayerische Industriellen-Verband als Modell des Einflusses von Wirtschaftsverbänden.* Berlin, 1976.

Eifert, Ch. "Frauenarbeit im Krieg. Die Berliner 'Heimatfront' 1914 bis 1918." *IWK* 21 (1985), 281–295.

Eisenbeiss, W. *Die bürgerliche Friedensbewegung in Deutschland während des Ersten Krieges. Organisation, Selbstverständnis und politische Praxis 1913/14–1919.* Frankfurt/M. et al., 1980.

Eley, G. *Reshaping the German Right. Radical Nationalism and Political Change after Bismarck.* New Haven, 1980.

Erhaltung und Mehrung der deutschen Volkskraft. Verhandlungen der 8. Konferenz der Zentralstelle für Volkswohlfahrt. Schriften der Zentralstelle für Volkswohlfahrt 12, new series. Berlin, 1916.

Die Ernährung im Wirtschaftsjahr 1917/18. Aufklärungsstelle des Kriegsernährungsamts, ed. n.p., n.d.

Essig, O. *Der hauswirtschaftliche Großbetrieb.* Frankfurt/M., 1920.

Evans, R. J. *The Feminist Movement in Germany, 1894–1933.* London, 1976.

—. "German Social Democracy and Women's Suffrage, 1891–1918." *JCH* 15 (1980), 533–557.

—. *Sozialdemokratie und Frauenemanzipation im deutschen Kaiserreich.* Berlin and Bonn, 1979.

Ewinger-Schenk, M. *Die Rüstungsarbeiterin im 3. Bayerischen Armeekorps.* Nürnberg, 1920.

Fächer, A. *Staatliche Mütterfürsorge und der Krieg.* Berlin, 1915.

Faust, M. *Sozialer Burgfrieden im Ersten Weltkrieg. Christliche und sozialistische Arbeiterbewegung in Köln.* Essen, 1992.

Feldman, G. D. *Army, Industry and Labor in Germany, 1914–1918.* Princeton, NJ, 1966.

—. "Die Demobilmachung und die Sozialordnung der Zwischenkriegszeit in Europa." *GG* 9 (1983), 156-177.

—. *Vom Weltkrieg zur Weltwirtschaftskrise. Studien zur deutschen Wirtschafts- und Sozialgeschichte 1914-1932.* Göttingen, 1984.

— et al. "Die Massenbewegungen der Arbeiterschaft in Deutschland am Ende des Ersten Weltkriegs (1917-1920)." *PVS* 13 (1972), 84-105.

Fenkner, W. *Die Stellung der Hausfrau im neuen Deutschen Reich.* Berlin, 1921.

Finger, E. *Der Krieg und die Bekämpfung der Geschlechtskrankheiten.* Wien and Leipzig, 1916.

Fischer, H. D., ed. *Pressekonzentration und Zensurpraxis im Ersten Weltkrieg.* Berlin, 1973.

Flemming, J. *Landwirtschaftliche Interessen und Demokratie. Ländliche Gesellschaft, Agrarverbände und Staat 1890-1925.* Bonn, 1978.

Flesch, M. "Der Entwurf eines Gesetzes zur Bekämpfung der Geschlechtskrankheiten und eines Gesetzes gegen die Verhinderung von Geburten im Deutschen Reich." *Annalen für soziale Politik und Gesetzgebung* 6 (1919), 145-148.

Fout, J. C. "Current Research on German Women's History in the Nineteenth Century," in J. C. Fout, ed., *German Women in the Nineteenth Century.* New York and London, 1984, 3-54.

Fränkel, B. *Maßnahmen zur Bekämpfung der Verwahrlosung der Jugend.* Breslau, 1916.

Fränkel, L. "Sexuelle Gefährdung der Frau durch den Krieg." *Zeitschrift zur Bekämpfung der Geschlechtskrankheiten* 17 (1916), 212-215.

Die Frau in der bayerischen Kriegsindustrie nach einer amtlichen Erhebung aus dem Jahre 1917. Beiträge zur Statistik Bayerns 92. Bayerisches Statistisches Landesamt, ed. München, 1920.

Die Frauenarbeit in der Metallindustrie während des Krieges, dargestellt nach Erhebungen im August/September 1916 in B. vom Vorstand des Deutschen Metallarbeiterverbandes. Stuttgart, 1917.

Frevert, U. "'Fürsorgliche Belagerung': Hygienebewegung und Arbeiterfrauen im 19. und frühen 20. Jahrhundert." *GG* 11 (1985), 420-446.

—. *Frauen-Geschichte: Zwischen Bürgerlicher Verbesserung und Neuer Weiblichkeit*. Frankfurt/M., 1986.

—. *"Mann und Weib und Weib und Mann". Geschlechter-Differenzen in der Moderne*. München, 1995.

Fridenson, P., ed. *The French Home Front 1914–1918*. Oxford, 1992.

Fries, H. *Die große Katharsis. Der Erste Weltkrieg in der Sicht deutscher Gelehrter und Künstler*, 2 vols. Konstanz, 1995.

Fürth, H. "Die Zentralküche als Kriegseinrichtung." *Archiv für Sozialwissenschaft und Sozialpolitik* 41 (1916), 464–474.

—. *Die deutsche Frau im Kriege*. Tübingen, 1917.

—. "Gemeinwirtschaftliche Förderung der Haushaltung und der Lebenskraft," in *Die gesunkene Kaufkraft des Lohnes und ihre Wiederherstellung*. (Schriften der Gesellschaft für Soziale Reform, vol. 69.) Jena, 1919.

Fussell, P. *The Great War and Modern Memory*. London, 1975.

—. "Der Einfluß kultureller Paradigmen auf die literarische Wiedergabe traumatischer Erfahrung," in K. Vondung, ed., *Kriegserlebnis. Der Erste Weltkrieg in der literarischen Gestaltung und symbolischen Deutung der Nationen*. Göttingen, 1980, 175–187.

Gaebel, K. and Schulz, M. von. *Die Heimarbeit im Kriege*. Berlin, 1917.

Geary, D. *European Labor Protest, 1848–1939*. London, 1981.

Geinitz, Chr. and Hinz, U. "Das Augusterlebnis in Südbaden," in G. Hirschfeld et al., eds., *Kriegserfahrungen. Studien zur Sozial- und Mentalitätsgeschichte des Ersten Weltkriegs*. Essen, 1997, 20–35.

Geiseler, U. "Die Frauendienstpflicht im Weltkrieg 1914–1918." Diss., Heidelberg, 1943.

Geiss, I. *Das Deutsche Reich und der Erste Weltkrieg*. München, 1985.

Genno, C. N. and Wetzel, H., eds. *The First World War in German Narrative Prose*. Toronto et al., 1980.

Gersdorff, U. von. "Frauen im Kriegsdienst. Probleme und Ergebnisse." *Wehrkunde* 14 (1965), 576–580.

—. "Das unbekannte Heer. In memoriam M.-E. Lüders." *Wehrwissenschaftliche Rundschau* 14 (1966), 319–323.

—. *Frauen im Kriegsdienst 1914–1945*. Stuttgart, 1969.

—. "Frauenarbeit und Frauenemanzipation im Ersten Weltkrieg." *Francia* 2 (1974), 502–523.

Giar, A. "Die Heimarbeit in der Offenbacher Lederwaren-industrie." Diss., Frankfurt/M., 1920.

Giesecke, K. *Im Kampf an der inneren Front. Meine Kriegserlebnisse als Staatsanwalt.* Leipzig, 1918.

Gilbert, S. M. "Soldier's Heart: Literary Men, Literary Women and the Great War." *Signs* 8 (1982/83), 422–450.

Glaeser, E. *Jahrgang 1902.* Berlin, 1931.

Gnauck-Kühne, E. *Dienstpflicht und Dienstjahr des weiblichen Geschlechts.* Tübingen, 1915.

Goltz, E. Freiherr von der. *Deutsche Frauenarbeit in der Kriegszeit.* Leipzig, 1914.

Grabinski, B., ed. *Weltkrieg und Sittlichkeit. Beiträge zur Kulturgeschichte der Weltkriegsjahre.* Hildesheim, 1917.

Graf, O. M. *Das Leben meiner Mutter.* München, 1981.

—. *Wir sind Gefangene. Ein Bekenntnis.* München, 1978.

Gravert, E. M. "Der Einfluß der wirtschaftlichen Demobilmachung auf die Entwicklung der Frauenarbeit." Diss., Hamburg, 1924/25.

Graves, R. *Goodbye to All That.* Harmondsworth, 1983.

Greenwald, M. W. *Women, War, and Work. The Impact of World War I on Women Workers in the United States.* Westport, Conn. and London, 1980.

Gregor, A. and Voigtländer, E. *Die Verwahrlosung, ihre klinisch-psychologische Bewertung und ihre Bekämpfung.* Part 1: *Die Verwahrlosung männlicher Jugendlicher.* Berlin, 1918.

Greven-Aschoff, B. *Die bürgerliche Frauenbewegung in Deutschland 1894–1933.* Göttingen, 1981.

—. "Sozialer Wandel und Frauenbewegung." *GG* 7 (1981), 328–346.

Groener, W. *Lebenserinnerungen.* Göttingen, 1957.

Grosz, G. *Ein kleines Ja und ein großes Nein. Sein Leben vom ihm selbst erzählt.* Reinbek, 1974.

Grünbaum-Sachs, H. *Zur Krisis in der Hauswirtschaft.* Veröffentlichungen des Instituts für Hauswirtschaftswissenschaft an der Akademie für soziale und pädagogische Frauenarbeit 4. Berlin, 1929.

Gruschwitz, K. "Die soziale und wirtschaftliche Lage der deutschen Textilarbeiterschaft, dargestellt an den Jahren vor, in und nach dem Krieg." Diss., Tübingen, 1922.

Günther, A. *Kriegslöhne und Preise und ihr Einfluß auf Kaufkraft und Lebenshaltung.* Jena, 1919.

——. "Die Folgen des Krieges für Einkommen und Lebenshaltung der mittleren Volksschichten Deutschlands," in R. Meerwarth et al., eds., *Die Einwirkung des Krieges auf Bevölkerungsbewegung, Einkommen und Lebenshaltung in Deutschland.* Stuttgart et al., 1932, 99–279.

Gutsche, W. et al. *Der Erste Weltkrieg. Ursachen und Verlauf. Herrschende Politik und Antikriegsbewegung in Deutschland.* Köln, 1985.

—— and Otto, H. "Der Erste Weltkrieg in der DDR-Geschichtswissenschaft," in J. Rohwer, ed., *Neue Forschungen zum Ersten Weltkrieg*. Schriften der Bibliothek für Zeitgeschichte 25. Koblenz, 1985, 91–103.

Guttmann, B. *Weibliche Heimarmee. Frauen in Deutschland 1914–1918.* Weinheim, 1989.

Haacke, H. *Barmen im Weltkrieg*. Barmen, 1929.

Haberda, A. "Gerichtsärztliche Erfahrungen über die Fruchtabtreibung in Wien." *Vierteljahresschrift für gerichtliche Medizin und öffentliches Sanitätswesen* 56, 3rd. ed. (1918), 55–104.

Hafkesbrink, H. *Unknown Germany. An Inner Chronicle of the First World War Based on Letters and Diaries.* New Haven, 1948.

Hagemann, K. *Frauenalltag und Männerpolitik. Alltagsleben und gesellschaftliches Handeln von Arbeiterfrauen in der Weimarer Republik.* Bonn, 1990.

Hagener, E. *"Es lief sich so sicher an Deinem Arm." Briefe einer Soldatenfrau 1914.* Weinheim and Basel, 1986.

Hager, P. E. and Taylor, D. *The Novels of World War I. An Annotated Bibliography.* New York, 1981.

Hammer, K. *Deutsche Kriegstheologie 1870–1918.* München, 1974.

Hammerich, K. and Klein, M., eds. *Materialien zur Soziologie des Alltags.* (*KZSS* special vol. 20, 1978.) Opladen, 1978.

Hanna, G. *Die Arbeiterinnen und der Krieg*. Berlin, 1916.

Hardach, G. *Der Erste Weltkrieg.* Geschichte der Weltwirtschaft im 20. Jahrhundert 2. W. Fischer, ed. München, 1973.

Harnack, A. von. *Der Krieg und die Frauen.* Berlin, 1915.

Hartewig, K. *Das unberechenbare Jahrzehnt. Bergarbeiter und ihre Familien im Ruhrgebiet 1914–1924.* München, 1992.

Hasenclever, Ch. *Jugendhilfe und Jugendgesetzgebung seit 1900.* Göttingen, 1978.

Haste, C. *Keep the Home Fires Burning. Propaganda in the First World War*. London, 1977.

Haumann, H., ed. *Arbeiteralltag in Stadt und Land*. Berlin, 1982.

Hausen, K. "Familie als Gegenstand historischer Sozialwissenschaft. Bemerkungen zu einer Forschungsstrategie." *GG* 1 (1975), 171–209.

—. "Women's History in den Vereinigten Staaten." *GG* 7 (1981), 347–363.

—, ed. *Frauen suchen ihre Geschichte. Historische Studien zum 19. und 20. Jahrhundert*. München, 1983.

—. "The German Nation's Obligations to the Heroes' Widows of World War I," in M. R. Higonnet et al., *Behind the Lines. Gender and the Two World Wars*. New Haven, Conn., 1987, 126–140.

— and Wunder, H., eds. *Frauengeschichte – Geschlechtergeschichte*. Frankfurt and New York, 1992.

Heer, H. and Ullrich, V., eds. *Geschichte entdecken. Erfahrungen und Projekte der neuen Geschichtsbewegung*. Reinbek, 1985.

Heinel, E. "Die Bevölkerungsbewegung im Deutschen Reich in der Kriegs- und Nachkriegszeit." Diss., Berlin, 1927.

Heinemann, U. *Die verdrängte Niederlage. Politische Öffentlichkeit und Kriegsschuldfrage in der Weimarer Republik*. Göttingen, 1983.

Heinz, W. and Schöber, P., eds. *Theorien kollektiven Verhaltens. Beiträge zur Analyse sozialer Protestaktionen und Bewegungen*, 2 vols. Darmstadt and Neuwied, 1973.

Heller, A. *Alltag und Geschichte. Zur sozialistischen Gesellschaftslehre*. Neuwied and Berlin, 1970.

—. *Das Alltagsleben. Versuch einer Erklärung der individuellen Reproduktion*. Frankfurt/M., 1978.

Hellwig, A. *Der Krieg und die Kriminalität der Jugendlichen*. Halle and Saale, 1916.

Henel, H. O. *Eros im Stacheldraht*. Hamburg-Bergedorf, 1929.

Hepelmann, H. "Beitrag zur Geschichte der Frauenarbeit im Weltkriege mit besonderer Würdigung der Verhältnisse im IV. Armeekorpsbezirk Magdeburg." Diss., Münster, 1938.

Herbert, U. "Zwangsarbeit als Lernprozeß. Zur Beschäftigung ausländischer Arbeiter in der westdeutschen Industrie im Ersten Weltkrieg." *AfS* 24 (1984), 285–304.

—. *Geschichte der Ausländerbeschäftigung in Deutschland 1880 bis 1980. Saisonarbeiter – Zwangsarbeiter – Gastarbeiter*.

Berlin and Bonn, 1986.

Herder, Ch. *Mein Kriegstagebuch 1914–1918*. Freiburg i. Br., 1955.

Hering, S. *Die Kriegsgewinnlerinnen. Praxis und Ideologie der deutschen Frauenbewegung im Ersten Weltkrieg*. Pfaffenweiler, 1990.

Herrmann, U. "Sozialdemokratische Frauen in Deutschland im Kampf um den Frieden vor und während des Ersten Weltkriegs." *ZfG* 33 (1985), 213–230.

Hetzel, P. H. "Die Bekämpfung der Arbeitslosigkeit und ihrer Folgen unter besonderer Berücksichtigung der Düsseldorfer Verhältnisse." Diss., Greifswald, 1924.

Higonnet, M. R. et al., eds. *Behind the Lines. Gender and the Two World Wars*. New Haven, Conn., 1987.

Hirsch, P. "Die Kriegsfürsorge der deutschen Gemeinden." *Annalen für soziale Politik und Gesetzgebung* 4 (1916), 261–348.

Hirschfeld, G. and Krumeich, G., eds. *"Keiner fühlt sich hier mehr als Mensch . . ." Erlebnis und Wirkung des Ersten Weltkriegs*. Essen, 1993.

— et al., eds. *Kriegserfahrungen. Studien zur Sozial- und Mentalitätsgeschichte des Ersten Weltkriegs*. Essen, 1997.

Hirschfeld, M. and Gaspar, A., eds. *Sittengeschichte des Ersten Weltkriegs*. Hanau, n.d. [1929].

Hitze, F. *Geburtenrückgang und Sozialreform*. M.-Gladbach, 1917.

Höh, G. "Vergleiche der Volksernährung im 3. und 4. Kriegsjahr des ersten und jetzigen Weltkriegs. Zur Beurteilung der Leistungs- und Arbeitsfähigkeit." Diss., Straßburg, 1943.

Hoffmann, M. "Das Gesetz betreffend die Unterstützung von Familien in den Dienst eingetretener Mannschaften vom 28.2.1888/4.8.1914 und seine Anwendung." Diss., Berlin, 1918.

Hoffmann, W. *Psychologie der straffälligen Jugend*. Leipzig, 1919.

—. *Die Lektüre der Frau. Ein Beitrag zur Leserkunde und zur Leserführung*. Leipzig, 1931.

Hofmiller, J. *Revolutionstagebuch 1918/19. Aus den Tagen der Münchener Revolution*. Leipzig, 1938.

Hohmann, L. A. and Reichel, E. *Die Dienstpflicht der deutschen Frauen*. Berlin, 1917.

Holz, H. "Der Anspruch von Kriegsteilnehmern auf ihre

Wiedereinstellung während der Zeit der wirtschaftlichen Demobilmachung." Diss., Jena, 1922.

Hong, Y.-S. "The Contradictions of Modernization in the German Welfare State: Gender and the Politics of Welfare Reform in First World War Germany." *Social History* 17 (1992), vol. 2, 251–270.

Huber, L. "Geburten und Sterbefälle in 61 größeren deutschen Städten während des Weltkrieges." *Kölner Statistik. Zeitschrift des Statistischen Amtes der Stadt Köln* 3/4 (Köln, 1920/21): vol. 1, 81–198; vol 2., 199–321.

Hüppauf, B., ed. *Ansichten vom Krieg. Vergleichende Studien zum Ersten Weltkrieg in Literatur und Gesellschaft.* Königstein/Ts., 1984.

—. *War, Violence, and the Modern Condition.* Berlin, 1997.

—. "Experiences of Modern Warfare and the Crisis of Representation," *New German Critique* 59 (1993), 41–76.

Husung, H.-G. "Arbeiterschaft und Arbeiterbewegung im Ersten Weltkrieg: Neue Forschungen über Deutschland und England," in K. Tenfelde, ed., *Arbeiter und Arbeiterbewegung im Vergleich. Berichte zur internationalen historischen Forschung.* München, 1986, 611–664.

Imbusch, H. *Arbeiterinnen im Bergbau.* Essen, 1917.

Jacobi, G. and Nieß, Th. *Hausfrauen, Bauern, Marginalisierte: Überlebensproduktion in "Dritter" und "Erster Welt."* Saarbrücken and Fort Lauderdale, Fla., 1980.

Jäckel, H. *Übergangswirtschaft und Textilarbeiter. Denkschrift des Deutschen Textilarbeiterverbandes, hg. im Auftrage seiner Kommission für Übergangswirtschaft.* Berlin, 1918.

Jäger, W. *Historische Forschung und politische Kultur in Deutschland. Die Debatte 1914–1980 über den Ausbruch des Ersten Weltkriegs.* Göttingen, 1984.

Jahrbuch des BDF 1915–1919. Berlin, 1915–1919.

Jahresberichte der Gewerbeaufsicht und Bergbehörden für die Jahre 1914–1918, 4 vols., official ed. Statistisches Reichsamt, ed. Berlin, 1920.

Jastrow, I. *Im Kriegszustand. Die Umformung des öffentlichen Lebens in den ersten Kriegswochen.* Berlin, 1914.

Jirgal, E. *Die Wiederkehr des Weltkriegs in der Literatur.* Wien and Leipzig, 1931.

Johann, E., ed. *Innenansicht eines Krieges. Deutsche Dokumente 1914–1918.* München, 1973.

Josczok, D. *Die Entwicklung der sozialistischen Arbeiterbewegung in Düsseldorf während des Ersten Weltkriegs.* Reinbek, 1980.

Jünger, E. *In Stahlgewittern.* Stuttgart, 1983.

Jungblut. "Die Geschlechtskrankheiten im deutschen Heere während des Weltkrieges 1914–1918." *Mitteilungen der Deutschen Gesellschaft zur Bekämpfung der Geschlechtskrankheiten* 21.1/2 (1923/24), 2–5.

Justus, Th. "Die weiblichen Hausangestellten in Frankfurt/Main. Ergebnisse einer privaten Erhebung vom Jahre 1920." Diss., n.p., n.d. [1924].

Kachulle, D., ed. *Die Pöhlands im Krieg. Briefe einer Arbeiterfamilie aus dem Ersten Weltkrieg.* Köln, 1982.

Karbe, A. *Die Frauenlohnfrage und ihre Entwicklung in der Kriegs- und Nachkriegszeit.* Rostock, 1928.

Kellner, F. *Die Kriegs- und Nachkriegsfolgen für die Gesundheit des deutschen Volkes.* Berlin, 1926.

Kennedy, D. M. *Over Here. The First World War and American Society.* New York and Oxford, 1980.

Kiegel, W. *Die soziale Hilfsarbeit der deutschen freien Gewerkschaften während des ersten Kriegsjahres.* Berlin, 1917.

Kielmansegg, P. Graf. *Deutschland im Ersten Weltkrieg.* Frankfurt/M., 1968.

Kinzinger, E. "Der Einfluß der Sozialpolitik der Nachkriegszeit auf die Arbeitsmarktlage insbesondere in Ludwigshafen a. Rh." Diss., Heidelberg, 1926.

Kirchgässner, B. and Scholz, G., eds. *Stadt und Krieg.* Sigmaringen, 1989.

Kleeis, F. *Die Geschichte der sozialen Versicherung in Deutschland.* Berlin, 1928; rpt., Berlin, 1981.

Klein, H. M., ed. *The First World War in Fiction.* London, 1976.

Kluge, U. *Die deutsche Revolution 1918/19. Staat, Politik und Gesellschaft zwischen Weltkrieg und Kapp-Putsch.* Frankfurt/M., 1985.

Knoch, P. "Feldpost - eine unentdeckte historische Quellengattung." *GG* 11 (1986), 154–171.

—, ed. *Menschen im Krieg 1914–1918.* Ludwigsburg, 1987.

—, ed. *Kriegsalltag. Die Rekonstruktion des Kriegsalltags als Aufgabe der historischen Forschung und der Friedenserziehung.* Stuttgart, 1989.

Knote, H. "Krieg und Säuglingssterblichkeit." Diss., Rostock, 1924/25.

Koch, E. "Kriegsmaßnahmen der Städte auf dem Gebiete der Lebensmittelversorgung." *Zeitschrift für Kommunalwirtschaft und Kommunalpolitik* 6 (1916), 1-6.

Kocka, J. "Weltkrieg und Mittelstand. Handwerker und Angestellte in Deutschland 1914-1918." *Francia* 2 (1974), 431-457.

—. *Klassengesellschaft im Krieg. Deutsche Sozialgeschichte 1914-1918*, 2nd expanded ed. Göttingen, 1978.

—. "Historisch-anthropologische Fragestellungen – ein Defizit der Historischen Sozialwissenschaft?" in H. Süssmuth, ed., *Historische Anthropologie. Der Mensch in der Geschichte.* Göttingen, 1984: 73-83.

Köfner, G. *Hunger, Not und Korruption. Der Übergang Österreichs von der Monarchie zur Republik am Beispiel Salzburgs. Eine sozial- und wirtschaftswissenschaftliche Studie.* Salzburg, 1980.

Köhne. "Die Jugendlichen und der Krieg." *Deutsche Strafrechts-Zeitung* 3 (1916), 13-18.

Köllner, L. and Kutz, M. *Wirtschaft und Gesellschaft in den beiden Weltkriegen. Berichte und Bibliographien.* München, 1981.

Koester, E. *Literatur und Weltkriegsideologie. Positionen und Begründungszusammenhänge des publizistischen Engagements deutscher Schriftsteller im Ersten Weltkrieg.* Kronberg/Ts., 1977.

Kohns, A. "'Wann mag dieses Elend enden?' Aus dem Kriegstagebuch einer Bonnerin." *Journal für Geschichte* 5 (1980), 28-34.

Konrad, H. and Schmidlechner, K. M., eds. *Revolutionäres Potential in Europa am Ende des Ersten Weltkriegs. Die Rolle von Strukturen, Konjunkturen und Massenbewegungen.* Wien and Köln, 1990.

Koppenfels, S. von. *Die Kriminalität der Frau im Kriege.* Leipzig, 1926.

Koszyk, K. *Deutsche Pressepolitik im Ersten Weltkrieg.* Düsseldorf, 1968.

—. "Pressepolitik und Propaganda im Ersten Weltkrieg." *Francia* 3 (1975), 465-475.

Kraft, H. *Staatsräson und Kriegsführung im kaiserlichen Deutschland 1914-1916.* Göttingen, 1980.

Kraus, K. *Die letzten Tage der Menschheit*, in *Werke von Karl Kraus.*, vol. 5. Heinrich Fischer, ed. München, n.d.

Die Kriegsgewerbezählung am 15. August 1917 in Bayern. Beiträge zur Statistik Bayerns 90. Bayerisches Statistisches Landesamt, ed. München, 1919.

Kriegsöffentlichkeit und Kriegserlebnis. Eine Ausstellung zum Ersten Weltkrieg. Compiled and ed. by H. Altmann et al. Regensburg, 1978.

Kriegsverwaltungsbericht der Stadt Neukölln 1914–1918. Statistisches Amt, ed. Neukölln, 1921.

Die Kriegsvolkszählungen vom Jahre 1916 und 1917 in Bayern. Beiträge zur Statistik Bayerns 89. Bayerisches Statistisches Landesamt, ed. München, 1919.

Kronecker. "Strafvorschriften gegen die Verwahrlosung Jugendlicher." *Leipziger Zeitschrift für deutsches Recht* 10.8 (1916), 576–584.

Kruse, W. *Krieg und nationale Integration. Eine Neuinterpretation des sozialdemokratischen Burgfriedensschlusses 1914/15*. Essen, 1993.

Kuczynski, J. *Darstellung der Lage der Arbeiter in Deutschland von 1900 bis 1917/18*. Geschichte der Lage der Arbeiter unter dem Kapitalismus, vol. 4. Berlin, 1967.

—. *Geschichte des Alltags des deutschen Volkes, Studien 4: 1871–1918*. Köln, 1981.

Künkel, H. "Die Wohlfahrtspflege, ihr Begriff und ihre Bedeutung, unter besonderer Berücksichtigung der Familienfürsorge in der Provinz Brandenburg." Diss., Würzburg, n.d. [1920].

Kuh, F. "Zur sozialen Wertung der gewerblichen Frauenarbeit." *Zeitschrift für Sozialwissenschaft* 8, new series (1917), 38–44.

Kundrus, B. *Kriegerfrauen. Familie, Politik und Geschlechterverhältnisse im Ersten und Zweiten Weltkrieg*. Hamburg, 1995.

Lamszus, W. *Das Menschenschlachthaus. Visionen vom Krieg 1. und 2. Teil*. Leipzig, 1923.

Landsberg, J. F. "Sexuelle Verwahrlosung der Jugend und ihre Behandlung." *Archiv für Sexualforschung* 1 (1915), 270–283.

Lasswell, H. D. *Propaganda Technique in the World War*. Cambridge, Mass. and London, 1971.

—, ed. *Propaganda and Communication in World History*, 3 vols. Honolulu, 1980.

Select Bibliography

Latzel, K. *Vom Sterben im Krieg. Wandlungen in der Einstellung zum Soldatentod vom Siebenjährigen Krieg bis zum II. Weltkrieg.* Warendorf, 1988.

Lauter, A. "Die deutsche Sozialversicherung vom Kriegsausbruch bis zum Frieden von Versailles." Diss., München, 1920/21.

Lebeck, R. and Schütte, M. *Propagandapostkarten I.* Dortmund, 1980.

Lederer, E. "Die Organisation der Wirtschaft durch den Staat im Kriege." *Archiv für Sozialwissenschaft und Sozialpolitik* 40 (1915), 118-146.

—. "Die Regelung der Lebensmittelversorgung während des Kriegs in Deutschland." *Archiv für Sozialwissenschaft und Sozialpolitik* 40 (1915), 757-783.

—. "Zur Soziologie des Weltkriegs." *Archiv für Sozialwissenschaft und Sozialpolitik* 39 (1915), 347-384.

—. "Die ökonomische Umschichtung im Kriege." *Archiv für Sozialwissenschaft und Sozialpolitik* 45 (1918/19), 1-39, 430-463.

Ledermann, F. *Zur Geschichte der Frauenstimmrechtsbewegung.* Berlin, 1918.

Leed, E. J. "Class and Disillusionment in World War I." *JMH* 50 (1978), 680-699.

—. *No Man's Land. Combat and Identity in World War I.* Cambridge, 1979.

Leidigkeit, H. "Die Fabrikarbeit verheirateter Frauen." Diss., Greifswald, 1919.

Lerg, W. B. *Das Gespräch. Theorie und Praxis der unvermittelten Kommunikation.* Düsseldorf, 1970.

Lessing, Th. *Geschichte als Sinngebung des Sinnlosen.* München, 1983.

Lewis, J. "Women Lost and Found: The Impact of Feminism on History," in D. Spender, ed., *Men's Studies Modified: The Impact of Feminism on the Academic Disciplines.* Oxford et al., 1981, 55-72.

Liepmann, M. *Krieg und Kriminalität in Deutschland.* Wirtschafts- und Sozialgeschichte des Weltkrieges, German series. Stuttgart et al., 1930.

Lindemann, A., ed. *Unsere Ernährung in der Kriegszeit. Neun Vorträge, gehalten bei dem Lehrkursus des Nationalen Frauendienstes im Stuttgarter Landesgewerbemuseum, 22.-24. Februar 1915.* Berlin, 1915.

Lindemann, C. H. *Die deutsche Stadtgemeinde im Kriege*. Tübingen, 1917.

Linse, U. "Arbeiterschaft und Geburtenentwicklung im Deutschen Kaisserreich von 1871." *AfS* 12 (1972), 205–271.

Lissmann, P. *Die Wirkungen des Krieges auf das männliche Geschlechtsleben*. München, 1919.

Liszt, F. von. "Der Krieg und die Kriminalität der Jugendlichen. Vortrag in der deutschen Juristischen Gesellschaft, gehalten am 12.2.1916." *Zeitschrift für die gesamte Strafrechtswissenschaft* 37 (1916), 496–516.

Löwenfeld, L. *Die Suggestion in ihrer Bedeutung für den Weltkrieg*. Wiesbaden, 1917.

Lorenz, Ch. "Die gewerbliche Frauenarbeit während des Krieges," in P. Umbreit and Ch. Lorenz, *Der Krieg und die Arbeitsverhältnisse*. Stuttgart et al., 1928, 307–391.

Losseff-Tillmanns, G. *Frauenemanzipation und Gewerkschaften*. Wuppertal, 1978.

Luckmann, Th. *Lebenswelt und Gesellschaft. Grundstrukturen und geschichtliche Wandlungen*. Paderborn et al., 1980.

Ludendorff, E., ed. *Urkunden der Obersten Heeresleitung über ihre Tätigkeit 1916–1918*. Berlin, 1920.

Ludewig, H.-U. *Das Herzogtum Braunschweig im Ersten Weltkrieg. Wirtschaft – Gesellschaft – Staat*. Braunschweig, 1984.

Lüders, M.-E. "Die volkswirtschaftliche Bedeutung der qualifizierten Frauenarbeit für die gewerblichen Berufe." In *Frauenberufsfrage und Bevölkerungspolitik Jahrbuch des BDF, 1917*. (Berlin and Leipzig, 1917), 3–12.

—. *Die Entwicklung der gewerblichen Frauenarbeit im Kriege*. Special publication of *Schmollers Jahrbuch* 44. München and Leipzig, 1920.

—. *Volksdienst der Frau*. Berlin, 1937.

—. *Das unbekannte Heer. Frauen kämpfen für Deutschland 1914–1918*. Berlin, 1937.

—. *Fürchte dich nicht. Persönliches und Politisches aus mehr als 80 Jahren*. Köln, 1963.

Lüdtke, A., ed. *Alltagsgeschichte. Zur Rekonstruktion historischer Erfahrungen und Lebensweisen*. Frankfurt and New York, 1989.

Maffei, G. von. "Die deutsche Volkswirtschaft bei Ausbruch des Weltkrieges." Diss., Erlangen, 1930.

Mai, G. "Burgfrieden und Sozialpolitik in Deutschland in der

Anfangsphase des Ersten Weltkriegs (1914/15)." *MGM* 20 (1976), 21-50.

—. "'Aufklärung der Bevölkerung' und 'Vaterländischer Unterricht' in Württemberg 1914-1918." *Zeitschrift für Württembergische Landesgeschichte* 36 (1977), 199-235.

—. *Kriegswirtschaft und Arbeiterbewegung in Württemberg 1914-1918*. Stuttgart, 1983.

—, ed. *Arbeiterschaft 1914-1918 in Deutschland. Studien zu Arbeitskampf und Arbeitsmarkt im Ersten Weltkrieg*. Düsseldorf, 1985.

Maier, R. *Feldpostbriefe aus dem Ersten Weltkrieg 1914-1918*. Stuttgart, 1966.

Malich, U. "Zur Entwicklung des Reallohns im Ersten Weltkrieg." *JbWG* 2 (1980), 55-70.

Marcour, J. "Arbeiterbeschaffung und Arbeiterauslese bei der Firma Krupp." Diss., Münster, 1925.

Marcuse, M. "Zur Frage der Verbreitung und Methodik der willkürlichen Geburtenbeschränkung in Berliner Proletarierkreisen." *Sexualprobleme* 9 (1913), 752-780.

Marquis, A. G. "Words as Weapons: Propaganda in Britain and Germany during the First World War." *JCH* 13 (1978), 467-498.

Marschalck, P. *Bevölkerungsgeschichte Deutschlands im 19. und 20. Jahrhundert*. Frankfurt/M., 1984.

Marsland, E. A. *The Nation's Cause. French, English and German Poetry of the First World War*. London et al., 1990.

Marwick, A. *The Deluge: British Society and the First World War*. New York, 1970.

—. *War and Social Change in the Twentieth Century. A Comparative Study of Britain, France, Germany, Russia and the United States*. London, 1974.

—. *Women at War. 1914-1918*. Glasgow, 1977.

Marx, L. "Die wirtschaftliche und soziale Lage der berufstätigen Frau bei Kriegsende in Mannheim." Diss., Heidelberg, n.d. [1920].

McMillan, J. P. "The Effects of the First World War on the Social Conditions of Women in France." Diss., Oxford, 1976.

Medick, H. "'Missionare im Ruderboot?' Ethnologische Erkenntnisweisen als Herausforderung an die Sozialgeschichte." *GG* 10 (1984), 295-319.

Meerwarth, R. "Die Entwicklung der Bevölkerung in Deutschland während der Kriegs- und Nachkriegszeit," in R. Meerwarth et al., *Einwirkung*, 1-97.

— et al. *Die Einwirkung des Krieges auf Bevölkerungsbewegung, Einkommen und Lebenshaltung in Deutschland.* Stuttgart et al., 1932.

Mendelssohn-Bartholdy, A. *The War and German Society. The Testament of a Liberal.* New York, 1971.

Meyer, G. *Die Frau mit den grünen Haaren. Erinnerungen.* M. C. Wiessing, ed. Hamburg, 1978.

Michaelis, G. *Für Staat und Volk. Eine Lebensgeschichte.* Berlin, 1922.

Michalka, W., ed. *Der Erste Weltkrieg.* München and Zürich, 1994.

Mihaly, J. ... *da gibt's ein Wiedersehen! Kriegstagebuch eines Mädchens 1914-1918.* Freiburg and Heidelberg, 1982.

Miller, S. *Burgfrieden und Klassenkampf. Die deutsche Sozialdemokratie im Ersten Weltkrieg.* Düsseldorf, 1974.

Minde. "Die zunehmende Verwahrlosung der Jugend." *Deutsche Strafrechts-Zeitung* 2 (1915), 501-506.

Missalla, H. *"Gott mit uns." Die deutsche katholische Kriegspredigt 1914-1918.* München, 1968.

Mleinek, G. "Frauenarbeit in der Kriegs-, Inflations- und Rationalisierungszeit." *Jahrbuch für Frauenarbeit* 8 (1932), 45-74.

Moeller, R. G. "Peasants, Politics and Pressure Groups in War and Inflation: A Study of the Rhineland and Westphalia, 1914-1924." Diss., University of California, Berkeley, 1980.

Möser, K. "Kriegsgeschichte und Kriegsliteratur. Formen der Verarbeitung des Ersten Weltkriegs." *MGM* 49 (1986), 39-51.

Momber, E. *'s is Krieg! 's ist Krieg! Versuch zur Literatur über den Krieg 1914-1933.* Berlin, 1981.

Mommsen, W. J., ed. *Die Entstehung des Wohlfahrtsstaates in Großbritannien und Deutschland 1850-1950.* Stuttgart, 1982.

—, ed., *Kultur und Krieg. Die Rolle der Intellektuellen, Künstler und Schriftsteller im Ersten Weltkrieg.* München, 1996.

— and Hirschfeld, G., eds. *Sozialprotest, Gewalt, Terror. Gewaltanwendung durch politische und gesellschaftliche Randgruppen im 19. und 20. Jahrhundert.* Stuttgart, 1982.

Mooser, J. *Arbeiterleben in Deutschland 1900-1970.* Frankfurt/ M., 1984.

Moses, G. *Zum Problem der sozialen Familienverwahrlosung*

unter besonderer Berücksichtigung der Verhältnisse im Krieg. Beiträge zur Kinderforschung und Heilerziehung 175. Langensalza, 1920.

Mosse, G. *Fallen Soldiers: Reshaping the Memory of the World Wars.* New York, 1989.

Most, O. "Kriegsfürsorge." *Handwörterbuch der Kommunalwissenschaften* 3. Jena, 1924, 169–184.

Mühsam, K. *Wie wir belogen wurden. Die amtliche Irreführung des deutschen Volkes.* München, 1918.

Müller, J. "Die Regelung des Arbeitsmarktes in der Zeit der wirtschaftlichen Demobilmachung." Diss., Erlangen, 1923.

Müller, K.-P. "Organisation, Themen und Probleme der Volksaufklärung in Baden 1914 bis 1918." *ZGO* 134 (1986), 329–358.

—. *Politik und Gesellschaft im Krieg. Der Legitimitätsverlust des badischen Staates, 1914–1918.* Stuttgart, 1988.

Müller, W. et al. *Strukturwandel der Frauenarbeit 1880–1980.* Frankfurt and New York, 1983.

Murdoch, B. *Fighting Songs and Warring Words. Popular Lyrics of Two World Wars.* London et al., 1990.

Nagl-Docekal, H. and Wimmer, F., eds. *Neue Ansätze in der Geschichtswissenschaft.* Wien, 1984.

Nicolai, W. *Nachrichtendienst, Presse und Volksstimmung im Weltkrieg.* Berlin, 1920.

Niecz, W. "Untersuchung der Lage der weiblichen Arbeitskräfte in der Textilindustrie während der Kriegs- und Übergangszeit." Diss., Frankfurt/M., 1923/25.

Niehuss, M. "Lebensweise und Familie in der Inflationszeit," in G. D. Feldman et al., eds., *Die Anpassung an die Inflation.* Berlin and New York, 1986, 237–265.

—. "Textilarbeiter im Ersten Weltkrieg. Beschäftigungslage und Fürsorgemaßnahmen am Beispiel Augsburg," in Mai, ed., *Arbeiterschaft*, 249–276.

—. *Arbeiterschaft in Krieg und Inflation. Soziale Schichtung und Lage der Arbeiter in Augsburg und Linz 1910 bis 1925.* Berlin, 1985.

Nielsen, L. "Die Verdrängung der Männerarbeit durch Frauenarbeit in der Industrie." Diss., Bonn, 1919.

Niethammer, L. "Anmerkungen zur Alltagsgeschichte." *Gd* 5 (1980), 231–242.

Niggemann, H. *Emanzipation zwischen Sozialismus und*

Feminismus. Die sozialdemokratische Frauenbewegung im Kaiserreich. Wuppertal, 1981.

Nürnberg während des Krieges. Wirtschaftliche Lage und soziale Fürsorge 1.8.–1.11.1914. Statistisches Amt., ed. Nürnberg, 1914.

Oppenborn, H. *Die Tätigkeit der Frau in der deutschen Kriegswirtschaft.* Diss., Erlangen, 1928.

Oppenheimer, H. and Radomski, H. *Die Probleme der Frauenarbeit in der Übergangswirtschaft.* Mannheim et al., 1918.

Patemann, R. *Der Kampf um die preußische Wahlreform im Ersten Weltkrieg.* Beiträge zur Geschichte des Parlamentarismus und der politischen Parteien 26. Düsseldorf, 1964.

Payer, F. von. *Von Bethmann Hollweg bis Ebert. Erinnerungen und Bilder.* Frankfurt/M., 1923.

Peukert, D. "Arbeiteralltag – Mode oder Methode?" in Haumann, ed., *Arbeiteralltag*, 8–29.

—. "Neuere Alltagsgeschichte und Historische Anthropologie," in Süssmuth, ed., *Historische Anthropologie*, 57–72.

—. *Grenzen der Sozialdisziplinierung. Aufstieg und Krise der deutschen Jugendfürsorge von 1878 bis 1932.* Köln, 1986.

Pfeiler, W. K. *War and the German Mind. The Testimony of Men of Fiction who Fought at the Front.* New York, 1941.

Philippi, K.-P. *Volk des Zorns. Studien zur "poetischen Mobilmachung" in der deutschen Literatur am Beginn des Ersten Weltkriegs, ihren Voraussetzungen und Implikationen.* München, 1979.

Polligkeit, W. *Die Kriegsnot der aufsichtslosen Kleinkinder.* Berlin and Leipzig, 1917.

Pomata, G. "Die Geschichte der Frauen zwischen Anthropologie und Biologie." *Feministische Studien* 2 (1983), 113–127.

Potthoff, H. *Die Bedeutung des Haushalts in der Volkswirtschaft.* Berlin, 1921.

—. *Hauswirtschaft und Volkswirtschaft.* Düsseldorf, 1928.

Prange, P. "Die Demobilmachung des Arbeitsmarktes im Deutschen Reich nach Beendigung des Weltkrieges 1914/1918." Diss., Würzburg, 1923.

Preller, L. *Sozialpolitik in der Weimarer Republik.* Kronberg/Ts. and Düsseldorf, 1978.

Pressel, W. *Die Kriegspredigt 1914–1918 in der evangelischen Kirche Deutschlands.* Göttingen, 1967.

Pribram, K. "Zur Entwicklung der Lebensmittelpreise in der

Kriegszeit." *Archiv für Sozialwissenschaft und Sozialpolitik* 43 (1916/17), 773–807.

Prölß. "Kriegsjugendschutz." *Deutsche Juristenzeitung* 22 (1917), 185–190.

Puhle, H.-J. "Vom Wohlfahrtsausschuß zum Wohlfahrtsstaat," in G. A. Ritter, ed., *Vom Wohlfahrtsausschuß zum Wohlfahrtsstaat. Der Staat in der modernen Industriegesellschaft.* Köln, 1973, 29–68.

Quandt, S. and Schichtel, H., eds. *Der Erste Weltkrieg als Kommunikationsereignis.* Gießen, 1993.

Rabenschlag-Kräußlich, J. *Parität statt Klassenkampf? Zur Organisation des Arbeitsmarktes und Domestizierung des Arbeitskampfes in Deutschland und England 1900–1918.* Frankfurt/M. et al., 1983.

Raithel, Th. *Das "Wunder" der inneren Einheit. Studien zur deutschen und französischen Öffentlichkeit bei Beginn des Ersten Weltkriegs.* Bonn, 1996.

Ratz, U. "Sozialdemokratische Arbeiterbewegung, bürgerliche Sozialreformer und Militärbehörden im Ersten Weltkrieg. Die 'Berichte des Büros für Sozialpolitik.'" *MGM* 37 (1985), 9–33.

Remarque, E. M. *Im Westen nichts Neues.* Köln, 1984.

Renn, L. *Krieg.* Frankfurt/M., 1929.

Reulecke, J. *Die wirtschaftliche Entwicklung der Stadt Barmen von 1910 bis 1925.* Neustadt a.d.A., 1973.

——. "Der Erste Weltkrieg und die Arbeiterbewegung im rheinisch-westfälischen Industriegebiet," in J. Reulecke, ed., *Arbeiterbewegung an Rhein und Ruhr. Beiträge zur Geschichte der Arbeiterbewegung in Rheinland-Westfalen.* Wuppertal, 1974, 205–239.

——. "Städtische Finanzprobleme und Kriegswohlfahrtspflege im Ersten Weltkrieg unter besonderer Berücksichtigung der Stadt Barmen." *Zeitschrift für Stadtgeschichte, Stadtsoziologie und Denkmalpflege* 1 (1975), 48–79.

——. "Wirtschaft und Bevölkerung ausgewählter Städte im Ersten Weltkrieg (Barmen, Düsseldorf, Essen, Krefeld)," in J. Reulecke, ed., *Die deutsche Stadt im Industriezeitalter. Beiträge zur modernen deutschen Stadtgeschichte.* Wuppertal, 1980, 114–126.

——. "Bürgerliche Sozialreformer und Arbeiterjugend im Kaiserreich." *AfS* 22 (1982), 299–329.

——. "Männerbund versus the Family: Middle-Class Youth

Movements and the Family in Germany in the Period of the First World War," in Wall and Winter, eds., *Upheaval*, 439–452.

—. "Vom Kämpfer zum Krieger. Zur Visualisierung des Männerbildes während des Ersten Weltkriegs." In Quandt and Schichtel, eds., *Der Erste Weltkrieg*, 158–175.

Richert, D. *Beste Gelegenheit zum Sterben. Meine Erlebnisse im Kriege 1914–1918*. A. Tramitz and B. Ulrich, eds. München, 1989.

Riebicke, O. *Was brauchte der Weltkrieg? Tatsachen und Zahlen aus dem deutschen Ringen 1914/1918*. Leipzig, 1936.

Riezler, K. *Tagebücher, Aufsätze, Dokumente*. K. D. Erdmann, ed. Göttingen, 1972.

Ringelnatz, J. *Als Mariner im Krieg*. Reinbek, 1977.

Ritter, G. *Die Tragödie der Staatskunst. Bethmann Hollweg als Kriegskanzler (1914–1917)*. Staatskunst und Kriegshandwerk 3. München, 1964.

Ritter, G. A., ed. *Vom Wohlfahrtsausschuß zum Wohlfahrtsstaat. Der Staat in der modernen Industriegesellschaft*. Köln, 1973.

Roerkohl, A. "Die Lebensmittelversorgung während des Ersten Weltkrieges im Spannungsfeld kommunaler und staatlicher Maßnahmen," in H. J. Teuteberg, ed., *Durchbruch zum modernen Massenkonsum. Lebensmittelmärkte und Lebensmittelqualität im Städtewachstum des Industriezeitalters*. Münster, 1987, 309–370.

—. *Hungerblockade und Heimatfront. Die kommunale Lebensmittelversorgung in Westfalen während des Ersten Weltkriegs*. Stuttgart, 1991.

Roesler, K. *Die Finanzpolitik des Deutschen Reiches im Ersten Weltkrieg*. Berlin, 1967.

Rohwer, J., ed. *Neue Forschungen zum Ersten Weltkrieg*. Schriften der Bibliothek für Zeitgeschichte 25. Koblenz, 1985.

Rouette, S. "Die Erwerbslosenfürsorge für Frauen in Berlin nach 1918." *IWK* 21 (1985), 295–308.

—. *Sozialpolitik als Geschlechterpolitik. Die Regulierung der Frauenarbeit nach dem Ersten Weltkrieg*. Frankfurt/M. and New York, 1993.

Rürup, R. "Der 'Geist von 1914' in Deutschland. Kriegsbegeisterung und Ideologisierung des Kriegs im Ersten Weltkrieg," in Hüppauf, ed., *Ansichten*, 1–30.

Ruge, A. *Die Mobilmachung der deutschen Frauenkräfte für den Krieg*. Berlin, n.d. [1915].

Rund, J. *Ernährungswirtschaft und Zwangsarbeit im Raum Hannover 1914 bis 1923*. Hannover, 1992.

Rupprecht. "Die Jugendstraffälligkeit in Bayern im Frieden und im Kriege." *Deutsche Strafrechts-Zeitung* 3 (1916), 128-134.

Saalmann. "Ein Beitrag zur Frage der Bevölkerungspolitik nach dem Kriege." *Zeitschrift für Bevölkerungspolitik und Säuglingsfürsorge* 10 (1918), 232-238.

Sachße, Ch. *Mütterlichkeit als Beruf. Sozialarbeit, Sozialreform und Frauenbewegung 1871-1929*. Frankfurt/M., 1986.

Salomon, A. *Charakter ist Schicksal. Lebenserinnerungen*. R. Baron and R. Landwehr, eds. Weinheim and Basel, 1983.

Saul, K. "Der Kampf um die Jugend zwischen Volksschule und Kaserne. Ein Beitrag zur 'Jugendpflege' im Wilhelminischen Reich 1980-1914." *MGM* 9 (1971), vol. 1, 97-143.

—. "Jugend im Schatten des Krieges. Vormilitärische Ausbildung - Kriegswirtschaftlicher Einsatz - Schulalltag in Deutschland 1914-1918," *MGM* 34 (1983), vol. 2, 91-184.

Schäfer, H. *Regionale Wirtschaftspolitik in der Kriegszeit. Staat, Industrie und Verbände während des Ersten Weltkriegs in Baden*. Stuttgart, 1983.

Scharrer, A. *Vaterlandlose Gesellen*. Berlin, n.d.

Scheck, M. *Zwischen Weltkrieg und Revolution. Zur Geschichte der Arbeiterbewegung in Württemberg 1914-1920*. Köln and Wien, 1981.

Schenck, E.-G. *Das menschliche Elend im 20. Jahrhundert. Eine Pathographie der Kriegs-, Hunger- und politischen Katastrophen Europas*. Herford, 1965.

Schenda, R. *Die Lesestoffe der kleinen Leute. Studien zur populären Literatur im 19. und 20. Jahrhundert*. München, 1976.

Schenk, H. *Die feministische Herausforderung. 150 Jahre Frauenbewegung in Deutschland*. München, 1980.

Schiffers, R. and Koch, M., eds. *Der Hauptausschuß des Deutschen Reichstags 1915-1918*. Quellen zur Geschichte des Parlamentarismus und der politischen Parteien 9, 4 vols. Düsseldorf, 1981.

Schilling, K. "Beiträge zu einer Geschichte des radikalen Nationalismus in der Wilhelminischen Ära 1890-1909." Diss., Leipzig, 1968.

Schirmacher, K. *Frauendienstpflicht*. Bonn, 1918.

Schlegel-Matthies, K. *"Im Haus und am Herd." Der Wandel des Hausfrauenbildes und der Hausarbeit 1880–1930*. Stuttgart, 1994.

Schmidt, E. H. *Heimatheer und Revolution 1918. Die militärischen Gewalten im Heimatgebiet zwischen Oktoberreform und Novemberrevolution*. Stuttgart, 1981.

Schönhoven, K., ed. *Die Gewerkschaften in Weltkrieg und Revolution 1914–1919*. Quellen zur Geschichte der deutschen Gewerkschaftsbewegung im 20. Jahrhundert 1. Köln, 1985.

Scholz, L. *Seelenleben des Soldaten an der Front. Hinterlassene Aufzeichnungen des im Kriege gefallenen Nervenarztes*. Tübingen, 1920.

Schorske, C. E. *Die große Spaltung. Die deutsche Sozialdemokratie 1905–1917*. Berlin, 1981.

Schracke, K. *Geschichte der deutschen Feldpost im Kriege 1914–1918*. Berlin, 1921.

Schramm, G. "Militarisierung und Demokratisierung. Typen der Massenintegration im Ersten Weltkrieg." *Francia* 3 (1975), 476–497.

Schüddekopf, O.-E. *Der Erste Weltkrieg*. Gütersloh, 1977.

Schütz, A. *Gesammelte Aufsätze*, 3 vols. Den Haag, 1971/72.

—. *Der Heimkehrer*, in Schütz, *Gesammelte Aufsätze*, vol. 2., 70–84.

—. *Der sinnhafte Aufbau der sozialen Welt. Eine Einleitung in die verstehende Soziologie*. Frankfurt/M., 1981.

— and Parsons, T. *Zur Theorie sozialen Handelns. Ein Briefwechsel*. Frankfurt/M., 1977.

— and Luckmann, Th. *Strukturen der Lebenswelt*, 2 vols. Frankfurt/M., 1979/84.

Schulte, B. F. *Die Verfälschung der Riezler-Tagebücher. Ein Beitrag zur Wissenschaftsgeschichte der 50er und 60er Jahre*. Frankfurt/M. et al., 1985.

Schulze, W., ed. *Sozialgeschichte, Alltagsgeschichte, Mikro-Historie*, Göttingen, 1994.

Schumacher, E. *Die Kriegspflichten der Hausfrau*. Bonn, 1915.

Schumacher, M. *Land und Politik. Eine Untersuchung über politische Parteien und agrarische Interessen 1914–1923*. Beiträge zur Geschichte des Parlamentarismus und der politischen Parteien 65. Düsseldorf, 1978.

Schwabe, K. *Wissenschaft und Kriegsmoral. Die deutschen*

Hochschullehrer und die politischen Grundfragen des Ersten Weltkriegs. Göttingen, 1969.

Schwarz, K.-D. *Weltkrieg und Revolution in Nürnberg. Ein Beitrag zur Geschichte der deutschen Arbeiterbewegung.* Stuttgart, 1971.

Segitz, M., ed. *Die Kriegsfürsorge in Bayern. Eine Denkschrift für die Kgl. Bayerische Staatsregierung. Nach statistischen Erhebungen des Landesvorstands der SPD und amtlichen Quellen bearb. v. M. S.* Nürnberg, 1915.

Seidel, A. *Frauenarbeit im Ersten Weltkrieg als Problem der staatlichen Sozialpolitik, dargestellt am Beispiel Bayerns.* Frankfurt/M., 1979.

Selig, P. "Der gewerbliche Arbeitsmarkt der Stadt Fulda seit Ausbruch des Weltkrieges." Diss., Gießen, 1924.

Sender, T. *Die Frauen und das Rätesystem. Rede auf der Leipziger Frauenkonferenz am 29.11.1919.* Publication commissioned by the Zentral-Vorstand of the USPD. Berlin, 1919.

——. *Autobiographie einer deutschen Rebellin.* G. Brinker-Gabler, ed. Frankfurt/M., 1981.

Shorer, M. "Roles and Images of Women in World War I Propaganda." *Politics and Society* 5 (1975), 469–486.

Sichler, R. and Tiburtius, J. *Die Arbeiterfrage, eine Kernfrage des Weltkrieges. Ein Beitrag zur Erklärung des Kriegsausgangs.* Berlin, n.d. [1925].

Sicken, B. "Die Festungs- und Garnisonsstadt Wesel im Ersten Weltkrieg: Kriegsauswirkungen und Versorgungsprobleme," in Kirchgässner and Scholz, eds., *Stadt und Krieg*: 125–222.

Sieder, R. "Sozialgeschichte auf dem Weg zu einer historischen Kulturwissenschaft?" *GG* 20 (1994), 445–468.

Skalweit, A. *Deutsche Kriegsernährungswirtschaft.* Wirtschafts- und Sozialgeschichte des Weltkriegs, German series. Stuttgart et al., 1927.

—— and Krüger, H. *Die Nahrungsmittelwirtschaft großer Städte im Kriege.* Berlin, 1917.

Smelser, N. J. *Theorie des kollektiven Verhaltens.* W. R. Heinz et al., eds. Köln, 1972.

Sösemann, B. "Die Tagebücher Kurt Riezlers. Untersuchungen zu ihrer Echtheit und Edition." *HZ* 236 (1983), 327–369.

Sogemeier, M. *Die Entwicklung und Regelung des Arbeitsmarktes im rheinisch-westfälischen Industriegebiet im Kriege und in der Nachkriegszeit.* Jena, 1922.

Sommer, R. *Krieg und Seelenleben.* Leipzig, 1916.

Sozialgeschichte und Kulturanthropologie. GG 10.3 (1984).

Sprondel, W. M. and Grathoff, R., eds. *Alfred Schütz und die Idee des Alltags in den Sozialwissenschaften.* Stuttgart, 1979.

Stark, G. D. "Cinema, Society, and the State: Policing the Film Industry in Imperial Germany," in G. D. Stark and B. K. Lackner, eds., *Essays on Culture and Society in Modern Germany.* Arlington, Tex., 1982, 122–166.

Stecher, M. *Ökonomik des Haushalts.* Veröffentlichungen des Instituts für Hauswirtschaftswissenschaft an der Akademie für soziale und pädagogische Frauenarbeit in Berlin 1. Langensalza et al., 1927.

Stegmann, D. *Die Erben Bismarcks. Parteien und Verbände in der Spätphase des Wilhelminischen Deutschlands. Sammlungspolitik 1897–1918.* Köln and Berlin, 1970.

—. "Die deutsche Inlandspropaganda 1917/18. Zum innenpolitischen Machtkampf zwischen OHL und ziviler Reichsleitung in der Endphase des Kaiserreichs." *MGM* 12 (1972), 75–116.

Stein, H. von. *Erlebnisse und Betrachtungen aus der Zeit des Weltkrieges.* Leipzig, 1919.

Stekel, W. *Unser Seelenleben im Kriege. Psychologische Betrachtungen eines Nervenarztes.* Berlin, 1916.

Stern, W. and Liepmann, O., eds. *Jugendliches Seelenleben im Krieg. Materialien und Berichte.* Zeitschrift für angewandte Psychologie 12. Leipzig, 1915.

Sternsdorf-Hauck, Ch. *Brotmarken und rote Fahnen. Frauen in der bayerischen Revolution und Räterepublik 1918/19.* Frankfurt/M., 1989.

Stickelberger-Eder, M. *Aufbruch 1914. Kriegsromane der späten Weimarer Republik.* Zürich and München, 1983.

Stockmann, R. "Gewerbliche Frauenarbeit in Deutschland 1875–1980. Zur Entwicklung der Beschäftigtenstruktur." *GG* 11 (1985), 447–475.

Stöcker, H. *Geschlechtspsychologie und Krieg.* Berlin, 1915.

Stöcker, M., *Das Augusterlebnis 1914 in Darmstadt.* Darmstadt, 1994.

Stoehr, I. "'Organisierte Mütterlichkeit.' Zur Politik der deutschen Frauenbewegung um 1900," in Hausen, ed., *Frauen,* 221–249.

Stransky, E. "Abhandlungen über Psychologie und Psychopathologie der Legendenbildung im Felde." *Wiener Medizinische Wochenschrift* 66 (1916), 1375–1385.

—. *Krieg und Geistesstörung*. Wiesbaden, 1918.

Strauß, B. "Die Konsumwirtschaft, Ihre Parallelentwicklung mit der Frauenberufsfrage." Diss., Frankfurt/M., 1929.

Stürmer, M. *Das ruhelose Reich. Deutschland 1866–1918*. Berlin, 1983.

Süssmuth, H., ed. *Historische Anthropologie. Der Mensch in der Geschichte*. Göttingen, 1984.

Syrup, F. "Die Arbeiterverschiebung in der Industrie während des Krieges und ihre Bedeutung für die Demobilmachung." *Jahrbücher für Nationalökonomie und Statistik* 111 (1918), 713-732.

—. *Arbeitseinsatz in Krieg und Frieden*. Essen, 1942.

Tampke, J. *The Ruhr and Revolution. The Revolutionary Movement in the Rhenish-Westphalian Industrial Region 1912–1919*. London, 1979.

Tenfelde, K. "Schwierigkeiten mit dem Alltag." *GG* 10 (1984), 376-394.

Thébaud, F. *La Femme au temps de la guerre de 14*. Paris, 1986.

—. "La Grande Guerre," in G. Duby and M. Perrot, eds., *Histoire des femmes en occident*, 5: *Le XXᵉ siècle*, sous la direction de F. Thébaud. Paris 1992, 31-74.

Thimme, H. *Weltkrieg ohne Waffen. Die Propaganda der Westmächte gegen Deutschland, ihre Wirkung und ihre Abwehr*. Stuttgart and Berlin, 1932.

Thönnessen, W. *Frauenemanzipation. Politik und Literatur der deutschen Sozialdemokratie zur Frauenbewegung 1863–1933*. Frankfurt/M., 1976.

Thoß, B. "Weltkrieg und Systemkrise. Der Erste Weltkrieg in der westdeutschen Forschung 1945-1984," in Rohwer, ed., *Neue Forschungen*, 31-80.

Tilly, Ch. et al. *The Rebellious Century, 1830–1930*. New York, 1975.

Tilly, L. and Scott, J. *Women, Work and Family*. New York, 1978.

Tobin, E. H. "War and the Working Class: The Case of Düsseldorf 1914-1918." *CEH* 18 (1985), 257-298.

Tornieporth, G. *Studien zur Frauenbildung*. Weinheim and Basel, 1979.

Travers, M. *German Novels on the First World War and their Ideological Implications: 1918-1933*. Stuttgart, 1982.

Twellmann, M. *Die deutsche Frauenbewegung. Ihre Anfänge und erste Entwicklung. 1843-1889*. Meisenheim/Glan, 1972.

Tyszka, G. von. *Der Konsument in der Kriegswirtschaft.* Tübingen, 1916.

—. "Die Veränderungen in der Lebenshaltung städtischer Familien im Kriege." *Archiv für Sozialwissenschaft und Sozialpolitik* 43 (1916/17), 841–876.

Ullrich V. *Die Hamburger Arbeiterbewegung am Vorabend des Ersten Weltkriegs bis zur Revolution 1918/19,* 2 vols. Hamburg, 1976.

—. "Die deutsche Arbeiterbewegung im Ersten Weltkrieg und in der Revolution von 1918/19. Anmerkungen zu neueren Veröffentlichungen." *NPL* 27 (1982), 446–462.

—. *Kriegsalltag. Hamburg im Ersten Weltkrieg.* Köln, 1982.

—. "Massenbewegungen in der Hamburger Arbeiterschaft im Ersten Weltkrieg," in A. Herzig, ed., *Arbeiter in Hamburg. Unterschichten, Arbeiter und Arbeiterbewegung seit dem ausgehenden 18. Jahrhundert.* Hamburg, 1983, 407–418.

—. "Kriegsalltag und deutsche Arbeiterschaft 1914–1918." *GWU* 43 (1992), 220–230.

Ulrich, B. and Ziemann, B., eds. *Frontalltag im Ersten Weltkrieg.* Frankfurt/M., 1994.

Umbreit, P. "Die deutschen Gewerkschaften im Kriege," in P. Umbreit and Ch. Lorenz, *Der Krieg und die Arbeitsverhältnisse.* Stuttgart et al., 1928, 1–305.

— and Lorenz, Ch. *Der Krieg und die Arbeitsverhältnisse.* Stuttgart et al., 1928.

"Ungeeignete Maßnahmen gegen Minderjährige." *Korrespondenzblatt der Generalkommission der Gewerkschaften Deutschlands* 26 (11.3.1916), 116–117.

Ursachen und Folgen. Vom deutschen Zusammenbruch 1918 und 1945 bis zur staatlichen Neuordnung in der Gegenwart. Eine Urkunden- und Dokumentensammlung zur Zeitgeschichte. Berlin, n.d.

Usborne, C. *The Politics of the Body in Weimar Germany. Reproductive Rights and Duties.* London, 1991.

Verhey, J. *The "Spirit of 1914". The Myth of Enthusiasm and the Rhetoric of Unity in World War I Germany.* Diss. Berkeley, University of California, 1991.

Vogel, W. *Die Organisation der amtlichen Presse- und Propagandapolitik des Deutschen Reiches von den Anfängen unter Bismarck bis zum Beginn des Jahres 1933.* Special publication of *Zeitungswissenschaft* 16.8/9 (1941). Berlin, 1941.

Voigtländer, E. "Veränderungen der Verwahrlosung während des Kriegs." *Mitteilungen der Deutschen Zentrale für Jugendfürsorge* 13 (1918), 24–26.

——. "Die Entwicklung der Verwahrlosung in den Jahren 1914–1920." *Zentralblatt für Vormundschaftswesen, Jugendgerichte und Fürsorgeerziehung* 13 (1921/22), 193–197.

Volkmann, H. and Bergmann, J., eds. *Sozialer Protest: Studien zu traditioneller Resistenz und kollektiver Gewalt in Deutschland vom Vormärz bis zur Reichsgründung.* Opladen, 1984.

Vondung, K. "Deutsche Apokalypse 1914," in K. Vondung, ed., *Das wilhelminische Bildungsbürgertum. Zur Sozialgeschichte seiner Ideen.* Göttingen, 1976, 153–171.

——, ed. *Kriegserlebnis. Der Erste Weltkrieg in der literarischen Gestaltung und symbolischen Deutung der Nationen.* Göttingen, 1980.

Vorberg, G. *Das Geschlechtsleben im Weltkriege.* München, 1918.

Waites, B. *A Class Society at War: England 1914–1918.* Leamington Spa et al., 1987.

Wall, R. and Winter, J., eds. *The Upheaval of War: Family, Work and Welfare in Europe, 1914–1918.* Cambridge, 1988.

Ward, S. R., ed. *The War Generation. Veterans of the First World War.* Port Washington, 1975.

Wehler, H.-U. *Modernisierungstheorie und Geschichte.* Göttingen, 1975.

——. *Das deutsche Kaiserreich 1871/1918.* Göttingen, 1988.

Weigel, H. et al. *Jeder Schuß ein Ruß, jeder Stoß ein Franzos. Literarische und graphische Kriegspropaganda in Deutschland und Österreich 1914–1918.* Wien, 1983.

Weinberg, M. *Unsere Hauswirtschaft und Volkswirtschaft in ihren wechselseitigen Beziehungen.* M.-Gladbach, 1922.

Wellner, G. "Industriearbeiterinnen in der Weimarer Republik: Arbeitsmarkt, Arbeit und Privatleben 1919–1933." *GG* 7 (1981), 534–554.

Wendt, B.-J. "War Socialism – Erscheinungsformen und Bedeutung des Organisierten Kapitalismus in England im Ersten Weltkrieg," in H. A. Winkler, ed., *Organisierter Kapitalismus. Voraussetzungen und Anfänge.* Göttingen, 1973, 117–149.

Weniger, J. "Die Verschiebung von Männer- und Frauenarbeit im Krieg mit besonderer Berücksichtigung von Industrie und Handel." Diss., Frankfurt/M., 1918.

Wernecke, K. *Der Wille zur Weltgeltung. Außenpolitik und Öffentlichkeit am Vorabend des Ersten Weltkriegs*. Düsseldorf, 1975.

Werner, L. *Der Alldeutsche Verband 1890–1918. Ein Beitrag zur Geschichte der öffentlichen Meinung in Deutschland in den Jahren vor und während des Weltkriegs*. 1935; rpt. Berlin, 1965.

Westermann, Ch. *Frauenarbeit im Kriege*. Berlin, 1918.

Wette, W. "Reichstag und 'Kriegsgewinnlerei' (1916–1918). Die Anfänge parlamentarischer Rüstungskontrolle in Deutschland." *MGM* 36 (1984), 31–56.

—, ed. *Der Krieg des kleinen Mannes*. München, 1995.

Wex, E. *Die Entwicklung der sozialen Fürsorge in Deutschland 1914–1927*. Berlin, 1929.

Whalen, R. W. *Bitter Wounds. German Victims of the Great War, 1914–939*. Ithaca, NY, and London, 1984.

Wicki, H. *Das Königreich Württemberg im Ersten Weltkrieg: Seine wirtschaftliche, soziale, politische und kulturelle Lage*. Frankfurt/M. et al., 1984.

Wieland, L. *Belgien 1914. Die Frage des belgischen "Franktireurkriegs" und die deutsche öffentliche Meinung von 1914 bis 1936*. Frankfurt/M. et al., 1984.

Williams, J. *The Home Fronts: Britain, France and Germany, 1914–1918*. London, 1972.

Winkler, H. A., ed. *Organisierter Kapitalismus. Voraussetzungen und Anfänge*. Göttingen, 1973.

—. *Von der Revolution zur Stabilisierung. Arbeiter und Arbeiterbewegung in der Weimarer Republik 1918 bis 1924*. Berlin and Bonn, 1984.

Winter, D. *Death's Men. Soldiers of the Great War*. Harmondsworth, 1987.

Winter, J. M. "Military Fitness and Civilian Health in Britain During the First World War." *JCH* 15 (1980), 211–244.

—. *The Experience of World War I*. London, 1988.

— "Catastrophe and Culture: Recent Trends in the Historiography of the First World War." *JMH* 64 (1992), 525–532.

Wippermann, K. W. *Politische Propaganda und staatsbürgerliche Bildung. Die Reichszentrale für Heimatdienst in der Weimarer Republik*. Köln, 1976.

Wohl, R. *The Generation of 1914*. Cambridge, Mass., 1979.

Select Bibliography

Wohltmann, F. *Unsere Volksernährung und die deutsche Hausfrau*. Berlin, 1915.

Wolff, O. A. *Zur wirtschaftlichen Lage der Handlungsgehilfinnen während des Krieges*. Stuttgart, 1918.

Wygodzinski, W. *Die Hausfrau in der Volkswirtschaft*. Tübingen, 1916.

Zahn, F. *Familie und Familienpolitik*. Berlin, 1918.

Zahn-Harnack, A. von. *Die arbeitende Frau*. Breslau, 1924.

Zepler, W. *Die Frauen und der Krieg. Kriegsprobleme der Arbeiterklasse* 15. Berlin, 1916.

Zickler, A. *Im Tollhause*. Berlin, 1919.

Ziemann, B. *Front und Heimat. Ländliche Kriegserfahrungen im südlichen Bayern 1914–1923*. Essen, 1997.

Zietz, L. *Zur Frage der Frauenerwerbsarbeit während des Krieges und nachher*. Publication of the Parteivorstand of the SPD. Berlin, 1916.

Zimmermann, W. "Die Veränderungen der Einkommens- und Lebensverhältnisse der deutschen Arbeiter durch den Krieg," in Meerwarth et al., *Einwirkung*, 281–474.

—, ed. *Beiträge zur städtischen Wohn- und Siedelwirtschaft*, vol. 1. Schriften des Vereins für Sozialpolitik 177. München and Leipzig, 1930.

Zinnecker, J. *Sozialgeschichte der Mädchenbildung. Zur Kritik der Schulerziehung von Mädchen im bürgerlichen Patriarchalismus*. Weinheim and Basel, 1973.

Zunkel, F. *Industrie und Staatssozialismus. Der Kampf um die Wirtschaftsordnung in Deutschland 1914–1918*. Düsseldorf, 1974.

Zweig, A. *Erziehung vor Verdun*. Ausgewählte Werke in Einzelausgaben, vol. 3. Berlin and Weimar, 1974.

—. *Junge Frau von 1914*. Frankfurt/M., 1980.

Name Index

Index

Subject Index

Aachen: textile industry 46
advertising 272
agriculture 56; cheating and
  black market 172; rural wives
  with Family Aid 188; urban
  gardens and animals 190–192;
  women's labor 278, 279
Aichach: women and prisoners
  of war 145
Alsace-Lorraine: employment
  statistics 43
Altötting: black-market trading
  205; war-weariness 233–234
Anhalt: civilian mortality rate 196
Association of German
  Housewives 193
Augsburg: Family Aid 188
Auxiliary Service Law:
  classification of trades and
  activities 82–83; effectiveness
  83–87; implementation 65;
  main stipulations 70–71;
  medical fitness 81–82; origins
  64–65, 65–71; war industries'
  preference for male workers
  81–82; women's jobs 84

Baden: employment statistics
  41–42; Family Aid 179
Barmen: Family Aid 178, 180;
  food riots 206; labor 27;
  prostitutes 142
Bautzen: textile industry 46
Bavaria: black-market trading
  204; conscription 130;
  employment statistics 41–42,
  45; Family Aid 178;
  gunpowder industries 46–48;

household statistics 137;
  independence 253–254;
  maternity benefits 159; rivalry
  with Prussia 239, 262–263;
  war-weariness 233, 237
Belgium: prostitutes 140
Berchtesgaden 198
Berlin: birthrate 135; chief of
  police complains about "war
  wives" 182–183; civilian
  mortality rate 196; Family Aid
  26, 179; food riots 250; morale
  flagging 232; political change
  with war 20; pre-war
  employment 48; youth army
  forced savings 167
Berliner Tageblatt (newspaper):
  on waiting in line 191
Britain: dilution of labor during
  war 102; German admiration
  for Scots 194
business and industry:
  apprentices and vocational
  training 98–100; classification
  of jobs for war effort 82–83;
  effect of mobilization 25;
  preference for male workers
  81–82; rumors about
  continuing war for gain
  244–245; textiles 46; wage
  patterns 94–98; war industries
  46–49, 54–55, 277–279

Central Office for Domestic
  Propaganda 255
Charlottenburg: Family Aid 178
chemical industries 279; wages
  95

Index

injustice 238–240; fluctuation in women's jobs 86–87; health and safety regulations 63–64; homework 57–58, 95–96, 278; institutional order and allocation of knowledge 9–10; men's statistics 276; mobilization of women 62–65, 87–89; no significant qualitative change in women's employment 276–278; professionalization of women 280; shortage 84–85; social relations of workers 104–105; statistics 24–27, 38–49, 276; structural changes in female employment 37–38; unemployment 58–62, 280–281; vocational training and qualification 98–100; wages 94–98, 281–282; wives and widows take husbands' jobs 54–55, 99; working women and working-class women 6; *see also* Auxiliary Service Law; *see also* business and industry
Lauben: Family Aid 187

The Marches: youth forced savings 169–170
Marne, Battle of the 32
Marxism: phenomenological sociology 8
military: Auxiliary Service Law and labor 85
mining: employment reports 40
money: black market and cheating 171–172, 197–207, 228–230, 283, 290; city and district debt 181; deprivation creates war-weariness 235, 238–241; enforced savings of adolescents 166–170; Family

Aid 50–54, 171, 185–189, 289–291; historical background to state assistance 173–176; household management 283; "moral economy" 224; paradigm of the "war wife" and Family Aid 182–185; rationing 171–172, 189–197; rumors about war bonds 245; "squirrels" 197–198; state expenditure on Family Aid 176–181; unemployment benefits 61–62; wages 56–57, 94–98, 281–282, 297; working-class women 28–29
Mülheim: labor 27
Münster: textile industry 46; youth army forced savings 168–170

National Committee for Women's War Work 77, 78
National Socialism 295–296
National Women's Service 73
National Women's Service of Germany 73
Neukölln: Family Aid 178
newspapers: criticism of war 236; government censorship 241
Nuremberg: lack of men for police 249

Oberhausen: labor 27
Office of Social Policy 255

Patriotic Women's Associations 73
Photograph and Film Office 256
police: lack of personnel 249
population: birthrates 128–138, 284–286; family planning 152–157; increase in female

Index

mortality rate 195–196; proportion of the sexes 133–134; racial hygiene 156
Post Office Board of Censors: sample letters for public opinion 251
Prussia: birthrate 135; conscription 130; employment figures 41–42, 56; Family Aid 179; historical background to state assistance to the needy 173–176; independence 253; minimum wage for military contracts 57; raising the birthrate 155–156; rivalry with Bavaria 239, 262–263; war-weariness 233
public opinion: attempts to lift morale 252–254; cinemas and advertising 255–257; folk poetry 265; joke about German versus Austrian morale 259; mediation of individual behavior 9; political opposition to war 246; polls 250–251; propaganda campaign 254–258; rumors subvert complete government control 241–244

railways: employment reports 43
Rhineland: textile industry 59–61

Saarbrücken: Family Aid programme 26
Saxony: birthrate 135; conscription 130; employment statistics 41–42; textile industry 59–61
sexuality: birth control 152–155, 216; changes 138–139; contraceptives 284; prisoners of war 144–147, 212, 287; prostitution and venereal

disease 139–144, 162, 285, 286–287; removed from marital context by war 286–287; secret lovers 143; see also families; population
Silesia: black market trading 205
Social Democrats: denounced measures against Family Aid 51
social history see historiography
social protest and unrest 246–250, 293; adolescents 287–288; defined 259; food riots 183–184, 206; tear-gas in Bavaria 268
sociology: approach to examining attitudes about women's labor 89–94; theoretical approaches 8–11; valuation of social conditions 163–164
"squirrels" 197–207, 290
Straubing 249
Stuttgart: black market 203

Tangermünde: food riot 247–248
textile industries: facing demobilization 105–106; stagnation during war 58–62, 68, 278; unemployment insurance 280–281; wages 95–96
trade unions: against forced savings 169; helpless to control rioting women 248–249; try to lift morale 254, 270–271; women 25

Universum-Film-AG 256
Upper Hesse: textile industry 46

Vorwärts (magazine) 183

Wartime Committee for Warm Underclothes 140